KU-022-582

Contents

PART IV: MODERN TIMES

796.358

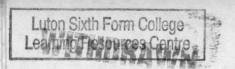

A SOCIAL HISTORY
OF ENGLISH CRICKET

Sir Derek Birley's other books include *The Willow Wand* (also published by Aurum Press) and the trilogy *Sport and the Making of Britain*, which won the British Society of Sports History's Aberdare Literary Award in 1995. He retired as vice-chancellor of the University of Ulster in 1991 after a distinguished career as an educational administrator. He died in 2002.

A Social History of English Cricket and *The Willow Wand* are acknowledged as two of the finest books ever written about cricket. In addition to winning the William Hill Sports Book of the Year award for 1999 – the premier award for sports books – *A Social History of English Cricket* was voted the Cricket Society's Book of the Year. John Arlott praised *The Willow Wand* as 'a quite unique cricket book... witty, scholarly, readable and thought-provoking, not only salutary but essential reading for every cricket-follower', and *Time Out* described it as 'a veritable tour-de-force... rips through the veil put up by orthodox cricket history'.

A Social History of
ENGLISH
CRICKET

DEREK BIRLEY

AURUM PRESS

First published in Great Britain
1999 by Aurum Press Ltd
25 Bedford Avenue, London WC1B 3AT

Reprinted three times

Published in paperback 2000

Reprinted five times

Re-issued in paperback 2003

A catalogue record for this book is available from the British Library.

ISBN 1 85410 941 3

7 9 10 8 6
2007 2006

Design by Roger Lightfoot
Typeset in Ehrhardt by Action Publishing Technology Ltd, Gloucester
Printed by Bookmarque, Croydon, Surrey

To my wife, Norma, with much love

Introduction

ONE OF THE CRISPER pronouncements about the nature of sport is that of Jonathan Swift: 'Most sorts of diversion in men, women, children and other animals are an imitation of fighting.' And, he might have added, some of them are imitations of out-and-out war. The English, who like to think that they are peaceable folk, slow to rouse but indomitable when they put their minds to it, also lay claim to the creation of a sublime diversion. Cricket is one of the more sophisticated latter-day war surrogates, a ritualised conflict in which each side in turn is required to attack and to defend. It is spiced with danger, but cunning is as important as physical strength. It requires strategy and tactics. It is a team activity, yet individual members operate in turn, and leadership is crucial. Not least, its techniques must change: as defence learns to cope with attack, new weapons and new stratagems must be devised.

This is an account of how the English took this game and made it into one of their most cherished institutions; how it was snatched from rustic obscurity by gentlemanly gamblers and in the late eighteenth century became the latest metropolitan fashion. In the nineteenth it became a symbol of the ideals of the new model public schools which undertook the task of training the leaders of Church and State as Britain took on the responsibilities – and the emotional trappings – of imperialism. A by-product of this powerful movement was the preservation of the values of this imperial heyday well into the present century, notably in the distinction between Gentlemen and Players. Similarly the game itself was freighted with extraneous moral overtones – such as 'not cricket' – of so elevated a nature as to promote a well-intentioned but ultimately sanctimonious literature derived from *Tom Brown's Schooldays* with the theme that cricket is 'more than a game ... an institution'. This notion inspired some fine cricketers in an age of privilege still referred to affectionately as 'cricket's golden age' but also exposed the law-givers to hypocrisy as professionalism began to emerge from the shadows with the insistent rise of competition which suffuses the ascendant forces of urbanisation and democracy, leading eventually to cricket becoming part of the leisure industry. In recent years cricket has struggled to keep pace with the tempo of the age, and has sometimes seemed to be lost in a dreamworld of past glories and outworn social attitudes. It now stands at a crossroads. One road points to profound and unprecedented changes in the structure of the game, and this is not a prospect that most cricket-lovers enjoy. However, the rewards are potentially enormous, and if the new England and Wales Cricket Board can forge a positive partnership with the county clubs and the Professional Cricketers' Association, they have an opportunity not merely to preserve the game but to make it better than ever.

Histories tend not to offer too much assistance in deciding future directions, but they may at least help to show how we got to where we currently stand, and, as a personal hope, this one may also offer a little entertainment along the way.

PART I

Peculiar Pastime

CHAPTER ONE

Cricket-a-wicket

ENGLISH CRICKET WAS BORN at some time in the later Middle Ages, of uncertain, though bucolic, parentage. Amongst its near relations, now defunct, are folk-games like stoolball (a unisex affair); the hard-ball variant, stowball; and the cat family (tip-cat, kit-cat, cat and dog, cat-in-the-hole), which used bits of wood as the missile. Its putative ancestor is *pila baculorea* (usually translated as 'club-ball'), which Edward III banned in 1369 as detrimental to his war effort. The usefulness of this impressive-sounding theory is somewhat limited by our ignorance of what 'club-ball' was. We do not even know whether it was a specific game, or whether, as seems more likely, it was a catch-all term to cover any form of ball-bashing the citizenry were apt to waste their time on.

The name, if not the game, almost certainly came over with the Normans, whose particular form of French was the official language of England for some three hundred years after the Conquest. Their word *criquet*, probably a diminutive of the Old Flemish *krick*, a stick, was the dialect name for a variant of *jeu de crosse* or *pila baculorea*.[1] This is not to suggest that the Norman ruling classes (or for that matter their Anglo-Saxon counterparts) played cricket themselves. Theirs was a chivalric society, in which the traditionalist nobility preferred such knightly pursuits as hunting or the tournament. Only the more raffish went in for ball games, and they played fashionable ones like tennis and bowls.

A certain licence was allowed to the young, however, and since the children of the great tended to be brought up amongst grooms, huntsmen and other servants, they sometimes acquired plebeian tastes. Thus Prince Edward (afterwards Edward II) had earned a reputation for idleness, pleasure-seeking and general moral turpitude in the company of Piers Gaveston, his Gascon boyfriend. Antiquarian rummaging through the Royal Wardrobe Accounts for 1299–1300 disclosed that £6 was paid out for the fifteen-year-old prince to play at *creag'* and other games at Westminster and Newenden in March that year. It has been suggested that *creag'* was short for creaget and the same as *criquet*. But even if it was – and who is to say? – no more was heard of it for close on three hundred years.

II

During this time, of course, games rarely appeared in the records except when the socially superior played them, or wanted to stop their inferiors doing so. From the early Middle Ages edicts were issued forbidding the lower orders from indulging in rowdy activities like football, gambling games that might lead to disorder, or anything that kept them from practice at the butts, which was required by law after church on Sundays. New statutes were still being issued in Henry VIII's time forbidding 'idle games' that interfered with archery.[2] But the very number of these prohibitions, increasing as the feudal system declined, indicates how hard they were to enforce.

At the other end of the social spectrum fashionable Renaissance writers expatiated on the sports, venatorial, militaristic and equine, thought suitable for the aristocracy and gentry. Ball games were of less reputable lineage, but court poets wrote verses about tennis and every great house had its bowling green or alley. Unfortunately, so did public houses: inn-keepers, ready to cater for every kind of frivolity, legal or otherwise, turned their yards into courts and alleys. When Thomas Wolsey was Henry's Chancellor, government agents were authorised to enter hostelries, inns and alehouses to seek out and burn '... tables, dice, cards, bowls, closhes, tennis balls' and other suspect devices. Bowls was a particular menace. In 1541 keeping alleys or greens for profit was forbidden. By this time the old stable, feudal society was gone. A degenerate church, dynastic wars, amalgamation and enclosure of land, the advance of merchants and speculators, and the encroachment of urban values as London and its trade increased – these had all contributed to a gradual erosion of the old hierarchies. The Tudor kings had reasserted central authority and either bypassed or reformed such hindrances as Parliament and Church. Henry VII, through skilled manoeuvring, the Star Chamber and the threat of artillery, emasculated the old feudal overlords and appointed his own local Justices of the Peace to impose some semblance of law and order.

A major task was to reduce the number of 'sturdy beggars': ex-soldiers from private armies or men put out of work by the drive for more efficient farming to feed the swelling population. Agriculture and the wool trade were still by far the most important industries, but there was constant concern about the effect of enclosure and the balance between pasture and arable land. Land, plentiful for centuries, was now in short supply. Rents for tenant-farmers rose sharply and prices fluctuated wildly. On the other hand, canny yeomen peasants, merchants with cash to spare, successful lawyers and ambitious gentry grabbed as much as they could.

The population growth was a springboard for greater productivity, a stimulus to trade, not least overseas, and to embryonic industries, eventually bringing unprecedented prosperity, but meanwhile Elizabethan society faced problems of adjustment, tensions between haves and have-nots, newly rich and newly poor, north and south. London, which had remained peaceful and prosperous during the Wars of the Roses, had continued to grow in stature and in size – from about 100,000 to 200,000 – throughout the sixteenth century. It had long been disproportionately significant to the existence of an essentially agricultural nation; now it became a civic and mercantile fastness.

What the powerful city fathers often had in common with the new squires was a liking for the modern religion, Protestantism, which idealised work and sanctified business, fortifying the successful and hardening their hearts against layabouts. New-style capitalists, claws sharpened by overseas competition, did not appreciate the old agricultural rhythms, casual and unreliable, nor the superfluity and haphazard nature of holy days which had long degenerated into holidays. The comprehensive regulation of wages, prices, hours of work and qualifications codified in the Statute of Artificers of 1563 was like an extra book of the Bible.

III

Cricket, if it was being played before Elizabethan times, was neither popular enough nor disruptive enough to achieve the distinction of specific prohibition, nor was it being played by people who mattered. Equally significantly, there is no record of commercial interest from innkeepers and the like, as there was with bowls and tennis. We first hear of it, in fact, as a game played by Guildford schoolboys in the middle of the sixteenth century on land also used for bear-baiting.[3] And, though word of it must have spread at least as far as London by 1598, when it appeared in John Florio's Italian–English dictionary, it does not come over as a very serious affair. Florio defines the verb *sgrillare* as 'to make a noise as a cricket, to play cricket-a-wicket, and be merry'.[4]

It was a good time for merry-making, by and large. The poor were still around, of course, but the economy was going very well, new industries were overcoming their teething troubles, and much of England was enjoying a golden age.[5] In the bustling metropolis, the theatre, music and leisure activities in general thrived under the patronage of the great, whilst licensing began to replace prohibition as a more practical – and profitable – way of controlling sport. It was not intended to encourage the common people in idleness: a public house might be licensed to allow men of substance[6] to engage in dice, cards, tables, bowls and tennis on condition that there was no blaspheming or swearing, and no play before noon on working days or during hours of religious worship on Sundays.

The insubstantial enjoyed no such privileges. And the way they spent

Sundays after church, their main lawful free time, was being viewed critically by the Puritans. Puritans basically tried to stop people doing things they enjoyed on the grounds that human nature, left to its own devices, fouls up the Creator's purposes. They had a good deal of evidence to support this view, however intemperately they were inclined to express it. Not many people, for example, will nowadays disagree with their condemnation of blood sports, which were the favourite amusement of high and low in the sixteenth century.

Bear-baiting was the royal preference as a spectator sport. For lesser mortals, there were public bear-gardens, notably the one behind the Globe Theatre, where both fashionable set and groundlings could enjoy the fun of seeing a blind bear whipped into action. Bull-baiting was a cheaper alternative, so popular that a special breed of dog, admired for the tenacity of its grip on the bull's tender parts, became a national emblem. Cock-fighting was the connoisseur's sport, and the gambler's. Textbooks were written about it, and it was so much part of the English way of life that on Shrove Tuesday mornings schoolboys got off lessons to try out the birds they had been training. After that they could watch the cock-shy, in which people threw things at a tethered bird until it dropped dead.

It is also easy to imagine (from our experience of modern rugby) that some of the local versions of football, which the pamphleteer Philip Stubbes famously denounced as more a 'bloody and murderous practice than a fellowly sport or pastime', might well invite 'enmity, malice, rancour, choler, hatred, displeasure, enmity' and so lead to 'fighting, brawling, contention, quarrel-picking, murder, homicide and great effusion of blood'.[7] Although football was popular with the more coarse-fibred university students and had caught the eye of at least one progressive schoolmaster, it did not commend itself to the authorities of the emerging towns, especially when it was played in the streets. Fear of the *mobile vulgus*, or mob for short, led to grave suspicion of all gatherings of common folk, especially if they made a noise, and the more paranoid believed these rowdy brawlings were a cover for subversive activity.

Sport also came under the Puritan lash if it attracted gambling, or was likely to disturb the peace or lead to drinking and/or illicit sex. The old May games, Whitsun ales and other seasonal frolics caused much head-shaking amongst the emergent middle classes who were the backbone of Puritanism. Did not the Devil make work for idle hands? Concern about how the lower orders spent their leisure naturally focused on Sunday, the Sabbath day that the Lord Himself had declared was to be kept holy. Attendance at church was a statutory duty, breach of which was punishable by a fine, but what went on afterwards depended on the locality and its religious affiliation. Puritans were strongly of the opinion that 'idle and lascivious' games ought to be banned, and looked to the local magistrates to put a stop to them, but in recusant Catholic areas all manner of liberties were allowed.

Lancashire was noted for strong feelings on both sides of the argument. The west and north were dominated by conservative gentry who stuck to the old faith, as of course did their rustic dependants. East Lancashire, however, was fervently Protestant. In 1616 the Manchester justices, already sick and tired of footballers, forbade 'piping, dancing, bowling, bear- and bull-baiting' and any other profanation of the Sabbath, and their lead was followed by adjacent districts. As a result a deputation approached King James I the following year as he made his way back through Lancashire from Scotland. He promised them support, and they went off gleefully to exercise their newly won freedom, with the result that the following Sunday orthodox Lancashire church-goers were disturbed by Catholic rebels piping and dancing and generally enjoying themselves. Solomon-like, James required the local bishop to draw him up a declaration to be read from every pulpit in the diocese. It rebuked 'Puritans and precise people' for inhibiting the people's lawful recreations, and ordained that these recreations be allowed after divine service on Sundays and other holy days.[8] In 1618, an expanded version of the declaration, popularly known as the Book of Sports, was ordered to be read in churches throughout Britain, and the tide of extreme Puritanism was held back – for a time.

IV

The game of cricket, presumably because it was obscure and relatively innocuous, was not mentioned in the king's Book of Sports. But in 1611 it at last surfaced as an adult activity, albeit a somewhat inglorious one. In the Sussex village of Sidlesham, south of Chichester, two men were prosecuted for playing cricket instead of going to church. Eleven years later at Boxgrove, north of Chichester, six cricket players were 'presented' by the church-wardens not only for profaning the Sabbath, but because 'they use to breake the church windows with the ball' and 'a little childe had like to have her braynes beaten out with a crickett batt'.[9]

It was hardly a crime wave, but then, in 1628, as the clouds of Puritanism gathered over Chichester, there was further trouble at nearby East Lavant. The Archbishop's Peculiar Court heard how ten men, one of them a systematic adulterer to boot, had been playing in, or watching, a game of cricket at service time: all had to pay the standard fine of 12*d.* for missing church; the players also had to make a public confession before the whole congregation, and the spectators before the vicar and churchwardens. A further eight were similarly dealt with at Midhurst, a dozen miles away, in 1637.

Kent was another early cricketing county. Indeed, in 1629, the curate of Ruckinge, on the edge of Romney Marsh, Henry Cuffen, censured when after evening prayers he 'did immediately go and play at Cricketts', defended himself on the grounds that it was played by persons of quality. On the other

hand, a Puritan minister, Thomas Wilson, thought it a vulgar affair entirely
unsuited to the clergy: he regarded Maidstone as 'a very prophane town'
where 'Morrice-dancing, Cudgels, Stoolball, Crickets ...' were played
'openly and publickly on the Lord's Day'. But, Sabbath-breaking apart,
cricket was emerging from the shadows. In 1646, at nearby Cox Heath, an
unenclosed common, an organised game for a wager of twelve candles was
taken so seriously that it led to a lawsuit.

V

By then England was deep into the Civil War, the inevitable outcome of
tensions between assertive monarchy and disaffected Parliament. The
Puritans set the tone and provided the rhetoric for the Parliament side, but in
victory Cromwell and his allies were more than anxious not to throw out the
baby with the bath water. Members of the Parliamentary assemblies they set
up needed a much bigger property qualification than before, and they had no
sympathy with fringe-group egalitarians. The peers – a few of whom were
themselves Puritans – were not strung up from the nearest tree; they merely
went out of fashion, and sometimes circulation, for a while. Most of the
Crown and Church land forfeited was broken up into affordable chunks and
sold, usually to Parliamentarians, successful New Model Army officers or
merchants. Surprisingly few individual Royalists forfeited their lands: they
might be taxed heavily or fined for malignancy, but most were able to keep
their estates. Nor did the new government interfere with the leisure pursuits
of the well-to-do. Both James and Charles had offended many of the country
gentry – not only those of the nobility who disapproved of the libertine
Jacobean court and London high life generally, but the squires, brought to
prominence by the Tudors, who saw themselves as the backbone of the real
England. Squires were also an influential section of the Parliamentary side.
Cromwell himself, a horse-lover and falconer, exemplified the type. His taste
in horseflesh was towards the sturdy and utilitarian rather than the freakish
type being bred for the newer trends in horse-racing, now firmly established
at Newmarket as the sport of kings and the more raffish of the aristocracy.
But he did not try to stamp out racing, merely to stop crowds gathering to
watch it.

Indeed the Protectorate government was particularly hot on any popular
activity, sporting or otherwise, that might attract unlawful assemblies. This
put football under a cloud, for it was suspected of being a cloak for protests
against land enclosure and Fen drainage, which Cromwell supported. They
also clamped down on bear- and bull-baiting, cock-fighting and the like, and
tried, with predictably varying success, to stamp out drunkenness, blasphemy, gambling, play-going and brothel-creeping. Similarly it was not so
much opposition to sport as support for godliness that led them to try to

suppress the old seasonal festivals in favour of a day a month set aside for fasting and prayer, and inspired them to even greater efforts to purify Sunday. Thus in 1654, at the start of the Protectorate, three Sabbath-breaking cricketers were arraigned by the churchwardens and overseers of Eltham, Kent, and fined 24*d.*, double the previous penalty.

But anyone with weekday leisure and the necessary funds could go hunting, shooting, fishing – *The Compleat Angler* first appeared in 1653 – or play tennis, bowls, or other ball games, provided they broke no other laws. Commonwealth London, now grown to some 400,000, was obviously a much duller place for people of fashion, theatre-goers, duellists and other bohemians, but it was not totally bereft of all entertainment – wine, women and song were still available, for example, if enjoyed discreetly – and certainly not bereft of sport. Given a bit of space, and provided they did not draw crowds, the leisured classes – or even working people after hours – could presumably play cricket during the week with impunity.[10] There is no evidence that many people took advantage of the opportunity, even in the game's south-eastern heartland. Clearly not many Kentish curates would now want to be seen leaping around with bats and balls in public, but what were the Cox Heath crowd doing? Perhaps with gambling so much out of favour the game seemed no longer worth the candle, as it were. It was doubtless a pleasant diversion in itself – probably something like underarm beach-cricket played with a hockey stick and a non-bouncing leather ball – but not, without the spice of a bit of a flutter, likely to set the Weald on fire.

Those who had most leisure and least interference from the guardians of public morality in the years of the interregnum were, of course, the aristocracy and gentry. Some undoubtedly had more time on their hands, and spent more time in the country, than before the war. Rusticated pleasure-seekers had less choice of amusement – no bears, for instance – and often less money. (What about the younger sons of the unfortunate minority of Royalist families whose deer-parks had been sold off in parcels to the politically correct?) It is possible that bored young blades, individually or in groups, might have joined in or commandeered ball games that their servants and villagers were playing, and this may have helped cricket not only to survive, but to begin its slow climb from obscurity. But they wrought no sudden transformation in the status of the game, in social, technical or organisational terms.

Much antiquarian endeavour has gone into the question of aristocratic involvement, the heritage of generations of well-intentioned seekers after a prestigious ancestry for the game, if only by adoption. These particular new players, if they existed at all, were perhaps condescending a little. Yet they were not the feudal overlords of the Norman ascendancy, temporarily *hors de combat* and viewing for the first time the strange antics their peasants were performing. They had almost certainly encountered it at school – not, of course, as part of the curriculum, but on the half-holiday allowed during the six-day week. It was probably being played at Winchester in 1647, and the young John Churchill, the first Duke of Marlborough, played it at St Paul's around 1655.

So, whatever was happening in adult circles, school cricket was alive and well during the interregnum. After a century or more of existence it must have been known to every schoolboy in the south-east. We need look no further for explanations of the social mix of early cricket teams. Schools, apart from Eton and Westminster, were not yet segregated by class and had very local intakes, so all but the high-and-mightiest and the poorest in towns like Maidstone or Guildford would have gone to the same grammar school. Those who kept their hands in after leaving school may well have been involved in the sort of game Henry Cuffen, the Ruckinge curate, took part in before the war. And they were likely to provide a core of the slightly more leisured, the artisan, the shopkeeper, the professional classes and the university students – and curates – of the next generation, set free by the Restoration to spend their spare time as they wished.

CHAPTER TWO

Publicans and Sinners

IN THE GREAT UPSURGE of sport after the Restoration there were two main strands. One was the excited resumption of the old, crude, forbidden popular favourites: animal-baiting, cock-fighting and inelegant variations like dog-tossing. The other was the equally feverish quest for pleasure amongst the fashionable set, led by Charles II himself. As in the theatre, where the hero of one of the biggest hits pretended to be a eunuch as an aid to seduction, the vanguard was London. There, goggling bystanders could marvel at imported élitist novelties like yachting, or, briefly, ice-skating on the Thames, and the eponymous Pall Mall. Old favourites like tennis, which had lost caste over the years, now flourished as His Majesty showed his prowess, trying to lose weight and keep himself in trim for work and womanising. And Charles's favourite out-of-town spot was Newmarket, where he was not only patron, owner-breeder and arbiter, but enthusiastic competitor. The Royalist John Evelyn confided to his diary his dismay at the sight of 'jolly blades racing, dancing, feasting and revelling, more resembling a luxurious rout than a Christian Court'.

Puritanism, it can be safely inferred, was in decline. It was manifestly not to the King's taste, and the Cavalier Parliament, though not prepared to indulge his softness towards Roman Catholicism, had tried in the Act of Uniformity of 1662 to bring Puritan clergy to heel. In fact nearly two thousand of them chose to give up their comfortable livings rather than conform, and the Dissenters, though browbeaten, were legalised in opposition. And there were plenty of stern moralists in all denominations, even before the Great Plague and the Great Fire of London, which were widely believed to be indications of divine displeasure on the lines of Sodom and Gomorrah.

The 1664 Act against 'deceitful, disorderly and excessive' gambling revealed growing alarm at the effects of the new dispensation, and tried to put the lid back on. It limited stakes to £100 'upon tick or credit or otherwise'[1], a generous enough amount since it exceeded the annual income of over 99 per cent of the population. In contrast with our own democratic times, kings and ministers rarely felt obliged to set an example to the lower orders: in 1667 Evelyn went to a 'wrestling match of £1,000' (with side-bets) 'in St James's Park, before his Majesty, a world of lords and other spectators ... Mr Secretary Morice[2] and Lord Gerard being the judges'. The preamble of the Act explained that it was not aimed at 'innocent and moderate recreations' in themselves but at their misuse, which led to 'idleness ... dissolute living' and the 'circumventing, deceiving, cozening and debauchery of the younger sort'. There was a good deal of that about, not least in racing, by definition a gentleman's sport, and in bowls and tennis, where impoverished idlers of good family could make a living out of their play, backed by shrewd betting and sharp practice. So it was, on the face of it, a good omen for the future of ball games that the government was trying purification rather than elimination. Likewise, though the 1667 Act 'for the better observation of the Lord's Day' was stern enough, it was not directed specifically at sport.

This was where the swing of the pendulum had reached when we first hear of cricket as a commercial enterprise. In 1668 the landlord of the Ram at Smithfield, London's medieval sports ground, paid rates for a cricket field, and in the same year the Maidstone justices benevolently waived excise duties on the sale of beer at a 'kricketing'. All cricketers will at once relax, assured that they are reading about the sport they know and love, for its connection with public-houses and their products is historic in every sense of the word. More specifically, the development is an indication that cricket had 'arrived', at least in local terms, for the brewery trade were the earliest and strongest sponsors of popular sport.

Another straw in the wind was the involvement, at last, of the aristocracy – or in stricter accuracy, of one aristocrat. This young man, Thomas Dacre, Earl of Sussex, who was married to one of Charles II's innumerable love-children, ensured immortality in 1677 by drawing £3 from his treasurer to go 'to ye crekitt match at ye Dicker'. The Dicker was a common near his estate at Herstmonceux, where his sixteen-year-old countess languished, less enthralled than he was with 'the prevailing amusements – hunting, hawking, nine pins, cricket'. Thereafter, for a couple of decades, another curtain of mist settles over the cricket players, at school or after, on public-house fields or commons, enjoying a flutter, but not on a scale to perturb the authorities or attract admiring attention. The mist is thicker because of the almost complete absence of newspapers (primitive affairs in any case) under strict government licensing laws designed to discourage sedition.

The passion for gambling was an indication of certain characteristics of the English upper classes, particularly the new town-bred sort, that came to flower in Restoration times – a reckless tendency to plunge into quarrels and a keen interest in money. The two were coming together as the sporting side of quarrelling became more and more commercialised: the venerable Masters of Defence, incorporated in Henry VIII's time, had turned their graduated tests into public spectacles, known as prize-fights. These were of three kinds, often on the same bill – swords, cudgels, and fists. All were highly popular but the British particularly fancied themselves at the last. The gentry not only patronised prize-fighting but took lessons, and sometimes joined in the informal, but widespread, London street sport of brawling. As Henri Misson de Valbourg, a Huguenot refugee, noticed in 1685, if even two little boys started fighting, crowds would gather 'not only of other boys, porters and rabble, but all sorts of men of fashion' pushing to the front and hiring seats if they could. The nobility also found clouting a good way of dealing with coachmen who charged too much. Misson recalled seeing the Duke of Grafton 'at fisticuffs in the open street with such a fellow whom he lambed most horribly'. It would never have happened in France, he reckoned.

As to money, the in thing was investment in the new overseas enterprises – East India, Royal Africa, Hudson's Bay. More and more merchants aristocratised themselves and vice versa: even the royal family played the market. Interest in agriculture – a harder way of earning money – declined amongst the bigger landowners, and enclosure lost momentum. Rents nevertheless went on rising, and the squires took advantage of their growing power in Parliament to secure import bans and export subsidies. They gained ground not only against the nobility but against most of those beneath them, the old yeoman class, who were now divided by the great rural caste-mark, the Game Laws. From 1671 the traditional right of every freeholder to take game that crossed his lands was restricted to the minority with at least £100 a year. Further down the social scale there were higher wages for skilled workers, and the London artisan in particular began to feel superior to foreigners with their lower living standards; but still further down about a million people, a fifth of the nation, needed assistance under the Poor Law, and the indigent could be ejected if they tried to enter another parish.

Towns were encroaching more upon the country as industry began to make inroads; rural Warwickshire, Durham, Northumberland, Scotland, Wales, all suffered. London, most of all, was spreading fast. Its population, barely checked by catastrophe, was over half a million (compared with the next biggest towns, Bristol and Norwich, with 30,000) and its splendid new, post-conflagration buildings, not least Wren's fifty-odd churches, were admired throughout Europe. Socially and culturally its dominance was even greater and in the early Caroline years, those of Pepys's diaries, hopes were high. But the Restoration, for all its talents – Dryden, Purcell, Wren, Newton, Boyle, Locke – and achievements – the founding of the Royal Society and the twin advances of science and classical scholarship, new styles of architecture, the first public library – soon turned sour. Its abiding image is of artificiality, cynicism, satire, double-dealing and sleaze.

We can, perhaps, draw a veil over its convoluted politics, but we must briefly note the emergence of two opposing parties – tribes really – of wealthy men, calling each other abusively Tory and Whig, after Scottish and Irish ne'er-do-wells, for they were to set the mould for over two centuries. The Tories, mainly squires or urban fellow-travellers, wanted to preserve the old rural values. The Whigs, great landowners and merchants, were for trade and commerce even if it meant change. When Charles's Catholic brother James II succeeded him, behaved vengefully, and produced an heir, the moderates of both parties closed ranks to secure Protestant succession and establish constitutional monarchy, offering the throne to Prince William of Orange. This 'Glorious Revolution' gave England a rabidly anti-Papal and Francophobe king from Holland, against whom she had fought three wars since 1650, and, as James went down fighting, upset the Irish apple-cart. Nobody liked William III much, but he shared the English love of money and, furthermore, knew how to look after it. He tried to pass on the secret, overhauling the government's ramshackle finances, but his fiscal policies, which involved steep increases in land taxes and heavy borrowing to pay for his anti-Catholic wars, were more popular amongst Whig financiers than Tory squires.

A less contentious effect of the Revolutionary Settlement was a relaxation of government censorship on printing, lifted entirely from 1696. Within a year the *Foreign Post* was reporting that

> The middle of last week a great match at Cricket was played in Sussex; they were eleven of a side, and they played for fifty guineas[3] apiece

and we may reasonably conclude that, but for the printing restrictions, other similar matches could have been recorded in the previous few years. The sum of money (£75 × 11) was considerable.[4] The individual bets were perhaps not in the same league as Charles II's £1000 at the wrestling or the £2000 Misson de Valbourg noted as a fairly common wager at Newmarket, but as a team effort it fully merited the adjective 'great' and mention in a metropolitan news sheet.

It may also have been thought newsworthy that such large sums should be gambled on so piffling an exercise, rather as the *Financial Times* today might report £100,000 at stake in a hopscotch competition. Cricket was still, after all, a regional idiosyncrasy with juvenile overtones and no pedigree. But the region included London, where sylvan attractions, nostalgic reminders of the rural past, from gardening and pet-keeping to racing pigeons, were in great demand. An advertisement in the *Post Boy* on 30 March 1700 read:

> These are to inform Gentlemen and others, who delight in Cricket-playing that a match at Cricket, of ten Gentlemen aside, will be played on Clapham Common near Fox-Hall on Easter Monday next, for £10 per head each game.

There is a distinct commercial message behind the polite language, and it is interesting that although the participants were all billed as 'Gentlemen', invitations to attend were issued to 'Gentlemen and others'. Clearly cricket, with big money at stake, had become a spectator attraction, and evidently the social status of the participants had a snob appeal. The combination of élite contestants and public display was as old as organised sport, but is worth pondering in the context of the commercialisation of leisure, accelerated by the ending of publishing restrictions. The middlemen in cricket were usually entrepreneurial innkeepers, some of whom provided grounds, and the gentry were content to perform before an audience – the ladies and gentlemen sitting in their carriages or in temporary grandstands, whilst such of the local populace as could find the time swelled the applause, cheering, shouting and cat-calling as beer and bets flowed. There were more of these idlers than the moralists wanted to see, but the publicans and bookmakers took a more liberal view.

Advertisements have survived from the next few years of similar games in Kent and London, and even of a contest between 'Kent' and 'Surrey' teams, but clearly, for all the increase in these 'great matches', the plebeian image continued. In the 1720 revision of Stow's authoritative survey of London, cricket, included for the first time, was listed as a recreation of 'the more common sort' of people. But one man's plebeian is another man's pastoral hero. In 1706 the schoolmaster William Goldwin, formerly of Eton and Cambridge, published *Musae Juveniles*, his youthful Latin verses, including *In Certamen Pilae*, the first description of the game. Cricket has always had a strong literary following, so this effort is just as fitting a milestone as the landlord of the Ram's rate-payment. Two teams are first seen carrying their 'curving bats' to the venue, choosing a pitch – 'happy chance! a meadow yields a smooth expanse' – and arguing over the rules to be played, until 'a Nestor ... a grey veteran ... a Daniel come to judgement' intercedes. They pitch two sets of wickets, each with a 'milk-white' bail perched on two stumps, toss a coin for first knock, the umpire[5] calls 'play' and the 'leathern orb' is bowled. They have four-ball overs, the umpires lean on their staves (which the batsmen have to touch to complete a run), the scorers sit on a mound making notches.[6]

Goldwin's game, conducted on lines presumably familiar enough to his audience for them to see the joke, reminds us of the vital part played by the schools in creating a game of such wide appeal. Not only had the folk elements of cricket been glued together in a distinctive shape by schoolboys, but the developed game, with teams, had thrived in the schools, particularly if they took boarders, where young fellows with energy and time to spare were corralled together. And Eton has always had a special influence in promulgating the virility cult: Horace Walpole remarked that when he went there in 1726 'playing cricket as well as thrashing bargemen was common ...' *In Certamen Pilae* depicts a game with rules similar to those adopted for 'great matches' later in the century. However, real-life games, at Eton as elsewhere, probably were more concerned with gambling than the characters in this rustic idyll.

Gambling was, increasingly, a national addiction. The fashionable spa towns, especially Bath, did much to civilise 'society', in the season at least, but positively encouraged gambling. William III, a punter of the shrewder type, was succeeded by his thoroughly English sister-in-law, Anne, who developed a passion for racing under the guidance of the royal trainer, and the change reflected the expansive mores of a more prosperous age. The Act of Union with Scotland promised harmony rather than competition. Soon the Whigs and their wars were temporarily in eclipse and the Tories were glee-fully demonstrating that peace treaties could be profitable, but then, as George I, the Elector of Hanover, came in, the Whigs were back and the war with France resumed.

Britain, as the conjoint kingdoms could now be properly called, continued to advance economically in war and peace, through improvements in agriculture, advances in mining and manufacture, assisted internally by better transport along canals and externally by colonial exploitation and the slave trade. The whole was inspired by the beguiling rhetoric of the marketplace, which provided all the justification needed for every kind of squalid deal. Perhaps the worst example, apart from regarding black people as a commodity, was the removal of restrictions on distilling and minimal taxation of spirits, because, as Defoe, the great reporter of the age, pointed out, it consumed corn and there-fore helped agriculture, the linchpin of the economy. The thirst for cheap gin was a major cause of the sharp increase in the death rate, particularly in London, and a host of attendant ills, such as child neglect.

For much of the time the minister who presided over all this, and over Georges I and II, was Sir Robert Walpole, the Cock Robin of the nursery rhyme, 'the drill-sergeant of the Whigs'. Walpole, the first premier to be expert in finance, was able to use this to gain more influence than the strict constitutional position allowed. He assumed in fact that the country's interest and his own were identical, demonstrating it most spectacularly in 1720 when the bubble of the South Sea Company, dedicated to redistributing the national debt, burst with a mighty splash, soaking almost everyone but Walpole and his monarch. But he stayed at the helm, and incidentally kept the ship off the rocks, for another twenty-two sleazy years.

It was not until mid-century, and a new generation of politicians, that the root cause of some of the social problems, such as cheap rot gut, began to be tackled. Meanwhile the debate was as much concerned with the superiority of good old English ale over new-fangled juniper as with the virtues of temper-ance preached by the Dissenters and other gloomy moralisers. 'Water bright' was not in fact all that bright, and polluted supply, especially in the towns, contributed to the health problems. George I was summed up by a modern critic as a 'dull, stupid and profligate king, full of drink and low conversation':

the drunkenness at least was one thing he had in common with his adopted countrymen. Drinking, scarcely checked by the new urban vogue for coffee, tea and cocoa, or sweetened by the pollutant tobacco and snuff, was the regular opiate of both men and women of all classes. The rich already had cheap port, as a result of a treaty deal; now the poor could get 'drunk for 1d, dead drunk for 2d, and clean straw to lie on for nothing'.

Drink was also a contributory cause of duelling and less ordered forms of violence. London, as ever, had the worst problems. Riots were frequent and the criminal underworld were more than a match for the crooked politicians and officials who, in the custom of the time, had either inherited or bought their places. Highwaymen and poachers were the rural menaces, and smugglers upset the digestions of those magistrates whose pockets and cellars they had not lined. Hanging and whipping were greatly enjoyed by the public, as were visits to lunatic asylums, and the old brutal animal sports.

It is easy to see the appeal of a healthy outdoor game like cricket compared with the alternative diversions available, and this indeed may have been one of its attractions, particularly to Londoners of the middling sort who were even taking up the back-breaking sport of rowing on the Thames to get air into their lungs. It was part of the early celebrity of a place that has as good a claim as any to be 'the cradle of cricket', a title much sought after in ancestor-worshipping circles. On the face of it, Islington, now in built-up North London, does not seem a strong contender, but in the early eighteenth century it was a village in rural Middlesex, famous for its fresh bread and milk when such things could not be taken for granted, and a place where stressed-out Londoners went for rest and relaxation. Amongst its amenities were a renowned old coaching inn, the Angel, with a 'field-keeper' for cricket, and the unspoiled White Conduit Fields, which today accommodate the environs of King's Cross railway station.

Their first noteworthy appearance in the saga was not auspicious. Back in Queen Anne's days the legal limit for bets had been reduced from £100 to £10, and informers were allowed to sue for four times the amount of an illegal one. So it was hardly a clamp-down, but more a matter of bringing in the law to protect honest gambling. And it was this that brought cricket into the law-courts. At White Conduit Field on 1 September 1718, according to the *Saturday Post*,

> was played a famous game of cricket ... by eleven London gamesters against eleven Kentish gamesters who call themselves the Punch Club Society, for half a guinea a man.

The game was not, this time, famous because of the social distinction of the gamesters or the size of the bets, but because, the writer alleged, after four hours the Kentish men thought they should be worsted and therefore to the surprise of a numerous crowd of spectators, three of their men made an elopement and got off the ground without going in ..., hoping thereby to save their money.

A fortnight later the Rochester men replied to the 'bragging hectors' of London, accusing them of 'forgery', blaming 'the violence of the rain' for their abrupt departure and offering a rematch at double the stakes, prophesying that 'sprightly Punch [would] easily overcome foggy Ale'. When the London gamesters declined, the Rochester team sued them and the match was ordered to be replayed the following year. The costs of this magisterial judgment were estimated at £200. London won.

London cricket may have got more publicity but the game was more deeply rooted in the rural south. In Sussex, for example, there was a regular circuit of inter-parish matches played on village greens, on commons, or in parks belonging to local squires. There may well have been betting by some of the players but if so it was incidental to the main purpose, which was enjoyment, laced with a keen local rivalry. The diaries of Thomas Marchant, a small farmer, record laconically the matches played between his own village of Hurst and eight or ten neighbouring parishes, and the odd one unavoidably postponed: 6 June 1721, 'Will went to Stenning with the rest of our parish to play a cricket match, but the weather was so bad they could not.'

On this infrastructure was overlaid a pattern of 'great matches' between the nobility and gentry leading teams drawn from their households, tenantry, village craftsmen and so forth. The highest-ranking of these innovators was the second Duke of Richmond. Twenty-two-year-old Charles Lennox, son of another of the illegitimate offspring of Charles II, gave up the family parliamentary seat of Chichester when he succeeded to the Dukedom in 1723. His first recorded game was a two-a-side challenge match in 1725 against Sir William Gage, MP, of Firle, near Eastbourne, a gentleman of distinguished lineage who was already active in these matches. Gage's reply to the challenge indicates how keenly aware the upper classes were of the gradations within their own ranks:

> My Lord Duke, I received this moment your Grace's letter and am extremely happy your Grace intends us the honour of making one a Tuesday ...

It continues in more playful style, but the courtesies had to be observed.

This applied even more to the socially mixed team games the Duke now embarked upon. In 1727 he played two matches against Mr Alan Brodrick, heir to Viscount Midleton, an Irish statesman now settled across the border in Surrey, which required articles of agreement complementing and clarifying the generally understood but unwritten rules of the game. Some of the more noteworthy of the sixteen points are:

that 'tis lawful for the Duke of Richmond to choose any Gamesters, who have played in either of his Grace's two last matches with Sir William Gage; and that 'tis lawful for Mr Brodrick to choose any Gamesters within three miles of Pepperharowe, provided they actually lived there last Lady Day.

(Residential qualifications were obviously important to avoid wholesale importation of new talent *ad hoc*: Lady Day was the usual hiring day for new servants.)

that twelve Gamesters shall play on each side; that each match shall be for twelve Guineas of each side; that there shall be one Umpire of each side; & that if any of the Gamesters shall speak or give their opinion, on any point of the game, they are to be turned out & voided in the Match; this not to extend to the Duke of Richmond and Mr Brodrick.

if any Doubt or Dispute arises on any of the afore-md. Articles, or whatever else is not settled therein, it shall be determined by the Duke of Richmond and Mr Brodrick on their Honours; by whom the Umpires are likewise to be determined by any Difference between Them.

The honour code, *noblesse oblige*, a legacy of the vows of medieval knighthood, was the ultimate sanction behind all the sporting contests, from the turf to prize-fighting, in which the nobility and gentry interested themselves. It clearly made its mark, as we shall see, on the integrity of umpires and the authority of gentlemanly captains in more modern cricket. Meanwhile it indicates how a duke might stoop to play with such social inferiors as were necessary to help him win his bet, and yet retain the authority due to his rank.

Kent's leading gamester at this time was a Mr Edwin Stead, a young gentleman of familiar type in the eighteenth century. He inherited his father's estate when he was eighteen and set about spending the proceeds. He found gambling of great assistance in this, and cricket a pleasant outdoor summer day-time method of disposal; while he lasted – he died at twenty-seven – he cut a tremendous dash. He began serenely enough with two twenty-five-guinea matches in 1726, one on Kennington Common, Surrey, the other at home on Dartford Heath, but then fell foul of the law in the shape of an Essex magistrate who took a poor view of sporting events. Convinced that a match between Mr Stead's men and a Chingford team was just a device 'to collect a crowd of disaffected people in order to raise a rebellion', he intervened 'with a constable and caused the Proclamation to be read in form to disperse the few well-meaning neighbours who were innocently at that play'. Recalling the Islington episode, *Mist's Weekly Journal* wrote:

The late Lord Chief Justice, Sir John Pratt, had made a rule ordering a cricket match to be played on Dartford Heath. Was it lawful to play cricket in Kent, but not in Essex?

Mr Stead went to Essex no more, but moved up the social ladder to safety. On 20 June 1728 his local *Weekly Post* announced that 'the Duke of Richmond and his club' were to play 'Edwin Stead Esq. and his company for a great sum' at Coxheath: this was the first of three similar matches that year. Sir William Gage was also active, playing the Duke at Lewes and Mr Stead three times. On the last occasion, in August, when they met 'at the Earl of Leicester's park at Penshurst for 50 guineas', Stead won by seven runs and the report ended: 'It is said this is the third time this summer that the Kent men have been too expert for those of Sussex.' The following year Sir William, out for revenge, cast his net more widely, with some effect. The *London Journal* for 6 September reported:

> A game of cricket was played at Penshurst Park ... between Kent, headed by Mr Edwin Stead, Esq., and Sussex, Surrey and Hants by Sir William Gage. The latter got (within 3) in one hand as the former did in two, so the Kentish men threw it up.

More relevant to our particular theme, the report continued:

> A groom of the Duke of Richmond's signalized himself by such extraordinary agility and dexterity to the surprise of the spectators which were some thousands and 'tis reckoned he turned the tide of victory which for some years has been generally on the Kentish side.

Aside from the throwaway comment about the crowd, which indicates the drawing power of these fashionable ventures, it is significant that the name of the hero, as distinct from his station in life, was not thought worthy of mention and that, conversely, the Duke of Richmond got the reflected glory even though he wasn't playing. Nevertheless the crowd, overcoming their surprise, were clearly impressed by what they saw, and the groom, Thomas Waymark, no doubt earned an extra shilling or two for his efforts.

Perhaps word of his entertainment value swelled the crowds at future matches. All the talk in the papers, though, was of the people of fashion now attending. (This tells us something not only about the newsmen but about the readership of these expensive ephemera.) Thus the report on the Duke of Richmond's match against a Mr Andrews of Sunbury, Middlesex, at Guildford in 1730 highlights the presence of the Rt. Hon. Lord Onslow (speaker of the House of Commons), Lord Midleton (formerly Alan Brodrick), a Sir Peter Soame, Mr Stead 'and a great many other persons of distinction'. However, the harsh reality behind the outward show shines through a later report:

A great match which was to have been played at Lewes in Sussex between the Duke of Richmond and Sir William Gage was put off on account of Waymark, the Duke's man, being ill.

The stakes in these 'great matches' were now getting bigger and bigger, likewise the crowds; and it all started to get very serious indeed. For the duke himself the trouble came to a head in two matches for 100 guineas in August 1731. The return match was scheduled to finish at 7 p.m. and in the delightfully unpolished prose of the local newspaper report,

> The Duke's hands came in first and got 79 before they were out; and Mr – Chambers's, going in, wanted about eight or ten notches when the hour agreed on being come, they were obliged to leave off though hands then played they had four or five more to go in. Thus it proved a drawn battle. There were many thousands of spectators of whom a great number were persons of distinction of both sexes.

So far so good, but the presence of the ladies does not appear to have assuaged the wrath of the local supporters, and at the foot of a report in the less circumspect *Fog's Weekly Journal*, on a sedate affair between Brompton and Fulham gentleman on Chelsea Common, appears this:

> The same night the Duke of Richmond and his cricket players were greatly insulted by the mob at Richmond, some of them having their shirts torn off their backs: and it was said a lawsuit would commence about the play.

(One of the idiosyncrasies of the English hereditary peerage is that their titles often bear no relation to where they live.[7] Thus the Earl of Leicester's seat was in Sussex, the Duke of Dorset lived in Kent and his son was the Earl of Middlesex. This is all very confusing for students of cricket, a game in which geographical counties still play a leading part, especially as the early aristocratic cricketers were themselves highly conscious of their local allegiances. In this instance the Duke of Richmond, whose seat was at Goodwood in Sussex, bore the name of a village in Surrey, whilst his opponent, a Mr Chambers, led the Richmond team, described in some reports as Middlesex men.)

The dignity of a duke was doubtless easily restored, but the episode may well have increased the sense of outrage that great men should be subjected – or should subject themselves – to such treatment. Richmond does not seem to have played much for a season or two. (He was, amongst other things, nursing a broken leg, which may or may not have been connected with his major interest, hunting: not the still rather socially suspect fox-hunting, but deer, for which he had over a hundred horses, a famous pack and an even more famous huntsman, Tom Johnson.)

There was plenty of activity below this elevated level, however. On Walworth Common, Croydon beat London, and London beat Brentford and Sunbury; 'in the field adjoining to the Wool Pack at Islington' London played the county of Middlesex for £20 a side; on Blackheath, London beat Greenwich; at Parson's Green Fulham beat Chelsea; for unspecified sums or for the fun of it. Most of the matches were evidently taken very seriously and at Ealing Common, when Ealing and Acton met London for £50, it was advertised as 'play or pay', which became the standard rule for money games, and deposits were required.

A new metropolitan venue was found – the Artillery Ground, Finsbury, an old archery field owned by the Honourable Artillery Company, which was evidently rather a rough wicket but had prestige value and crowd-handling facilities. When London played Surrey in June 1732 the notice read:

> At the request of two gentlemen who have laid a very great sum of money, the ground is to be staked where all gentlemen are desired to keep to the outside of the rope which will be round the ground.

The London team – or one of the several who called themselves London – seem to have been the current cracks. When in September they played 'the whole of Middlesex' in a game which ended when time was called six minutes before the appointed hour, *Appleton's Original Weekly Journal* (surely a usually reliable source) commented:

> The London gamesters intend to go to law for the money, there being upward of £100 depending upon the game. This is the thirteenth match the London gamesters have played this year and not lost one match.

The most important development in London cricket was, however, the arrival in its midst of Frederick Louis, Prince of Wales – 'Poor Fred' in a famous epitaph – whose desire to be English was such that he had had cricket bats shipped out to Hanover, where he was educated. He couldn't play very well, but he was keen – a not infrequent combination amongst cricket-lovers – and couldn't resist the chance to become a patron and lead serious players. He is first reported heading the list of illustrious spectators at a match in 1731 at Moulsey Hurst between Surrey and Middlesex, when he was pleased to 'order a guinea to be given to each man for their dexterity'. In 1732 and 1733 he was still a spectator, first at a 'great match' at Kew and then at a game in Hyde Park 'between several persons of the highest rank', and later in 1733 'the Prince's men' – but presumably not the prince – won the silver cup he had presented for a contest with Edwin Stead's Kent. But two years later we read of HRH 'with several persons of distinction diverting himself at cricket in Kensington Gardens, it being the first time he ever play'd'.

So far the effect of the royal presence had been uplifting but intangible, but this now changed dramatically. The banner of Kent cricket had passed with the demise of Edwin Stead to the hands of the illustrious Sackville family at Knole, near Sevenoaks, and in particular to the two sons of the first Duke of Dorset, Charles, Earl of Middlesex and his brother Lord John Sackville. The earl was a particular crony of 'poor Fred' and in July they played a match at Moulsey Hurst for £1000 a side, a quite staggering sum. 'His Royal Highness,' we read, 'came into the field between 12 and 1 o'clock and the stumps were immediately pitched.' Hardly surprising in the circumstances. However, the deference ended there. The prince, leading eight men of the London club and three of Middlesex, lost this and the return at Bromley Common.

Meanwhile the Sussex connection was being maintained by Sir William Gage. His bi-annual matches with Kent had continued, home and away, first with Mr Stead and then with the Sackvilles. In August 1735 the tutor to Horace Walpole, son of Sir Robert, wrote to him from Lewes:

> I have spent the whole day at a cricket match between the Gentlemen of Kent & Sussex, which was won by the latter at which they seem as much pleased as if they had got an Election. We have been at supper with them all. I have left them at this one o'clock in the morning laying bets about the next match. Ld. Middlesex and Sir Wm. Gage are the rivals of the bat ...

Both the Sackvilles took part in this and the return match at Sevenoaks. Two years later Gage also played the Prince of Wales 'for a considerable sum' and it is clear that the ante, in the best circles at least, had been raised. The prince's next notable match was against the Duke of Marlborough's London men, for 500 guineas. When he led his own 'Surrey' men out against Lord John Sackville's 'Kent' at Kennington Common in 1737 the *London Evening Post* reported that 'a pavilion was created for his Royal Highness who was accompanied by several persons of distinction'. The crush outside was so great that 'a poor woman by the crowd bearing upon her unfortunately had her leg broke, which being related to His Royal Highness, he was pleased to order her ten guineas'. (She was lucky: this was about three months' pay for a craftsman.)

Already the contrast between these grand occasions, generated by gambling and promoted for commercial gain, and the rustic inter-parish encounters at, as it were, the game's grass roots, was startling. It is salutary, too, to consider the nature of the exercise they were indulging in, whether for 1,000 guineas or for who bought the drinks. When the Swiss traveller Cesar de Saussure saw the English at play in 1728 he was not much impressed by cricket, which he found baffling: 'they go into a large open field and knock a small ball about with a piece of wood.' It might be less disgusting than beating young cockerels to death and less uncouth than football, which involved 'a score of rascals in the street kicking at a ball', breaking the windows of houses or coaches, knocking down pedestrians and roaring with laughter at the sight, but cricket's finer points were lost on him. And the first illustration of a cricket match, by the French artist Gravelot in 1739, does nothing for its image as a manly recreation or an alternative to the turf.

Still less can it have been thought an entirely suitable recreation for such personages as the Prince of Wales and the Duke of Richmond FRS, LLD and MD (Cantab), Lord of the Bedchamber, Master of the Horse and Privy Councillor. By this time Richmond was lending benign support to a new development in professionalism – a team from the nearby village of Slindon. This was built around some of the duke's old players like Waymark and Stephen Dingate, a barber drafted in from Surrey, and the three Newland brothers, born in the village. The eldest, Richard Newland, was not only a local hero, but probably the best player in England. Under his leadership Slindon had a run of forty-three games with only one defeat. So when Richmond wrote to the Duke of Newcastle in 1741 about his fears for 'poor little Slyndon against almost your whole county of Surry' Newcastle would have appreciated the joke without the postscript: '... we have beat Surry almost in one innings.'

Slindon's impressive record and Newland's prowess were emphasised in the publicity for a game at the Artillery Ground, 'the greatest ... that has been played for many years between the famous parish of Slendon in Sussex and XI picked gentlemen of London', in 1742. The term 'gentleman' was, as we have already seen, freely interpreted in cricket advertisements to mean anyone worth flattering for profit. In this one, for instance, earnest hopes were expressed that gentlemen (i.e. the public) would not crowd in because of the large numbers expected. Also, a large sum was said to have been bet on whether one gentleman from Sussex would get forty notches himself. Newland, the person in question, was not, by the criteria of the polite circles of the day, a gentleman, but of yeoman stock. Yet, though he certainly played for money, he was no mere hireling. Indeed, he was a good enough player to back himself, if not rich enough or reckless enough to bet large sums. The money he made went to help him qualify as a surgeon – not yet separated from Dingate's trade as a barber but respectable enough.

On their visit to the Artillery Ground, Newland failed and Slindon lost narrowly, then were swamped in a second game, and a challenge to the Londoners to yet another match was, apparently, not accepted. Nevertheless they were a major attraction, despite their lack of social graces. When Newland led Three of England[8] against Three of Kent in 1743, his own team included a bricklayer and a nondescript, and Kent's a clock-maker and a tanner, but the crowd at the Artillery Ground was estimated at 10,000. The match, furthermore, was for 500 guineas – the same as that at Bromley

Common, in which Lord John Sackville's Kent XI beat Lord Mountford's men before the Prince of Wales, Lord Waldegrave, Lord Baltimore and other notables.

Middle-class society did not much care for this, and its new voice, the *Gentleman's Magazine*, expressed disapproval in an article reprinted from the more ephemeral *British Champion* in 1743. After making incredulous noises about what things were coming to, the author took specific exception to the 'public advertisement' of cricket 'to draw together great crowds of people who ought, all of them, to be somewhere else', particularly 'apprentices and servants whose time is not their own' and people truanting from work 'to the ruin of their families'. He went on:

> Noblemen, gentlemen and clergymen have certainly a right to divert themselves in what manner they think fit, nor do I dispute their privilege of making butchers, cobblers, or tinkers their companions, provided they are gratified to keep them company. But I very much doubt whether they have any right to invite thousands of people to be spectators of their agility, at the expense of their duty and honesty. The time of people of fashion may, indeed, be of little value, but in a trading country the time of the meanest man ought to be of some value to himself and to the community.

The article adds, almost as an afterthought,

> It is a most notorious breach of the laws, as it gives the most open encouragement to gaming – the advertisements most impudently reciting that great sums are laid ...

Yet the nobility and gentry – and soon even the clergy – were cavorting round the Artillery Ground for that very reason, taking up with riff-raff not for the pleasure of their company but because it was profitable. And if a little of the profit trickled down, was that not the way a trading nation operated?[9]

CHAPTER THREE

Patrons and Plebeians

I T WAS HARDLY to be expected that the aristocratic denizens of the Artillery Ground, conscience-stricken, would at once forswear money-matches or decline to hire professionals after the attack in the *Gentleman's Magazine*. The promoters probably thought it good publicity. They were secure in the patronage of men like the Prince of Wales, his brother Augustus, Duke of Cumberland, the Duke of Richmond, and Admiral Vernon, who in 1744 went to the Artillery Ground to watch 'the greatest cricket match ever known' between 'the county of Kent', led by Lord John Sackville, and 'All-England', led by Newland.

The game is remembered for a number of reasons, all indicating that cricket was beginning to be mentionable in the same breath as boxing, which had been elevated into a noble art by Jack Broughton, teacher of the aristocracy, and in the next breath to racing, the sport of kings and of every crooked Tom, Dick and Harry in the land. The influence of public-school men, notably from Eton and Westminster, was already marked in popularising cricket as the latest gambling vogue. Now the extraordinary social mix of the great game of 1744 was made part of the joke in a set of celebratory verses by the pseudonymous James Love, late of Merchant Taylor's and (degreeless) Oxford, a disappointed aspirant to political preferment turned comedian.[1] His mock-heroic in the inflated poetic diction of the day has the advertising man's tongue-in-cheek.

It begins with a piece of copy that was to be the staple of journalists and reverential cricket historians for two hundred years:

> Hail Cricket! glorious, manly, British game!
> First of all Sports!

and so on for a page or two. The high-flown rhetoric is leavened by a few wisecracks – one, for instance, at the expense of the venue and its owners:

> A place there is, where City-warriors meet,
> Wisely determin'd not to fight, but eat.

Love is careful to give 'illustrious Sackville' his due – 'Swift as the Falcon, darting on its prey' – even when he is out first ball, and 'valiant' Newland, 'the Champion', gets carefully graduated epithets, but Love has fun with some of the humbler occupations on show. Bryan, the bricklayer, for instance, is a 'swain'

> ... whose cautious Hand could fix
> In neat dispos'd Array the well-pil'd Bricks:

And the climax comes when the groom, Waymark – 'As sure a Swain to catch as e'er was known' – puts one down and loses the game.

II

The 'laws' of cricket were settled at this time by the 'Cricket Club', who played at the Artillery Ground.[2] There is the ring of bitter experience about them. As much as possible was made specific and the umpires were declared sole judges of 'all outs and ins, of all fair and unfair play or frivolous delays, of all hurts real or pretended ...'. This was in line with 'Broughton's Rules' for boxing, 'agreed by several gentlemen' at the amphitheatre in Tottenham Court Road the year before. These provided that 'to prevent disputes ... the principals shall ... choose from amongst the gentlemen present, two umpires who shall absolutely decide all disputes ...'. In neither sport did it prevent improper influences, nor did it remotely imply that noble and gentle patrons left important decisions to their social inferiors: it was simply that when it came to gambling, honour was an intangible commodity. The government, taking a similar view, renewed and reinforced the old Queen Anne statute on gaming.

Perhaps the most startling thing in the 'laws' is the provision that the stumps be 22 inches high and the bail across them 6 inches. It does not seem a big target at which to bowl (i.e. trundle) a 5–6 ounce ball 22 yards, particularly as there were no limits to the shape or size of the bat.[3] Yet the bowlers appear to have more than held their own: forty notches was a very big score. Speed was the bowlers' main weapon, of course, and the prospect of a rap on the shins (unprotected save for the knee-length stockings of the day) would be a powerful deterrent to 'standing unfair to strike'. So the manliness of the game, which everyone bragged about, was a reality from the start. So was its Britishness. The laws are highly complex: it is easy to understand de Saussure's bafflement that merely bashing a ball with a bit of wood could involve such inexplicable rituals. They provide, furthermore, a detailed catalogue of deviations from the path of righteousness, suggesting that ingenuity on the part of players and vigilance on the part of umpires were quintessential features of the game, even in its primitive form.

Another memorable feature of the Kent v. All-England encounter was the crowd trouble. Ropes were already in use at the Artillery Ground both to mark the boundaries and to separate the riff-raff from the 'civil spectators'. It was an important part of the ground-keeper's duties to control the rabble: the Artillery Ground leaseholder, George Smith, is featured in Love's poem wielding 'with strenuous arms the cracking whip'. Smith, landlord of the Pyed Horse in adjoining Chiswell Street and possessor of the catering and drinks concession, also imposed financial controls. He had recently introduced a payment for entry to the civil ring 'which it is hoped will not be taken amiss, each person to pay no more than 2d admission'. Now, after the disorderly scenes at the Kent–All England match, he scented further profit, citing conversations with 'noblemen and gentlemen' as prelude to the proposal that in future

> each person pay for going into the Ground sixpence, and there will be for the better conveniency of all gentlemen that favour me with their company, a ring of benches that will hold at least 800 persons.

This was brought in at a match three weeks later, but failed miserably. As the *Penny Daily Morning Advertiser*, serving the cheaper end of the market, grumbled:

> the small appearance of the company is a plain proof of the resentment of the Public [at] the price ... being raised from twopence to sixpence; it is thought there were not 200 people present when before there used to be 7000 to 8000; which plainly verifies the old proverb, 'all covet, all lose'.

Smith appeared set in his covetous ways, however, and relented only for hurling matches, which the London Irish held at the ground. For a Munster v. Leinster game in September 1747 he announced:

> This is the last match of the season, and as it is not attended with so much charge as Cricket, to oblige the Town the door will be only 3d.[4]

By the following season Smith was beginning to get the message, his perceptions no doubt clarified by a spell of bankruptcy, and by 1749 he was contrite:

> Numbers of my friends have intimated that the taking of sixpence admission has been very prejudicial to me. This is to inform them that for the future they shall be admitted for twopence, and the favour of their company gratefully acknowledged. Their Humble Servant George Smith.

Smith had a monopoly at the Artillery Ground, but there was serious competition at unenclosed venues from mobile caterers. One of the best-known, George Williams, landlord of the White Lion at Streatham (and captain of Streatham), travelled to Bromley Common for England v. Kent and to Moulsey Hurst for Surrey v. Sussex in 1745 'with his grand tent and flying squadron of Red Caps', smartly dressed waitresses in distinctive livery. But outsiders were not always welcome; for a match at Duppas Hill, Croydon the rule was: 'No person to bring in liquor that don't live in the parish.'

III

All of this is a corrective to the view that early cricket was about simple rustics basking in the benevolence of kindly squires. The distinguished historian G. M. Trevelyan contributed to this agreeable myth by his charming but romantic little sketch in *English Social History*. Referring to a match in 1746 when, he says, Lord John Sackville was a member of a Kent team 'of which the gardener at Knole was the captain', he goes on:

> Village cricket spread fast through the land. In those days, before it became
> scientific, cricket was the best game in the world to watch, with its rapid
> sequence of amusing incidents, each ball a potential crisis! Squire, farmer,
> blacksmith and labourer, with their women and children come to see the fun,
> were at ease together and happy all the summer afternoon.

There may have been games of this kind at holiday times, and squires may have made their parkland available to local teams, but for the most part the involvement of the gentry in the cricket games of their inferiors was a by-product of their penchant for gambling.

Village-style cricket had certainly 'spread fast through the land', but so had other kinds. By mid-century the net had got beyond the initial group of Hampshire, Surrey, Kent, Sussex, Middlesex and Essex to Berkshire, Bedfordshire, Oxfordshire, Cambridgeshire, Suffolk, Norfolk, Nottinghamshire, Warwickshire, Yorkshire and even remote Durham. The process was not quite osmotic, nor entirely through inter-parish encounters. There were pockets of activity around schools and universities and a natural transmission by interested clergy, schoolmasters and others educated at southern boarding schools. The game was spread, too, by the army and navy, those missionaries of all sports who had taken the game abroad before it was properly rooted at home.

And always, just as influential as parson or squire, there were the innkeepers, looking for novel ways of making money, and capable of overcoming any difficulties – even the absence of teams and equipment, as in this 1745 advertisement:

On Tuesday, May 28, will be played for at Cricket at the Crown Inn,

Stokeferry, Norfolk, by any gamesters that please, 11 pair of buckskin gloves of 2 guineas value, every gamester to put in 1/-. N.B. The gamesters are desired to bring bats and balls, there being none good to be had in the place.

In another interesting co-operative venture, when the bachelors of Barnet challenged any two parishes within seven miles 'for not more than 10s 6d', the landlord of the King's Head donated eleven pairs of silver sleeve buttons for the winners to flaunt.

The tightening of the gaming laws had had some effect, and a certain coyness came into promoters' blurbs, particularly at lower social levels, where the contestants did not see themselves as above the law. A London magistrate, ruling on a disputed wager in 1748, conceded that cricket – 'a manly game' – was not bad in itself, but condemned its 'ill use' by betting above £10, the 'legal' limit. Not surprisingly, precise sums were mentioned less frequently, and increasingly money gave way to innocuous-sounding stakes like eleven pairs of gloves, or eleven velvet caps. These were not negligible stakes, but unlikely to warp the souls of the contestants or land them in the courts.

IV

The most unromantic and least kindly of cricket's patrons now hurtled across the sky. This was the egregious William Augustus, Duke of Cumberland, George II's younger son. Sent by his father to quell the 1745 rising, Cumberland had dealt so harshly with the Scots at Culloden that he was known as 'the Butcher' ever after, north and south of the border. Cumberland had been schooled at Eton, picking up a taste for animal cruelty, pugilism and gambling. He was assisted, particularly in the last, by a younger schoolfellow, the Earl of Sandwich, who greatly impressed Cumberland by his inventions to save time for gambling, such as sticking chunks of meat between bits of bread and a method of rolling dice on horseback to while away the long waiting periods in hunting.

Resting on his Culloden laurels, Cumberland made the life of leisure a full-time, highly expensive occupation, with lavish investment in hunting of the deer-cart variety, exotic animal shows and, above all, reckless gambling. First and foremost he loved the turf, impatiently trying to buy success in matches at Newmarket, and becoming one of the horsy set that frequented the Star and Garter in Pall Mall. He was a fervent supporter of prize-fighting, keen to persuade Jack Broughton out of retirement to put the young upstart Jack Slack in his place. But he also tried his hand at cricket patronage for a while, turning his jaundiced eye on the Star and Garter's Cricket Club, of which his brother and severest critic, the Prince of Wales, was the leading light. In this he was prompted by Sandwich, who saw cricket as potentially more useful politically and economically than drudgery at his desk as First Lord of the Admiralty.[5]

Cumberland made a fool of himself, to everyone's satisfaction, by preparing for a big match against Sandwich by hiring two teams to battle it out for the honour of selection and choosing the winners – who then lost. He was also faring badly in boxing, losing £10,000 on Broughton in 1750, and after a season or two decided to omit cricket, which he had never entirely fathomed, from his repertoire. Sandwich, after making a splash in 1751 as the sponsor of Old Etonians against the Gentlemen of England (at Newmarket) for 1000 guineas, lost his Admiralty post and had to draw in his horns for a while. Neither was any great loss to the game. But several of its real linchpins were withdrawn around this time. The Duke of Richmond's death in 1750 signalled the end of an era for the Sussex connection. The following year poor Frederick Louis, a true cricket fan, was snatched from the scene, killed, according to one account, by the delayed effects of a blow from a cricket ball. His old cronies the Sackvilles, no longer young and beset by family problems, ceased to fly the Kent flag in great matches.

The Jockey Club was formed at the Star and Garter: as the London smart set's pendulum of summer fashion swung, with Cumberland's rank and money, over to racing. The rules for its first 'contribution Free Plate', at Newmarket, were published in 1752. The Star and Garter's Cricket Club, cited as a leading authority by the publishers of the first printed booklets on the 'Articles' of the game, was by no means dead, but cricket was no longer the acme of fashion, and the sudden shortage of big money chilled the air of the Artillery Ground. It was a straw in the wind when George Smith gave it up in 1752 and bought the late Duke of Somerset's house at Marlborough for conversion to an inn.

V

Even London cricket wasn't all about gambling, of course. The *Daily Advertiser* that May carried a notice from a club seeking members 'desirous of playing for diversion only'. Two days later the new manager of the Artillery Ground, advertising foot-races, added a postscript, 'Gentlemen may be supplied with bats and balls.' An even more compelling invitation came in 1754 from White Conduit House, Islington, where Robert Bartholomew offered 'Bats and Balls for cricket and a convenient place to play in'. He had recently converted the old inn, adding tea-rooms, and clearly had in mind the health-conscious minority. 'My cows eat no grain, neither any adulteration in the milk and cream' his publicity read. A start had been made on one of the worst of the city's problems, with the raising of the tax on spirits in 1751, and the death rate was beginning to fall, but there was still a long way to go. In 1755 a spoof advertisement offered an instant suicide potion for

men of pleasure, who have by fast living, now commonly called sporting, formerly stigmatised by the name of whoring and drunkenness, brought upon themselves at the age of forty all the pains, aches and infirmities of fourscore.

In London, with a population of nearly a million, a sixth of England's total, townspeople were no longer simply country folk living a little closer together. But cricket was, fundamentally, the same wherever it was played. No doubt the White Conduit players got the same thrill from it as the countless hundreds of Kent or Sussex locals showing off to their wives and girlfriends once a week. We certainly need not subscribe to the view that true cricket can only be played on the village green with church bells pealing and blacksmiths bowling to curates, as implied in the nostalgic waffle characteristic of much of the traditional literature. The value of eighteenth-century cricket was as a healthy and pleasant alternative to the many squalid pursuits still common amongst all classes in the country as well as the towns.

In the next decades, however, another dimension was added to the town–country division by the supersession of the old cottage industries. Britain's industrial revolution not only swelled and reshaped the towns, but gave a new meaning to the old 'North–South divide'. The inventions that transformed the Lancashire cotton industry; the Darbys' success in coal-coke smelting of iron, profoundly affecting South Yorkshire, Tyneside and South Wales; James Watt's improved steam engine and its application to mass-production not only in textiles but in the pottery and engineering factories of the Midlands – all were part of a new dispensation. The most obvious immediate effect, however, was a surge in national prosperity. Trade multiplied rapidly, assisted by improvements in transport, notably the canal network initiated by the entrepreneurial Duke of Bridgewater. Exports doubled. Agriculture was having its own revolution: corn prices rose and attracted more enclosure, and gave a spur to scientific advances such as those of Viscount 'Turnip' Townshend and the Leicestershire stock-breeder, Robert Bakewell. Landowners did extraordinarily well out of all this: apart from farm profits, direct and indirect, many benefited from enhanced rents for industrial and commercial development, some from exploitation of mineral resources.

Colonial exploitation – that is, importing cheaply the almost limitless supply of raw materials the colonies seemed to have in return for manufactured goods – was an important factor in this equation. The slave trade, at its height in the second half of the century, was inextricably linked to the Lancashire cotton industry, and the source of Liverpool's wealth. To the original American settlements had been added India and Canada, won by outsmarting the French, and Australia, won by Captain Cook's discovery. The fiercely British George III, son of the cricketing Frederick Louis, distanced himself from Hanoverian ambitions in Europe, and by concluding the Peace of Paris in 1763 and divesting the Duke of Newcastle, the Whig puppet-master, of his extensive powers of patronage, allied himself, willy-nilly, to the Tory squires. The loss of the American colonies, squeezed to help reduce Britain's massive European war debt, and the expensive settlement with the USA's European allies, went down badly with the populace. The more volatile, especially in London and the new industrial centres, were learning through rabble-rousers like John Wilkes to express their grievances by mass meetings, pamphlets and the free press – with the implied or actual menace of physical violence in the wings. As a counterweight, unifying all factions, the frequent wars and their humiliating and expensive settlements greatly increased xenophobia, already an integral part of our island mentality.

The French had now been cast in the role of historic enemy number one, in succession to the Spanish and Dutch. Hogarth's *The Gates of Calais* depicted French tyrants starving their citizens to submission whilst the British enjoyed not only liberty but roast beef. The French were also widely blamed in provincial Britain for the disgusting and, well, Frenchified London manners that glamorised sin and sophisticated pleasure beyond recognition. The tale of the simple country girl who sets off to London in search of work and ends up as a whore was a common theme in eighteenth-century moralistic literature and art. The social upheavals of the industrial and agricultural changes now beginning added male victims, including cricketers, to the parable.

VI

The bridge between cricket's two worlds, initially constructed by the schools, was now strengthened by the old-boy rivalries that were beginning to harden. There were natural battlegrounds at the universities, where cricket was now being played, albeit in fairly casual fashion. Thus the Revd James Woodforde played for 'the Winchester against the Eaton' at Oxford in 1760. The sharpest rivalry, however, was between the old boys of Eton and Westminster, the oldest and hitherto most prestigious public schools. It was to one such match at Moulsey Hurst that the dissolute William Hickey made his way through brothels and brawls in 1768, arriving just in time to avoid a fine, so hung over that he almost lost the match through poor fielding, and so dejected afterwards that he could not eat the 'magnificent dinner' or even enjoy the champagne.

This rivalry and its ancillary betting run as an explicatory thread through the otherwise puzzling developments that now caused fashionable cricket to be born again, not in London but in rural parts – and fresh ones at that. In the words of the Revd John Mitford, editor of the *Gentleman's Magazine*, sketching the history of the game fifty years later,

It was somewhere between the years of 1770 and 1780, that a great and decisive improvement took place and that cricket first began to assume that truly skilful and scientific character which it now possesses. The pretty and sequestered village of Hambledon in Hants, was the nursery of the best players; the Down of Broad Halfpenny the arena of their glory ...

Mitford does not go on to explain why this should have been so. In fact, although the Hambledon Club had played at the Artillery Ground against a Dartford team as early as 1756, it had not made any great stir until well into the 1760s. Its captain was the landlord of the Bat and Ball inn, Richard Nyren, who had learned his cricket from his uncle, Richard Newland. Playing skill was one thing, but the turning point was the setting up of a gentlemen's social club at the Bat and Ball: Nyren ran the team, with their financial backing, and also arranged matches for individual members at the ground or elsewhere.

The 'gentlemen of Hambledon' who played a Chertsey team at the Artillery Ground in 1764 were called Squire Lamb's Club, but the driving force behind the transformation was the Revd Charles Paulet (or Powlett), younger son of the disreputable Duke of Bolton and his mistress-turned-wife, the actress Lavinia Fenton. Paulet, a lad about town until rusticated to Itchen Abbas, near Hambledon, in 1763 when still in his thirties, found an outlet for some of his passions in gambling on cricket. His partner in this was an old schoolfellow from Westminster, Philip Dehany, son of a wealthy Bristol merchant. The bulk of the members were local, but with an annual membership fee of 3 guineas – over a month's pay for a labourer – they must have been prosperous. Assiduous researchers have discovered that at its peak the 157 members included eighteen with titles, six MPs, two county sheriffs, twenty-seven army or navy officers, four clergymen and two wine merchants. Its secretary in its later years was Henry Bonham, of a prominent local family, radical in politics.

The members' main function was to entertain themselves. Nyren provided dinners for a shilling.[6] Port was two shillings a bottle, sherry three. The price of table wine is less clear, but the club was awash with it. One entry in the minutes reads, 'A wet day: only three members present: nine bottles of wine.' The club seems to have bought them in bulk. They ordered first a wine cistern and then a bin. William Barber, who took over when Nyren moved to the George, was given a corkage fee of 'sixpence per bottle for drinking the club wine', and also had the task of collecting the empty bottles and returning them to the wine merchant. Members would also take it in turns to contribute wine, either voluntarily or as penalties for misdemeanours. A dozen claret was the standard fine, but occasionally solids might be substituted. The president was supposed to provide venison for the annual dinner, and when Jervoise Clerk Jervoise neglected to do so he was fined a whole buck. The minute book records 'An Extra Meeting to Eat Venison and Drink

Bonhams and Fitzherberts Claret'. Famously, the earliest surviving minute book includes:

Standing Toasts
1 The Queen's Mother
2 The King
3 Hambledon Club
4 Cricket
5 To the Immortal Memory of Madge
6 The President

– which suggests stamina as well as laddish wit. 'Madge' – a what rather than a who – probably does not present as much difficulty to modern readers as it did to the innocents of the 1920s when the book was first unearthed.

The players, though segregated, seem to have had as good a time after the matches as the members. This is strongly emphasised in the memoirs of John Nyren, the landlord's son. Nyren, musically inclined himself, notes their singing and instrumental skills as well as what they did on the field, and grows lyrical at what they ate and drank 'Two or three of them would strike dismay into a round of beef', and there was 'punch that would make a cat speak! Sixpence a bottle!' and 'The ale too! ... This immortal viand (for it was more than liquor) was vended at twopence per pint.'

VII

Amongst the wealthy cricket addicts and patrons who graced Hambledon were the latest Sackville, John, now the third Duke of Dorset, another Old Westminster; his Kent neighbour, Sir Horace Mann, a Carthusian; and his keenest rival, Lord Tankerville, of Eton and Surrey. They often raised teams to play against Hambledon, sometimes dipping into the pool of professional talent that the club attracted from the surrounding district and further afield. Tankerville and Dorset, fairly good gentleman cricketers, would sometimes play in the great matches to make up the numbers, and Dorset, in particular, liked to show off to his numerous women friends. But when big money was at stake, as it almost invariably was, they often thought it best to leave it to the experts. Sir Horace rarely exposed himself at any level.

The squad of players Hambledon could draw on for their teams were not retained professionals, but paid on a match basis. Regular practice matches were held at which sides would be chosen from players present. For these games they were paid 'four shillings if winners, and three shillings if losers', not a lot in terms of port and sherry but reasonable compared with a farm labourer's eight or nine shillings for a six-day week. Certain players were allowed, exceptionally, half a crown or so to hire horses to let them travel in from a distance. Wage rates are not recorded for the players chosen for 'great matches', which were held weekly during the season, usually for £500 but occasionally for £1000, but when they played away they seem to have received between seven and nine shillings a day. In addition a guinea was awarded for the team's lodgings, and transport was provided – by caravan.

'Hambledon', even at the start of its fame, has to be regarded as a term of art rather than a precise description of the players' birthplace: it always included men from the surrounding villages. Some of its most famous players came from quite far afield: Barber and the swarthy Noah Mann were from Sussex; the Walker brothers from Churt, the Wells brothers, Francis and the greatest of all, 'Silver Billy' Beldham, from Farnham, all in Surrey. Even John Small, whose first game was in 1755, was from Empshott, 10 miles away. Travel, in fact, was a part of daily life for them: Beldham and John Wells, saddle-sore from riding 54 miles to Hambledon and back, set about building themselves a cart, only to be hit by a new government tax. At least their frequent trips to London were now pleasanter as the licensed turnpike trusts' improved roads came into commission, and the Post Office's new mail coach, though it cost at least fourpence a mile inside and twopence outside, was reported to have done a trial run from Bath to the capital at seven miles a hour.

The lucky ones were those with occupations that gave them a certain independence, or at least flexibility – and of course could keep them all the winter. The attractions of being a publican are obvious: Barber gave up shoemaking, and Andrew Freemantle carpentry for it. Peter Stewart, whom they called Buck because of his natty dress, was another innkeeper; so was Noah Mann, twenty miles away. George Lee, better still, was a brewer. Thomas Brett, the great fast bowler, was a shoemaker, as were Edward Abarrow, known inexplicably as Curry, and John Small before he turned to bat and ball manufacture. But the great majority were farmers, or somehow got their living from the land. Richard Nyren himself had a farm, though his son, John, ended up in London as a calico printer.

John Nyren's recollections, edited by a man of letters with a taste for nostalgia, were not published until 1833, forty years after Hambledon's heyday, and are rather more reverential towards authority than their present-day counterparts tend to be. Lamborn, whom everyone called 'The Little Farmer', was thought entertainingly shocking when he narrowly missed bowling the Duke of Dorset.

> The plain-spoken little bumpkin, in his eagerness and delight, and forgetting the style in which we were always accustomed to impress our aristocratical playmates with our acknowledgement of their rank and station, bawled out, 'Ah! it was tedious near you, Sir!' The familiarity of his tone, and the genuine Hampshire dialect in which it was spoken, set the whole ground laughing.

The Duke of Dorset also figures in a story about the dignified John Small:

> The Duke ... having been informed of his musical talent, sent him as a present
> a handsome violin, and paid the carriage. Small, like a true and simple-hearted
> Englishman, returned the compliment by sending his Grace two bats and balls,
> also paying the carriage.

Nyren admired these qualities in his own father, who, at a slightly higher
social level than the rustics, acted as a intermediary between them and the
great men:

> I never saw a finer specimen of the thoroughbred old English yeoman than
> Richard Nyren. He was a good face-to-face, unflinching, uncompromising,
> independent man. He placed a full and just value on the station he held in
> society, and he maintained it without insolence or assumption. He could differ
> with a superior without trenching on his dignity, or losing his own. I have
> known him hold an opinion with great firmness against the Duke of Dorset and
> Sir Horace Mann, and when ... proved ... right, the latter has afterwards
> crossed the ground and shaken him heartily by the hand.

VIII

If this last sentence means, as it seems to do, that Sir Horace was more
amenable to suggestion from inferiors than the Duke, it would be in line with
the evidence we have of the character of both men. Sir Horace, who was no
great shakes as a player, seems to have been amiable but weak, and so firmly
hooked on cricket – and betting on it – that he went bankrupt and had to give
up the Bishopsbourne estate where he staged his matches. Great crowds were
attracted there – a reputed 20,000 for Kent v. Hambledon in 1772 – and afterwards a certain discipline was required:

> People are requested to keep their dogs at home, otherwise they will be shot, as
> at the last match they greatly obstructed the players.

Sir Horace is shown, in Nyren, deep in conversation with Aylward, a
Hambledon player, who, it later appears, has been lured away by a job as a
bailiff, at which he proved notoriously bad without keeping his form as a
cricketer. Mann's obituary categorised him as 'rather dedicated to pleasure
than business', and he ended his days commuting between Bath and Margate
in pursuit of whist and similar diversions.

Dorset, on the other hand, was a much smoother, harder type, a political
animal though not a hyperactive one, charming but lethal with women, and in
cricket either a calculating rogue or a benevolent patron, bestriding the
famous Vine Ground at Sevenoaks and hero of anecdotes illustrating his

nobility of character, according to taste and political persuasion. In the noble mode the *Morning Post*'s report of 1773 deserves quoting because it is the sort of story that passes on from generation to generation with the names changed to fit a later hero. This one was told in the 1940s, with elegant variations, by Neville Cardus about Archie MacLaren:

> The Duke ... having run a considerable number of notches from off strokes, the [opposing fielders] very unpolitely swarmed round his bat so close as to impede his making a full stroke; his Grace gently expostulated with them on this unfair mode, and pointed out their danger, which having no effect, he, with proper spirit made full play at a ball and in so doing brought one of the gentlemen to the ground.

By contrast a year later, the *Morning Chronicle*, on the even more familiar 'things aren't what they were' theme, snarled:

> The game of Cricket ... has too long been perverted from diversion and innocent pastime to excessive gaming and public dissipation ... The increasing evil our magistracy ought to suppress in the Artillery Ground. It is confidently said, that a set of idle fellows, or more properly a gang of dextrous gamblers, are hired and maintained by a most noble lord, at so little expense as £1,000 a year.

The paper seemed to have a point: a full-scale riot broke out at the Artillery Ground in 1775 when things started to go wrong for the Duke's team in a match against All-England.

Unable to stop the bandwagon, however, it appears to have jumped on it, and by 1782 it was admiringly describing the preparations for 'a fete which is to conclude the cricket match at Sevenoaks' and adding: 'His Grace is one of the few noblemen who endeavour to combine the elegance of modern luxury with the more manly sports of the old English times.' The *Whitehall Evening Post*, a year later, seemed unimpressed by what Dorset had done with his life – 'at cricket, tennis and billiards His Grace has hardly any equal' – but put an approving spin on his role as a patron: 'The Duke of Dorset's cricket establishment, entirely exclusive of any betting ... or consequent entertainment, is said to exceed £1,000 a year.'

This spin derived from the teachings of Adam Smith, whose *The Wealth of Nations* (1776), advocating the trickle-down theory of economics, argued that rich wastrels seeking the 'gratification of their own vain and insatiable desires' were often 'led by an invisible hand' to confer incidental benefits on mankind. This well-intentioned but lethal doctrine thereafter provided a respectable-looking cloak for prostitution, literal and metaphorical. Spin apart, the figure of £1000 a year that the Duke spent, whilst making him a contender for the Smith prize for philanthropy, was a very much cheaper option than that chosen by many of his contemporaries, the turf. Lord Grosvenor, an addict, had recently offered £11,000 for Eclipse, the property of a former sedan-chairman, and been refused. The reprobate Prince of Wales in his first spell as an owner had lasted only two years before he bankrupted himself and had to withdraw.

Dorset's Star and Garter crony and 'Surrey' rival attracted little praise for philanthropy, or anything else. He is encapsulated neatly in the *St James's Chronicle*: 'the Earl of Tankerville, renowned for nothing but cricket-playing, bruising and keeping of low company'. He was one of the coachman-thrashing types, having indeed been up in court for it. The chief weapon in his cricketing armoury was his retainer Edward Stevens, a.k.a. Lumpy, who could even master the Duke of Dorset:

> His grace for bowling cannot yield
> To none but Lumpy in the field.

Instead of trundling the ball in the old style, Lumpy pitched a length, and was adept at doing so 'o'er a brow' – and at choosing a strip of turf to suit him.

Whatever their moral worth or motives, these three were the great patrons who made the 'Hambledon era' possible, the foils to Paulet and Dehany, who appear to have been utterly crooked. (One of John Nyren's most celebrated anecdotes illustrates the honesty of John Small and Richard Nyren in a match against 'England', when Paulet and Dehany 'began to quake' because things looked bad, hedged their bets, and then when the Hambledon stalwarts made a stand cried, 'You will win the match and we shall lose our money.') Dorset, in particular, though he was usually leading the opposition, called the shots at Hambledon. When he found Broad Halfpenny too draughty they moved to Windmill Down. Money was the grease that oiled the wheels of cricket, at Hambledon just as much as in London.

Hambledon was, in fact, a rustic amalgam of the Star and Garter and the Artillery Ground, with the leading team in the country forming the apex of a triangle. John Small, the 'old reliable', was at the centre of the game's technical development and respected everywhere. As a bat-maker he was in a good position to respond to the new, sneaky 'length' bowling of the type Lumpy and Hambledon's own David Harris favoured. When the ball bounced and moved about, a bat shaped like a hockey-stick was not much use, so Small made himself a straight bat – the shape of blade that not only facilitated movement back and forth from the crease, the new batting style adopted by Beldham, but exemplified the undeviating courage that has been expected of true English batsmen ever since. Less excitingly, the other old English tradition of blocking also began with the new bat.

With the old curved bat it had not been found necessary to specify size, but John Small's innovation put ideas into defensive-minded heads, and in 1771 the Reigate player Thomas 'Shock' White came to the crease with a bat as wide as the wickets. Unfortunately the opponents were Hambledon and the result was a resolution signed by Nyren, Brett and Small 'that four-and-a-quarter inches shall be the breadth of a bat forthwith'. And Small was again at the wicket at the Artillery Ground four years later when Lumpy sent the ball through the stumps on three separate occasions. This was felt 'to be a hard thing upon the bowler' and Hambledon decreed a third stump for future matches.

Decreeing is one thing; enforcing another. The third stump was still not being used at the Duke of Dorset's home ground at Sevenoaks (nor, indeed, was the narrow bat) in 1776, presumably because the Duke, a batsman, felt the bowlers had it easy enough already: he was heard to say that 'if he missed a ball he was sure to be out'. However, for All-England v. Hampshire the following year, Sevenoaks Vine's first 1000-guinea match, three stumps were specified 'to shorten the game'. As Nyren predicted, this did not happen – the batsmen merely batted more cautiously. So fair play came in, very hesitantly indeed, amid much head-shaking from the traditionalists. It did not become 'law' until 1785. By this time the Duke of Dorset had gone off to Paris to become Ambassador to France, a burst of civic activity that amazed his critics, leaving Sir Horace and the Earl of Tankerville to their own devices. The upper reaches of cricket were about to meander round the next bend.

PART II

Growing Pains

CHAPTER FOUR

Lord's, MCC, Lord Frederick and the Squire

THE STAR AND GARTER was still the place for upper-class sportsmen when they were in town. It was here that the laws of cricket had been revised in 1774, and again ten years later, by a 'Committee of Noblemen and Gentlemen of Kent, Hampshire, Surrey, Sussex, Middlesex, London'.[1] (There was a special section relating to bets.) The regulars nowadays preferred to play at White Conduit Fields, although there were certain difficulties. *The Times*, a brash newcomer, sarcastically advised the 'Lordling Cricketers' to 'procure a Act of Parliament for inclosure' after a 1785 clash with some 'spirited citizens' who resisted attempts to shoo them off a public footpath. The following month, however, it was respectfully reporting a match for a thousand guineas 'between the gentlemen who usually play there' and 'the gentlemen of Kent', and next day printed a full score-sheet.

The leading name on the list of the 'White-Conduit Club' was that of George Finch, Earl of Winchilsea. Winchilsea, an Etonian, was already thirty-two years of age but had not previously troubled the notchers, having spent four of his formative years in the army taking in the American wars. He and Col. the Hon. Charles Lennox, later fourth Duke of Richmond (an Old Westminster), continued the friendly old-school rivalry into the new era. Winchilsea, a bachelor who went on for many years, was better known as a patron/captain, and a schemer on and off the field. Lennox, a better player, was a regular soldier and diplomat who spread the game in fashionable circles wherever he served, including Edinburgh, and Ireland, where he was Lord-Lieutenant. He made himself popular with the regiment, we are told, by playing cricket with the common soldiers, 'then an unusual condescension'.

Both were Hambledon members. Indeed Winchilsea was president from 1787, but he seems to have looked on the club almost as a nursery, and to have corrupted a few country lads' morals in the process. One former player, confessing in old age to selling a match, explained how as an eighteen-year-old farm-worker, on ten shillings a week, he had been spotted by Winchilsea, and taken from the fields to play for Hampshire against England at White-Conduit. The temptations were too much for him, as he was taken, awestruck, to the professional cricketers' equivalent to the Star and Garter, the Green Man and Still in Oxford Street. There the 'foremost in the game ... met together, drinking, card-playing, betting, and singing' and eating such meals as even top money – 'three guineas a game to lose and five to win' – couldn't sustain long. They 'were soon glad to make money some other way'.

According to Nyren, the 'modern politics of trickery and "crossing" were ... as yet a "sealed book" to the Hambledonians': only one poor wretch ever sold out, to his own remorse and everyone else's sorrow. It would not have been surprising had there been dozens, and cricket's first historian, the Revd James Pycroft (1851), noting that all the scoundrels of the turf had been involved in cricket, stated flatly, 'the idea that all the Surrey and Hampshire rustics should either want [i.e. lack] or resist temptation to sell is not to be entertained for a moment'. Nor can there be much doubt that the patrons were at it, too. Certainly the 'blacklegs'[2] skulking in the Green Man were quick to tell the lads, 'Your backers, my Lord this, and the Duke of that, sell matches and over-rule all your good play so why shouldn't you have a share of the plunder?'

II

It was not all a question of naïve rustics being deceived by city slickers and wicked aristocrats. Cricket's diaspora and the incipient industrial changes had already created a few provincial centres of activity. Nottingham was one. In 1771 they and Sheffield played two matches, in the away leg of which their opponents made use of local material to good advantage by putting coal slack on the wicket after a downpour. This story was repeated in the same spirit as in the inter-war years, when Sheffield steelworks' chimneys were supposed to be ready to put out clouds of smoke when Yorkshire's opponents came in to bat. However, in the early days, in pugilism as well as in cricket, it was the Nottingham 'lambs', the rough element in the crowds, who exercised a decisive influence on sporting contests staged there. It was at Nottingham that several notorious games against London clubs went sour, but they also had difficult problems with provincial neighbours. In 1772, for instance, there was a bitter dispute with Leicester, involving public challenges and alleged sharp practice over the eligibility of players, about which contrasting accounts were given in the respective local papers.

Then Leicester themselves became involved in a disastrous series of games with Coventry. These were a species of county match and were not held in the towns named. In 1787, at Hinckley, the proceedings began with assurances 'that each party entertained the highest opinion of each others character as players and as gentlemen'. Sadly, by the second day 'great animosities' arose:

The Leicester youths having left the field of honour and retired to the Bull Inn
to regale themselves ... a large body of colliers [Coventry supporters from
Bedworth and Nuneaton] made their appearance ... using every gesture that was
hostile and alarming.

The Hinckley inhabitants were 'obliged to have recourse to blows for their
own defence'; at four o'clock the shopkeepers put up their shutters and 'a
scene of bloodshed ensued scarcely to be credited in a country [i.e. district] so
entirely distinguished for the arts of humanity.' Or so wrote the *Leicester
Journal*, whose readers weighed in with corroborative detail about Coventry's
skulduggery, including threatening the Leicester umpire.

The following year, at Lutterworth, there were no expressions of mutual
esteem, and the *Coventry Mercury* scented trouble when at the end of the first
day's play in a scheduled two-day match the Leicester captain, Mr Needham,
'fearful they should be beat in one innings', cursed his 'own' umpire, 'a man
whose character ever stood unimpeached'. This paragon thereupon resigned
and went home (taking their 'notcher' with him), and next morning a Mr
Brown, a man of doubtful integrity, replaced him. A Leicester batsman, Clarke,
who had been given out the previous evening by the Coventry umpire, reap-
peared at the crease. Shooed away, he was joined by Mr Needham, shouting,
'Clarke, keep to your stumps; damn ye Brown, why do you not call play?' It
appears that poor Clarke had played the ball forward, but it had spun back
towards the stumps and he had blocked it with his bat. The Coventry umpire
decreed that he had 'struck himself out' and refused to change his decision. It
was finally decided to postpone the game until the following Monday, to allow
time to consult 'the first reputed Cricket Society in the Kingdom'.

The decision went in Leicester's favour, Clarke was allowed to resume and
Leicester saved the innings defeat and got a good lead. Coventry contained
themselves until they lost three quick wickets in their second innings, but
then refused to continue and left the ground. They managed to recover from
one stakeholder their five-guinea deposit, and to persuade him to give them
the ball (the usual trophy for winning a match). However, the main stakeholder, Mr Belgrave of Lutterworth, 'judged from the written articles in his
possession and upon which he held the money' that the Leicester players were
entitled to the fifty-guinea stake, and he handed it over, amid threats of legal
action from the Coventry players.

Amongst the interesting features of this affair are the elaborate precautions
the teams took to prevent games running aground. It was quite common to
find clauses in agreements that 'matches shall be played out'. The system of
appointing umpires seems to have boiled down to each team having their
own, biased one. The Coventry umpire in this match was a Mr Banbury,
landlord of the Golden Cup Inn, where the Coventry team held their meetings: indeed they were known as Banbury's Club. The disputants were given

technical advice by the leading cricket society, presumably either Hambledon or the Star and Garter crowd, but the laws themselves weren't much use, because when challenged about his decision, Banbury 'urged the prerogative of his situation and the unlimited extent of his office'.

The problem, and the related one of disorderly behaviour, was general. In 1787 *The Times* coupled the two in a jokey anecdote in which two magistrates sent instructions to stop a match, and the players sent the messenger back saying they would be glad if 'the worthy Magistrates, for the sake of the peace, would do them the honour of coming to be umpires'. The disorder was no joke. Things had quietened a little in London since the frightening episode of the Gordon riots, when 450 people had been killed or wounded, and – always of great concern – considerable damage had been done to property. There was pressure for Home Rule in Ireland, and everywhere religious tensions exacerbated the old arguments over enclosure, the paranoiac protection of the Game Laws, the price of corn, poor relief and the drift into industrialisation. Despite repressive legislation the working classes – and the out-of-work ones – were extremely volatile.

III

As the French overthrew their tyrannical rulers, and Burke, commending nobility as 'a graceful ornament to the civil order', warned that the contagion might spread, Tom Paine's *The Rights of Man* sold like hot cakes. But apart from a few radicals and rabble-rousers the English tended to think their own system of government, based on Habeas Corpus, was the sort of thing God, that well-known Anglophile, had in mind. Both the Gordon riots and the anti-Unitarian outburst in Birmingham a decade later were by mobs who thought they were upholding the constitution, which as everyone knew was vested in King, Lords and Commons, another blessed trinity. We could teach those Frenchies a thing or two.

Cricket had seemed a distinct possibility for inclusion in the syllabus with the choice of that ardent devotee of the manly British game, the Duke of Dorset, as Ambassador to France, and the satirists had a field day, what with cartoons of French fieldsmen surrounding him making wisecracks and suggestions about what he was up to with Marie Antoinette. He had certainly wasted no time before showing the French how to put their splendidly situated Elysian Fields to proper use. *The Times* had reported from Paris in 1786 on a match played by

> some English Gentlemen in the Champs Elysées. His Grace of Dorset was, as usual, the most distinguished for skill and activity. The French, however, cannot imitate us in such vigorous exertions of the body, so that we seldom see them enter the lists.

The following year it killed a few birds with the same facetious stone:

> Horse-racing is already on the wane in France, as it is in England. Cricket, on
> the recommendation of the Duke of Dorset, is taking its place, and making a far
> better use of the turf.

Dorset hurriedly abandoned his mission when the revolution started, so we
shall never know whether a longer exposure to his methods might have given
a reprieve to the *ancien régime*. This question has entertained cricket followers
since Trevelyan's neat epigram at the end of the lyrical paragraph quoted in
the last chapter: 'If the French *noblesse* had been capable of playing cricket
with their peasants, their chateaux would never have been burnt.' The apparent bonhomie of the British *noblesse* for their inferiors was greatly assisted by
the expertise of the lower orders in the three main gambling sports of the day
– racing, pugilism, and cricket.[3] Also, of course, the virility that was so
important to the sporting English and their eccentric game encouraged
respect and admiration.

Generally speaking, however, the mixing ended when the game was over –
sheep went to the Green Man and goats to the Star and Garter.
Furthermore, the demarcation on the field was about to become sharper. Old
boys' teams and superior regimental sides were already active, and the
universities were dabbling – provoking criticism from those who thought
they should be places of learning – but now the élite social clubs that were all
the rage began to take up the game. The White Conduit club, one of whose
rules stated 'none but gentlemen ever to play', became the latest vogue. It
soon attracted nobility and gentry who wanted to play and to have a bet and
to stage 'great matches', but were no longer patrons in quite the old style.
Into their midst came an ambitious young provincial, Thomas Lord, looking
to the wine trade to help him out of the poverty trap his family had fallen
into. He also had a useful sideline in cricket (which he had learned in
Norfolk) and was working as a net bowler and attendant at White Conduit
when his big break came.

Astutely matching the 'Lordling cricketers' desire for privacy with his own
desire for money, and armed with assurances of support from Winchilsea and
Lennox, Lord leased a stretch of land in the Marylebone district from the
Portman family estate, put a high fence around it, added a storage shed, made
a few groundsman-like gestures to the grass and opened for business.
Presumably White Conduit started playing their practice games there, but the
first 'great match', in 1787, was a miscellaneous affair, such as might have
taken place at the Artillery Ground, and certainly not gentlemen only. Lord
himself was playing, and only half a dozen Esquires leavened the mixture. A
year later, however, the leading White Conduit socialites, headed by
Winchilsea, appear to have formed themselves into a 'Marylebone Club'

based at Lord's new ground. There they played and beat the gentlemanly remnant of White Conduit, who thereafter faded from the picture.

The mantle of the Star and Garter Committee fell naturally on this new club. Its most notable member was the Duke of Dorset, who now had a London-based assignment as a Steward of the Royal Household, but was, so far as cricket was concerned, a wasting asset. (His seeming sinecure had special reference to keeping an eye on the dissolute Prince of Wales, currently lurching from pugilistic to racing scandals, and, under the guidance of the cynical opposition leader, Fox, angling for a Regency as George III periodically had his funny turns.) He was joined by his old adversaries Sir Horace Mann and the misanthropic Tankerville; and by the smart operator Sandwich, now back in favour at the Admiralty. And the movers and shakers were the current Hambledon President and White Conduit luminary, Winchilsea, Col. Lennox and the new wave. However, the notion that MCC at once, or even soon, became some kind of supreme governing body is quite wide of the mark. Neither they nor the other autonomous clubs would have recognised such a concept. True, they did put out a revised code, including a section on betting, but like the Jockey Club they made rules for their own matches; if other clubs wanted to use them, they could, but that was as far as it went. The laws were no easier than they ever had been to implement, still less change.

The early interest in MCC, in fact, is in their playing, because, although they did not practise a White Conduit-style apartheid, there were many more aristocratic performers on show, exciting great public interest. They certainly dazzled the provincials, including, in 1791, Nottingham, last seen in a dispute over a 'debt of honour' with their Leicester neighbours. The MCC encounter arose from a light-hearted challenge on behalf of the locals by Col. the Hon. Charles Churchill, one of the Marlborough family, who was garrisoned at Nottingham. MCC, led by its two military men, Winchilsea and Lennox, and with seventeen-year-old Lord William Bentinck and 'sundry lords and honourable gentlemen' in their wake, made the journey in their own carriages, and beat the local champions in fine style.

The spectators, estimated at 10,000 (probably exaggerated as usual), including all the local notables, were duly impressed. The MCC party stayed the week, amusing themselves with 'cocking, milling,[4] or some kind of gentlemanly entertainment'. The citizenry may have been disappointed not to see any duels, only horseplay, from the MCC party, for Lennox had already fought two, in the first of which Winchilsea had acted as his second. His opponent was his own commanding officer, the 'Grand Old' Duke of York, George III's second son, a fellow MCC member, who had tried to quash Lennox's promotion.

IV

There was particular interest, of course, in the contests between MCC and Hambledon, which were features of the 1790s. The cross-membership of Winchilsea and the like made little difference, for people like Dorset, Tankerville and Mann had always been backers of Hambledon's opponents. The decisive effect of the change was the concentration of so many potential patrons in one strategically placed club near the centre of London. There were still a few individual big-money backers, but increasingly it was a question of syndicates. This gave scope to a new kind of sponsorship – by people who didn't want to spend £1000 a year on hiring their own personal teams but didn't mind a share in the action. For well-informed, serious gamblers this brought profit on a much smaller outlay.

The earliest and best-known of this type was also the first gentleman player to be as good as the leading professionals. The Revd Lord Frederick Beauclerk was one of the long line of younger sons of the aristocracy brought up with the habits and interests of a gentleman – huntin', shootin', fishin' and the turf, tennis, billiards, cards – but then, thanks to the English law of primogeniture, left without money to indulge them. It had long been the custom for the younger sons to be put to appropriate professions – the army and navy, the church as well as the less prestigious but lucrative ones like law, and to various permutations of commerce, including marrying the daughters of rich merchants. Church of England clergymen, in particular, could be found livings and given a certain status in society, but needed outside financial support to keep them in the style to which they were accustomed. Thus Parson Jack Russell, the most famous of the scores of hunting parsons, had a rich wife, and Beauclerk, a bachelor, turned to cricket as a pleasant way of augmenting his income in the summer. £600 a year was his own estimate – and he played for thirty-five seasons.

Beauclerk, son of the Duke of St Albans, and later Vicar of St Albans, was first 'discovered' by the well-known talent spotter, Winchilsea, as a slow bowler at Cambridge University, and he played his first game for MCC in 1791. He had, as they say, an old head on young shoulders, carefully studying opposing batsmen and setting fields accordingly. He made bets with the same forethought and was desperately keen to win them. His reputation, like that of self-centred modern professionals, was for being quicker to run for his own hits than his partners'. Though he was an athlete and won many bets in furlong races, one of his legs was slightly shorter than the other and he knew how to hobble to advantage. The new club soon built up a reputation for canny tactics, and Beauclerk from the beginning was a shrewd exploiter of the laws. He was completely devoid of Christian charity, and also very bad-tempered, a weakness the experienced professionals did their best to exploit.

So far as the Hambledon professionals were concerned, the best of them became even more the hired assassins they always in principle were, however strong their emotional ties to their rural base. Thus MCC's first century-maker was old Tom Walker, one of Nyren's pair of 'anointed clod-stumpers', and the second, in the same match against Middlesex in 1792, was 'Silver Billy' Beldham, the 'in-comer' from Farnham. Their achievement can be measured by the fact that 110 was regarded for betting purposes as the 'norm' for a whole team. Beldham's century was less surprising, for he had always been a stylist and an innovator: his way of dealing with 'length' bowling was to use his feet to get to the pitch, leaving his crease if necessary. Tom Walker was known as 'Old Everlasting', both for his long career and his adhesive batting style; as Nyren wrote, 'I have frequently known Tom go in first and remain to the very last man.'

It was a stern tussle when Walker first faced Beauclerk's teasingly slow bowling at Lord's. His Lordship, resplendent in his red sash and white beaver hat, bowled the first (four-ball) over, every one of immaculate length. 'First four or last four made no difference to Tom … Every ball he dropped down just before his bat. Off went his Lordship's white hat – dash down upon the ground … calling him at the same time "a confounded old beast".' This anti-democratic sentiment drew no response: '"I doan't care what he zays", said Tom when one close by asked if he had heard …'. Tom Walker could play Beauclerk because he was himself a steady bowler in the 'home and easy' style. Nyren 'never thought much of Tom's bowling' but admits that in Hambledon's heyday they were so well served that Tom just wasn't used.

The greatest of the many Hambledon bowling stars was David Harris, a potter, the best bowler in England by general consent. 'Twisting' or 'bias' was already well-known. Leg-spin was the natural way for underarm, and Lambourn had invented an off-break without having the wit to know where to pitch it. Keeping a length was the spinner's secret, then as now. David Harris's success came from careful choice of a wicket (like Lumpy Stevens but with more concern for his opening partners) and endless practice to hit a length. He was equally meticulous in his technique, always the same, and beautiful to watch. His delivery, says Nyren, was 'very singular': 'he would bring it from under his arm by a twist, and nearly as high as his arm-pit', pushing the ball up the pitch. As a result it fizzed off the wicket, picking up pace off the pitch, as cricketers unscientifically but graphically say. But the batsmen were accustomed to speed. Beldham recalled that Tom Walker was the first 'lobbing slow bowler' he had ever seen, adding: 'When in 1792 England played Kent I did feel so ashamed of such baby bowling; but, after all, he did more than even David Harris himself. Two years after … Tom Walker, with his slow bowling, headed a side against David Harris, and beat him easily.'

'Old Everlasting' also lasted better than Harris, who was racked with gout but so much sought after that towards the end he would bring a chair on to the field and sit down when he wasn't actually bowling. Tom Walker never moved quickly enough to wear himself out. What he lacked in athleticism he made up for in 'manliness'. Nyren grows lyrical about his 'hard, ungain, scrag-of-mutton frame' with a 'skin like the rind of an old oak' and says that though his knuckles were 'handsomely knocked about', he never bled. Beldham, who was not always respectful about the Nyrens or the standards of the old players, denied this: 'I have seen Tom Walker rub his bleeding fingers in the dust! David Harris used to say he liked to rind him.' It sounds a pretty tough game. In the course of describing the customary dress of knee breeches and stockings Beldham laconically says, 'We never thought of knocks ... Certainly, you would see a bump heave under a stocking, and even the blood came through; but I never knew a man killed ... '.[5]

Technically the game had now climbed its first mountain and had reached a plateau. Beauclerk improved his batting (and thus his chances in single-wicket contests) and his tactical acumen, which made him a natural captain, a role both temperament and rank demanded. As a batsman he modelled himself on Beldham – the complete professional, correct but bustling – yet without anything like his natural flair. Beldham, supreme as a batsman, was also a more than useful change bowler. Both continued at the top for another thirty years, and the extraordinary Walker for twenty. During this time there were no more bowling innovations. Back in the eighties Tom Walker had experimented with what Nyren called 'throwing' – raising his arm to waist level – but had promptly been told by a 'council of the Hambledon Club' that it was considered foul play.

The batsmen, generally socially superior to bowlers, tended to hold sway in these matters, and this did not change with the advent of MCC. There was, however, one further advance in batting in response to 'length' bowling. Young William Fennex, from Buckinghamshire, was an elegant stylist who, instead of jumping out to the pitch of the ball, stretched forward and played it from the crease. This astonished his father, who shouted, the first time he saw it, 'Hey! Hey, boy! What is this? do you call that play?' This was a doubly historic moment, for apart from the innovative technique it was the first recorded complaint of 'not cricket' about something that was within the laws. Fennex profited from his immoral play, however, and wicket-keepers' frustrations increased. Fennex was also an excellent orthodox bowler and thus well-equipped to take advantage of the current vogue for single-wicket matches. These had an additional appeal for the 'legs' because they were easier to fix, and sadly Fennex proved well-equipped to take advantage of this vogue, too.

V

The two major events of 1793 were the single-wicket match at Lord's for 1000 guineas between Winchilsea and the Earl of Darnley, and the outbreak of war against the French. The Chief Minister, William Pitt, had no enthusiasm for the war, but this did not spare him from scurrilous attacks by pamphleteers:

> Sending troops to be swamped where they can't draw their breath,
> And buying a fresh load of taxes with death.

Pitt's taxation policy had been more rational than anything that had gone before; it depended heavily on increased trade through reduced duties on French goods. Still, he was now aligned with the extreme conservatives and the Royal Family, who had a vested interest in stemming the tide of Jacobinism, and fair game for the Radicals. There had been a bad harvest, the price of bread had gone up and there were spasmodic food riots. The government were extremely nervous, and feared not only invasion by the French but subversion and conspiracy within. Habeas corpus was suspended, and a witch hunt began for spies.

An incidental casualty was the Hambledon club. Though its cricketing supremacy was now at an end it carried on merrily until 1795. The cost of dinners had gone up to two shillings but the forty-nine members present at one meeting spent fourteen shillings a head on wine. On 29 August, however, whilst there were only three members present, there were twelve guests, including one recorded as 'Mr Thos Paine, Author of the Rights of Man'. It seems unlikely that Citizen Paine, forbidden to enter the country, would have smuggled himself in simply to discuss cricket, despite his youthful interest in the game, or that his infamous book would have been mentioned unless to make a political point, or that so many guests would have turned up except to hear him. The activities of radical notables such as the Bonhams were no longer exempt from government enquiry and the disapproval of orthodox public opinion, so the membership may have walked, or been pushed, out. Either way, on 21 September the minute simply read, 'No gentlemen present.'

The war had few other substantial effects on the higher echelons of cricket or any other gentlemanly sport. At lower levels the dangers of allowing crowds to gather, or of anti-enclosure protests by staging football or cricket matches, was given an extra edge. And the hedgerows became a battleground as agitation grew for still greater tightening of the Game Laws. But for the 'enjoying classes' the war could be left to the regular forces, with the navy, according to Pitt's master-plan, playing the lead role in the colonies and providing a protective scarf for the homeland, whilst the Allies – suitably subsidised – did the land fighting. Unfortunately this did not quite work out, but the better sort were inconvenienced remarkably little. The turf had a few problems with crowds at places like Epsom, so near to London, and a serious outbreak of horse-poisoning engineered by crooked bookies, but the Derby never had fewer than thirty entries and some of the other great races, such as the Ascot Gold Cup and the 1000 and 2000 Guineas, were actually inaugurated during the war. They were great times for pugilism, too, with Tom Cribb the popular hero, and the government as interested in the results of these illegal but morale-building contests as the thousands who went into remote parts of the countryside to watch them.

Cricket also had its crowd troubles, and if the sixpenny standard charge at Lord's reduced the numbers slightly, it increased the number of pickpockets and hucksters. Pitch invasions when play closed without a result grew more frequent as batsmen strengthened their mastery of bowlers and MCC increased the size of the wickets as a palliative.[6] The once-rustic pastime could now claim, as the nineteenth century began, a recognised place in the nation's array of sports. The antiquarian Joseph Strutt's *The sports and pastimes of the People of England* (1801) was only slightly patronising: 'From the club-ball I doubt not originated that pleasant and manly exercise . . .', and he conceded that of late years it had become 'exceedingly fashionable, being much countenanced by the nobility and gentlemen of fortune'.

This aspect caused some concern to Dr Anthony Willich, author of *The Domestic Encyclopædia* of 1802. 'This sport was formerly confined solely to the labouring classes,' he complained, 'but is now becoming daily more fashionable among those whose rank and fortune entitle their countrymen to expect a very different conduct.' It was also 'in all respects too violent, and, from the positions into which players must necessarily throw themselves, cannot fail to be productive of frequent injury to the body . . . dislocations of the hip joint in particular are by no means uncommon from the awkward posture occasioned by employing both arms at the same time.'

It was from the schools that the danger was spreading. Not that it was usually encouraged by the masters, but increasingly in the 'public' schools, in which headmasters were not the owners but employees, the authorities had to heed parental, and indeed as more and more boys stayed on to a riper age, pupil opinion. Boys and old boys had made cricket into a favourite game of all classes, and in spite of its gambling associations it was an improvement on the old cruel animal sports that still survived. (Parliament, inspired by an impassioned defence from the Secretary for War, had recently rejected a bill to abolish bull-baiting.) In boarding schools, too, cricket was an excellent way of keeping twenty-odd boys occupied and out of worse mischief. Nevertheless, headmasters were decidedly unkeen on inter-school encounters for reasons that deserve our sympathy.

When Harrow, a relatively late butterfly to emerge from its Elizabethan grammar school chrysalis, entered into competition with Eton in 1805, the initiative to hire Lord's ground came entirely from the boys. Lord Byron (who fancied himself, in spite of his lameness, as a boxer and a cricketer) appears to have arranged the match during the school holidays. He left an entertaining account, though apparently exercising poetic licence over his own part in it, of a game in which Harrow 'were most confoundedly beat'. After the match the true sporting spirit prevailed:

> ... we dined together and were extremely friendly, not a single discordant word was uttered by either party. To be sure, we were most of us rather drunk and went to the Haymarket Theatre, where we kicked up a row, as you may suppose, when so many Harrovians and Etonians were in one place ...

The fixture then seems to have lapsed. Challenges were renewed every year, but could not be fitted in. There was no problem in hiring Lord's. The ground was let for 'pedestrian' events, pigeon-shooting matches, hopping contests, and, in 1802, a famous (French!) balloonist, to augment the rather meagre cricket programme, and Thomas Lord's income. Nor was there yet much enthusiasm for the ultimate declaration of social realities, matches of gentlemen against teams of paid players. Beauclerk, who had been doing well in contests between MCC teams and the local 'county' Middlesex or clubs like Hampstead or Highgate, had fancied the idea as early as 1798. He challenged a team of professionals including Walker, Beldham and the leading wicket-keeper, Hammond, but was defeated so thoroughly that the idea was dropped. By 1806, however, a 'Gentlemen v. Players' match was arranged with Beldham and a new star, William Lambert, as 'given' men for the Gentlemen. This produced a huge but hollow victory. The distinction was not very meaningful anyway, as Pycroft later recalled, for in London 'nearly all the play was professional; even the gentlemen made a profession of it'. MCC, apart from tours and special occasions, normally played against Middlesex, Hertfordshire or similar, local aggregations; but they also had a 'B' team, a mixture of members and paid players, ready to take on one or other of the various 'England' groupings.

VI

Some social change took place, during, if not because of, the war. Religion was the great dividing issue: Pitt resigned when he could not bring George III to accept Catholic Emancipation. But oppression turned it into a driving force, particularly in Ireland and such overspill areas as Glasgow and Liverpool. Similarly, Protestant Dissent, from Quaker and Unitarian intellectualism to Baptist and Congregationalist populism, strong in the new industrial areas, was behind most of the reforming movements now springing up. Methodism, which had begun as a movement within the Established Church, was swept by evangelical fervour to separation.

The climate for new ideas was greatly improved by the spread of literacy, now gathering momentum. Printing and publishing were thriving. Education, narrowly conceived and, for the poor, usually seen as an instrument of sectarian indoctrination, nevertheless became more widely available. The two great poets of this time, Burns and Blake, were not the products of public schools and universities. And when working-class radicalism was suppressed, the new wave – Wordsworth, Coleridge, Shelley, Byron – were sympathisers from the privileged classes. Bentham's intensely radical notion of using the law to promote the greatest good of the greatest number appealed not only to foreign intellectuals but to pragmatic northern industrialists and entrepreneurs. William Wilberforce, as a reforming evangelical Tory, was also a profound practical influence for good when radicalism was bad news: the ending of the slave trade in 1807 was one of the few achievements of the lacklustre 'Ministry of All the Talents', otherwise noted chiefly for its interest in pugilism.

If religion was a divider, Bonaparte was a great uniter. Yet there was a level below which hunger did not allow patriotic sentiments to come into play. In 1808 hordes of starving weavers, ruined by the blockade that prevented the import of American cotton, swarmed into Manchester and had to be dispersed by the army. But if these were below the patriotic level, others were above it. MCC, with its professional soldiers and sailors pursuing their careers, came into this category. Lord's and Lord himself were doing quite well out of the arrangement with the club. With crowds of 4–5000 for a big match, the sixpenny admission meant receipts of £200 or more, quite apart from the food and drink concession. They were good times for the players too: the best could command fees of six guineas to win and four to lose. Only the MCC were feeling the pinch, with the demise of old-style patronage, and backing a team costing £70 a time in players' wages. Now you would see a subscription list pinned up at Lord's for matches between Surrey or Kent and the Rest of England and find notices at Brooks's and other clubs[7] seeking guarantors. The members could still get practice and coaching on Mondays, Wednesdays and Fridays, but now there was a Marylebone Thursday club for the non-titled.

As the old grandees departed, the membership began to take on a slightly less aristocratic look. Some new members greatly strengthened the playing strength, like the Etonian civil servant E. H. Budd, a thorough sportsman, who clouted the ball many a mile with his three-pound bat, would bet on anything and back himself in most things, including Beauclerk's specialisms, but had no blue blood. Nor had William Ward, a Wykehamist who wielded a four-pound bat, who became a banker and a Member of Parliament. Some lacked both lineage and athleticism, notably Benjamin Aislabie, a rich wine merchant, who was so fat he could hardly walk. A jolly and a generous fellow, Aislabie had become by 1822 MCC's first honorary secretary. These were men of a new kind, the upper middle class – tremendous swells but not in the Duke of Dorset class.

The shortage of aristocratic patrons notwithstanding, MCC were rubbing along happily enough until Lord, faced with a demand for a higher rent, decided to find a cheaper place. He still kept on his old one, but in 1809 MCC members read in their *Morning Post*:

> CRICKET GROUND ... LORD begs to inform the Noblemen and Gentlemen that he has levelled and enclosed at the top of Lisson Grove, a short distance from his old Ground, which for size and beauty cannot be excelled ...

The Noblemen and Gentlemen were not impressed and declined to move: Lord was obliged to let the new field to the local St John's Wood Club. There were greater hardships. A bad harvest sent up the price of bread, already more than twice the pre-war price, and the new military hope, Sir Arthur Wellesley, later Lord Wellington, was in grave trouble in Iberia.

The Prince of Wales, Regent at last, was widely expected to take the Whig line and pull out the troops. He surprised everybody by holding firm. However, his mind was on other things. He spent the following summer in Brighton with Mrs Fitzherbert, earning stern criticism from the *Sporting Magazine*, not for neglecting the war effort, but for neglecting the Brighton Cricket Club. As recently as 1788 *The Times* had taken him to task for his cavortings there – driving his own coach in public and making 'his own lamp-lighter a partner at a game of cricket'. But his patronage had made Brighton – a 'shopocracy' as the snobbish called it – into a powerful club. Now the *Sporting Magazine*, recalling the time when Brighton had been a match for 'all-England and the Mary-le-bone Club', sneeringly commented that 'as nothing flourished in this part of the world without the renovating rays of the Heir Apparent' they had 'degenerated into their former insignificance'.

Back at Lord's, meanwhile, another belligerent non-combatant in the struggle against Bonaparte was taking the stage. This was George Osbaldeston, regarded in later life as the epitome of the sporting squire. Heir to a Yorkshire estate, he was born in London and brought up by his doting widowed mother in Bath, taught to ride by the celebrated Dash and nothing much by anyone else. His stay at Eton was brief and stormy, and his achievements were not scholastic: 'I could beat any boy at single-handed cricket, or any boy of my age at fisticuffs.' He also enjoyed shooting, fishing and making fireworks, rowing, hiring horses in Windsor and going to Ascot races. Required to leave, he spent two years at a crammer's near Brighton, acquiring his first pack of hounds. At Oxford he kept two hunters, annoyed the master of his college – 'I can't bear a Yorkshireman because he always offers to back his opinion by a bet' – and became a tearaway fast bowler.

After Oxford the young squire became a fearsome MFH, a renowned shot, a steeplechase rider, and a compulsive gambler. His aggressions increased as he lost his estate, chiefly by his ambition to own the finest pack of hounds and run the finest hunt in the country. He also developed a strong dislike for sporting parsons, arising from his experience of a neighbouring incumbent in Yorkshire, and a fierce jealousy of anyone with a title. When he joined MCC, therefore, he soon locked horns with Beauclerk, fourteen years his senior, who was both a clergyman and an aristocrat. Their first clash came in 1810 when Osbaldeston challenged Beauclerk to a double-wicket match for fifty guineas, each to play with a professional: Beauclerk with T. C. Howard and Osbaldeston with the new star, William Lambert. Osbaldeston was ill on the day, but it was 'play or pay', and Beauclerk refused to postpone or to allow a substitute. Osbaldeston staggered to the wicket and scored one notch before staggering off. Lambert saved the day by going on alone, and furthermore, winning by deliberately bowling wide and causing Beauclerk, as was his wont, to fly into a temper. This was a victory that Osbaldeston and poor Lambert were to regret, for Beauclerk had a long memory. Meanwhile, his immediate response was to secure a change in the laws, prohibiting wide balls, and MCC duly obliged in 1811.

By this time they were a club without a ground. Lord transferred the turves from the old pitch as an inducement so that the members could play 'on the same footing as before', but although they now had to give up the old ground they were so unenthusiastic about the new one that they played no games for two years and the club seemed to be on the way out. These were hard times for everyone. Much of industry was disrupted by Luddite riots as textile workers feared replacement by machines; the countryside was riven by repressive Game Laws. Magistrates, scenting Jacobin influence, bore down hard. A thousand spectators watched the public hanging of a racecourse tout at Cambridge. There was another bad harvest. The Prime Minister was assassinated by a madman. The Americans declared war and began to threaten Canada.

But the war news began to improve as Wellington broke the stalemate in Iberia, Napoleon bit off more than he could chew on the road to Moscow and the Allies closed in for the kill. The MCC was saved by a government decision to cut a new canal, named in honour of the Prince Regent, right through the Lisson Grove field. In 1813, aided by the £4000 compensation, Lord was able to buy his third ground, at St John's Wood, remove the turves again, and build a pavilion, a tavern, and various outbuildings. This time everyone was happy.

The war seemed to be over too. Napoleon was in exile, and the Americans, after the army had vengefully set fire to Washington, were ready to make peace. There was a little drama left, and the cricketers played their part in it. In March 1815 Napoleon escaped from Elba and marched on Paris, a hundred days, without a shot being fired. As the tension mounted, Wellington, now a Duke and Ambassador to the restored Bourbons, was recalled. An army was found for him only with difficulty. The Radicals at home gleefully expected Napoleon to win, and Wellington in Brussels had to instill calm into his troops and their wavering allies. Like Francis Drake facing the Armada, he turned to sport. Horse races, organised in Newmarket style, were one outlet, but cricket, MCC-style, was another. General Charles Lennox, now Duke of Richmond, was resident in Brussels, and whilst his Duchess gave a ball for Wellington's officers, his own contribution to morale was a cricket match. Wellington went to both, before getting down to business.[8]

CHAPTER FIVE

March of Intellect

IF THE WAR had scarcely touched the enjoying classes, the peace did little to ease the burdens of the poor. This was hardly surprising since all that had been achieved was restoring a reactionary regime across the channel to protect a reactionary one at home. Protecting the farmers from cheap imported grain was the chief objective of the Corn Laws of 1815, but it left the masses at the mercy of the British weather. Another bad harvest the following year brought riots and rick-burnings in the rural south, and machine-smashing in industrial districts, where thousands were forced on to poor relief by the recession. E. H. Budd recalled the anxieties about the crowd when MCC went to play at Nottingham in 1817. The ground there, in the Forest on the old racecourse, was unenclosed and so admission was free:

> the concourse was very great: these were the days of the Luddites ... and the magistrates warned us that unless we would stop our game at seven o'clock they could not answer for keeping the peace.

After a brief recovery, trade slumped again. Popular anger was sharpened by a growing sense of frustration at the political system. In 1819 troops were brought in to control a huge crowd assembled to hear a speech on parliamentary reform at St Peter's Field, Manchester. The resulting 'Peterloo' massacre outraged liberal opinion but brought stern reaction from the government. The accession to the throne of the Prince Regent added to the polarisation of opinion, and gave weight to the arguments of radicals who wanted to sweep out not just cobwebs, but the whole 'dead weight' of privilege and patronage. This was the telling phrase of William Cobbett (a near-contemporary of fellow-Farnhamite, William Beldham), who swung from extreme Toryism to pungent radicalism in a new vein of inspired 'common-sense' writing and politics. George IV was not only a moral disaster, he was manifestly an anachronism, still trying to pull the strings of government for his own benefit.

II

Cricket, too, was full of anachronisms at a time when change was sorely needed. To say that MCC showed lack of leadership is to mouth a truism that could have been uttered at any time in cricket history; but it is also to miss the point. Why should this once-voguish, now cliquish, gentlemen's club have been expected to give a lead in a pastime that was already country-wide in its extent, and appealed to all classes? Who should order these things? We have no answer even today. Still less can we fairly criticise these long-dead characters, cavorting around the bumpy, sheep-grazed Lord's ground in bizarre uniforms, for not having the vision to introduce an evolving system, authoritative yet democratically inclined, capable of reconciling all the vested interests and solving all the problems that still defy solution.

These fellows were seeking what everyone seeks in joining an élite social club – enjoyment and an escape from the real or imaginary troubles of the world outside. Unfortunately, some of them chose to play cricket in public and to allow money to be charged for the privilege of watching them, and the experts they hired, try to win their bets. A few were derided at the time, including the unfortunates singled out by the Revd John Mitford:

> There is not much to be said in favour of Messrs Kynaston, Woodhouse or Romilly when the bowling is first-rate; and Col. Lowther and Lords Strathaven and Clonblock ought to play in private, especially the Colonel who was designed rather to stand for the stumps than to hold a bat.

Many more were indulged because of their social eminence, indulged not only as players but as legislators and setters of standards.

The cricketers may have stood comparison with those of the previous generation, but the 'great matches' were fewer and lacked the resonance of times past. This may have been partly a natural or at least inevitable phenomenon, resulting from the demise of the old patrons, but it was also a reflection of the extent of gambling, which had long removed the first flush of healthy youth from cricket's cheek. 'The constant habit of betting will take the honesty out of any man', declared Pycroft. Morality apart, it made backers less forthcoming, taking the stuffing out of big cricket. The repentant sinner, Fennex, whose confession Pycroft published, exudes a world-weary sense of geese that laid golden eggs being killed off:

> matches were bought and matches were sold, and gentlemen who meant honestly lost large sums of money, till the rogues beat themselves at last. They over-did it; they spoilt their own trade ...

He goes on: 'One match up the country I did sell – a match made by Mr Osbaldeston at Nottingham.' And Pycroft adds, 'From information received,

I could tell this veteran that ... his was not the only side that had resolved to lose. The match was sold for Nottingham too ...'

Osbaldeston had established his Nottingham connection when Master of the Burton Hunt. He had already made several single- and double-wicket matches there against players from what he calls 'the County Club', with the assistance of his old accomplice, Lambert, then generally acknowledged to be the best player in England. The squire did not play himself in the double-fix match – leaving things to Lambert – but his enemy Beauclerk did. Lord Frederick was far too combative to put himself on the losing side even for gain: indeed he tried so hard to prevent his team winning the race to lose the match that, as Pycroft relates, 'he broke a finger trying to stop a designed and wilful overthrow' and had to bat with one hand in the second innings. Nottingham won in spite of themselves, and Beauclerk found himself worsted once more by Osbaldeston and Lambert. Osbaldeston, as a gentleman, was out of his reach.[1] Lambert, as a professional, was not. Men who would sell a cricket match would sell a fellow-professional, and Lord Frederick was able to find witnesses to Lambert's implication in the swindle and to ensure that he never afterwards appeared in a match at Lord's.

Eventually a stroke of good fortune delivered the squire into Beauclerk's hands. It was the result of Osbaldeston's inordinate vanity. 'I could beat anyone at single-wicket, even my friend Lambert,' he wrote in his autobiography, 'and nobody ever attempted to play against me singly.' The Brighton Club had recently come back into the news, largely because of a lightning-fast bowler, George Brown, about whom stories were told surpassing those about Osbaldeston – that he needed several longstops and that he had once killed a dog through a coat held out by a nervous boundary fielder. What was true was that his wicket-keeper surreptitiously and in (understandable) violation of the virility code wore a stuffed sack under his shirt. 'Osbaldeston,' recalled William Ward, 'had boasted a little too loudly that he could beat any man in England at single-wicket ... and of his extraordinarily fast bowling'. Ward and his friends saw a way of beating Osbaldeston at his own 'force and rough play' by suggesting that Brown might be faster than he. 'This,' commented Pycroft, 'resulted in Osbaldeston's challenge and defeat, which he bore with no good humour; for his hangers-on who usually came to crow ... [started] chaffing him on his overthrow. He was so angry that he went to the Pavilion and scratched his name off the list of members.'

Beauclerk's pleasure was complete when, some time later, Osbaldeston, through his friend E. H. Budd, asked to be reinstated. The answer was predictable, for despite widespread hostility to him, MCC revolved around Beauclerk. Aside from such internal matters as Osbaldeston's membership, he was also the acknowledged authority on the laws. When, for instance, the Oakham and Melton Mowbray clubs got involved in an inter-county dispute about the laws in 1818 and referred the matter to MCC, it was he who replied, delivering the judgment of Solomon. In Norfolk, another county with which he had close connections, disputants wrote to him direct. No one dared challenge his authority – based on rank, long service and intensive study of the laws – or, if they did, sooner or later unpleasant things would happen to them.

All very well, perhaps, if his own conduct had been exemplary, or had occasionally displayed a glimpse of Christian charity or aristocratic chivalry. The old professional, John Bowyer, was still indignant years later when he told the Wykehamist Fred Gale about how Beauclerk had treated him. There was quite often, in a big match, a guinea-a-man sweepstake on the player making the highest score. On one occasion Beauclerk had drawn his own name, while Bowyer's had been drawn by Lord Ponsonby, who had promised him two guineas if he won for him. This he seemed to have done, but Beauclerk

> went backwards and forwards to the scores to count his notches and mine, and the end of it was he got 64 and I got only sixty. Though he did give me a guinea, Lord Ponsonby would have given me two, and I call that sort of thing ... cheating.

When the rhymester Baxter described MCC's players in 1830 he commented on Beauclerk:

> My lord comes in next and will make you all stare
> With his little tricks, a long way from fair.

Osbaldeston is not a reliable witness, perhaps, but he adds a good story to the collection:

> Lord Frederick had a trick of raising his left shoulder higher than the other to make spectators who did not know better think he was deformed; to add to the deception he used to put his pocket-handkerchief under his cricketing waistcoat to increase the pretended deformity.

III

The most trenchant and perceptive comment on Beauclerk – and on the depths to which 'first-class' cricket had sunk – came from an unexpected source. Women so far played only a minor role, feminine rather than feminist, in this professedly 'manly' game.[2] The writer Mary Russell Mitford was herself no player, but a fervent supporter of her parish team. In 1823, aged forty-six, she wrote to a literary friend about a match she had seen between 'Hampshire with Mr Budd' and All-England. Her high expectations led to intense disappointment:

There they were – a set of ugly old men, white-headed and bald-headed (for half of Lord's was engaged in the combat, players and gentlemen, Mr Ward and Lord Frederick, the veterans of the green) dressed in tight white jackets ... with neckcloths primly tied around their throats, fine japanned shoes, silk stockings and gloves ...

After comparing them unfavourably for looks, dress and 'glowing, bounding youthfulness' to her own village team, she comes to the root of the matter:

There they stood ... silent solemn, slow – playing for money, making a business of the thing, grave as judges, taciturn as chess players – a sort of dancers without music, instead of the glee, the fun, the shouts, the laughter, the glorious confusion of the country game.

She concludes with a display of romantic idealism that would make a fine topic for discussion in any bar or university seminar:

I was never so disappointed in my life. But everything is spoilt when money puts its ugly nose in. To think of playing cricket for hard cash! Money and gentility would ruin any pastime under the sun.

Characteristically, 'Old Lord Frederick, on some real or imaginary affront, took himself off in the middle of the second innings,' and she took pleasure in the frustrated conclusion, 'for the degrading of my favourite sport into a "science", as they were pleased to call it, had made me quite spiteful': 'So be it always when men make the noble game of cricket an affair of bettings and hedgings and, maybe, of cheatings.'

Mary Mitford's denunciation of Beauclerk and the corrupt *ancien régime* can be directly related to the winds of change, perceptible during the war and now blowing more powerfully than ever. The flames of reform were fanned by such influences on public affairs as Wilberforce's Clapham Sect and the Methodists, remorselessly driving the country's leaders (with the notable exception of the king) towards a sense of shame, almost a conscience, that began to show itself in a collective prudence. Going on to the gold standard in 1821 not only stabilised the currency, it helped to create a collective integrity. The notion of free trade, Adam Smith modified by Jeremy Bentham, brought a measure of enlightenment into the blundering self-interest of protectionism. The march of intellect was the in-phrase amongst optimistic believers in progress: it was the sarcastic description given by reactionaries to anything they disliked, and hence it was the term used by the opponents of the innovative style of bowling that was disturbing cricket's equilibrium.

IV

The background to the prolonged and acrimonious dispute over bowlers'
actions was the continued domination of batsmen in the upper reaches of the
game. The MCC, who made the laws, were entirely complacent about this,
because batting was the enjoyable part of the game and the one most members
liked. The club employed bowlers to give the members batting practice: they
did not employ batsmen to give them bowling practice.[3] In the bigger
matches bowlers had occasionally tried to produce something a bit different,
and been cried down. When the professional Tom Walker had done it,
Hambledon had simply told him to stop. When gentlemen tried it, they were
made unwelcome in the best circles. John Willes, a Kent farmer, had
appeared at Lord's back in 1806 with a wide-sweeping arm movement (said
derisively by his critics to have been learned from playing with his sister,
Christina, swinging her arm above her hooped skirt) but did not venture back
for sixteen years.

No one knew what went on in the provinces, but there was sufficient
anxiety at Lord's for MCC to attempt controlling legislation. In 1816 they
ruled as follows:

> The ball must be delivered underhand, not thrown or jerked, with the hand
> below the elbow at the time of delivering the ball. If the arm is extended straight
> from the body, or the back part of the hand be uppermost when the ball is deliv-
> ered, or the arm extended horizontally, the umpire shall call no ball.

This appears to have settled matters for a while, and in 1819, as a palliative,
the size of the wickets was increased slightly, to 26 by 7 inches. John Willes
had not given up, however, and he began making the headlines again, as a
disruptive influence in Kent matches. As Pycroft put it:

> Mr Willes and his bowling were frequently barred in making a match, and he
> played sometimes amid much uproar and confusion. Still he would persevere
> until 'the ring' closed in on the players, the stumps were lawlessly pulled up and
> all came to a standstill.

Who would be an umpire ruling against a dubious action in circumstances
like that, with money at stake? The answer is that none would. Crowds apart,
the umpires' actions were subject to the superior force of gentlemanly
opinion, and this was divided. Beauclerk's views on Willes, according to Lord
Harris, a later reincarnation, were simple: 'When he played on the side of
Lord Frederick his bowling was fair, when against him, the contrary.' The
showdown came in 1822 when Willes played for Kent against MCC – and
Beauclerk. Sure enough, he was no-balled, and, revealingly, no one can say
with certainty who the brave umpire was.[4] The real decision-maker was

Beauclerk. At any rate Willes knew the jig was up, and, so it is said, stalked off the field, leapt on his horse and rode off into the sunset.

Another palliative to fend off imitators was tried in 1823, when the wicket size was increased to 27 by 8 inches; and again things quietened down for a while. The next significant event was the retirement of Beauclerk in 1826. He became president for a year, and remained a brooding presence thereafter, but he was no longer an interested party. Resistance among the active cricketers now centred on William Ward, who had been a prolific scorer off the old bowling but was less comfortable with the new. (Ward's opinion was doubly important because he owned the lease of the ground, having bought it from Lord the previous year when that immortal businessman had threatened to start building houses in the outfield.) The next bout of lawlessness came from Brighton, where the Sussex club was struggling into existence. It was master-minded by William Lillywhite, christened, in the high-flown journalistic style of the day, 'the Non-pareil'. From his pictures he looks anything but a demon bowler – a portly figure in a top hat and broad cotton braces holding up narrow-legged trousers. Nevertheless, he and his slightly younger partner, James Broadbridge, caused great commotion in 1827 by what their opponents claimed was 'throwing'.

There was sharp criticism from the old guard and from the cricket corre-spondent of the *Sporting Magazine*, William Denison. The renegades had a powerful supporter, however, in Mr G. T. Knight, an influential MCC member who was himself a 'march of intellect' bowler. Knight had already put the case for a change in the law before the committee without success, but he persuaded Mr H. Kingscote, Beauclerk's successor as president, to sanc-tion a series of 'experimental matches' in which an All-England side would play the Sussex innovators. Not only would the new bowling be put to the test, but to add further spice to the contests they were played for 1000 guineas.

They provided no neat solution. Sussex won the first two games, but Ward made runs in the second one and seemed better disposed to the new bowling than did England's professional players. Nine of them (including young Will Caldercourt, later the leading umpire) signed a statement refusing to play in the last match, 'unless the Sussex players bowl fair; that is, refrain from throwing'. They were either talked out of it or replaced, and England, includ-ing four gentlemen players – Ward, Budd, Osbaldeston and Knight – won this third contest, which was played at Lord's. The match was closely contested and 'it was supposed that £250 was taken at the door in sixpences'. Even this does not seem to have reconciled the proprietor to the monkey tricks on the pitch, and Denison concluded his report:

The old captain of stumps, Lord, a good fellow ... waxed desperately hot on the occasion, and neither civil nor adverse treatment could recover his good humour. Still he smiled at the victory; and the hand that guides this pen he clasped with fervency upon the event.

Nevertheless, the bowling issue was still wide open. When Knight appeared for Kent in an end-of-season game against Sussex, Denison accused him of 'throwing' and took the opportunity to rubbish the new style:

> it is not allowed by the articles of cricket, and I have yet heard no sufficient reason for its introduction. It is agreed that the game is now generally too long; and, it is said, it would be curtailed by the throwing. This I do not admit. I think fewer runs would be obtained, but that the game after a time would be equally long.

He certainly had a point there, but his remaining arguments were unconvincing: 'The fine lively scientific hitting would be lost. There would be comparatively no cutting to the point or slip; and no driving forward.' His assertion that nine-tenths of the cricket world were against it was, however, probably correct – all batsmen and experienced underarm bowlers. Denison concluded with a call for MCC to do their duty:

> The Mary-le-bone Club are looked up to as the legislators in cricket; their authority has never hitherto been disputed; and if they mean to preserve their power and influence, let them, like other wise law-givers, respect the feelings of their subjects.

Knight responded with two extremely long letters, which, interspersed with Denison's replies and comments from 'cricket-lovers' and seekers of fair play, took up large chunks of the *Sporting Magazine* in February 1828. The gist of Knight's argument was that bowlers should be given 'a larger field for the exertion of science than they now enjoy'. He objected strenuously to the 'throwing' label, pointing out, reasonably enough, that it was the very opposite, i.e. straight-armed. He added, rather less convincingly, that it was impossible to bowl dangerously fast in this mode. Notwithstanding this rather stilted exchange, the matter was to be decided not by debate or by committee edict but by a demonstration of the growing power of market forces.

Knight went back to MCC in May, proposing that only balls delivered from shoulder-height or above be illegal; and after long debate the legislators agreed to a compromise – deliveries with hand or arm above the elbow would be no-balled. This utterly impractical ruling gave enough licence to Lillywhite and Broadbent for them to restore the balance between bat and ball and thus to start a fashion. The old underarmers suddenly began to seem antiquated, particularly when, predictably, first the Sussex pair, and then their imitators all over the country, began to raise the arm higher and higher. Superior provincial clubs that wanted to observe the law found themselves frustrated when local umpires felt obliged to go by Lord's practice rather than MCC theory. The St Austell Club beyond the Tamar decided that games should be played by MCC rules, 'but if the majority of the members wish to play the rough game, they may do so'. MCC were now in effect following the trend, not setting it. They found themselves agreeing first to Knight's original proposal and then, in 1835, to legitimising any ball not thrown or jerked in which the hand or arm did not go above the shoulder. Lillywhite now bowled whatever he liked – that is, what the public liked – and after him came the deluge.

V

In this climate of uncertainty there were unprecedented openings for skill, and the top professionals were beginning to realise it. There was no open defiance of MCC, however. How could there be? After all, the Marylebone club was far and away the biggest source of match-fees and of regular summer-time employment: in 1825 they hired four practice bowlers and two young fielding 'scouts' and the total went up to ten in the next decade. This apart, in 1827 they increased pay for the big games to £6 a win, £4 a loss for three-day matches, £5 and £3 for shorter ones. It is no coincidence that the professional stars of the new era were mostly bowlers. As James Cobbett, of Middlesex, sixteen years on the Lord's ground staff, told Pycroft, 'We have no practice but in bowling; our batting must come of itself, except with Pilch and one or two others.' Young Fuller Pilch was a highly accomplished batsman from Norfolk and it is a measure of his greatness that even in the Lillywhite era there were ambitious clubs down in Kent seeking his services as a potential match-winner and box-office draw.

That, with very rare exceptions, run-of-the-mill professionals could outstrip the best the gentlemen could produce had long been obvious. When the disastrous Gentlemen v. Players idea had been tried again in 1819, with the same formula of star professionals 'given' to the Gentlemen, there had been a similar lack of interest in the outcome. Two years later the Gentlemen, having batted first and made 60, fielded for many hours whilst the Players made 270 for 6; then 'gave up'. This was the Coronation match, celebrating the accession of George IV, and it was a suitably murky affair. As Beldham recalled it:

> I was hurt and could not run my notches; Still James Bland and the other 'Legs' begged of me to take pains for it was no sporting match, 'any odds and no takers'; and they wanted to shame the Gentlemen against wasting their [the 'Legs'] time in the future.

Nevertheless, the fixture struggled on. In 1835 the match was enlivened by the performance (for the Gentlemen) of a young Nottingham professional,

Sam Redgate, who clean bowled Pilch twice for nought, bowling fast round-arm stuff. The Lord's pitch of those days 'in a hot summer was clay baked to the hardness of brick' and the ball flew around rarely. The following year the Gentlemen, fielding eighteen against the Players' eleven, brought out an even faster round-armer, Alfred Mynn, a strapping fellow of six foot two and some eighteen stone, coached by Willes. He and a seventeen-year-old Winchester schoolboy called Lowth[5] – and the Lord's pitch – wrought havoc.

The advent of young Lowth was an omen of better things to come. After a long interval, another Eton v. Harrow match had been arranged in 1818. By then it was apparent that the schools' reputations were based on more than scholarship. *The Times* advised Eton, who lost, to look to their laurels: 'They should contrive not to lose a characteristic which has been thought to distinguish them as much as making centos of Latin verse.' By 1822 the encounter had become a regular fixture, and Harrow set a new trend by hiring a professional coach, Will Caldercourt, from Lord's. Lord himself was delighted, for the fixture brought in crowds of two or three thousand schoolboys, outside the short London 'season' at a time when the gentry had gone off in search of birds to shoot. These matches should not be thought of as pleasant, innocent frolics. Byron had indicated what the lads might get up to after the match, and as Pycroft observed laconically of the 1825 game, 'There was much betting in those days.'[6]

But they soon became highly fashionable. *The Times* reported in 1833, 'We noticed upwards of thirty carriages containing ladies ...' By this time the élite circle had widened sufficiently to admit Winchester. At first, Pycroft tells us,

> little was known of them. Then Price was seen repeatedly bowling down a single stump at Lord's the day before the match, the odds altered at once, and men were in a hurry to hedge.

The criterion was, however, social not athletic. It was said of Harrow twenty years later that they still only recognised themselves, Eton, Westminster, Winchester and Charterhouse as public schools anyway; and Pycroft recounts that when Shrewsbury wrote asking for a fixture, Eton replied, 'Harrow we know, Winchester we know, but who are ye?' But the gradual improvement in the standard of amateur cricket over the next thirty years stemmed from these encounters and the subsequent rivalry at the universities. 'At this time the Wykehamists were the best players of the day,' wrote Pycroft of his time at Oxford. They played an annual match against the rest of the university and once won a match against 'the two Universities'[7] at Lord's.

It was the dawn of muscular Christianity in the public schools, and Winchester's contribution certainly emphasised the muscular. They were 'particularly famous for fielding. Their rush in to meet the ball, their clean scoop up and quick return were remarkable ... they used to qualify by prac-

tising till they could throw over a certain building in the neighbourhood.'
There were six Wykehamists in the first Varsity match against Cambridge in
1827. The driving force behind this, however, was the Harrovian, Charles
Wordsworth (nephew of the poet and afterwards Bishop of St Andrews), and
it was Harrow who produced the best amateur bowler of the early thirties, the
fast underarm C. J. Harenc. 'I bowl the best ball of any man in England,' said
Lillywhite, dispensing with false modesty, 'and Mr Harenc the next.' The
Etonians had their muscular Christian 'dry-bobs', too: notably (Revd) J. H.
Kirwan, who wrought havoc 'with a kind of undetected jerk' and a decade
later (Revd) F. W. Marcon, who may have been faster than Brown or
Osbaldeston. 'Fast as he is, I'll have a crack at him,' said one young hopeful.
The first ball that came took his bat clean out of his hands and right through
the wicket. Marcon, who broke a batsman's leg before going off to cure souls
in Cornwall, was talked about in hushed tones for years. His team-mate
Harvey Fellows was the first hero of a basic cricket joke: the story went that
when Fellows started bowling, the fifty-year-old Lillywhite, usually a stubborn tail-ender, walked across to the scorers' tent and said, 'No – put down
Lillywhite absent.'

VI

Amongst the more welcome changes in the world beyond Lord's were
improvements in health. Lower death rates augmented the fast-growing
population. By 1831 there were some 14 million in England and Wales,[8] the
biggest growth occurring in the industrial towns. With the stimulus of
reduced and simplified import duties the mechanisation of industry developed apace, bringing prosperity to employers and offering better job
opportunities, but fitfully, and mainly to skilled workers. For those in work
long hours were expected – to keep the machines in use – for children as well
as adults. All but the most sentimental liberals saw this as a valuable extension
of the devil-makes-work-for-idle-hands policy. Invading job-seekers, especially from Ireland, which was in desperate straits, were hotly resented. There
were disturbances in all the major cities, and racial and religious feelings
added ginger to sporting contents.

When the ultra-conservative Wellington became Prime Minister his object
was to preserve society from incipient chaos. The Metropolitan Police force
was set up in 1829 to quell disorder as well as fight crime. Even Wellington
gritted his teeth and supported Catholic emancipation to avoid rebellion in
Ireland, but he wanted nothing to do with parliamentary reform. He had this
in common with his old adversary and new king, William IV, a randy old
sailor and long-time patron of illegal prize-fights, who, regardless of his many
faults, had the immense advantage of not being George IV. Wellington soon
bowed out and the Whigs came in to face mounting disorder, particularly in

the countryside. Kent was terrorised by a mysterious Captain Swing, who left notes after his midnight rick-burnings. The workers' plight was pitiful and their wage demands moderate; indeed, the new government awarded a shilling a week increase in wages, but not before hanging or transporting the ringleaders. Emigration doubled in a year. Throughout their period of office the Whigs maintained a tough policy towards the looming shadow of trade unionism, entering the hall of infamy by creating the Tolpuddle Martyrs.

The Whig leader, Earl Grey, did, however, see parliamentary reform as a way of placating the burgeoning middle classes and fending off mob rule. One in six suitably qualified men were given the vote, after two years of continuing disorder, politically motivated strikes, Commons' argument, Lords' resistance, and royal obstruction. The Reform Act was equally moderate in its after-effects. There had been every expectation that the reformed Parliament would sweep away the Dissenters' grievances by doing away with an Established Church altogether, but it preferred milder measures. These reduced the gap between rich and poor clergy, reduced the scope of sporting parsons like Beauclerk, lightened the burden of tithes and shifted it from the tenant-farmer to the landowner – all of which lessened hostility to the Church and the clergy, allowing them to take a worthier part in the social-reform movement.

The redistribution of seats also recognised the new urban realities, and the Municipal Reform Act of 1835 extended the principle. The power of the landed classes was dented a little in favour of the new bourgeoisie, and there was some realignment of the old political tribes. A new Conservative Party began to develop under Sir Robert Peel, determined to hold the line against radical ideas, but amenable to organisational improvement and more sympathetic to industry and commerce. The Whigs were still some distance from being Liberals, but they had achieved middle-class backing and the parliamentary support of the Irish Catholics.

Their new leader, Lord Melbourne, was no progressive, but he rode the waves of change with impressive suavity, presiding over some important advances – the abolition of slavery, the first substantial Factory Act addressing the problems of women and children, the first modest government grant in support of elementary education, reform of local government, and, not least, reform of the hated Game Acts in favour of a licensing system. This last greatly depressed the fox-hunting traditionalists, whilst opening the door to urban middle-class *arrivistes* seeking gentrification or escape back to nature through the wholesale slaughter of game birds. The fox-hunters were also bitterly resentful of the incursion of the railways which now disfigured the countryside, accelerating the pace of industrialisation and shrinking the distance between town and country.

Mary Russell Mitford, with her series of books on 'Our Village', launched a new genre, a literature of place, and her works, along with Cobbett's more

pungent *Rural Rides,* were part of a rediscovery of the countryside that was to
have a powerful appeal to the new massed inhabitants of industrial towns.
Cricket was part of it, and Mary Mitford herself produced a rhapsodical
account of a village cricket match in which she gave full rein to her romantic
– and suppressed sexual – yearnings, alloyed by touches of shrewd observation and wit. It is a longish piece, not easily divisible into representative
snippets, but perhaps a stripped-down version of its celebrated opening will
sufficiently illustrate its theme:

> A village cricket match is the thing – where our highest officer ... is but a little
> farmer's second son; where a day-labourer is our bowler, and a blacksmith our
> longstop; where the spectators consist of the retired cricketers ... the careful
> mothers, the girls and all the boys of two parishes, together with a few
> amateurs, little above them in rank, and not at all in pretension; where laughing
> and shouting, and the very ecstasy of merriment and good humour, prevail.

In 1833 the changing times also evoked, from the London-based Nyren and
his London literary ghost, their dollop of undiluted nostalgia about
Hambledon. This was not only a sylvan idyll, but a paean of regret for
cricket's lost soul. The section sternly headed

PROTEST AGAINST THE MODERN INNOVATION OF THROWING,
INSTEAD OF BOWLING THE BALLS

might have been commissioned by Denison for his *Sporting Magazine*
campaign, and he quoted approvingly from it in his own book:

> If the present system [of throwing] be continued a few years longer, the elegant
> and scientific game of cricket will decline into a mere exhibition of rough,
> coarse, horse play.

Protesting his complete lack of prejudice, he concludes:

> I have, therefore, no hesitation in declaring that none of the players who have
> risen with the new system, can compare for a moment in the standard of excel-
> lence ... with the eminent men I have named.

John Mitford's strange 'review' of Nyren (he does not refer once to the
book in two long articles) is similarly rhapsodical about the Hambledon era as
the defining moment when cricket crossed an important threshold, but
without suggesting that civilisation had been given notice to quit by
Lillywhite and Broadbridge. He takes the new bowling as given, and his criticism is rather more measured: 'We are convinced that the present style of
bowling will never again fall back into the straight old underhand mode; but

we hope also that it will not advance into throws, to which it is approaching; and which, if allowed, will destroy the game altogether.' His rhapsody is, indeed, for cricket itself: he is in no doubt about its value in the great scheme of things, being particularly concerned, for instance, that notable cricketers going into the Church should not let their parsoning interfere with their true vocation. Of Mr Knatchbull, a great hitter to whom a corner of Lord's was dedicated, Mitford writes:

> We hope and trust that his professional engagements in Norfolk will never detain the reverend gentleman from the classical ground of Marylabourne. A curate can easily supply his place in the church, but who is to supply it in the field? ... He ought to have the living of St John's Wood, when he could play and preach alternately. Could it not be obtained?

VII

Mitford is also interesting as an early exponent of the xenophobic (and some-times racist) streak that characterises much English cricket writing. Here it is jocularly intended:

> Cricket is the pride and the privilege of the Englishman alone. Into this, his noble and favourite amusement, no other people ever pretended to penetrate: a Frenchman or a German would not know which end of a bat they were to hold.

Similarly he has no doubt about the best in England:

> Kent has always stood proudly pre-eminent; Kent is emphatically the field of the cricketer's glory.

Sussex, Hampshire and Surrey come next. Middlesex's recent celebrity stems from the fortuitous presence of MCC. The most promising newcomers are Norfolk, for the great Pilch, and Yorkshire, for the 'extraordinary accom-plishment' of Thomas Marsden. As a batsman Mitford found Marsden 'wanting in temper and judgement and discretion'; he was 'a good player, and had he been brought up at Marylabourne, among fine players, would have been eminent'. Nevertheless, he was the pride of Sheffield, with 'a great name in Yorkshire'.

The implication, of course, was that without southern nurture, northern natural talent could not hope to flourish. There was also a suggestion of the uncouth in the reports southerners took back from their missionary ventures. Thus John Bowyer told Fred Gale of an early game in Sheffield, memorable because he got a £10 fee and all expenses paid, out and home: the organisers took £1200 at the gate; but the game lasted four days because the stumps had to be 'drawn each day at a quarter to six before the factories closed, as they were afraid of the roughs'. Clearly the better sort of Sheffield – who were the ones who got up the games and flocked to watch them – were just as apprehensive of violence from their social inferiors as Londoners traditionally were, but the impression of a harsh industrial wasteland is misleading.

In its way this brief report from the early *Manchester Guardian* about a match in 1826 paints as idyllic a picture as Nyren, without Cowden Clarke's hyperbole:

> A cricket match was played at Huddersfield, on Monday last, between eleven of the Huddersfield old club and eleven of the Manchester new club, which was won after a good contest by the former ... This match excited considerable interest amongst the connoisseurs of the game: the Huddersfield club were saluted by 'a merry peal from the church bells on retiring from the field. They spent the evening together with the utmost conviviality, and the harmony was kept up by a company of glee singers.'

One way and another, things seemed to be looking up for the northerners. The first of the 1828 'experimental matches' against Lillywhite and Broadbridge was played in Sheffield, and the 'England' side included some local heroes, including the young Marsden, who had made a double-century on his début the previous year against Leicester. Afterwards the *Sporting Magazine* reported that the Yorkshire players 'displayed great skill and convinced the cricket world that the South must not, as heretofore, presume to wear the wreath for ever'. Since then Marsden had not looked back until he was beaten at single-wicket in 1833 by Pilch. Others, such as James Dearman, had also done well in Yorkshire teams, whilst Nottingham had had much success with Sam Redgate. Eventually the commercial possibilities of a North v. South match were realised. This took place at Lord's in 1836, after the new law had been passed, and the Northerners so far forgot their manners as to win.

The symbolism in social terms was most powerful: in cricketing terms it did not last long, though. A return match was arranged at Leicester for £500 a side, which the South won by 218 runs. The match demonstrated first that Lillywhite under the new dispensation was unplayable, and second that fearful physical injuries could be inflicted by round-arm bowling, as its opponents predicted. The situation was exacerbated, of course, by the virility cult, which decreed that 'leggings' be not worn. (Lord Frederick, still the arbiter of taste, thought they were acceptable in practice but unfair to bowlers in a match.) Ironically, the sufferer was the fast bowler, Alfred Mynn.

Mynn had injured his leg in practice, but was, as the local paper put it, 'doctored up' for the match. He needed a runner when he went into bat, but he made 21 not out, fielded, bowled briefly at the end of the North's first innings, taking a wicket, and then went in a second time and made 125 not out. The North's leading bowler, Redgate, said afterwards, 'The better I bowled the harder he hit me away.' Sometime during North's second innings Mynn decided to confess to Lord Frederick that he was in difficulties, showed his swollen and battered limbs and was despatched at once for home. He was, reported the *Leicester Journal*, 'obliged to be packed up, as it were, and laid on the roof of the stage coach, and in that position he rode from Leicester to London'. There he lay, first at a tavern in St Martin's Lane, then at St Bartholomew's Hospital, narrowly escaping amputation, taking a long enforced rest from cricket.

CHAPTER SIX

Reformers and Reactionaries

IT SEEMED TO HERALD a new dawn when the young Victoria succeeded her rough old uncle in 1837. Tennyson wrote a poem about it. The Prime Minister, Lord Melbourne, was aroused from his pose of world-weary cynicism by Victoria's freshness and direct simplicity and took delight in gently instructing her in her new duties. Then Prince Albert of Saxe-Gotha, an altogether superior human being, came into her life. He was a firm believer in progress through science, free trade and similar serious subjects, which inevitably made him seem both comic and sinister to the cheerfully disorganised and xenophobic British. If Victoria's accession had symbolised advance, the reaction to Albert epitomised the obstacles in its path.

Indeed, Parliament's first experiment in Benthamite progress, the Poor Law of 1834, had not been a great success. Four years later the workhouses it created featured in *Oliver Twist*, a grim melodrama serialised by the new sensation, Charles Dickens. Reform was not foremost in the mind of Peel, back in office in 1841 for five years. He put his trust in industry, where his father's fortune had been made, and where the economic fruits of change were beginning to ripen. Protectionist agricultural policies put a brake on foreign trade and brought temporary recession in the important new cotton trade. Redemption came through expansion of the railways, improving the links between coal- and iron-fields, factories, ports and home markets, and injecting fresh life into trade and industry. Exports almost doubled in value between 1830 and 1850, two-thirds of them in cotton goods. There were dramatic increases in profits and investments, which, if God were in His heaven taking tea with Adam Smith, meant that the workers would get their share sooner or later.

There was still some way to go in wealth redistribution: only 10 per cent of the population had incomes over £100 a year. Male industrial workers mostly earned from 15s. to 30s. a week, some even less (like all women). The new industries certainly brought more jobs – an increase from 340,000 to 570,000 in textile factories alone – but the gap between rich and poor increased rather than lessened. From the turn of the century to 1850, the annual average income of the top 10 per cent went up from £130 to £200, but wage-earners' gains were much smaller. In agriculture, which provided work for a million families,[1] the fitful protection of the Corn Laws was no help against manipulation of the market by speculative importers: nothing seemed able to lift the farm labourer from his lowly status, still earning around ten shillings a week in areas where there was no industrial alternative.

Over the same period the cost of living fell by almost a third, and this was the main cause of complacency about drifting along with the industrial tide. Lower prices were the manufacturers' moral and economic goal. This gingered up the town–country, north–south debate and provoked bitter opposition to the older agricultural interests, still hankering after higher prices. Hence the mounting agitation for free trade amongst the urban middle classes. Neither side put the workers' interests first. By 1844 the German radical Engels, working in his father's factory in Manchester, was confidently predicting revolution; and four years later he and Karl Marx, from their base in London, invited the workers of the world to unite. But such radicals as there were amongst the British proletariat had been seduced by the Chartist vision of total (male) parliamentary democracy, or diverted into the bourgeois Anti-Corn Law League. Revolution broke out all over Europe, but the pragmatic British workers preferred to keep their capitalist shackles.

II

In the cricket world, it was thought a revolutionary act to raise the bowling arm above the elbow. All such disturbing matters were set aside, however, as MCC members commemorated their fiftieth anniversary in 1837. Their main concern was whether the funeral of the old king would get in the way of the celebrations. These included a Jubilee Match benevolently arranged 'for the benefit of the Players', each of the 170 or so members being asked to contribute £1. Lord Frederick and the Earl of Thanet chose the two teams and, to the satisfaction of some 3000 spectators, North, even with the aid of two 'given' southerners, proved no match for the South, with Lillywhite rampant. Indeed, the only fly in the MCC ointment was the sorry performance of the Gentlemen against the Players in both that year's fixtures. The first, christened the 'Barn Door Match', was eleven a side, but the Players were asked to defend giant stumps (36 by 12 inches); they still won by an innings. In the return match the Gentlemen were allowed sixteen men, but again lost by an innings.

In truth, since Beauclerk's retirement and the decline in gambling MCC did not take cricket as seriously as before, showing more interest in the purely social side of things. Lord's had changed hands again the previous year when James Dark bought the unexpired portion of the lease from William Ward.

Dark, the son of a saddler, had been a professional cricketer and umpire in his extreme youth before moving into property-owning. He began an ambitious programme of developments – extending and improving the pavilion, installing gaslight, adding a billiard room, a real tennis court and a running track and planting 400 trees. Only the pitch remained in a primitive state, bumpy, undrained and sheep-cropped. Nor can the outfield have been improved by some of the extra attractions Dark staged, such as pony races and Red Indian encampments.

But he set to with great energy, bringing his whole family in on the act. His brother Ben set up a bat-making business at the ground with his wife Matilda, and their younger brother Robert, once apprenticed to John Small, not only supplied all the balls used at Lord's (and took money at the gate) but also developed a range of equipment, including pads and gloves. Even before Mynn's battering at the hands of his fellow round-armers, batsmen had begun to take advantage of the change in sartorial fashion to slip padding inside their trousers surreptitiously. Now the interest quickened, especially outside public-school circles, where muscular Christianity was thought protection enough. A Nottingham professional, Thomas Nixon, patented cork pads in 1841, and two years later the London Toy Repository advertised 'knee pads' for cricket. And a whole range of products came on to the market as the potential of the American Charles Goodyear's invention of vulcanised rubber began to be realised.

One of the first to respond was an agreeable and ingenious young schoolmaster, Nicholas Wanostracht, known as Felix. In his delightful book *Felix on the Bat* (1845) he strongly recommended 'paddings' for protection against 'the uncertainty and irregularity of the modern system of throwing'. His preference was 'longitudinal socks' of linen filled with strips of rubber, worn under the trousers. He also invented one of the earliest practical batting gloves, using tubular rubber strips. He sold his patent in 1848 to Duke & Sons, the ball and equipment makers, but the same year Robert Dark advertised himself as 'sole inventor and manufacturer of the Tubular India-Rubber Gloves and the Improved Leg Guards'.

Diehards, of course, scorned such protection, pointing out that pads hampered stroke-play, but they appear to have been pretty adroit at keeping their shins out of the firing line. (Fuller Pilch's admired stance would not be approved today.[2]) Felix, who saw no purpose in needless heroics, devoted a chapter of his book to the cut shot, a suitably distant stroke. Another chapter was given over to the 'draw'. This, which involved lifting up the front leg and deflecting the ball underneath it, gradually disappeared from the canon as pads and pad play came in, in later, more cynical times. Felix poked gentle fun at the masochists. (In one of his illustrations a boundary fielder is watched by admiring spectators as he bends back to catch a ball in his teeth.) They were given even more scope as the new bowling became the norm; sharpening controversy about the ethics of protective clothing for wicket-keepers and longstops.

Wicket-keepers were not expected to stop every ball, but rather to look out for stumping chances and other attacking moves. Herbert Jenner (later Sir Herbert Jenner-Fust, a MCC luminary), the admired wicket-keeper of the twenties, had worn neither gloves nor pads, but the new bowling changed things slightly. Wenman, the great Kent professional, wore only 'a common leather glove on one hand' in 1836, surprising Pycroft, who reflected, however, that there were not so many games in those days. Wenman rarely kept wicket twice a week. Pycroft expected professionals, as horny-handed sons of toil, to have an in-built advantage over the gentlemen, who, of course, were accustomed to wear gloves in ordinary life. Others argued that rowing was the best way for a gentleman to toughen up the palms. The longstop, an essential and honoured fielding position, filled the defensive role, and was correspondingly more likely to put protection before mobility: Pycroft's friend, John Marshall, wore thick 'leggings'.

Another hazard of facing the new 'rough' bowling, even with a superior willow bat, was that it jarred the hands badly. Bats were still carved out of a single piece of wood until around 1837, when splicing was introduced, to allow more 'give'. At first this simply meant removing the handle from the blade with a V-shaped cut and sticking the two bits together again. This helped a little, and experiments with strips of other material in the handle produced even better results. In 1840 you could buy a bat with a steel 'spring' for half a guinea, but most people preferred whalebone, the standard stiffening for women's corsets, which was lighter and more flexible.

Cricket, in short, was becoming a scientific affair. The ultimate was another of Felix's inventions, the catapulta, a bowling machine. 'A block of wood was struck by the recoil of a strong spring. You could set it to any length, and vary the power ...' wrote Pycroft. Like Crompton's Mule and Hargreaves' Spinning Jenny fifty years before, the catapulta must have sent shivers down the spine of manual operatives. But the bowler's art – and more particularly the practice bowler's income – was safe: '... the precision was not exact,' added Pycroft, recalling how, at Cambridge, Lillywhite had backed himself against the catapulta and won.

III

Lillywhite, now well into his fifties, was by this time looking back somewhat ruefully over his long career. He had started his working life as a bricklayer, first under his father on the Duke of Richmond's Goodwood estate, then moving to Brighton, combining cricket with managing brickyards until in 1837, at the height of his fame, he became landlord of the Royal Sovereign and proprietor of a cricket ground – the classical combination. Unfortunately, despite his renown, it was not a success. He staged some early matches of the Sussex County Club (founded with high hopes in 1839, but sporadic in its operation), then his ground 'had to be abandoned to building requirements'. The pub didn't do well either. In 1844, aged fifty-two, Lillywhite moved to London, where he became a ground bowler for MCC, was allowed a benefit match and set up a sports equipment shop with his two sons. They, with nothing like their father's cricketing ability, reaped more reward than the old man did.

Still, to have provided so well for his family was a not inconsiderable achievement and one that many of his contemporaries must have envied. Witness poor Fennex, who had died in the workhouse a few years earlier. It is easy to make fun of Victorian moralising about the evils of drink, but a public house could be a dangerous place for a sporting hero. This apart, it needed a special temperament to handle the twin tasks of being a celebrity and running a public house at the scene of your triumphs. Sometimes lesser mortals did better than the big stars. Thus Tom Adams, a much less famous round-arm bowler than Lillywhite, who started out as a factory-hand in Gravesend at 12s. a week, and was sponsored for his £5 match fees by the Town Malling Club gentry, was soon able to take over the Bat and Ball Inn, gradually levelling and fencing the adjoining ground. Without ever reaching the pinnacle, he had a good career with Kent, but he also worked hard at his ground-keeping and augmenting his public-house business – for example, by holding fairs in conjunction with the cricket matches – whilst his wife handled the catering. The critical step for many was that between working for wages and entrepreneurship. For example, Daniel Day, another round-armer, moved to Southampton to become ground bowler and pro for the superior South Hampshire Club, and also secured the tenancy of the Antelope Inn. But when he moved to nearby Itchen to set up his own ground, the venture failed.

Kent was undoubtedly the county to be in just then, if you were a cricketer. There were good clubs in every small market town. Dickens' *Pickwick Papers* (1837) offers an agreeably irreverent account of an encounter between Dingley Dell and the impressively named All-Muggleton. Dickens' piece, whilst open to criticism on technical matters, conveys well the seriousness with which the bourgeoisie in the Kentish skirts of London took this most idiosyncratic of their sporting pleasures and its attendant social ceremonies. And above this level – cricketing and social – there was extraordinary eagerness amongst the gentry not only to bring in professionals as ground-keepers and coaches at their clubs but to build them into a team and to try it out against the best in the land. This is how the Town Malling Club came to recruit the best batsman in England, Fuller Pilch.

Pilch, born in Norfolk, had gone looking for work in Sheffield as a lad and had learned his cricket there. He moved back, first to Bury St Edmunds then to Norwich, taking up a post in which Mitford saluted him bizarrely: 'Come forth from thy public house at the bottom of Surrey Hill, Norwich, which thou keepest, with thy sister as thy bar-maid, Fuller Pilch!' He came forth to take another pub in Town Malling, with the added inducement of £100 a year as ground-keeper. He also took on an assistant at £60 a year, Will Martingell from Surrey.

Pilch's backers were headed by Mr Thomas Selby (a business man turned squire, who took sides around the country like a modern version of Sir Horatio Mann), the like-minded Silas Norton, and the third Lord Harris, an Oxford man and later one of the emerging breed of colonial administrators. Between 1835 and 1842 Kent sides chosen by Selby and his associates played eleven matches at Town Malling against neighbouring counties or against 'England' sides chosen by MCC. They proved highly popular: the crowds were so great that a 'ring-keeper' was employed who, like George Smith at the old Artillery Ground, proudly used 'his long lash with energy and some noise' – presumably for demonstration purposes only. The railway network had not yet spread this far, but people walked, rode or drove conveyances of all kinds to see the great cricketers whom the new, racy sporting press described so glowingly. Given its distinctive flavour by Pierce Egan earlier in the century, sports journalism was now established firmly amongst all ages of the literate population:[3] *Bell's Life*, started back in 1822, had become essential Sunday reading.

In between these occasional 'county' games Pilch and Martingell (one of the great bowlers of the day) might be chosen for the Players or for MCC, but they also had to be ready to turn out for the Club, to coach its members and to give them practice. Pilch, the great batting star of the era, but also a countryman of the old style, saw nothing wrong with this and fully accepted the social divide on which it was based: 'Gentlemen were gentlemen, and players much in the same position as a nobleman and his head keeper maybe.' Similar attitudes were prevalent amongst Kent's home-grown professionals like Edward Wenman, the great wicket-keeper. Wenman was a carpenter and wheelwright in his home village of Benenden, and there he stayed all his life, working at his trade. He played regularly for Kent for almost twenty years, was awarded a benefit match in 1843 and still played occasional games until he was over fifty. Wenman was a countryman, like Pilch, and they tended to know their place better than some of the sharper, towny types. Denison referred to the great esteem in which Wenman was held, citing his 'quiet and respectful demeanour' as a major reason for the esteem – and the benefit.

For all the dominance of the gentlemen off the field and their enthusiasm for playing cricket on it, the great Kent sides in the period of their supremacy, from about 1830 to 1850, were nearly all professional. Matches were becoming longer – usually three days – and increasingly difficult to fit in with any business that needed year-round attention. Thus Kent's two regular amateurs might as well have been professionals – they could not afford to play as much as they did without making something out of their cricket – if it were not for the perceived social stigma. Their cases were otherwise quite different.

Felix had so many talents apart from cricket – inventive, artistic, musical, literary – he had such a privileged start in life, and was so universally liked and admired for all his attributes, that it is surprising that he did not achieve more. While still a young man he had inherited a private school in Camberwell and had been serious enough about it to write textbooks. A neat, stylish and thoughtful cricketer, he took up the game as enthusiastically as all his other interests, but when he started playing publicly he adopted the name Felix lest his image of scholastic seriousness be tarnished amongst parents. Then he moved his school to Blackheath and began to play for the congenial and convivial Kent XI. And there he struck up an alliance with the beefy Alfred Mynn, a giant in all but intellect. They made an engaging if improbable pair.

The fourth son of a gentleman farmer, Mynn had no settled profession, and, with a wife and family to support, was, unfortunately, cut out for nothing but playing cricket. His return to the game after his leg injury was delayed not only by the slow process of recovery but by financial worries brought on by the death of his father, who had subsidised his cricketing. A benefit match at Lord's – 'very well supported,' says Pycroft, for Mynn was every schoolboy's hero – helped keep the wolf from the door for a while. After trying his hand at his brother's hop-making business he returned with relief to cricket in 1838 – an even deadlier bowler, more accurate and off a shorter run. That season, decked in a straw hat[4] with a red ribbon, he beat the Yorkshire challenger James Dearman at single-wicket, home and away, before thousands of spectators. It was eight years before he was challenged again – by his friend Felix. A small man, expert at the cut, Felix was handicapped because shots behind the wicket did not count. Nevertheless they played a game so exciting that old men described it to their grandchildren.

Presumably they took a share of the gate on such occasions. Mynn in particular was in chronic need of money, several times becoming bankrupt and imprisoned for debt, and he was granted another benefit match in 1847. Yet the rewards of professionalism were not enough to compensate for the loss of social status. In any case, first-class cricket was a precarious business. Rising costs and reduced gates ended the Town Malling venture. After that the task of arranging Kent matches fell to a number of county families, the Bakers of Canterbury and the Brenchleys of Gravesend being the most prominent. Pilch cut his losses and entered the service of the brothers Baker, on whose estate the Beverley Club played its matches, also becoming landlord of the Saracen's Head at Canterbury. The most celebrated of the Beverley Club's promotions was an annual Kent Cricket Week, originally played on the Bakers' estate, but soon outgrowing this and transferring to the St Lawrence's hospital ground. The week's main cricketing feature was a game between

Kent and 'England', which for some years took its place amongst the leading fixtures along with Gentlemen v. Players and North v. South, but the unifying theme, apart from a lot of eating and drinking, was an interest in amateur theatricals. This formula proved highly attractive, for fairly obvious reasons, to a group of young Cambridge men, the more dedicated of whom began styling themselves 'The Old Stagers', establishing a tradition that helped to compensate for the variable quality of the cricket over the years.

It also gave a strong amateur flavour to the proceedings at a time when the relationship between amateurs and professionals was being hotly disputed at the universities in the socially superior sport of rowing, which in its highest team form, eights, was the foremost battleground for muscular Christians. Powerful factions, first in Cambridge, then in Oxford, had forsworn the use of professional coaches and coxes. They believed that 'waterman's practice' was a bad influence on the sport, which was at a crossroads between the old, gambling win-at-all-costs mode and the new high-minded team-spirit approach. Their disagreement was such that the Boat Race was not held for several years as diplomatic relations became strained in the late thirties and thereafter were resumed only fitfully until 1849. The cricketers did not, of course, tread the same path as the oarsmen, which eventually led to the complete exclusion of the watermen in the leading schools and the universities. But there were some similarities. Eton eventually got around to appointing a cricket coach, Sam Redgate of Nottingham and England, in 1840, but there was no question of his enjoying the same status as the masters.

The incursion of university amateurs at Canterbury was an indication of a growing interest in casual country-house cricket. The enthusiasm of many well-to-do families for the game tended to be fitful, usually strongest as the junior members and their friends passed through public school and university, and as much social as purely cricketing. At this level a cricket match was a good way of entertaining friends, neighbours, tenants and villagers, and of bringing in eligible young men for daughters to meet. Talented young amateurs would come along for the wine, women and song and the greatest of professionals for a modest fee; all you needed was a large country house with a few acres. There were plenty of these in Kent. Pilch told Fred Gale how he particularly enjoyed country-house cricket: at close of play he would take his supper in the butler's pantry and the young master would come round later, after dinner with the family and their guests, to smoke a cigar, drink with him and talk cricket.

The same activists on the theatrical side of things at Canterbury – the Hon. F. Ponsonby (the future Earl of Bessborough), his brother, Sir Spencer Ponsonby-Fane, and Mr J. L. Baldwin – were the prime movers in founding a unique club in 1845. This was called, with deliberate exoticism, I Zingari ('The Gypsies' in Italian) because their intention was to own no ground of their own but to play at any country house where they would be given suitable hospitality and entertainment. They also levied no subscription, which allowed them to bring in more of their own kind, young men who even after university were still, in Pycroft's phrase, 'drawing on the governor'. They hired no professionals, with the avowed intention of ending the dependency of the gentlemen on professional bowling. The sprigs of aristocracy had come a long way since the fashionable thing was to hire a few pros to help you win your bets.

IV

That same year the young Ponsonbys were persuaded that it was incumbent on them to become founder-members of a proposed Surrey County Club. The Hon. Fred came over from Ireland (where his father was shortly to become Lord Lieutenant) to chair the inaugural meeting, which was also graced by William Ward. The urge to form county clubs was part of the latest phase in the battle between town and country. There was an element of nostalgia in this, for already cricket was an emblem of Britain's blissful rural past. There was also an element of snobbery, for the first thing socially aspirant industrialists did when they could afford it was buy a 'place' in the countryside, not to live in but to use for leisure and prestige. Otherwise it was swimming against the tide, and town clubs in places like Leeds, Sheffield, Birmingham, Bristol, Liverpool and Manchester might have been expected to become the dominant organisations of the future. It was a long time before the battle was resolved in favour of gentrification.

After Sussex's hesitant start only three other county clubs surfaced during the 1840s,[5] and all, like Sussex, owed as much to 'shopocracy' as to aristocracy. The Nottingham Old Club had earlier established supremacy in the north and had twice mounted successful challenges to Brighton/Sussex. Their main man was a one-eyed bricklayer turned innkeeper, William Clarke, who set up an enclosed money-taking ground beside the Trent Bridge Inn, invited Sussex to play an inaugural match there and in 1841 called a meeting of interested local worthies and set up the county club.[6] Next came Cambridgeshire, essentially Cambridge town, complementing Cambridge gown, both still playing on the vast public ground, Parker's Piece.[7] And then came Surrey, which did not live up to its initial promise. Ponsonby became vice-president, but the presidency went to a Mr Houghton, of the old-established Montpelier Club, seventy of whose members formed the nucleus of the proposed Surrey Club. Houghton also became the proprietor of their new ground, Kennington Oval, a converted market garden.

The first secretary was none other than W. Denison, Esq., now bowling slow round-arm (!) with some success, but with so many irons in the fire that he made a mess of the job. In his absence the president decided to boost the cricket income by organising such attractions as a Walking Match and a

Poultry Show. This dismayed the traditionalists. All were alarmed to be told at the start of the 1847 season that they were £70 in debt, and so might not be able to fulfil all their fixtures. There was a motion to close the club. All eyes fixed on the noble vice-president as he began to speak. If they were expecting a handout, they were disappointed. Instead he proposed that the debt be covered by allowing six people to become life members for £12 apiece. He became one of them. And the club survived.

                                        V

Things were not going much better for Nottinghamshire. The public, having had free cricket on the old racecourse for a hundred years, were not flocking to Trent Bridge. So the remarkable William Clarke, at the age of forty-seven, decided to expand his activities. He left the pub and ground in the care of his son-in-law for the summer and went to London to seek his fortune. He had been playing cricket for thirty years, and was a byword in the North and Midlands, but had only once appeared in a big match at Lord's, for the North in their first historic victory over the South back in 1836. He was a very crafty spin bowler in the old underarm mode, and the advent of the 'march of intellect' had given him a rarity value, which he was now ready to exploit.

In 1843 Clarke had appeared for 'England' against Kent at the Canterbury festival, and two years later renewed acquaintance with Mynn, Felix and Pilch at a MCC v. North match at Trent Bridge. That season he had joined Lillywhite as a ground bowler for MCC. Dark, who handled these matters, had increased the numbers, and, though the pay he offered was not great, ground staff were well placed to catch the selector's eye for big matches. That season Clarke was the latest bowling sensation, and nobody could play him freely: few could play him at all. Felix, who had started out by scoring runs against him, never managed it again.

The reasons for Clarke's success were part technical, part social, reflecting the conventions of the time. Bowling for catches was not a thing that occurred to many bowlers – it was not until 1836 that they were even credited with wickets taken that way – and to most it would have seemed almost like bowling for run-outs. Clarke saw it differently, and thrived on it. Similarly, Bob Thoms, a team-mate, felt Clarke had the great advantage of bowling at fast-footed batsmen, who were also bound by convention:

> It was considered infra dig. to go out to him, although many men knew well enough that would be the best way to play him. I remember that Joe Guy [great Nottingham batsman] said to me, 'I could do the jump right enough, but they don't like you to do it.'

Clarke himself, in one of the pithy remarks for which he was famous, told

Felix, 'If a man is fast-footed he is ready money to me.' But he was full of tricks, including, according to an amateur cricketer of the next, purer-minded generation,[8] 'his custom of preying on the terrors of his victims by making caustic and cocksure remarks'. One such, playfully recorded by Pycroft, became a classic: Clarke enquires politely of an incoming batsman if he's from Harrow, then ostentatiously moves a fielder to somewhere between point and the wicket, telling him to 'stand there for the "Harrow drive"'.

But 'Old Clarke' had more on his mind than taking wickets in 1846. At the end of the MCC season – which was shorter than anyone else's so that the gentlemen could get off to the moors by the 'glorious twelfth' of August – he assembled an All-England XI to play three matches, in the unfashionable but prosperous North, against twenty-two of Sheffield, eighteen of Manchester and eighteen of Yorkshire. Any old team had often called itself 'England' in the past but these really were, as near as makes no difference, the best players in the land. They included Joe Guy and the up-and-coming George Parr from Nottingham; Lillywhite and Dean from Sussex; Denison and Martingell of Surrey; and most of Kent's great men – Pilch, the brilliant bowler Hillyer, and, significantly, the two impoverished gentlemen, Felix and Mynn. As Pycroft euphemistically put it: 'with both, pleasure at last spoilt business', so they needed to make the pleasure pay.

Clarke was the one who made the real profit. The clubs he visited were, says Pycroft, so proud of the honour of receiving the star players that, besides paying 'a subscription of some £70, and part or all of the money at the field-gate', they also extended 'much hospitality'. Out of this largesse Clarke paid his players a fee and expenses and kept the rest himself. He did not pay well – £4 to £6 a game – but this matched MCC rates, which, with masterly timing, they had just reduced (to take account of the greater rapidity of travel in the railway age). This no doubt encouraged further recruits to the All-England, notably 'the little marvel', John Wisden from Sussex. Clarke took them north again – to Manchester, Liverpool, Leeds, York, Stockton, Sheffield, Birmingham, Newcastle and Stourbridge, all in August and September, after a season in which Clarke and Lillywhite tore the Gentlemen apart for the Players, taking all twenty wickets between them.

MCC's ill-timed economy drive was followed in 1848 by a somewhat pathetic attempt to ensure punctuality, on the Hambledon principle of exclusion for latecomers. This was like ordering the removal of deckchairs from the deck of the *Titanic*, for Clarke had decided that the time had come to withdraw his services: All-England became a full-time organisation, playing seventeen matches throughout the season. The programme continued to expand, amid increasing friction over availability for big matches, until in 1851 the rebels, playing thirty-four matches, had become a serious nuisance. Not to everyone, of course. Robert Dark, the equipment-making brother, told Pycroft, whose history came out that year, that he had been amazed at the idea of taking cricket to such outlandish places but that his sales had demonstrated its success. And Pycroft himself, Oxonian, southern Tory to the gills, and clearly thinking this 'travelling circus' somewhat vulgar, conceded that Old Clarke's team 'tend[ed] to a healthy circulation of the life's blood of cricket, vaccinating and inoculating every wondering rustic with the principles of the national game'.

VI

In *The Cricket Field* Pycroft makes social and ethical claims for the game that match this missionary spirit:

> It is no small praise of cricket that it occupies the place of less innocent sports. Drinking, gambling, cudgel-playing insensibly disappear before a manly recreation, which draws the labourer from the dark haunts of vice and misery to the open common ... where 'The squire or parson o' th' parish Or the attorney' may raise him without lowering themselves, by taking an interest if not a part in his sport.

His analysis conveniently ignores the fact that it was enthusiasm for gambling that brought the various classes together. Still, Pycroft was a slightly newer model clergyman than Paulet, Beauclerk or Mitford, and the forerunner of a type that regarded MCC's laws, written and unwritten, as a fifth gospel. It was he who first committed to print the famous phrase everyone remembers about the English and their game – 'not cricket'.

Pycroft did not, of course, give it the metaphorical spin that afterwards made the phrase celebrated. In truth, it was a metaphor for which there had so far been little call. But conscience was now jostling privilege in almost every aspect of life, even politics. Repeal of the Corn Laws came in 1846, after Peel's conversion, to the fury of his party and the embarrassment of the Opposition. After a brief Whig interlude the indolent Lord Derby, racing addict and translator of the *Iliad*, was borne in, provoking Prince Albert to protest about his filling places at Court with 'the Dandies and Roués of London and the Turf'. Yet it was the Tory Chancellor, Disraeli, who warned of the emergence of 'two nations', ending his novel of industrial life, *Sybil* (1845), with a symbolic workers' riot against exploitation.

There was, however, little danger of conscience dislodging the cornerstone of the kingdom, which was freedom under the law. This beguiling phrase impaled the country on the horns of the *laissez-faire* dilemma. Corn Laws apart, whilst free trade brought unprecedented prosperity as the driving force of industrial development, the consequent, equally unprecedented housing needs of an expanding and shifting population also bred slum landlords, jerry-builders and lodging-house keepers. These man-made problems were increased by the added impact of the potato famine that afflicted Ireland, shrinking its eight million population in four years by one million through starvation and disease and another one and a half million through emigration, much of it to English cities. It was 1848 – following an outbreak of cholera – before the first Public Health Act began to encourage the new urban authorities to do something about living conditions.

Needless to say the chief sufferers of the 'hungry forties' were the labouring classes and the small farmers. However, the better sort, paying income tax at seven old pence (under 3 per cent) in the pound, were at least tightening their belts. And it was Lord Shaftesbury, who called Socialism and Chartism 'the two great demons in morals and politics', who sponsored the Ten Hour Act (1847), reducing the daily stint required of women and children in the textile industries. This, and the 1850 requirement for the mills to close at 2 p.m. on Saturdays, were the first small steps towards freeing the workers to join in the new leisure activities which the emerging new health-conscious and moralistic middle classes of the public schools were shaping.

Cricket was not, of course, to become one of these. It was already, at its highest, most influential levels, freezing, if not frozen, into the patterns of a pre-industrial age, of the privileged besporting themselves with their retainers. Establishment mythology has usually represented Old Clarke's initiative as an assault upon a citadel, an attempt to overthrow authority. In fact it was an attempt to fill a vacuum: on the one hand bringing first-class cricket to places that had never known it; on the other hand providing regular employment for professionals throughout the summer months. Neither of these objectives would have been recognised by MCC as any of their business. What they did do, apart from running their own teams, having ceremonial dinners and pontificating about the laws, was arrange a few prestigious matches such as North v. South and Gentlemen v. Players, and for these the All-England players were still available. MCC was dying from self-indulgence without any help from Old Clarke.

MCC's arbitrary traditions, inherited from Beauclerk, continued. Lord Frederick himself had remained a persistent symbol of insensitive autocracy long after his retirement. Until his death in 1850, he was a frequent visitor to Lord's matches, accompanied by a nasty, yapping dog. To everyone else the rule was, 'No dogs allowed'. After Beauclerk, presidents had been elected annually by the committee until 1841, after which democracy was discarded and the retiring president nominated his successor. The basis of selection, unremarkable at first, seems to have settled from 1835 fairly firmly on social rank. There followed a sequence of seventeen earls, three marquises, three viscounts, eight barons and two baronets, punctuated by a single commoner. No doubt they were all jolly nice chaps, which was a change, but they do not seem to have been willing or able to raise the post above figurehead status.

Continuity was provided by the secretaries, honarary and otherwise. The fat Etonian vintner Benjamin Aislabie continued until 1842, chiefly remembered for the red 'Subscribers to Matches' book he carried hopefully around. His successor, for the next sixteen years, was another Etonian, the same Roger Kynaston of whose batting John Mitford had spoken so disparagingly. Administratively he is characterised, even by the kindly official chroniclers, as a man of dictatorial edicts masking good intentions. His was the punctuality rule, and, again in 1848, he replaced the existing bonus system for good play by one for good conduct, payable in case of illness or accident. In short, the management style was crude. Another crudity was the state of the ground: the pitch was a public scandal, even after Dark had had it drained 'at his own expense'. It is an irony, saying much for the power of the virility cult, that the wicket at this club of gentlemen batsmen should be so appalling.

The member who had most influence on the ethos of MCC was the Hon. Robert Grimston, who began as a young fogey and worked his way up to *eminence grise*: he was an utter reactionary, and greatly admired for it. Fred Gale, Grimston's biographer, whose own *nom de plume* was 'the old Buffer', gives an example of Grimston's 'old Toryism'. Dark had borrowed a mowing machine and was watching the cutting with the owner when Grimston walked past

> and, not saying a word … went straight to the top of the ground, where some navvies were at work [and asked] 'Do any of you fellows want to earn a sovereign?' Of course they said 'Yes, master' and brought their pick-axes. 'Now then', said he, 'slip into it and smash that "infernal machine" up.'

Clarke's activities were regarded by the likes of Grimston as a perversion of the natural order of things. And MCC's growing irritation with professionals chimed with the new ideals of amateurism emerging in the public schools and universities. Another powerful influence was I Zingari, which spawned the first of its many imitators amongst alumni of Cambridge (Quidnuncs, 1851) and Oxford (Harlequins, 1852). This was reflected in the influential 'county' circles, where cricket was a feature of the social calendar. In Kent, for example, the 1849 Cricket Week match, between Gentlemen of England and Gentlemen of Kent, was given a long and fulsome notice in *The Times*, with every Mr put in each time a participant was mentioned. Apart from the cricket

> the ground presented the most elegant and fashionable attendance. There was an immense ring of carriages from which the fair occupants alighted, and either paraded along the upper portion of the ground, or took their seats in the canvassed pavilion, which, as heretofore, had been provided for their accommodation by the 'Cricket Committee'.

Another thing Old Clarke aroused was the latent southern hostility towards the crude but increasingly prosperous 'jumped-up' northerners. 'Northernness' Clarke could not deny. But this apart, he was no revolutionary, nor even the obstacle to county cricket he was later supposed to be. True, Nottinghamshire, who had been by far the most active county, were laid low when Clarke first went on tour, and they played no matches at all from 1846–50. However, by 1851 they were back in action, in harness with Clarke, ready to take on the best of the southerners again. The best were not hard to find. Sussex and Cambridgeshire were still doing pretty well, in a casual sort of way, but Norfolk had folded in 1848 and did not resume for fourteen years. In Kent meanwhile the Beverley Club's bid for county status faltered not only for lack of money, but because of preoccupation with the Canterbury Festival, the theatre and its side-shows. After 1849 the Brenchleys of Gravesend weighed in with sponsorship, but there was no concerted effort, and less and less interest in, and money for, professional cricket. So when Notts went to the Oval in 1851 to play Surrey there was no doubt that they were taking on the best.

Surrey, after spending a couple of years getting rid of Denison, and getting the lease back from Houghton, had built up a good side, including the young batsmen Julius Caesar and William Caffyn. They won all their matches in '49, '50 and '51, but it was not until they beat Notts with all their stars, including Guy, Parr and Clarke himself, that they really felt they had come of age. Spurning the services of Pilch, who had offered himself, they had decided to stick to players born in the county – the first time such a rule had been adopted. This enabled them to field N. Felix, who had a birth qualification, but it did not prevent his continuing to play for Kent – or for Clarke's circus.

VII

The Harrovian Anthony Trollope, intensely money-conscious but feeling himself part of some loftier establishment, afterwards wrote nostalgically, not of Hambledon but of the world Beauclerk had created – when professionals were 'proud of being asked to play. They came up to Lord's and earned their five pounds for winning a match. They were civil and contented.' It was, he reckoned, an 'evil hour for cricket' when Clarke, performing the 'quasi-episcopal function' of 'propagating cricket in distant parts', had intervened with commercial gain in mind. Trollope, who would never have written a line had he not been paid for it, was even more scathing about the gold rush that followed. This was hardly of Clarke's making: all he had done was discover the seam.

The cricket industry, like the textile, had moved out of its cottage. Sports equipment played an honoured part in Prince Albert's Great Exhibition of 1851, a celebration of progress through science, manufacture and trade with as centrepiece a great glass exhibition hall christened the Crystal Palace. Fittingly, Duke & Son (est. 1760), who had just begun to make bats as well as the triple-sewn balls for which they were famous, won a prize medal. Clarke's part in the transformation, as the Eleven travelled to ever more distant sport-hungry places, was not merely as a purveyor of equipment but as a bringer of delight. A future captain of Notts, Richard Daft, a very different, more idealistic type than Clarke, later wrote nostalgically of those pioneering times:

> ... one never sees such holiday-making and high jinks as we used to see in the All-England days. The match was the topic of conversation months before the event took place. Special committees were formed to get up entertainments in the evenings, and when the day arrived the excitement was often intense.

Clarke, however, like many another captain, of industry and of cricket, was not generous to his subordinates. He paid as well as MCC and more often, but he himself made a good deal out of his enterprise and as time went on some of the players began to feel they should be getting a bigger share. Dissatisfaction was particularly strong amongst the southerners: they were prominent in 1852 when a group of players declared that 'in consequence of the treatment ... received from Clarke at Newmarket and elsewhere' they would not play for or against his teams, 'county matches excepted'. That year young John Wisden, as entrepreneurial as Clarke, and his Sussex colleague Jemmy Dean led a breakaway group, calling itself the United XI of England, on a rival but complementary circuit.

The two Elevens still had much in common and neither showed any sign of wanting to go back to dependence on MCC. In fact all were coexisting, with MCC's collective head going deeper and deeper into the sand. Some of its individual members were even lending their names, or even their private pitches, to one or other of the Elevens when they visited their local fiefdoms. There was a nasty moment in 1854 when Clarke – possibly out of pique for not being chosen himself – refused leave to a couple of his men to turn out for the Players against the Gentlemen, but even this evoked little reaction. Clarke's death two years later brought no change of policy from All-England: a meeting of the players agreed to continue on the same lines under George Parr. Parr was Wisden's partner in managing a ground at Leamington. By 1857 the two Elevens had agreed to play each other at Lord's, with the proceeds going to a new Cricketer's Fund Friendly Society,[9] which had received donations from some well-disposed supporters. The spirit of goodwill between the elevens was such that the 1858 match, watched by 6000 spectators, was 'for the exclusive benefit of George Parr'.

PART III

The Authorised Version

CHAPTER SEVEN

Slithering into the Future

PARR'S BENEFIT MATCH was a personal triumph for John Jackson, his young team-mate at Notts and All-England, who, having scored 45, then took 6 for 40 and 6 for 28. Jackson was a product of the new system. Clarke, in a modern version of Lord Winchilsea's talent-spotting in rural Hampshire, had discovered him as a youth playing for one of the eighteens or twenty-twos eagerly taking on All-England. Soon he was the most feared bowler in the land, and the hero of those stories told of 'demon bowlers' in every generation: a batsman facing Jackson is hit on the pads and starts to walk away; the umpire says, 'Not out' and the batsman says, 'Maybe not, but I'm going.'

The new satirical magazine, *Punch*, already making great play with the transformation of cricket since round-arm, depicting batsmen and fielders clad in huge padded suits with eye-hole slits, produced the classical comment on Jackson let loose among the 'wondering rustics'. A batsman explains his battered appearance to a spectator:

> I 'ad a hover of Jackson; the first ball 'it me on the 'and; and the second 'ad me on the knee; the third was in my eye; and the fourth bowled me out. Jolly game![1]

The deplorable state of some of the wickets up and down the country, including Lord's, undoubtedly assisted Jackson, but he did not always need their help: as William Caffyn recalled, he slipped in a 'beamer' now and again. He had that kind of simple philosophy. When asked if he had ever taken all ten wickets in an innings, Jackson replied,

> No, but I once did something as good. It was in North versus South at Nottingham. I got nine wickets and lamed Johnny Wisden so that he couldn't bowl. That was as good as ten, eh?

II

The latter-day quest for speed and mayhem, appealing to spectators if not to batsmen, increasingly disturbed the old order of things, in which display and artifice were the admired qualities. The new trend had been set as much by gentlemen – Osbaldeston, Marcon, Mynn – as by Brown of Brighton or Jackson: doubly significant in view of the much smaller share of bowling done by gentlemen in top-level cricket. Such enthusiasm for the virility cult is a reminder of Jonathan Swift's aphorism: 'Most sorts of diversion in men, women, children and other animals are an imitation of fighting.' Hunting, the tournament, sword-play, wrestling and such like were until modern times what was meant by outdoor sport; and still in the mid-nineteenth century bare-knuckle pugilism was the admired sport of everyone from Palmerston, the Prime Minister, and the Marquis of Queensberry to thousands of school-boys using fist-fights as the accepted way of settling differences and pecking order. And cricket, without putting too much strain on the imagination, can be seen as a more sophisticated transmutation of primeval bellicosity into psychologically – and socially – useful channels, much as the Pacific Island elders told the colonial administrator Arthur Grimble, 'We old men take joy in watching the kirikiti of our grandsons, because it is a fighting between factions which makes the fighters love each other.'[2]

Unfortunately, just as the virility cult was given a quasi-ethical cloak by muscular Christianity, cricket was soon to be festooned in high-falutin' nonsense. There are two main sources, from which later Victorian and Edwardian writers drew freely. The first, from Pycroft in 1851, though written by a Church of England clergyman, relies on pre-Christian ethics but still goes some way over the top:

> The game of cricket, philosophically considered, is a standing panegyric on the English character: none but an orderly and sensible people would so amuse themselves. It calls into requisition all the cardinal virtues, some moralists would say. As with the Grecian games of old, the player must be sober and temperate. Patience, fortitude, and self-denial, the various bumps of order, obedience and good-humour, with an unruffled temper are essential.

(Cricket-playing readers should mark themselves out of ten on this test – two points for sobriety – and then seek a second opinion.) There follows an equally daunting list of intellectual requirements and such racially oriented quips as:

> we require not only the volatile spirits of the Irishman Rampant, nor the phleg-matic caution of the Scotchman Couchant, but we want the English combination of the two: though, with good generalship, cricket is a game for Britons generally.

Pycroft then goes off into flights of chauvinistic fancy: '... the game is essentially Anglo-Saxon. Foreigners have rarely, very rarely imitated us', and so forth, spicing his argument with reference to 'frogs, sourcrout or macaroni' and a ferociously bad anti-Irish joke.

This is depressing stuff, but jocularly intended: many of Pycroft's claims for English primacy are based on the superiority of ale over whisky and similar brews. The other, even more celebrated source is blatantly serious, dripping with piety and good intentions, in dialogue about as convincing as that in those television commercials when gaily clad young housewives talk solemnly to each other about the relative merits of washing powders. In *Tom Brown's Schooldays* (1857) the author, Thomas Hughes, a Christian socialist alumnus of the brash new public school, Rugby, presents a 'pop' version of the stern Dr Arnold's intensely religious philosophy. The scene is the cricket field, where Tom Brown, a nineteen-year-old giant with whiskers, is leading the eleven, in his last match before leaving for Oxford, against an MCC side led by Old Mr Aislabie.

A friendly young master – the future Head of Marlborough – is moralising about this and that to the hearty Brown and his intellectual team-mate Arthur, when he breaks off to applaud the cricket. This turns out to be a mistake, for he reveals his gross ignorance by only enjoying big hits like the common herd. He tries to redeem his gaffe by speaking of higher things:

> 'What a noble game it is, too!' 'Isn't it? But it's more than a game. It's an insti-tution,' said Tom. 'Yes,' said Arthur, 'the birthright of British boys old and young, as habeas corpus and trial by jury are to British men.' 'The discipline and reliance on one another which it teaches is so valuable, I think,' went on the master, 'it ought to be such an unselfish game.'

This second piece has been more influential than poor Pycroft's *jeu d'esprit*, measured by the number of people who have trotted it out like a familiar hymn with threadbare sentiments that gets by on the strength of its tune. (What on earth has cricket to do with habeas corpus or trial by jury? Is playing baseball the same as pleading the Fifth Amendment?) Thus the Anglo-Scottish essayist Andrew Lang in 1893 prescribes Hughes like a medicine – 'Cricket ought to be to English[3] boys what Habeas Corpus is to Englishmen, as Mr Hughes says in Tom Brown.' The most-quoted bit over the years, however, has been '"... it's more than a game. It's an institution."' The cutting edge of this maxim has been blunted somewhat in recent times by our increased regard for games and markedly reduced veneration for institutions, but it certainly seemed both profound and unanswerable to Victorian pundits and their many followers who sought to invest cricket with moral qualities.

Similarly, '"The discipline and reliance on one another which it teaches is so valuable ... it ought to be such an unselfish game,"' the young master says.

Well, perhaps it ought, and it very often is. But equally, when played by a technically accomplished but self-centred player it manifestly is not. In modern times Boycott is the obvious example of a player who had claims to being the greatest English batsman of his time, but was renowned amongst his colleagues as a selfish cricketer. No one doubted that he was a cricketer, however, and a good one at that. A ball game, no matter how elaborate, is ethically neutral: any moral qualities it exhibits are those brought to it by the players. The Victorian establishment's view of cricket needs the corrective of Swift's intellectual perception, and beyond this the old Pacific islanders' wisdom.

III

Sadly, in the 1850s and 1860s the conflict raged not only on the field but off, making it hard for the combatants to learn to love each other. One of the factors was that the gold rush amongst the professional elevens began in earnest. (Such metaphors became popular after the discoveries of the real stuff in California in 1849 and Australia two years later.) The first of the new prospectors, the United All-Ireland XI, started by the London professional Charles Lawrence, who was working for the fashionable Phoenix Park Club in Dublin, was exploring new territory: its attempts to enlarge the Anglophile circles of Trinity College, Dublin and Belfast's North of Ireland Club resulted in invitations to English professional elevens as well as I Zingari. However, a serious scramble for the English spoils soon began. Two new teams, each calling itself the New All-England XI, sprang up in 1858. Each was Surrey-based, another sign of the growing strength of that county and its consequent rivalry with Notts, the northern stronghold. Neither of these All-Englands lasted long, but one was briefly resurrected in 1862 as Another New All-England XI, and then a much more soundly based outfit, the United South of England XI, appeared in 1864. Meanwhile the north had produced its own New England XI in 1860, another England XI in 1862 and An Eleven of the North of England in 1863.

The commercial struggle amongst the various All-England XIs, suffused with glarings across the north–south divide, was soon complicated further by arguments over selection for overseas touring sides. The first of these, in the autumn of 1859, had been utterly harmonious. Mr W. P. Pickering, formerly of Eton, Cambridge and Surrey and now a member of the Montreal Club, conceived the idea of bringing the 'travelling circus' on a tour of Canada. The game had taken root there, beginning amongst the military and the superior sort of colonist, to the extent that they had already played an 'international' match for $1,000 against the United States in 1844. The tour was set up at the British end by the president of the new Cricketers' Fund Benevolent Society on behalf of the two original elevens. The party of twelve, six from each, was led by George Parr and included the 'rival' captain, John Wisden, who was not only Parr's business partner at Leamington but now played for North v. South.

Travelling some 7500 miles in two months, including two two-week Atlantic crossings, they played five matches in Canada and the States, attracting large and fashionable crowds. (On 8 October *The Times*, receiving intelligence from Montreal 'per Electric and International Telegraph', reported on the match played on 24 September. The two sons of Old Lillywhite went on the tour, John as a player and Fred as scorer: Fred took his tent and not very portable printing press with him, and afterwards wrote a book about the trip.) The tourists, who included Hayward and Carpenter, prodigious batsmen from Cambridgeshire, as well as Jackson and the Surrey stars Caesar, Caffyn and all-rounder H. H. Stephenson, had been guaranteed £50 plus expenses. They actually netted £90 apiece, a pretty good return, for this spectacular romp. (The phlegmatic Britishers were loath to show undue enthusiasm, however: Jackson, when told that 1,500,000 gallons flowed over Niagara every second, replied, 'Aye well, Ah wouldn't dispute that – there's nowt to stop it, is there?')

The trouble began two winters later. The proprietors of the Café de Paris, Melbourne, Messrs Spiers and Pond, having failed to interest Dickens in a lecture tour of the Antipodes, offered a guarantee of £150 a man and first-class travel to a team of English cricketers. Britain's Australasian colonies were regarded as remote, wild and woolly. Only Western Australia and Tasmania were still penal colonies, but the aura of convicts and remittance men remained, and to this was now added the glint of gold. Whether Parr declined the trip or whether he was manoeuvred out by the machinations of Billy Burrup, Surrey's artful secretary, is not clear. But six Surrey men were chosen, including H. H. Stephenson as captain; there were four other Southerners, and only two from the North, both Yorkshiremen. The insult to the North in general, and Notts in particular, was deeply felt.

The following summer, on 26 August 1862, when their season was almost over, MCC were dragged back into the picture by a bowling dispute. Surrey were playing All-England, and the Kent left-armer Edgar Willsher was bowling, with his usual jerky action that had gone unchallenged for years. Suddenly, out of the blue, he was no-balled six times in a row and, like Willes reincarnate, theatrically flung down the ball and stalked off the field. His eight professional colleagues walked off after him (but not the gentlemen V. E. Walker and Hon. C. G. Lyttleton). The umpire, John Lillywhite, was replaced, allowing the match to continue, but only after Surrey had put out a statement saying that he had 'fulfilled his duties as umpire according to his honest convictions' and *The Times* reporter had called the decision 'perfectly justified'.

There were dark rumours that Lillywhite had been nobbled, but no evidence and no agreement about who was doing the nobbling. Oddly, and casting doubt on the conspiracy theory, no other umpire seems to have followed Lillywhite's lead and no action was taken against Willsher. It could be that the two men, who were friends and prospective business associates, contrived the incident between them as a device to try to get the law changed. Whatever the cause, MCC found themselves having to pronounce on this long-ignored problem, on which opinions were now coloured by extraneous factors like Gentlemen v. Players, North v. South, Surrey v. Notts and almost everybody against MCC.

The hostility to MCC showed up clearly in the press. Newspapers were becoming more and more popular, and arguably, influential. The sporting press, now being infiltrated by public-school men, was eagerly devoured. *Sporting Life*, which was eventually to take over the sixty-five-year-old *Bell's Life*, began to campaign for a Cricket Parliament, to replace or at least restrict MCC; and its correspondence columns were filled with pseudonymous letters, some no doubt sent covertly by the county clubs. Press apart, MCC seemed scarcely capable of handling their own domestic affairs, let alone giving a lead to the nation. When Dark told the committee in 1857 that he wanted to retire and offered to sell them the freehold of Lord's, they declined. And when three years later it came up for auction they did not bid, leaving the field clear to a property speculator who picked up a bargain at £7000.

They were incapable of speedy decisions, and barely capable of decisions at all. Twelve months after the Willsher incident they voted not to change Law X (defining fair bowling). This did not please Willsher's Kent supporters. W. South Norton, Carthusian Hon. Secretary of the emergent Kent County Club, saw it as 'vengeance on Willsher'. He added, in a private letter,

> I begin to be jealous of MCC as law-givers and am inclined to favour the suggestion of a congress of representatives for the cricketing counties with a view to superseding its authority.

As well as such gentlemanly dissent MCC had to contend with the brash, highly professionalised and highly successful Surrey, who had a far better ground, pitch and team than anything at Lord's. They also had more members – over 1,000. But these were, of course, by MCC's faded-glory standards,[4] rather low-grade chaps.

IV

In the most recent cosy in-house chronicle of MCC, *Double Century* (1989), the author, Tony Lewis, diligently forking around the haystack for nice things to say about his subject's ancestry, is most enthusiastic about R. A. FitzGerald, their twenty-nine-year-old new secretary – MCC's 'first constructive move in 1863'. He was certainly more energetic than his predecessor Alfred Bailey, described by Lord Bessborough as a nice young chap with nothing to do.

FitzGerald was assiduous in getting his young friends on to the committee (where they were ignored); and by 1867 he had talked his way into being paid £400 a year, which helped keep him in the top 2 per cent of the population. He persuaded the committee to buy their ground (for £18,313), at the same time filling the coffers by increasing the membership. (This virtually doubled in five years, passing that of the dreaded Surrey with considerable dilution of the aristocratic content but no reduction of pomposity.)

FitzGerald also put up the charges for Eton v. Harrow and Oxford v. Cambridge to pay for policing to prevent further crowd trouble at these rowdy affairs. He began extensions and built a new tavern; he even got the ground re-levelled and started trying to improve the pitch. But he was scarcely a great progressive. At the critical meeting on Law X in 1864 he spoke eloquently against legalising overarm or 'high' bowling, which, he declared, was responsible for the recent crop of big scores and the deterioration in the standard of bowling.

Double Century provides no details of that epic meeting, of which not the least surprising feature was that two of the influential advocates of change were the Hons. F. Ponsonby and R. Grimston. Grimston in particular was as reactionary on social matters as he was on grass-cutting: 'It is our duty,' he declared, 'to keep cricket as a game and not as a gate-money business.' This sounds an admirable sentiment but it was MCC and their aristocratic predecessors who had created the system of professionalism. The establishment's subsequent distaste for paying customers was to prove a millstone around the necks of the emerging county clubs, which tended to have MCC-style committees. It also drove them into amateurism, not only from conviction but as an economy measure.

When Mr Norton and his colleagues had started the new Kent County Club in 1859 finances had sunk to such a low ebb that they could only afford to stage a few matches each year. The retirement during the fifties of all their great stars – Pilch, Felix, Hillyer, Wenman and eventually Mynn – brought a reduction in the team's drawing power, and even if replacements had been available the club could not have afforded to hire them, so they dwindled into dependence on available amateurs and lesser professionals. So, too, the Beverley Club, at whose Canterbury Festival the Kent team in the annual match against England was obliged to field sixteen players to make a game of it. The gentlemen of Middlesex found things just as difficult. When in 1864 the first two of the six Walker brothers of Harrow, Cambridge University and Southgate launched the new county club, the intention was to share the burden of sponsorship: John Walker had footed the bill entirely for a game against Kent the previous year. Fielding amateurs did not produce winning teams, but winning – without the incentive of a serious bet – was becoming less fashionable in the best circles.

This was part of the pure doctrine of amateurism as practised by the wandering clubs. I Zingari were already a celebrated and prestigious adornment of anyone's fixture list. Now, in addition to Quidnuncs and Harlequins, there arose travelling troupes galore: in the Midlands, Free Foresters started in the Forest of Arden (1856), the Band of Brothers (1857) in Kent, and Incogniti (1857) in the superior North London suburbs. After that a steady stream, first of relatively serious and explicable foundations like Emeriti (for Catholics), Eton Ramblers and Yorkshire Gentlemen, then of clubs about whom the best thing was the name – Perambulators, Etceteras, Knickerbockers, Accidentals, Inexpressibles, Anomalies, Gnats, Active Fleas, Caterpillars, Grasshoppers, Limits, Jolly Dogs, Odds and Ends. These gaily coloured, beribboned good-time Charlies seemed to determined, two-way snobs like Trollope just as much of an annoying deviation from orthodoxy as the professional circuses.

The elevens were still in full spate. George Parr and his associates had refused to play in matches involving Surrey players in 1863, but buried at least part of the hatchet that winter when the gentlemanly Melbourne Cricket Club invited Parr to take another party to Australia. Diplomatically, Parr included Caffyn, Caesar and Lockyer of Surrey, as well as Jackson and two others from Notts. He also chose the new demon bowler 'Tear 'em' Tarrant along with Hayward and Carpenter from Cambridgeshire, George Anderson of Yorkshire – and, surprisingly, a gentleman, the twenty-two-year-old Bristol medical student, E. M. Grace, of whose inclusion more later. The fee this time was £250 plus expenses for the eight-month trip, roughly seven times an average wage-earner's annual £37, and nearly three times a skilled worker's £90. (Grace, as an amateur, got £500 expenses.) Despite this largesse the tourists shocked their Australian hosts by their rapacity – selling equipment, buying up cheap gold and jewellery, soliciting gifts and making pigs of themselves at welcoming functions. The Australians issued no more invitations for a decade and then aimed much higher socially – with mixed results.

Parr's team returned to face the first season of legal overarm bowling. MCC's decision on 10 June 1864 was something of a damp squib after all this time (for Willsher since the Oval incident had gone on bowling much as before), though it did remove one pretext for the warring tribes not to play against each other. It also took a little of the steam out of the debate about MCC and its role. There had been some not very promising developments during the winter. Kent had come out in favour of the Cricket Parliament idea, and Notts against it. FitzGerald's reply in April 1864 to the *Sporting Life*'s months-old proposal was a supreme example of pompous impenetrability. It said in essence that MCC had been dealing with the laws in their own way since 1787, saw no reason to do things any differently and that nobody needed to follow them if they didn't want to.[4] This, without FitzGerald's elaborate, bourgeois sarcasm, was the approach of the Jockey Club, to whose status MCC's neo-aristocratic layer of leadership aspired. Surrey's annual report that year called MCC 'the only true cricket club in England' but urged them to abandon their normal routine and get out amongst the populace.

There followed another aimless summer of futile wrangling. The belated relaxation of Law X had changed nothing. But the spotlight had shifted from MCC to the warring professionals. The formation of the United South of England XI in November, with the apparent antagonists of the Oval no-balling incident, Edgar Willsher and John Lillywhite, as secretary and treasurer, seemed likely to add a new dimension to the problem. And there were indeed unpleasant clashes, withdrawals, overlapping fixtures and strikes in 1865. After a disputed victory at the Oval, Surrey refused to play Notts. Yorkshire CCC, founded only two years earlier around a nucleus of the old Sheffield club, was hit by a strike of five leading professionals, including their captain, Roger Iddison, who had gone with Stephenson to Australia. They were suspended for refusing to play against Surrey, and although reinstated for the match against Notts, then refused to play in the return at the Oval.

V

MCC wobbled indecisively throughout the season and the following winter, disconsolately contemplating the nettle they seemed to be required to grasp. Be bold, Grimston urged them:

> let the men who want to choose their own elevens do so, and pay for them themselves on their own speculation, but don't let them dictate to committees of their grounds; and if they do, we must not allow these clubs to play here.

Then, at Whitsun 1866, the northern players withdrew at the eleventh hour from the annual Cricketers' Benefit Society match. MCC's minutes read, in characteristic FitzGerald style: 'Northern players secede from Lord's on the day of the Two Elevens Match, played for benefit of Professionals, the ground being given to them for that purpose. Gratitude!' North v. South, Gentlemen v. Players and the Canterbury Festival were similarly affected.

In August *The Times* commented:

> the cause ... is to be found in the too prosperous conditions of the players. So long as they can earn more money by playing matches against Twenty-Two's than by appearing at Lord's – so long as they can be 'mistered' in public houses and stared at in railway stations, they will care very little for being absent from the Metropolitan Ground. But they are wrong. They may be certain that the 'Gentlemen' will not give way in the struggle.

MCC, reminded of their duty to preserve the nation from such outrageously egalitarian pretensions, decided that in future they would only select for Lord's matches those professionals 'willing to play together in a friendly manner'. Then the following May they put the boot in: the president announced a new Marylebone Club Cricketers' Fund, available only to Lord's professionals and to 'cricketers who, throughout their entire career shall have conducted themselves to the entire satisfaction of ... MCC'. A Middlesex v. England match would replace the Two Elevens' games and the proceeds would go to the new fund.

The elevens did not instantly realise the error of their ways, apologise and disappear into the woodwork. The original two by this time were both exclusively northern, so they played their 1865 match at Manchester, which had long been supportive of their efforts. The stripling *Manchester Guardian*, as far back as 1847, had said of Clarke's efforts, 'These matches will always be anticipated with great pleasure by the Manchester gentry.' But times were changing, and the kind of match that had seemed so novel and exciting in 1847 – 'Eleven of All-England v. Seventeen of Manchester with a wicket-keeper given' – no longer gripped the imagination so tightly. For this the very success of the professional circuses was partly responsible. The general improvement of standards of play and the discovery of gifted young cricketers outside the confines of the pre-Clarke empire coincided with the greater sense of regionality, not least northernness, stimulated by the Industrial Revolution. Now the Manchester club, which had imported the Cambridgeshire player Fred Reynolds as club professional and manager of their splendid new ground at Old Trafford in 1860, had launched a more ambitious enterprise.

Manchester itself was now a town of over 300,000, an industrial and commercial centre, highly conscious of its importance as a focus of culture and thought, for the region if not the nation. It also had a large number of highly prosperous people who wanted to spend their money acquiring gentility, educating their sons at public schools and so forth, and a great deal of more or less friendly rivalry with the rich and newly rich elsewhere in the county. And there was enough of the requisite admiration for anything 'county' to lead, in 1864, hard upon Yorkshire's decision the previous year, to the formation of the Lancashire County Cricket Club. 'Fifteen Gentlemen of Lancashire', as *Wisden* called them, formed the committee, and the Earl of Sefton (president), the Earls of Derby and Ellesmere, Lord Skelmersdale and a couple of Members of Parliament (vice-presidents) adorned their masthead.

But Lancashire started with a largely amateur team. County cricket was not yet a serious alternative to the elevens as a source of employment for the scores of good players now seeking it. The tension between reliance on membership subscriptions plus amateurism on the one hand and gate-money plus professionalism on the other was not easy to resolve: indeed it never would be. The professionals, brought back from the brink of out-and-out independence by MCC's show of strength, and not by nature revolutionary, merely at worst mercenary and at best pragmatic, continued to make themselves available for whoever would pay them. The United South of England XI prospered, and a new North of England counterpart was started up in 1869. MCC perched precariously on top of a still volatile, highly disorganised sub-structure until the situation was transformed by accident, or, as some would see it, the hand of destiny.

VI

The accident, if such it was, did not wait to happen. It was first inspired by Old Clarke and George Parr and later hijacked by MCC, but it originated in some gene that fulfilled itself through a middle-class Bristol family. The Graces were not orthodox, according to any of the canons that were being developed at the public schools and universities. This is hardly surprising, for they were not public-school and university types. Had they been they would scarcely have countenanced E.M.'s trip to Australia with Parr's team of professionals in 1863–4. Admittedly cricket's social orthodoxy, like that of other sports overtaken by the changes of early Victorian times, was still fairly undefined, but there were limits.

In fact E.M., the third of five cricketing sons of a cricket-mad provincial doctor and a equally keen mother, had first been noticed in 1854 as a thirteen-year-old longstop playing against All-England for West Gloucestershire, a team got up by his father. He had, furthermore, been presented with a bat – the customary recognition of a good local performer – by William Clarke himself, who, like a true missionary, had also given the boy's mother, Martha Grace, a book of cricket instruction. Four years later Martha had actually written to George Parr asking him to consider E.M. for that year's All-England XI.

Nothing had come of it, but E.M. had stuck to his cricket in the summers whilst trying to acquire qualifications at the Bristol medical school, then a humble satellite of the better-known London and Edinburgh schools. His next notable appearance, in 1861, was for the South Wales Club. This, the creation of a Captain George Homfrey, played five or six games a year, including a short London tour with matches against the fashionable metropolitan clubs, like MCC and Surrey Gentlemen. Presumably this was one of the reasons why the twenty-year-old E.M. came to be playing for South Wales. It paid off – quite apart from whatever he made in 'expenses' – for his London appearances brought selection for Gentlemen v. Players, followed by an invitation to join Parr's team on the tour of Australia. This not only, or merely, subsidised his medical studies but fulfilled his mother's ambition for him of playing for All-England.

It also brought him the honour of appearing in *Wisden's Cricketer's Almanack*, which came out for the first time in 1864, price one shilling or 'post-free for 13 stamps'. E.M.'s recognition was the greater because few of its 112 pages contained anything about the contemporary cricket scene. In its

twelve-page almanac section, for example, the 1 January entry informed
readers that the British Museum closed on that day, and the entry for 10 May
commemorated the Battle of Lodi in 1796. True, it printed 'the Laws of
cricket as revised by the Marylebone Club', but it also gave the rules of quoits
and knur and spell – and, even more bizarrely, a short history of China, the
dates of foundation of learned societies, results of the classic horse races, and
useful facts about the coinage and canals.

However, amongst the accounts of ancient matches and remarkable bits of
batting and bowling at the Artillery Ground, there appear a few brief reports
of Parr's team in Australasia. These included score-cards of matches in which
E. M. Grace and either Jackson or Tarrant had taken on and heavily defeated
elevens of places like Otago and Castlemaine. On one occasion Mr Grace (as
Wisden was careful to call him in contrast with the stark surnames of the rest
of the team) had afterwards singly challenged the best six of the opposition,
batting first and making an unbeaten century.

Purse replenished, E.M. spent the next three years getting qualified, by
which time he had been overtaken as a cricketer by his young brother, Gilbert.
W.G., seven years younger, but bigger and stronger, had already been
mentioned in Martha's letter to George Parr as potentially better than E.M.
because his back play, at the age of ten, was sounder than that of any of his
brothers. By 1864, barely sixteen, W.G. was already playing for the South
Wales Club against MCC and Ground at Lord's, impressing *The Times* with 'a
fine innings of 50'. Later on the same tour he made a good impression with bat
and ball against a glittering I Zingari team, including the Hon. S. Ponsonby and
R. A. FitzGerald, and ended by scoring a century against Sussex Gentlemen at
Brighton. The following year he was invited to play for the Gentlemen, helping
them to a rare victory over the Players. True glory came in 1866 when the young
all-rounder, still only eighteen, scored 224 not out for 'England' against Surrey,
leaving the match in such a state that on the fourth day he was allowed time off
to go and win a hurdle race at Crystal Palace.[5]

A third brother, G.F. – known as 'Fred' – was now emerging. When a
Gloucestershire team went to Lord's in 1868 to meet and beat MCC and
Ground, all three Graces played, along with a bevy of young men from the local
public schools, Clifton, Cheltenham and Marlborough. Bristol, its wealth
diminished somewhat by Liverpool's advance, was nevertheless a town of some
166,000, and an important regional centre, linked easily to both Birmingham
and London by rail: its cricket club, built up, one way and another, by the
Graces' father, now eclipsed the Cheltenham and Gloucester club that had been
fielding occasional 'Gloucestershire' teams. Within a couple of years a county
club was formed at Bristol with Cheltenham's president, Lord Fitzhardinge,
becoming vice-president under the Duke of Beaufort.

But the Graces ran the show. E.M., who was now settling in to a local
medical practice and marrying the first of his four wives, was chosen as secre-

tary. (This put him in charge of expenses, a source of scandal that was to surface before the end of the decade.) And there was no other choice as captain than W.G., who at twenty-one was already the talk of the cricketing world. He was also a hot property commercially, his drawing power enhanced as, scorning the puny modern fashion of moustaches, he grew an enormous black beard. Playing for South v. North at Sheffield in 1869 W.G. faced the best bowler in the country, George Freeman of Yorkshire, hitting 122 in the first innings and being bowled for a duck in the second. Freeman, an auctioneer, played only five seasons before turning back to business, and this might well have been W.G.'s chosen path had he not been following in the footsteps of an elder brother who had shown how to get the best of both worlds.

W.G. was already being wooed by the United South of England XI, who rightly recognised him as the kind of attraction the professionally run game needed if it was not to stagnate further. But MCC – guided by the commercially astute FitzGerald – were also in effect bidding for his services, and in 1869 W.G. became a member, proposed by the treasurer and seconded by the secretary. If they thought this would keep him from the enemy camp, they were sadly mistaken. Thereafter, whilst proudly displaying MCC colours (and collecting only whatever expenses were allowed), he cashed in on his fame. W.G. 'organised' matches for the United South for payment throughout the 1870s, and coincidentally played for them for expenses only, travelling all over Britain and Ireland to satisfy the vast public appetite to see him. MCC obviously knew what was going on, but considered the price – an extra layer of hypocrisy – well worth paying for this splendid new recruit to the amateur ranks.

VII

The difference between amateurs and professionals has long been socially meaningless but in the mid-nineteenth century the Victorians were beginning to make an enormous fuss about it. In part this was because class divisions were growing more complex with the expansion, urbanisation and industrialisation of the country and the consequent blurring of distinctions. The 1867 Reform Act had continued the 1832 redistribution of seats to take into account the industrial changes, and the franchise was extended to bring in skilled workers and more of the lower middle classes. In 1868 the picture of society painted by the economist Dudley Baxter showed the basic pyramid structure not much changed, but the groups below the top 2 per cent and above the bottom 65 per cent of the population were much elaborated.

Class	Annual income	Numbers	% (approx.)
Upper	£5000+	7,500	0.0075
Upper middle	£1000–£5000	42,000	0.42
Middle	£300–£1000	150,000	1.50
Lower middle (1)	£100–£300	850,000	8.50
Lower middle (2)	Up to £100	1,003,000	10.03
Skilled labour	Up to £100	1,230,000	12.30
Less skilled labour	Under £100	3,819,000	38.19
Agricultural/Unskilled	Under £100	2,843,000	28.43

It was no longer enough to divide society up simply into gentry and the rest. An increasing number of 'the rest' had now achieved the income and leisure that put them in the boss class but had not been born to it; they were particularly anxious that any of their new-found thunder be not stolen by even newer arrivals in that station. In the dream world of sport the people who had originally paid the piper, and still called the tune, wanted to preserve the old divisions: the modern vulgar realities were not welcome. But by mid-Victorian times these vulgarities were a persistent nuisance in the old sports and a serious threat in the new ones that had been born of increasing middle-class prosperity. So an uneasy coalition emerged to prevent further encroachment from below.

This whole tiresome business was actually an inheritance from the aristocratic taste for gambling, and the aristocratic habit of hiring the lower orders to perform on their behalf. On the turf, the most plutocratic sport, the gentry had long become non-starters as serious performers because of the fashion for speed-trials with lightweight horses requiring minuscule riders. In the newer styles of horse-racing – steeple-chasing, point-to-point and so on – where heavier horses were required and gentlemen could still take part without making fools of themselves, the attempt to keep out riff-raff meant trying to define gentlemen. This was easy enough at the top end – judges, bishops, Members of Parliament – and in defined categories such as army and navy officers, but these excluded vast numbers of manifest gentlemen. So the lists grew more elaborate, including members of specified West End clubs, for instance, and eventually, as a fatuous catch-all, 'persons generally received in society as gentlemen'. This in practice left the judgement about eligibility to the stewards of individual meetings: Lord Derby is once said to have allowed a man in because he spoke French and wore a gold ring.

In the revised hierarchy of sport that was being created in the public schools, those which best satisfied the criteria of muscular Christianity came first. Rowing was ideal, especially the eight-oared team version, for it was almost masochistic in its denial of the flesh, and did not lend itself easily to commercialisation. The gambling and prize-money elements were correspondingly easier to eliminate, and by the same token the bumping and boring and pinching the other fellows' water that had once been part of the fun could be tagged as 'waterman's practice' and purged by simple exclusion of professionals from amateur competition, coaching and so forth. In rowing the decision-making on eligibility was based at first on straight class lines: there were separate clubs for gentlemen, for tradesmen and for watermen, and when in 1868 a sculler was accused of professionalism, the Henley Regatta stewards dismissed the charge on the grounds that he was a member of a gentlemen's club. Meanwhile the élite Amateur Athletic Club broke new ground in 1866 by regarding competing for prize money (which everybody had done hitherto as a matter of course) as grounds for exclusion from amateur competition. Even so, they began their first definition 'An amateur is a gentleman who ...', followed by the exclusion of menials, etc. on rowing-club lines.

As higher-minded university men felt the call to take on responsibility for keeping the sport free of professionalism, this particular method did not survive more than a year or two, but its spirit lived on. When modern football emerged from the public schools, both its rugby and soccer codes were riven by fierce controversy about 'broken-time' payments that allowed working men to be able to afford to participate at the highest level. In boxing the gentlemen sought to distance themselves from the 'pugs', by wearing vests, keeping a straight left and above all, not getting into the same ring. Golf, the Scottish game, had to make sudden adjustments when English amateur competitions were introduced. The concocted social hybrid, lawn tennis, considered a mere fad or a debasement by real tennis players, soon attracted enough of the new self-conscious middle class to make the distinction between new- and old-style amateurism a contentious issue.

The conflict in cricket between independent professionals of the lower classes and latter-day representatives of the old feudal system was thus part of a wider struggle. Before long, MCC, easy victors in their own little battle, became smug about the turmoil afflicting the newer sports, but they achieved this complacent superiority only by the accident of time and with the help of extra large doses of hypocrisy. The need for hypocrisy had a lot to do with the Graces, and W.G. in particular, for he became a synonym for cricket and Britishness and perhaps the most famous and most hero-worshipped man in the country, but he made a nonsense of most of the emerging canons of the game.

CHAPTER EIGHT

Grace Notes

THE RECRUITMENT OF THE YOUNG W. G. Grace was a masterstroke by MCC. Future history was rewritten in an instant, and the establishment chronicler H. S. Altham was still excited about it sixty years later:

> Nothing in all his monumental history is more remarkable than the stark figures which illustrate WG's decisive impact on the Gentleman v. Players match.

Or to put it another way, without W.G. this moribund fixture might have had to be abandoned a hundred years before it actually was. And the truly remarkable thing is that he was deemed eligible to play for the Gentlemen, for he undoubtedly made more money from playing cricket than any professional. By the same token, whilst he rescued the establishment, he was not part of it. MCC had made him a member, but he was never to inhabit the corridors of power. Not that he wanted to: he did not slink along corridors, but strode unhesitatingly to centre stage, where he knew he belonged.

II

He was not our first great national sporting hero: Tom Sayers, whose fight with the American J. C. Heenan in 1860 had engaged the emotions of both countries, was just the latest in a line of battlers – Jack Broughton, John Jackson, Tom Cribb – with whom Britons high and low were proud to identify, whether or not they ever saw a fight. But W.G. was of that order, transcending the limits of cricket, which excited only a section of the population. He was soon as well known as anyone in England – by name, by appearance and by that indefinable quality of newsworthiness that the burgeoning press fed upon. It was no accident that almost all our previous heroes had been soldiers, sailors or fighting men of some kind. In the mid-nineteenth century we needed a hero badly, especially after the Crimean disasters. The Prime Minister, Lord Palmerston, 'Old Pam', brought in to save the situation, was much admired for his pugnacious and aggressive reputation, but now in old age pursued a policy of 'judicious bottle-holding' rather than actually fighting. This kept the country out of major wars for another fifty years but left it flexing its muscles. The Indian Mutiny persuaded the sturdy patriot Victoria that what India needed was direct rule by the Crown and what Britain needed was a vast standing army properly supported by Parliament. The great upsurge in sport that followed was by turns surrogate and preparation for war.

But sport was also, it now seemed, in its own right an aspect of British superiority, as a whole array of games and pastimes, new and refurbished, bore testimony to the middle-class genius for playing, organising and writing about them for pleasure, profit and proselytism. First rowing, then cricket, boxing, athletics and football had been purged by public-school and university fervour; and cycling, croquet, badminton, golf and lawn tennis came to beguile suburbia. W.G. was both a standard-bearer and an emblem of this process. Success was what counted in the new enterprise culture, and cricket, still rooted in Pickwickian etiquette, was due for a shake-up. Here was a young cricketer, uninhibited by mere convention, who dwarfed his contemporaries on either side of the social divide. In 1871 he scored 2,739 runs, averaging 78.25, whereas his nearest competitor, Richard Daft, the Notts captain, averaged 37, less than half.

E.M.'s Australian trip showed the Grace family's disregard of conventional etiquette, and both he and W.G. already displayed its considerable regard for making money. E.M. also had a reputation for flouting the conventions on the field. His unorthodoxy was still shocking enough in 1900 for an otherwise reverential critic to write sorrowfully, 'with all his great qualities he never played with a straight bat'. In the best circles hooking and pulling were not merely considered bad form, but immoral; yet that is how E.M. got many of his runs. W.G., who was utterly ethical in this respect at least, explained why. Their father had let E.M. use a bat far too big for him, which had got him into the habit of dragging it across the line and relying on his eye: this brought him lots of runs, but, conventions apart, it was not safe.

Dr Henry Grace did not make the same mistake when coaching his younger son. W.G. was so big a lad that he could in fact have used a heavier bat, but his father made him continue with a small size long after he had grown bigger than most men. Even when he reached his enormous adult size and strength W.G. used a far lighter bat than the great strikers of the past like E. J. Budd (3lb+) and William Ward (4lb). He was able to do this because of the continued improvement in bat design and construction. The great breakthrough had been made back in 1853, by Thomas Nixon, the same man who had devised the first cork knee pads. His idea was to make the spliced handle springy, not by putting flexible strips of whalebone into an inflexible wood, but by making the whole handle out of a springy wood. He chose cane, and once the cane-handle principle was accepted all sorts of refinements became possible by 1860 – just in time for W.G. to take advantage.

Taking advantage was second nature to the Graces, never infringing the laws but exploiting them to the full. In bowling, too, E.M. was the trailblazer, using the old underarm method. Fred Gale, the influential Wykehamist defender of the old order, severely criticised him in 1871:

> The only painful exhibition I ever saw in amateur cricket was when Dr Grace tried to pitch a ball right up in the air so as to drop on the bails, leaving the batsman powerless. It was within the laws of cricket, but that was all.

W.G. himself was twice censured in *Wisden* for his bowling habits by the Etonian Lord Harris, the fourth Baron, who had known him from boyhood: once in a tribute in 1895 and secondly in an obituary article.

The very British concept of 'not cricket' had now come to include unnecessarily appealing to the umpire.[1] Harris thought W.G. 'depended rather too much on the umpire for leg before ...' when he was bowling. W.G., a roundarmer, bowled leg breaks: he was an exceptionally good field to his own bowling, so he had a straight mid-on and covered the off himself. Harris, having duly praised W.G.'s splendid fielding, commented,

> He crossed the wicket so far to the left himself that he could not ... judge whether the ball pitched straight or not, and I don't think a bowler ought to ask for leg before unless he is pretty sure as to the pitch.

In the obituary he was even more disapproving, seeing the tactic as giving him

> the additional chance of the umpire making a mistake ... he could not possibly see whether the ball would have hit the wicket, but he generally felt justified in appealing.

Doing his best to speak nothing but good of the dead, Harris put the best gloss he could on another aspect of W.G.'s reputation for infringing the spirit of the game:

> WG was desperately keen for his side to win, and consequently was led, in his excitement, to be occasionally very rigid in demanding his full rights ...

The Australians were made fully aware of this when he first toured their country in 1874. At a time when proper colonial reverence was the norm, one local newspaper sadly reported:

> Now it may be confessed, if only in a shame-faced way, that in Australia we

did not take kindly to 'WG'. For so big a man he is surprisingly tenacious on very small points. We duly admired him at the wicket, but thought him too apt to wrangle in the spirit of a duo-decimo lawyer over small points of the game.

He was just the same in England, out to win at all costs. A. G. Steel, of Marlborough, Cambridge University and Lancashire, another called upon to pay tribute in W.G.'s lifetime, told a story about an episode in the North v. South match in 1878:

> Barlow, the Lancashire professional, was batting and WG was fielding at point. Now Barlow had a trick of playing the ball away after he had played it, and occasionally, in order to excite a laugh from the onlookers, would scamper down the pitch for a yard or two and then back again.

This time Barlow dead-batted the ball and after it had stopped, tapped it towards point and 'went through his performance of dashing down the pitch and back again'. W.G. at point appealed for hitting the ball twice, and as Steel commented, 'out Barlow had to go'. In the same season, playing against Surrey, W.G. had run three when the throw-in lodged in his shirt and, taking advantage of the existing laws,[2] he ran three more – and then refused to give the ball back himself in case he was given out 'handling the ball'.

Perhaps the most notorious episode of this kind occurred at a crucial stage in the England–Australia match of 1882. As *Wisden* records, the young Australian S. P. Jones had completed a run 'and thinking wrongly but very naturally, that the ball was dead, went out of his ground' to repair the wicket. Grace put down the wicket and appealed for run out. As in the Barlow incident the batsman had to go, but it was not within the spirit of the game. *Wisden* made light of it:

> There was a good deal of truth in what a gentleman in the crowd remarked, amid some laughter, that 'Jones ought to thank the champion for teaching him something'

However, the champion seems to have deliberately misled Jones by carrying the ball over to the bowler, by which time the batsman was well out of his ground, then walked back and broke the wicket. The umpire, Bob Thoms, on appeal replied, 'I'm sorry to say the gentleman is out.'[3] Joe Darling, one of the most respected of Australian captains, and one of the most critical of W.G., claimed that Thoms actually added, 'It's not cricket.'

WG's encyclopaedic knowledge of the laws, disregard of convention, dominant personality and standing with the public put umpires in awe of him, and he grew worse as his fame spread. When cricket matches could be advertised as 'Admission threepence. If W. G. Grace plays admission sixpence' it is not surprising that umpires were reluctant to give him out until the spectators had got their money's worth. And as Lord Harris said in his obituary tribute, W.G. was so popular that accounts of his gamesmanship 'more often than not added to the fund of humorous stories about him'. In particular the public loved – and still love – to hear the one about him being bowled first ball, replacing the bails and brushing aside the protesting umpire with 'Don't be silly. They've come to see me bat, not you umpire.' (A better version of the same story, to my mind, is that about Harry Jupp, the Surrey professional, a Dorking man, who, batting at his home ground, was out first ball. When he replaced the bails and took guard again an opposing player asked, 'Aren't you going, Harry?' 'Not at Dorking, I ain't,' said Jupp.)

III

It is often remarked that W.G. was an unlikely hero for the straight-laced Victorian era, but this is to over-simplify a very complex period of our history, and to underestimate the influence of the competitive ethos unleashed by the Industrial Revolution and the worship of success that came in its wake. It is also greatly to underestimate the capacity for hypocrisy in a country that since Chaucer's day had been perfecting the art of laughing at the foibles of pillars of society, until by the end of the nineteenth century it was thought remedial action enough to laugh at the jokes in *Punch* or *Iolanthe*.

This apart, the thing about W. G. Grace was that he approached cricket as if he were fighting a small war – which Swift would have acknowledged as inevitable – not spreading a gospel of sweetness and light, as later apologists were apt to claim. The more serious charge against him, and those who installed him on his pinnacle, is that he blatantly abused the concept of amateurism, whilst fully sharing in its privileges – and not treating his more honestly professional colleagues any too well, either socially or materially. Of this more later. Meanwhile, however, we should put the Grace family in context, for, though important, they were by no means the only factor in the revival of amateur fortunes, or, as it were, the only stealers of the professionals' clothes.

The critical factor in this revival was the great improvement in public-school and university cricket, as post-Industrial Revolution affluence produced a stream of neo-Tom Brownites able to spend long years acquiring a straight bat, a fancy cap and an accent to match. To the muscular Christian advocates of sport in the public schools were now added those who saw games as important to the defence of Empire as it spread and its significance impinged on the British consciousness; those who saw them as essential character-builders, especially for leaders; and that happy band who liked playing them and perhaps hoped to make an agreeable living out of organising them or writing about them. The stern scholastic regimes that had, at best, left the organisation of games to the pupils now gave them an honoured place in their brochures. There was a symbiosis between the leading schools and universities. At Oxford the great debate between those who wanted to concentrate on scholarship and learning and those who wanted to make it into an extension of public school, with an emphasis on service to the nation, was won decisively by the latter, at Cambridge there was no contest.

One of the results was a broadening of university admission standards, with the different colleges competing with each other in trying to attract potential Blues as well as potential Firsts. In turn schools began to look for 'rounded' personalities from Oxbridge on their staffs, and these were now encouraged to coach in the favoured sports. Rowing, of course, had set the lead: Dr Edmond Barre, a classics master who was also a dedicated rowing coach, eventually became the headmaster of Eton. But cricket was now an acceptable alternative, especially in those otherwise distinguished schools that did not have a river. Eton itself, however, had the most famous cricket coach to come from the ranks of the gentlemen.

This was R. A. H. Mitchell, who won a Blue in all his four years at Oxford (1862–65) and was captain for three. Considered one of the best bats of the day, he nevertheless played only a few first-class games after becoming a master at Eton, where he spent the whole of his working life, devoted to its cricket. Facilities, tuition and endless leisure – these essentials were now applied to the amateur cause with spectacular results. During the 1870s and 1880s a succession of privileged young men followed Mitchell in getting a Blue for four years running: at Oxford S. E. Butler, C. J. Ottaway, R. D. Walker, the Hon. George (afterwards Lord) Harris, E. F. S. Tylecote, M. C. Kemp, H. V. Page and K. J. Key; and at Cambridge C. A. Absolom, Clement Booth, C. E. Green, the Hon. C. G., the Hon. Revd E. and the Hon. A. Lyttelton, C. I. Thornton, W. Yardley, A. P. Lucas, D. Q. Steel, A. G. Steel, C. T. Studd, G. B. Studd, C. Aubrey Smith and the Hon. Ivo Bligh. Many of these were still able to spend their summers on cricket after university, captaining or playing for the counties or England. And, of course, they were a great adornment to the University match and to the Gentlemen.

Eton v. Harrow was now firmly part of the London season, and in a class of its own. Unfortunately, its social glitter was no guarantee of civilised behaviour either on the field or amongst the spectators. In 1870 the Hon. George Harris, the product of 'Mike' Mitchell's gentlemanly tuition at Eton and later so censorious of W.G.'s gamesmanship, committed an act that his biographer records as an instance of his courage, but most of us would think 'not cricket':

> An incident occurred when as a bowler he ran out the batsman at his end who was backing up too eagerly. He checked his delivery on the crease, and instead of bowling put the wicket down, an unusual mode of dismissal which evoked a noisy expression of disapproval from the Harrow partisans.[4]

Three years later MCC issued a statement of pained disapproval at this 'unseemly conduct' of spectators, adding, 'Such scenes ... would not occur if the partisans of both schools were to assist the authorities in checking the immoderate expression at the conclusion of the match.'

The greatest disincentive to civilised conduct at Lord's was, however, the state of the pitch. There were many complaints about it, but the issue was greatly confused by the virility cult that had always been part of cricket and was now enormously strengthened by the influx of public-school men. Eton had always been a stronghold, and Lord Harris was a modern exemplar. He wrote in his autobiography of a serious accident to a school friend, Lord Wenlock:

> The ball hit him in the mouth, driving his lips through his teeth, and in writing him a letter of sympathy I could not help adding that I should advise him in future not to put his head where his bat ought to be.

In 1870 a batsman was killed at Lord's in circumstances when similar advice might have been given.

The pitch does not seem to have been an especially bad one. Indeed, MCC had begun to use a heavy roller that season, and Wisden says 'the wickets were excellent'. But it was not free of small pebbles, and the ball, hurled at great force by a young fast bowler, John Platts, making his début for MCC, probably hit one of them. The ball shot up and felled the batsman, George Summers, who was carried off the field. Richard Daft, the Nottinghamshire captain, next man in, recalled that he was laughed at by MCC's fielders for wearing a towel round his head.

Apart from W.G., who was an indestructible type, the MCC team included a number of hard men like V. E. Walker and C. I. Thornton who still scorned the use of pads and gloves. Thornton told 'Old Ebor': 'I shall never forget Richard Daft coming in next with a towel round his head covered with a scarf tied under his chin.' C. E. Green, who was MFH of the Essex Hunt, was more explicit, revealing scorn for the professional. Daft, he said, who was 'always dapper and rather full of self-importance', looked 'ludicrous'. The wicket-keeper, William Yardley, who later became a dramatic critic, produced a suitably theatrical, masochistic version of Harris's sadistic joke:

> If Summers had been able to duck and avoid the ball I must inevitably have got it between the eyes. I have always felt sorry since that it was not I who was struck, for I don't suppose that the result would have been more than a pair of lovely black eyes, whereas Summers was struck in a vital part ...

IV

Such blemishes apart, the future for establishment cricket looked brighter than for many a day – a welcome if surprising side effect of the Industrial

Revolution. Furthermore, the new generation of amateurs included many who believed cricket was much more than a game. One such was the Hon. George Harris, who had demonstrated his creed in the Eton and Harrow match. His father, the third Baron, was the president of a new Kent county club, reconciling the warring factions by amalgamating with the old Beverley Club in 1870. The following season, aged twenty and in his first year at Oxford, young Harris became Kent's 'moving spirit', and in 1875, now the fourth Baron, was formally appointed captain. His mark remained on Kent and on MCC, to whose committee he acceded as of right, until the end of his long life. In particular, at a time when MCC's old guard were highly suspicious of the counties as breeding grounds of obstreperous professionalism, Harris demonstrated that restoration of the old feudal values was possible and led the movement that gradually brought county cricket back into favour in the best circles.

It was not yet, however, a homogeneous or even a coherent entity. From the mid-1860s there had been talk in the press of a 'champion county', though there was not the remotest attempt to create a system for deciding such a thing. The few counties that had managed to get off the ground played whoever they liked, or whoever their pros would play against, and wondered where the money was to come from to stage the season's fixtures. Notts were generally the hardest team to beat in the 1860s and 1870s. According to their captain, Richard Daft, in his engaging book *Kings of Cricket*, his own team, Cambridgeshire and Surrey were the strongest sides, whilst Yorkshire, Kent and Sussex 'were each able to put good elevens in the field'.

Notts had adjusted well enough to what George Parr called 'committee cricket'. Their frankly professional culture happily embraced the genuine amateur but rejected the type who wanted lavish expenses. Richard Daft, who owned a small brewery and a high-street sports shop (which he greatly neglected), had started out as an amateur but had turned professional when it became clear that he couldn't afford to play cricket all summer on genuine expenses only: he had joined the All-England XI, emerging as the best professional batsman in the land. His views about the place of violence in the game were strictly those of one who earned his living from batting, as we have seen. Lord Harris, who clearly thought he had ideas above his station, recalled in his autobiography how Daft had once been painfully struck on the foot by a ball, 'and he turned to me and said in his most superior way "This is not cricket, my Lord. This is not cricket."' Daft may have been 'superior' but he was a fine captain, and with George Wootton, J. C. Shaw (and later the great Alfred Shaw) in their attack, and Will Oscroft, Tom Bignall, Jack Selby and himself as batsmen, Notts were the leading county for the next decade and more.

On the other hand, Surrey, their old rivals and spiritual enemies, suffered from a string of undistinguished amateur captains, who failed to make use of good professional talent – Jupp and the Humphrey brothers with the bat, wicket-keeper Pooley, and the fine left-arm spinner Southerton. No one called them 'champion county' again for over twenty years. Yet they were constantly in the limelight. In 1871 they secured as their secretary (£200 a year) Charles W. Alcock, another of the new journalist-organisers, assistant editor of the *Sportsman*, editor of Lillywhite's *Cricketer's Annual*, and of the *Football Annual*, and already making a name for himself as honorary secretary of the new Football Association, inaugurating international matches and planning a new FA Cup competition that winter based on the Cock House competition at his old school, Harrow.

Alcock had big plans to make the Oval a national sports centre and he staged international matches there in rugby football as well as soccer. For Surrey he soon built up the membership to 1,200, with an annual income of £3,500, and the future looked bright. By contrast, Cambridgeshire, a survival into the machine age, were at their last gasp. Heavily dependent now on their two great batsmen, Hayward and Carpenter, they never recovered when both retired in 1871, and thereafter took second place to the university not only socially and economically but as a cricketing force.

Kent were certainly capable of good things, but they were inconsistent. Edgar Willsher was the last of their great professionals for a while, and the good elevens Daft spoke of were dependent on the presence of Harris himself and their Cambridge Blues, the free spirit C. A. Absolom, the brilliant William Yardley, the great hitter C. I. Thornton, the talented Ivo Bligh, and batsman/wicket-keeper E. F. S. Tylecote, all wonderful cricketers but not always there. Middlesex, whom Daft does not mention, were also reliant on amateurs, like C. J. Ottoway, C. E. Green, the Studd brothers and, most of all, the Walker brothers, who held the club together through some very precarious years. Middlesex played only a handful of matches and had no ground suitable for raising gate-money, but were buoyed by an increase in membership. Sussex simply lacked distinction, for they had few good amateurs, and their professionals, apart from the stylish batsman Charlwood, known as the 'hope of Sussex', and the notable bowler James Lillywhite, were not of the highest standard.

Yorkshire were like an imperfect copy of Notts. The county's early years were blighted not only by the general bloody-mindedness that afflicted cricket, but by internal strife. The county club had been formed at Sheffield, largely due to the efforts of M. J. Ellison, a former town club amateur who had now become the county president and treasurer. But by this time Sheffield had lost its pre-eminence as a source of great professionals. There was now greater strength in the woollen districts around Bradford and Huddersfield, but new contenders came from all over this big sprawling county. Only two Sheffielders were in the side that played George Parr's All-England XI at Bramall Lane in 1865: both opening batsmen came from

Stockton-on-Tees, over the Durham border. Roger Iddison, the captain from 1863 to 1870, was from Bedale in north Yorkshire, also the home of the veteran George Anderson.

Apart from geographical rivalries there was also an aristocratic interest in a politer kind of cricket. A more gentlemanly club at York, a city redolent of gracious pre-industrial days, was a strong claimant to take over the county mantle, and it enjoyed the backing of such worthies as the Earls of Harewood, FitzWilliam and Effingham and Viscount Milton, recently president of MCC. The second Baron and first Earl of Londesborough (whose father had acquired some 60,000 acres in the East Riding, with an annual income of £100,000) was the glue that held the county's cricket together. There were two groups, the gentlemen based on York and the professionals based at Sheffield, but also playing at such places as Hunslet, an industrial suburb of Leeds, in keeping with the well-known Yorkshire maxim, 'Wheer th's mook, th's munny.' In 1869, when they played Cambridgeshire there, winning with great ease, Roger Iddison scored 115, which earned him 'a present of £5, and loud hearty cheering from the thousands present'.

The coming of the railway in 1845 had revived Scarborough's faded reputation as a fashionable spa town, bringing well-to-do folk from the cities to fill their lungs with uncontaminated air. Local cricket clubs and private patrons were happy to give games to enthusiastic young visitors (and their fathers) and to arrange matches against them. This conviviality grew until, in September 1871, the Cambridge University captain, C. I. Thornton, brought a side including two of the Middlesex Walker brothers to play Lord Londesborough's team, which included the leading Yorkshire professionals. Over the years this London link grew into the Scarborough Festival, with Londesborough offering accommodation and hospitality at his house to induce the best amateur players to come to Scarborough as a season's end relaxation.

Meanwhile the county's talented but spiky and intemperate professionals – as colourful as their fashionable modern uniforms[5] – performed well when it suited them, but were not noted for reliability or sobriety. Yorkshire's gentlemen grew steadily more impatient. They surely envied Lancashire the tight amateur control they exercised through the Rowley and Hornby families and their public-school-educated sons, but cannot have been entertained by their un-neighbourly habit of hiring footloose professionals as required. Lancashire's first century was scored by Yorkshire's captain, Roger Iddison, who played for both counties from 1865 to 1870.

V

Iddison – an independent-minded character – took the leading part in founding the United Northern XI in 1869. Lord Londesborough, with his refreshing catholicity, became its president. The team did as well as could be expected, in a shrinking market for exhibition cricket, with Grace's United South XI getting the cream of the fixtures all over the country. W.G. was now playing cricket more than any professional – and with a greater say over who he played for and against – and this constant practice, coupled with amazing physical fitness, helped keep him at the top year in year out.

Increasing leisure was now opening up further opportunities for the entrepreneurs. The first Bank Holiday, in 1871, aroused fierce controversy but was popular with the growing lower-middle-class electorate: this was a promising development for the three-day format that had become established in big cricket. The industrial working classes were more regimented than before. The haphazard, rural collection of Saints' Day holidays gave way to the rhythm of the factory and the town. The old ways were not entirely eradicated: 'Saint Monday'[6] was still popular, and in areas like Sheffield, which had small cutlery-making workshops, Mondays were commonly taken as holidays. But in most of industrialised England workers tended to get 'wakes weeks', unpaid annual holidays when the factories closed for maintenance. This too lent itself to the establishment of regular annual attractions – such as local 'derbies'[7] – and the gate-money-conscious clubs reacted accordingly.

Had cricket, at this time of the great expansion and commercialisation of games, been a new creation, a stylised public-school and university version of an old folk-game, like soccer, perhaps its leading practitioners would have exposed it to market forces then, rather than a century later, and it would have become a genuine complement to soccer – as baseball is to American football – not an élitist pursuit kept out of the hands of the undiscriminating majority. But then, as every traditionalist will instantly point out, it would not be cricket. As early as 1875 a *Times* essayist was suggesting one reason: '... all Englishmen love the game – scarcely so much, perhaps, for itself as for its many associations.' But why three-day cricket? He thought a village match the quintessence and 'scientific' cricket rather a bore, but he knew it was blasphemy to say so.

Logic pointed to an accommodation with the stern facts of life that all but the privileged had to cope with. Only a tiny minority of even the upper and middle classes had time to play, or to watch, first-class cricket. The working classes had marginally shorter hours, and Saturday half-holidays were now becoming standard practice. This restricted them to games that could be finished in a few hours. In soccer, where ninety minutes was all that was required, the working-class professionals soon came to dominate the game. In cricket, where it was assumed, by MCC, county committees and their membership, public-school and university men and high-grade professionals alike, that three-day games were sacrosanct, the game remained frozen in a neo-feudal posture.

All that was needed to obliterate the professional elevens from serious consideration was to create a pattern of committee cricket in which the brilliant new amateurs from the public schools could continue after they left university. There were temptations, such as that prompted by the new FA Cup, and MCC, left to their own devices, might well have succumbed. Indeed in January 1873 they proposed 'with a view to promoting county cricket, and to bringing counties into contact which otherwise might not have had the opportunity of competing with each other', to offer a silver cup for a knock-out competition. But only two counties, Kent and Sussex, accepted, and though they played a match on 'a very dangerous pitch' at Lord's the competition was abandoned. It had been assumed, perhaps, that Alcock of Surrey, on whose football original the idea was based, would be in favour, but, on the contrary, he was strongly opposed. He can have had no idea of the extent to which soccer would be overrun by professionalism, but, with an obvious eye to the United XIs that were always on the look-out for more business, he strongly advised MCC not to meddle with cups lest they encourage others to take up the idea and thus threaten the emergent county game.

This was expanding at last. The progress made by Yorkshire, Lancashire and close neighbours Notts had now aroused ambitions in Derbyshire. Derby had won renown for its porcelain and silk industries and was now an important rail centre. The county had played their first match there in 1863 but there was not enough support to form a club. No one took them seriously until in 1870 they beat MCC. Even then, for their first three seasons only Lancashire would play them on level terms – and they probably wished they hadn't when Derbyshire had them out for 25 in 1871 at Old Trafford. Much more spectacular, of course, was the advance of Gloucestershire. They played five games in their first season, including two against a team calling itself Glamorgan. Two years earlier W.G., the erstwhile hero of the South Wales Club, had gone to Neath with the United South XI, where, according to the records, he 'was "ciphered" by a professional called Howitt' in both innings.[8] He certainly took his revenge when 'Glamorgan' came to Bristol, where he scored 197 and took nine wickets and E.M. seven, and Gloucestershire won by an innings and 268. Glamorgan disappeared from the firing-line until 1888.

But Gloucester had a fine team, all amateur (if the term be stretched to include the Graces), and no one questioned their right to be amongst the nine counties who in 1873 drew up a set of rules of players' eligibility for county matches. The ignominious failure of their Silver Cup scheme quenched the tiny flame of initiative in MCC's breast and soured their relations with the counties. They decided to leave them to their own devices, and, reverting to the style attributed by W. S. Gilbert to the House of Lords,

> did nothing in particular, and did it very well.

Surrey, masterminded by Charles Alcock, took the lead in proposing the qualification rules, which in essence provided that no cricketer, amateur or professional, should play for more than one county in the same season and that everyone should be free to play for the county of their birth or their residence for the previous year or their family home if it was still open to them to live there. The counties, who wanted MCC to settle disputed cases, asked their formal approval. MCC suggested an amendment giving amateurs an extra option, playing for a county in which his parents held, or if deceased, had held property. The counties respectfully rejected this, and MCC sulkily resolved to let them stew in their own juice, or words to that effect. And so the situation remained, stewing and sulking, for the next fourteen years. Meanwhile, in the absence of formal rules, it fell to the press to determine who was champion county.

CHAPTER NINE

Imperial Intimations

THE GENTLEMEN OF ENGLAND were beginning to find a cause to justify their existence in the new, questioning age. The concept of leadership was emerging, a self-fulfilling prophecy, from the public schools and universities, educating the sons not only of the great landowners and the squires who still monopolised Parliament, and of the professional classes, but of the new men who aspired to their agreeable condition. Palmerston had convinced everyone who mattered that the British constitution was the finest in the world. Now its operation needed to be perfected by good administration, at home and in the exciting new dimension of Empire.

There was one snag. Gladstone, no imperialist or flag-waver, had discovered a novel political device, an electoral campaign based on national issues, which allowed him to stump around the country speaking directly to the enlarged electorate, and the moral quality he exuded won him the 1868 election. More important, he carried through a series of reforms – the 1870 Education Act, which inaugurated a national system of elementary schools; competitive examinations for the top layer of the Civil Service; the abolition of religious tests for university admission; reform of the armed services and the legal system, and improvement in local and central administration. This was splendid stuff, though not heart-warming. Nor was the Liberals' sponsorship of a Licensing Bill, trying to restrict drinking hours, which failed miserably, after cementing an alliance between the brewers and the Conservative Party. Gladstone was swept from power 'in a torrent of gin and beer'.

The Queen, an imperialist ex officio and by conviction, was delighted not be addressed like a public meeting, but to be coaxed and flattered by the silver-tongued Disraeli. After years of seclusion, mourning Prince Albert, she was ready again to help unite her burgeoning kingdoms – always with the incorrigible exception of Ireland, of course. The new Tory Government concentrated on social reforms with a greater appeal to the ordinary worker, including a Trades Union Act giving limited freedom from prosecution; an

Artisans' Dwelling Act, a Public Health Act, and similar measures outside Gladstone's bleak moral gaze. The Conservatives also launched a policy of 'Imperial consolidation' and an 'Imperial tariff' which contrasted sharply with Gladstone's unromantic free-trading view of Britain's overseas territories.

The seeming prudence of protecting the vast tracts of land, haphazardly acquired, annexing or otherwise manipulating buffer states and making strategic alliances, got off to a great start with Disraeli's purchase of a majority share-holding in the French-built Suez Canal to protect the route to India. The declaration of Victoria as Empress, in 1876, was highly popular. Soon she was urging the government to declare war on Russia, threatening the lifeline, as the music halls resounded to a new song:

> We don't want to fight
> But by Jingo! if we do
> We've got the ships, we've got the men
> And got the money, too.

Her reaction to the 'peace with honour' settlement was widely shared: it wasn't quite the total victory Disraeli claimed, but the Liberals would have done a good deal worse. Gladstone, protesting that he too harboured 'the sentiment of Empire ... innate in every Briton', yet warned against 'excess'. And sure enough, setbacks – a battalion lost to the Zulus in South Africa, legation staff massacred in Afghanistan – soon diluted the gung-ho spirit.

II

These outlandish parts were far beyond the ken of most Englishmen. Indeed, when the gentlemen of the Montreal Club wrote to R. A. FitzGerald asking him to arrange a tour of Canada in the winter of 1871–2 he displayed the great wit for which he was renowned. The Montrealers, he wrote, had first explained 'where Canada was and who the Canadians were. The precaution was necessary as great ignorance prevailed in England at this time respecting its colony.' Canada, in fact, had become a Dominion in 1867, its first Governor-General had set aside land at the Vice-Regal Lodge for practice, and the Prime Minister had declared cricket the national sport. This did not save the Canadians from a severe mauling by FitzGerald's team: 'The British Lion,' reported *The Times*, had made 'exceedingly short work ... of the very weak teams the colony could bring into the field'.

The expenses of the all-amateur touring team were met by their hosts. They were fortunate to be able to afford W.G., who was obviously the main attraction, the one everyone wanted to see. When in the winter of 1872–3 Melbourne CC invited him to take a team to Australia, he asked £1500, plus expenses, which was beyond the colonists' reach. The following winter, however, negotiations were concluded satisfactorily – for the Grace family, that is. For W.G., just married, it was a honeymoon trip and he took his brother Fred along, too. The professionals were not so well served. They got only £150 plus second-class travel and £20 expenses: consequently it was not as strong a team as it might have been. Nor did it diminish W.G.'s reputation for peasant-like thrift. C. B. Fry told a slightly barbed story about this tour:

> The English team had gone to play an up-country match, and WG and his company were welcomed by the hotel proprietor of a quadrangle of iron shanties, who said, 'Pleased to meet you, Dr Grace, but we can't do you here like they do in the cities. Not much in the way of bloody bathrooms and such-like.' 'That don't matter,' squeaked WG. 'We Graces ain't no bloody water-spaniels.'

The next venture, in 1876–7, was all professional, led by James Lillywhite of Sussex, who had been on the Grace tour. Lillywhite had met a fast bowler from Victoria, John Conway, a journalist by profession, and when Lillywhite decided to take a team himself, Conway made the arrangements. Most of the matches were against local eighteens or fifteens, at odds, but at the end of the tour Lillywhite agreed to play a combined Victoria and New South Wales XI on level terms. Thus casually was arranged what Conway called a 'grand combination match' but was afterwards designated the first 'Test' match, a term the newspapers coined. The colonists won handsomely, and Charles Bannerman, born in Kent, made the first century for them.

The result was received with equanimity in England, partly because little interest was taken – in polite circles – in professional ventures in distant places, partly because Lillywhite's already weakish side had been further stricken by the detention of their brilliant but dissolute wicket-keeper, Edward Pooley, in a New Zealand jail. *The Times* was philosophical: 'It began and ended in good temper and Lillywhite's pecuniary success must have consoled him for his defeat.' Further solace was on the way: a return match was played a fortnight later for the Englishmen's benefit. (They also managed to salvage a little of their reputation by winning.) Lillywhite paid the Australians £20 a man in gratitude, and the tour as a whole was such a financial success that he was able to pay the players double what he had guaranteed. He also struck up a warm relationship with Alfred Shaw, of Notts, who became his assistant, learning a few tricks of the developing colonial trade.

The Australian captain, D. W. Gregory, with John Conway at his elbow, clearly thought the time now ripe to reverse the flow of traffic, and took a team to England in the summer of 1878 as a speculative, profit-sharing venture. Lillywhite agreed to make the arrangements in England. These were not the first Australians to make the trip, for the former All-Ireland XI organiser Charles Lawrence, who had settled in Australia, had brought over a side of Aborigines ten years before. These agreeable, unsophisticated young fellows had proved to be pretty good cricketers, who had led MCC on first innings at Lord's, but were chiefly memorable for their unusual colouring and hairstyles, and for the displays of throwing the boomerang and other exotic arts with which they augmented their programme.

This gave rise to much racist comment when Gregory's team arrived, notably the story that when they took the field at Nottingham a spectator called out, 'Why, they ain't black!' This, Lord Harris recalled, 'was heard and resented by the team'. The president of Cambridge University CC, the eccentric heavy-weight Revd Arthur Ward,[1] apparently persisted in this misapprehension, giving rise to similar stories: when Cambridge came up to Lord's, A. G. Steel, who was with F. R. Spofforth, the Australian fast bowler, mischievously intro-duced him to the president as 'the demon nigger bowler'. Spofforth was apparently less amused before the MCC match by members' casually racist enquiries about the tourists' form. He certainly took his revenge.

The match was not well attended. Initial curiosity had attracted crowds of 7,000 for the first day's play at Nottingham and 10,000 for the second, but the Australians had lost by an innings in the chilly, damp weather and no one gave them much chance against a strong MCC side which included W.G. and A. N. Hornby and no fewer than four Notts players, among them Alfred Shaw, who happened to be Lord's professionals that year. The 4,000 who did show up saw a totally unexpected MCC defeat by nine wickets in less than five hours' play, and a particular humiliation for 'the Champion', who made four in the first innings and nought in the second. As *Punch* put it, in a famous parody of Byron:

> The Australians came down like a wolf on the fold:
> The Marylebone cracks for a trifle were bowled;
> Our Grace before dinner was very soon done
> And Grace after dinner did not get a run.

The Australians 'were loudly cheered by the assembled multitude', and their bowlers Fred Spofforth (6–4 and 4–16) and Harry Boyle (3–14 and 6–3) became instant celebrities, with Spofforth receiving the accolade of a carica-ture in the fashionable weekly, *Vanity Fair*.[2] Not least, the financial success of the tour was assured.

The Graces were quick to grab a share of the spoils and three weeks later all three, plus a rather seedy cousin, played for the Gentlemen of England against the tourists at the élite Princes' Club. The admission charge, a shilling, did not deter crowds of 11,000 and 6,000. Australian press reports commented that the 'so-called Gentlemen Cricketers Messrs WG Grace and WR Gilbert[3] received the sum of £60 for their services, and when Mr Conway raised an objection to it, it was asserted that WG Grace, GF Grace and WR Gilbert were invariably paid for playing'. (E.M.'s omission must have been an oversight.)

For their part the Australians normally took 80 per cent of the gate-money and shared it out between them. This was a sore point with the English players, for the Australians were regarded as amateurs – and given the usual courtesies of Mr or Esq in press reports and on score-cards. Resentment surfaced when C. W. Alcock of Surrey made the Oval available to the Australians in September for a match against James Lillywhite and a team of leading professionals (mostly Notts stars, recruited by Shaw). It was intended as a sequel to the 'Test' matches the previous winter, but before it could take place the *Sporting Life* published the following letter:

> Sir, – Having observed at the Oval that we are announced to play the Australians there ... we wish, through your columns, to inform the public, so that they may not be misled, that we are not engaged at all in the match and do not intend to play. We also beg to inform the public that it is not the intention of any of the recognised Yorkshire players to take part in the match. If, sir, any letters may be addressed to you on the subject of our remuneration, we beg to inform the public that we only asked for what we paid the Australians in our benefit match in the Antipodes.

The signatories – Shaw himself, Oscroft, Selby, Morley, Shrewsbury, Barnes and Flowers of Notts; Jupp and Pooley of Surrey – had asked for £20 but the Australians offered £10. Undeterred by the defections, the tourists went ahead with the game against a substitute team of lesser lights, and this still drew crowds of 10,000 and 12,000. Having made their point, the Australians increased the agreed rate of pay from £10 to £20, and gave a £5 bonus to Ted Barrett of Surrey, who took all ten wickets in one innings. Their restored reputation for generosity did not last long. After a hastily arranged match at Princes' Club against 'The Players of England' three weeks later, which attracted only 10,000 spectators in all, *Bell's Life* and the *Sportsman* reported that the Australians had received some £36 a man.

The Graces' 'amateur' status was also an inflammatory issue and MCC were sharply criticised as parties to the sham. Their protestations of innocence impressed nobody but they stalled for time by the long-established process of appointing a sub-committee to investigate. It reported in November that MCC had spent only 'trifling sums' on refunding 'reasonable expenses', but proposing 'that no gentleman ought to make a profit by his service in the cricket field' – a curious way of saying 'playing cricket' – and that in future anyone taking more than his expenses would be ineligible to play for Gentlemen v. Players. The report went on to refer to 'statements which have been made to us that sums much in excess of actual expenses have been frequently paid to gentlemen by other clubs or individuals'. On this, in a wonderful bit of question-begging, it concluded:

We have not thought it desirable to go into this question at any length, because
we hope that if the committee of the MCC should adopt our suggestion ... that
course will have the effect of checking a system which might grow into a serious
abuse, and which even now as alleged to be practised is open to grave objection.

MCC, of course, as connoisseurs of double talk, approved this unanimously.

III

The English professionals were not the only ones who felt obliged to withdraw their labour during the Australian tour of 1878. So did the Australians,
infuriated by W.G. The bone of contention was one William Midwinter, born
in Gloucestershire but taken out to Australia by his father, who was a small
and unsuccessful part of the gold rush. Out there Midwinter junior had done
well as an all-round cricketer, impressing W.G. in 1873–4 and eventually
earning selection for the first 'Test' against Lillywhite's team. Deciding to try
his luck in England, he sailed back in April 1877, appearing for W.G.'s
United South of England XI at Birmingham, Holbeck and Barrow-in-
Furness, before playing for Gloucestershire at the Oval, helping them (7 for
36 and 4 for 46) to a celebrated victory over 'England'. Later in the season he
saved the day against Yorkshire, scoring 68 in four hours, during which a
collection was taken and Mrs Grace 'presented him with £15'. 'This
happened to be,' wrote a later Gloucestershire secretary,[4] 'one of those Grace
testimonial matches. With brotherly solicitude EM raised the gate money
from 6d to 1s without informing his committee.'

When Gregory's team arrived in England they brought only eleven players
and picked up Midwinter later: he had already played for the United South of
England XI and for MCC before joining them at Nottingham in May. He
played for the Australians against MCC, making top score (10), and stayed
with them until, a month later, he was padding up waiting to open the innings
at the Oval when he was nobbled by a marauding party from Gloucestershire.
This comprised W.G., E.M. and the very large rugby international, J. A.
Bush. W.G., arriving at the Oval a man short, had apparently dashed across to
Lord's to get Midwinter, bundled him into a waiting cab, and taken him off
without consulting poor Gregory. As soon as he realised what was happening
Gregory, accompanied by Conway and Harry Boyle, who was Midwinter's
friend, set off in pursuit, catching the fugitives at the Oval gates, where, in
the course of an 'unhappy altercation' in front of amazed bystanders, W.G.
called the Australians 'a damned lot of sneaks'.

They protested bitterly, but got nowhere. In the long wrangle that ensued,
with charges and counter-charges, it is hard to find anything to excuse the
Graces' conduct apart from Midwinter's evident duplicity. W.G. tried to get
away with an evasive half-apology, but only the Australians' threat of with-

drawal from a potentially lucrative fixture brought a suitable climb-down and eventual reconciliation. Midwinter's reward was, it seems, £56 for the seven matches he played that year and re-engagement at the same rate of £8 a match for 1879. He may also, however, have been allowed in on the racket the Graces operated at away matches, where the hosts paid expenses. This was exposed in January 1879, when at a special meeting of the county club, it emerged that E.M. had submitted an exorbitant expenses claim to Surrey (for the match in which Midwinter was kidnapped) but Surrey had declined to pay it. This had brought to light the accounts, which the committee normally did not see, and revealed that, as against the standard expenses of £4 10s. for the bulk of the team, E.M. had claimed £20 for himself, £15 for W.G., £11 for G.F., £10 for Midwinter and £8 for W. R. Gilbert. The chairman reported that Surrey had agreed to pay a reduced claim. He also ventured to suggest that the accounts had not been in good shape and that they prevented the committee knowing what the players received.[5]

There followed a protracted and stormy meeting, with E.M. protesting innocence, denying charges, and generally behaving in a way that made his guilt even clearer, and W.G. supporting him at every turn, with the same result. The committee did agree stricter rules for the future, and the appointment of a finance committee, but E.M. remained in post, with everything short of a vote of confidence. By then he was coroner for West Gloucestershire and a pillar of his local community, and he stayed in post until 1909. W.G., of course, had grown far too big, and too popular with the public, for anyone to venture criticism. And Gloucestershire had not only held their own in the upper echelons but had been proclaimed county champions in 1876 and 1877.

It need hardly be said that serious criticism of W.G. – as distinct from amused head-shaking – was confined to envious persons, anarchistic professionals, cricket-haters and similar warped characters. The right-thinking folk of Gloucestershire started a testimonial fund for the great man, and it was taken up with enthusiasm throughout the country. The MCC, with scant regard for their new policy, endorsed the idea and in 1879 Lord Fitzhardinge made a presentation to him of £1,458, a marble clock and two bronze ornaments. The purpose of the gift – worth, say, £75,000 in current money – was to help him to buy a medical practice, for he had at long last satisfied the examiners, becoming MRCS and LRCP at the ripeish age of twenty-nine. As C. B. Fry wryly commented, W.G. was 'the only man who ever became a Doctor of Medicine on account of successful operations on the cricket field'.

IV

There was a higher moral tone amongst some of the newer leaders of amateur cricket. They tended to be public-school and university men who could afford to spend some years enjoying themselves before turning their attention to such tiresome matters as earning a living, running their estates and so forth. The most priggish of these was Lord Harris, a purist on residential qualifications and any other device to keep professionals in their divinely ordained slot in life. He was practically the King of Kent by now and his crown was renewed annually at the Canterbury Festival. The Old Stagers' week of drama at the local theatre ended with an epilogue on some topical issue. In 1877 Harris used the occasion to utter an indignant protest against the 'obstructives' threatening his feudal dream:

> Hold! I protest for here I represent
> All – MCC, I Zingari and Kent.
> Ne'er shall such trivial, childish schemes be found
> To desecrate our famed St Lawrence Ground.
> There, let Kent's white-horse banner be unfurled
> Against All-England – aye, 'gainst All The World.

His Lordship, whose father had been Governor of both Trinidad and Madras, was himself inclined towards colonial governance and he regarded cricket as an important educative force in such matters. He had made an apprentice trip with FitzGerald to Canada, finding the natives congenial and biddable, and when, in 1878–9, the reverential Melbourne club, anxious to experience the true-blue amateur spirit in action, invited him to lead an expedition to Australia he felt it his duty to begin the education of the colonies there.[6] Harris's team was originally to have been all amateur, but the Walkers of Middlesex had to withdraw because of a bereavement, so the two Yorkshire professionals, Tom Emmett and George Ulyett, were taken, mainly to perform the bowling chores. Their principal encounter, with David Gregory's returned heroes, was billed as 'Gentlemen of England (with Ulyett and Emmett) v. the Australian XI' and is now regarded as the third Test match. It was a sporting disaster for England, mainly due to Spofforth, who took 13 wickets including a hat-trick, but socially it went well. It was conducted reasonably amicably in the reasonably refined Melbourne atmosphere, and Lord Harris also found a reasonable umpire. The custom in Australia was to use amateur umpires, but Harris thought it better to hire a Melbourne professional, Coulthard, on trial. He was so satisfied that he decided to take him on to the next match, against New South Wales in Sydney.

Hiring a Victorian to officiate in New South Wales was not a diplomatic thing to do: hiring this one was a very bad idea indeed, for he first of all gave Harris a second 'life', a blatant error, and then, next day, gave Billy Murdoch, NSW's star player, run out. With the lively Saturday crowd getting restive, Gregory – captain again! – asked Harris at the pavilion gate to change the umpire. His lordship declined and returned to the wicket to defend his employee, around whom the crowd were now swarming. One of the 'larrikins', aiming at Coulthard, caught Harris with a stick, and A. N. Hornby, a keen amateur boxer, grabbed him and 'conveyed his prisoner to the pavilion in triumph'. Some accounts have the two professionals each grabbing a stump and standing guard on their noble leader, muttering, 'Nothing but sons of convicts.' The crowds dispersed temporarily and the Australians twice sent batsmen to the wicket, but when, at Harris's insistence, Coulthard remained, the crowds returned to the pitch and play had to be abandoned for the day.

The Australian establishment were mortified, and the newspapers were full of expressions like 'disgrace', 'profound regret', 'rough and excited mob' and 'deplorably disgraceful affair': the *Australasian* asked, 'What will they say in England?' The NSW Cricket Association waited upon Lord Harris and grov- elled. In reply he said 'he did not place any blame on the Association, or on the cricketers of Sydney, but it was an occurrence it was impossible he could forget'. The game was finished without incident on the Monday, the Englishmen duly won, a couple of ringleaders were charged, and it seemed possible that the thing might turn out to be a nine days' wonder. Sadly, Harris was not the forgiving type, and he had been less than straightforward in saying that he did not blame the Association or the cricketers. He sent a long letter to a friend, clearly intended to be published, and it duly appeared in the *Daily Telegraph* and the sporting press. Connoisseurs of righteous indignation should read the *Wisden* account.[7]

Harris's concluding words, 'We never expect to see such a scene of disor- der again – we can never forget this one', seemed to be literally true eighteen months later when another Australian team arrived. Gregory had gone and the affable Billy Murdoch was at the helm, but no one seemed to know about their arrival or to want to play them. As Harris wrote in his autobiography: 'They asked no one's goodwill in the matter, and it was felt this was a discour- teous way of bursting in on our arrangements; and the result was they played scarcely any counties and were not generally recognised.' He added, speciously, 'We felt we had to make some protest against too frequent visits.' The cold-shoulder treatment worked and the Australians, unable to get county games, were reduced to old-style odds matches against XVIIIs. They offered to play 'England' and devote the proceeds to MCC's Cricketers' Fund, but they were snubbed. When W.G. tried to arrange for a similar match in July, Lord's was 'not available'.

However, despite the generally poor quality of the opposition, the Australians drew big crowds and the counties began to regret the lost revenue. In the end it was Charles Alcock who proposed a match at the Oval in September, and managed to persuade Harris to choose and lead an England side. He mustered a surprisingly strong team, considering that some of the amateurs were on the moors. The Graces were all there and W.G. began the match with a century. The visitors lacked Spofforth, disabled by what *The Times* called 'some questionable bowling at Scarborough'. So although Billy Murdoch surpassed Grace's score in the second innings, the Australians found themselves in the admired role of gallant losers. That, assisted by the record attendance of nearly 45,000, assured them of a warmer welcome on their next visit and added a new dimension to the growing enthusiasm for the game of cricket.

V

The main focus of that enthusiasm was county cricket and its championship, which was beginning to excite public interest. The idea of championship was the inevitable outcome of commercialised leisure in age of competition – cups and their more developed counterparts, leagues, were in the air, notably in the newest public-school sport, football, that was sweeping the country. Apart from providing outlets for old-boy extensions of school and university loyalty they helped ordinary folk, particularly city-dwellers and factory-workers, to identify with some life-enhancing chance of success. Since the new idea represented a shift from older values stemming from the gentlemanly honour code to a system based on merit – something like competitive examinations for the Civil Service, which was also highly controversial – it did not appeal to everyone.

In cricket, for example, people like Fred Gale thought it deplorably vulgar and said so. The diehard section of MCC opinion, too, swung against excessive competition after the ignominy of its Silver Cup venture. Indeed, in 1874 MCC announced a new system of regional matches – with themselves picking all the teams! – patently designed to upstage and bypass the counties. In practice their scheme was a half-baked affair that merely lowered further the standard of play at Lord's. This, already greatly diminished, was not helped by the standard of the pitch. A basic levelling had been completed in 1875, and it was slowly improving, but its reputation lingered.

FitzGerald, whose authoritarian idiosyncrasies, prejudices and neglect of basics were widely held responsible for a situation in which England's premier club could no longer raise a decent team for a match at Lord's, defended himself vigorously – and made things even worse. In a speech in late 1874 he blamed the apparently poor quality of cricket at Lord's on two factors: first, the advent of W.G. – when he wasn't playing, standards seemed to have dropped; second, the excessive amount of cricket being played, which *inter alia* made it hard to tell Gentlemen from Players. He was roundly taken to task by county supporters, most succinctly in a letter to *Bell's Life*:

> Let the Marylebone Secretary, if he has the time, pay a visit to the Kennington Oval, or to Prince's, whilst a good county match is proceeding without Mr Grace, and he will at either place receive a direct denial to his preposterous

statement. The real fact of the case is that the public are more fond of cricket than ever, but they will not visit any ground that does not lay an attractive programme before them.

Poor FitzGerald, as it happened, was beaten not by his enemies or the force of progress, but by ill-health, which obliged his early retirement and precipitated his death. His successor, Henry Perkins – £500 a year from the start – was a good deal brighter and more businesslike and less concerned with buttering up the committee. He extended the membership considerably, again with the effect of diluting the aristocratic share: in 1877, 337 of the 2,291 total were titled and by the end of his twenty-year reign the total passed 4,000 with no increase in the titled, and not much change in the self-perpetuating committee that ran things to the extent that their assertive little secretary would let them. There was, however, much spiteful comment about the elevation of Mr W. Nicholson, a noted benefactor of the club who owed his fortune to the distilling trade.

'Perkino' did his best to improve the club's playing strength, amateur and professional, but his most lasting contribution was perhaps his first. In 1877 he concluded an arrangement with Middlesex to share the ground, rent-free at first and later making a contribution according to the state of their finances. This was not an entirely logical arrangement, given MCC's ambivalence towards the counties, but it showed that the Old Pals' Act had not been entirely repealed and filled a huge gap in the Lord's programme without putting MCC to the trouble of finding attractive fixtures for an age with which it had little sympathy.

VI

So the counties and their doings loomed larger in the cricket scheme of things. Gloucestershire, who were very good at looming large in any event, added to the excitement by becoming champions in 1874, 1876 and 1877. In 1878, on their first visit to Old Trafford to play Lancashire, they caused so much excitement that the ground record was broken: some 16,000 were estimated on the Saturday and 28,000 for all three days, with receipts of some £750. And, money aside, there was romance in it. It proved unforgettable to one young medical student, an even worse one than W.G., for he never finished his course and ended up in London out of work and addicted to drugs. This was Francis Thompson, who years later rendered his poignant recollections of the match in verses of the kind that reverberate with memorable sounds and echoing rhymes, but do not bear too much close analysis. They are called *At Lord's*, so we may imagine poor Thompson, the expatriate Lancastrian, whiling away the tedium of an inconsequential MCC game and thinking about his lost youth:

> It is little I repair to the matches of the Southron folk,
>> Though my own red roses there may blow;
> It is little I repair to the matches of the Southron folk,
>> Though the red roses crest the caps, I know;
> For the field is full of shades as I near the shadowy coast,
> And a ghostly batsman plays to the bowling of a ghost,
> And I look through my tears on a soundless-clapping host
>> As the run-stealers flicker to and fro,
>>> To and fro:
> O my Hornby and my Barlow long ago!

The names of Lancashire's openers have the right mournful, hollow associations and sit well with the most hallowed of nostalgic phrases, 'long ago', so we must be forever grateful that Thompson thought better of his original intention to use their nicknames – 'O my Monkey and Stonewaller long ago!' Thompson presents 'new-risen Lancashire' as a tiny flower being crushed by bats used as maces, and a 'long-whiskered Doctor that laugheth rules to scorn'. There was indeed a contentious episode in the match. Lancashire's W. R. Patteron drove the ball to the boundary, the crowd shouted 'four' and the batsmen stopped running – and some Gloucester wiseacre knocked down the stumps. The appeal was upheld, stopping the game for several minutes, during which the small but pugnacious Hornby argued with W.G., finally persuading him to go down in amongst the spectators, who convinced him that the ball had crossed the boundary.

Characteristically, Thompson does not mention the relatively cheerful fact that Lancashire drew their match with Gloucester. In fact Gloucester never won the championship again and soon were in real decline. Young Fred Grace died suddenly in 1880 and, though he had not made the grade at international level, some felt the county was never quite the same without him. Meanwhile, for the next three years Lancashire shared the honours with Notts. They had now settled into a pattern. They had aggressive amateur batting in Hornby, A. G. Steel, his brother 'Mr D.Q.', and the Revd Vernon Royle, a sinuous and swift cover-point. But they also had a core of strong professionals: the solid batting of Barlow; a great wicket-keeper in Dick Pilling; and a string of bowlers complementing A. G. Steel's leg spin, including three, McIntyre, Crossland and Briggs, from Notts. And the whole was held together by firm amateur leadership, first from E. B. Rowley, who had once made over 200 in a memorable victory over Yorkshire Gentlemen, and then from Hornby, 'the Boss', impulsive and short-fused but generous. As Barlow said of him, 'He runs you out, then he gives you a sovereign.'

The Nottinghamshire team, by contrast, were utterly professional and positively hostile to such feudal concepts. They had a brilliant young batsman, Arthur Shrewsbury, who had fought his way into the side through the competitive hierarchy of local cricket – Meadow Imperial CC, works cricket for a lace firm, Nottingham Commercial, Castle Gate Club, then the annual Easter trial for the Colts, twenty-two aspirants against the county side, selection for Fifteen Colts of England against MCC and for the Next Fifteen against Notts first Eleven. Held back a year by rheumatic fever, he made the first eleven in 1875.

VII

Becoming a county professional was not a full-time job, even in the summer. The counties (with the partial exception of Surrey) could not afford to retain professionals as coaches for their members, so the usual practice was to seek a job with a gentlemen's club and play for counties on a part-time basis for match fees. Notts, who played more than the usual half-dozen or so county matches, offered contracts for some thirty-six days, and their players spent the rest of their time at leading clubs up and down the country, sometimes including, as we have seen, four at MCC. The young Shrewsbury, who would soon be a qualified draughtsman, did not fancy the cricketing equivalent of 'domestic service'. He took a contract but kept his lace-trade option open. This independent spirit explains why in 1878, at the age of twenty-two, he was a leader of the strike over pay in the Australian match. Amongst those persuaded by his arguments was the great Alf Shaw, fourteen years older, but infinitely less sophisticated (and as a former farm worker with fewer expectations of a prosperous life outside cricket).

Whatever their precise individual sociological slots, however, the Notts professionals collectively were a pretty hard-nosed bunch, and the county committee were much exercised as to how to deal with them. They had no amateur tradition – Daft had been too honest – and they were obliged to appoint the veteran Will Oscroft, another striker, when Daft retired in 1880. So they put their trust in their honorary secretary, Captain Henry Holden, universally known as 'Hellfire Jack', whose day job was chief constable of the county, to instil a proper sense of values into the mercenaries. He had disciplined Shrewsbury in 1878, over a minor infringement, by leaving him out of the team, but quickly found it impractical to repeat this – the youngster was too good. Furthermore, he was a teetotaller, and an introverted, slightly prissy, bachelor, concerned about his premature baldness, and so got into none of the usual cricketers' sorts of trouble. He kept his eye implacably on the main chance and, whilst quietly spoken, did not like to be messed about.

In 1880, after touring with Richard Daft's team in North America, Shaw and Shrewsbury set up in business together in a Nottingham 'Sports Depot', with Shrewsbury manifestly the sharp end of the outfit. That season, after Notts had won the championship, they had another run-in with Captain Holden over pay for an extra match at the end of the Australian tour, outsmarting – and infuriating – him by arranging a profitable North of England game of their own at the new Bradford Park Avenue ground. In 1881 they broke off diplomatic relations with Holden and insisted on dealing with the committee direct over their right to arrange a 'county' match with the Bradford faction of the equally anarchic Yorkshire club. As a result Shrewsbury and Shaw led seven Notts players into a long wrangle over contracts, which so divided the committee that they turned to MCC's new secretary, Perkins, for arbitration. Holden ignored his decision and the strike resumed.

The establishment held its breath. Charles Alcock, wearing one of his 'unofficial' hats, wrote in *Lillywhite's Annual* (1882) blaming the Australians 'for the sudden and extraordinary change which took place in the bearing of professionals who had comported themselves most becomingly' and warning that this 'deliberate combination against recognised administration ... vitally affected the interests of any club of any importance'. But all was well. One by one five of the rebels gave in, leaving Shaw and Shrewsbury high and dry. After a winter's reflection they conceded defeat, apologised and were reinstated, turning their attention to the greater avenues of profit that lay in running the sports depot and organising overseas tours.[8] In the intervals they helped the county to the championship five years running, from 1882 to 1886.

Surrey, meanwhile, had to settle for second best. They had, however, found an amateur disciplinarian captain in the Wykehamist John Shuter, and gradually began to get results. The pattern of the team was similar to Lancashire's: largely amateur batting with Shuter, the great Walter Read and the dashing K. J. Key and W. E. Roller, bolstered by the extraordinary little professional, Bobby Abel, gradually perfecting the art; professional bowling, headed by the magnificent George Lohman with a strong supporting cast; and a fine wicket-keeper, Harry Wood. When Nottinghamshire's day was past, Surrey were ready to take over.

In Yorkshire, by contrast, it was still the case that no one seemed able to make a team out of their gifted but scarcely house-trained professionals – George 'Happy Jack' Ulyett; Edmund Peate, first of the great left-arm bowlers; Billy Bates, a wonderful all-rounder; Ephraim Lockwood, known as 'Mary Ann', the epitome of Yorkshire's traditional claim 'We may be rough, but we're ready'; the congenial Allen Hill; and the brilliant but inconsistent Tom Emmett. Their performances and rough-hewn image were no doubt an embarrassment to Lord Londesborough, who became president of MCC in 1876. The gentlemanly wing of the club had grown more and more dissatisfied at the professionals' lack of success under a string of idiosyncratic leaders. After Iddison, and the veteran Joe Rowbotham (1871–75), came Ephraim Lockwood (1876–77) and the delightfully eccentric Tom Emmett (1878–82), who claimed to have the reddest nose in cricket and to have earned it. He was fond of telling the story of how one morning after a binge he had immersed his nose in a wash-basin and 'it made the water fair phizz'.

Drink was, in fact, Yorkshire's biggest problem. Louis Hall, a Nonconformist lay preacher, who joined the club in 1873 as an opening bat in the Barlow mould, was reputedly the first teetotaller ever to play for them and, though he kept one end dry, he made few converts during his long stay. Their new captain, taking over in 1883, had the task, it was said, of leading nine drunks and a chapel parson. He also had to unite the club's geographical and social factions and try to produce a winning team. The chosen Messiah was the Hon. M. B. Hawke, an Etonian who had come down from Cambridge prepared to make cricket the most serious thing – almost the only thing – he did with the rest of his life. This autocratic, opinionated, utterly self-confi-dent sprig of the aristocracy, a disciple of Lord Harris, was not immediately successful. It was ten years before Yorkshire were reorganised and set free from the old Sheffield domination, and, coincidentally, won the champi-onship. But he set about the task of instilling discipline and sobriety into his wayward troops and soon Yorkshire, restored to feudalism, were ready to play the establishment game.

VIII

The imperialist 'excess' that Gladstone feared exposed British troops to attack in remote corners of the globe, and the Liberals, back in office, found themselves forced into ceding the Transvaal to the Boers, 'scuttling' Kandahar, quelling a nationalist revolt in Egypt, trying to evacuate a garrison from the Sudan and then rescue General Gordon from Khartoum. With Ireland a sword pointed at its heart, the Empire was lurching towards crisis. But Britain was now committed to her self-appointed task of leadership, and everywhere they went the British took, as part of their cultural baggage, their games, not least cricket. It was the badge of Englishness in divided Canada (and Ireland) and the bounty conferred on the native élites in India and the West Indies. *Tom Brown* was required reading and manly sports were part of the curriculum in the superior schools of Nigeria and East Africa – and in racially mixed South African mission schools before discriminatory policies took hold. 'In the history of the British Empire it is written that England has owed her sovereignty to her sports,' declared the Revd J. E. C. Welldon, the young headmaster of Harrow, afterwards Bishop of Calcutta.

Australia was foremost of the cricketing colonies, and it had its cultural strongholds, such as St Peter's College, Adelaide, which was deliberately modelled on Rugby School. Cricket was also administered to Aboriginals, as part of 'the civilising process', by missionary schools. Unfortunately, by the same token, it became an important route to social improvement for the less privileged, and at its higher levels seemed to have fallen into the hands of mercenary-minded types with no breeding. Or so Lord Harris thought.

Meanwhile, however, like was speaking unto like and in the winter of 1881–2 Lillywhite, Shaw and Shrewsbury took off on another tour to Australia and New Zealand, this time by way of America.

It proved a rather precarious venture. America was disappointingly unenthusiastic; elsewhere the weather was variable, likewise gates; there was a scandal over Ulyett and Selby, who were accused of selling a match; and the tourists lost two of the four Test matches and drew the other two. They still did well enough financially to pay the players £225 plus expenses and to make a profit of £700 each. But was the well running dry? Worse, was English cricket in decline?

When the Australians brought another team in 1882 it cannot have pleased either the MCC and county establishments or the professionals to read *The Times*'s leading article on the subject. After comments on individual stars, complete with prefix Mr, it hailed the visitors as a welcome break from 'the monotonous round of matches between county and county, between North and South, and gentlemen and players'. In a comment that could still be written today it continued, 'The pitch of interest felt in county matches by all except the players is far from high.' After demolishing the other staples of the fixture list it criticised all English games as 'mere opportunities for the display of individual skills', whereas the Australians offered 'the spectacle of a team that is nothing if not united', and added, 'When a nation is tired out with internecine feuds, a common enemy exerts a rallying influence.'

So far from Britain conferring blessings on its colony, it seemed, the colony was coming to the mother country's rescue. Then, brutally, *The Times* exposed the reasons why this might be so. The Australians did not play cricket day in day out, but normally only on Saturdays, whereas our best players felt they had to play full-time. There was an affinity between gentlemen and players, 'that both make a business of the game, in the sense that for a certain time during the year, both do nothing else'. It was tempting to wonder whether the gentlemen had 'any other taste or occupation in life'. The professional was lucky in that he could take pleasure in his work:

> He is generally a capital fellow whose only failing is to spend improvidently what he earns easily ... That his head is seldom turned with praise, and that his success does not very often sink him in dissipation speaks well for the general manliness and healthy character of the class. The cricket professional is more deserving than most of those who minister to human pleasure. It is only lamentable to think that the goal of his aspirations is, too frequently, to be the proprietor of a public house.

This might have been easier to bear had not the part-timers, with Spofforth rampant, won the only Test match. *Punch* began its verse commentary with a handsome acknowledgement:

> Well done Cornstalks! Whipt us
> Fair and square!

But then it turned to an uglier aspect:

> England's star
> Seems to some, at least, here to have sunk
> Through that worst of captains, Captain Funk.

(The actual captain, the Hon. Alfred Lyttleton, one of five cricketing sons of the 4th Baron Lyttleton, just down from Cambridge, was a future Colonial Secretary.)

Amongst all the recriminations, however, little was made of the only jarring note, W.G.'s running out of S. P. Jones, referred to in Chapter Eight. But Spofforth, who did the damage, is said to have been fired up by the incident. The defeat, an ironic sequel to *The Times*'s hope for a common enemy exerting a rallying influence on England's jaded and complacent cricketers, was commemorated in various mock obituaries, of which the best known, in the *Sporting Life*, gave the name to the prize for which future series were fought:

> In Affectionate Remembrance
> of
> ENGLISH CRICKET
> Which died at the Oval
> on
> 29th August, 1882,
> Deeply lamented by a large circle of sorrowing
> friends and acquaintances.
>
> R.I.P.
>
> N.B. The Body will be cremated and the
> ashes taken to Australia.

CHAPTER TEN

Amateur Ambuscade

IT WAS ENTIRELY PREDICTABLE that the expedition despatched 'to bring back the ashes' the following winter would be thoroughly well-bred. To the delight of fashionable Antipodean society and particularly its female section, Melbourne CC's invitation was picked up by the Hon. Ivo Bligh, the future Earl of Darnley, a twenty-two-year-old bachelor. (The appetite of his Kent captain and fellow Etonian Lord Harris for colonial tours was now sated.) 'Ivo's Twelve' included five four-year university Blues – Bligh himself, A. G. Steel, E. F. S. Tylecote, C. T. and G. B. Studd (both of whom were later to become missionaries in China) and one three-year, C. F. H. Leslie, together with Surrey's Walter Read and G. F. Vernon of Middlesex, whose original vocations (scholastic and legal) were to be neglected over the years in favour of touring. They were supported by four professional work-horses, one of whom, Fred Morley, was so conscious of the honour of selection that he withdrew from his last county match for fear of injury, and during the tour went on bowling in spite of a shipboard accident that later caused his death.

After a happily contested three-match series against Murdoch's tourists, narrowly won by the Twelve, a group of young ladies 'cremated' a bail, put it in a little urn and presented it to the English captain. Or so the agreeable legend had it. Whether this is true, or whether the presentation took place at a country-house Christmas party before the series began and was actually of an incinerated ball,[1] makes little difference to the spirit of the affair. The gold plate on the urn is inscribed with verses of baser metal:

> When Ivo goes back with the urn, the urn
> Studds, Steel and Tylecote return, return:
> The Welkin will ring loud.
> The great crowd will feel proud,
> Seeing Barlow and Bates with the urn, the urn;
> And the rest coming home with the urn, the urn.

but they no doubt brought a warm glow to Anglophile hearts. They presumably also sustained the team when they lost an extra, fourth 'Test' match. Ivo took the urn home anyway, and it was afterwards deemed that such extra games did not count as 'Ashes' matches.

The continued advance of gentlemanly cricket, even discounting the question-begging contribution of the Graces, was a highly gratifying feature of the cricketing scene. The partisan excitements and the social dazzle of Eton v. Harrow and Oxford v. Cambridge were augmented now by some fine cricket. The first real star of the Varsity match was William Yardley, who not only scored the first century, in 1870, but also, two years later, the last until the 1920s. The 1870 match also had a meteor, F. C. Cobden. Oxford needed three runs to win with three wickets to fall when Cobden took a hat-trick to finish the match. It was his finest hour.[2] Individuals apart, there were whole families of magnificent cricketers – headed by the Lyttleton dynasty – ready to fulfil the public-school prophecy of future leadership, in intellectual and spiritual life, in statesmanship and above all in empire-building and defending.

A particular and welcome bit of imperial defence had come in 1878, when the Hon. Edward Lyttleton's Cambridge team defeated the touring Australians. Oxford had their own stars – Ottoway, Harris, Tylecote and A. J. Webbe – and when they got their own ground, the Parks, in 1881, it seemed a symbolic advance. To some senior members of the university it no doubt seemed a step nearer the Greek ideal of a healthy mind in a healthy body, though the mathematics don, Revd Charles Dodgson (aka Lewis Carroll), considered it a piece of élitist self-indulgence:

> The man of wealth and pride
> Takes up the space that many poor supplied:
> Space for the game and all its instruments,
> Space for pavilions and for scorers' tents:
> The ball, that raps his shins in padding cased,
> Has wore the verdure to an arid waste;
> His Park, where these exclusive sports are seen
> Indignant spurns the rustic from the green.

To the unreflecting cricketers, spurning the odd rustic was a small price to pay for the advance in standards demonstrated by Oxford's victory in 1884 over both Cambridge and the Australians.

II

MCC also, with revenue leaping from £3,012 in 1873 to £15,065 in 1884, had grounds for optimism. However, though Ivo had vanquished one enemy, there was work to be done in combating another, the recalcitrant English professional. Unfortunately for the establishment, the counties, despite the raising of tone and improvement of standards by amateur leadership and example, were still deplorably dependent on professionals, some of them far too big for their boots. Notts, for example, though grooming a couple of young amateurs for the future, had been obliged to appoint Alfred Shaw as captain in 1883. He admittedly steered them to the championship three times but his extra-mural activities grew no less as retirement loomed, what with the sports goods business, organising tours, publishing books about them, and now coaching for the munificent Earl of Sheffield, the president of Sussex CCC, who had his own private ground.

The championship, in any case, though the public were beginning to get very excited about it, was something of a shambles. The press, in their self-appointed task of awarding the laurel wreath, generally determined that the county that lost fewest matches was the best. Thus in 1883 Notts (played 12, won 4, lost 1) were judged by the scribes to be better than Yorkshire (played 16, won 9, lost 2). And it was still up to each individual county what opponents they played and how many times, making the notion of a championship, in the modern sense, a nonsense. It also encouraged conservatism. Notts were severely criticised at their AGM for not extending their fixture list so that they could give a chance to young players. Both Surrey and Lancashire were currently doing this, playing several of the 'minor' or 'second-class' counties, and employing a few promising young players as ground staff. Notts' failure to respond left them unprepared for the expansion that was to come.

Of more immediate concern to the Notts committee was Lancashire's Jack Crossland, a ferocious fast bowler who starkly contravened the bowling laws. Several counties were chary of meeting Lancashire because of this. In 1882 Wisden reported 'a most unseemly exhibition of feeling in the Surrey v. Lancashire match', and, whilst commenting that it 'seems impossible that so thorough a cricketer as Mr Hornby would countenance a style of bowling which he was not convinced was fair', added that 'many independent critics condemn Crossland's style, and take occasion to point out that the present unsatisfactory manner in which umpires are appointed is the real cause ...'; and in 1883 'Crossland's success with the ball in the first innings of Surrey gave rise to a similar exhibition of feeling to that displayed in the corresponding match last year.' Notts, who had extra reason to disapprove of Crossland because he was a Nottinghamshire man, had declined to play Lancashire for two seasons, and relations between the two clubs had got to the stage of exchanging abusive Christmas cards.

Kent were also at odds with Lancashire, and Lord Harris, who had strong views on the unfair bowling question, was exasperated at what he thought was umpiring weakness. In a famous exchange Harris had snapped at Robert Thoms, 'When are you umpires going to do something about this?' and Thoms had replied, 'My Lord, we are going to do nothing. It is you gentlemen who have got to do it.' The dependent position of the umpires, essentially unchanged since the Duke of Richmond's match with Alan Brodrick in 1727, was exposed. In December 1883 the county secretaries met to discuss the question of unfair bowling, and tried to get a gentleman's agreement, the nineteenth-century equivalent of the honour code, 'not to employ any bowler whose action is at all doubtful'. Yorkshire, Kent, Middlesex, Derbyshire, Nottinghamshire and Surrey signed, but Lancashire, who as well as Crossland had a questionable slow bowler, George Nash, did not.

They did, however, drop Nash when Kent came to Old Trafford in 1884, and Harris decided not to press the matter of Crossland. But when he came back in 1885 and found both Crossland and Nash in the side he felt the time had come to protest. He protested at length, pompously and sententiously, more in sorrow than in anger. Lancashire replied tersely, more in anger than in sorrow. They also, foolishly, tried to go over Harris's head to the Kent committee and were suitably rebuked. Kent refused to play Lancashire in the return match. Indeed, Lancashire might have found themselves totally without fixtures had not Nottinghamshire reported Crossland's breach of residential qualification regulations to MCC: he had spent the winter at home in Sutton-in-Ashfield. These qualifications were another matter on which Lord Harris felt strongly, and wearing his MCC hat he was able to kill two birds with one stone.

That was the end of Crossland's career with Lancashire, whether they liked it or not. George Nash went back to his native Buckinghamshire, and so the matter blew over – for the time being – with bad feeling all round. The gentlemanly code of honour had not been much use. In the exchange with Kent the Lancashire committee were clearly in the wrong, and ill-mannered into the bargain, but this makes it no easier to sympathise with Lord Harris. Neither would show up well before a modern industrial tribunal, as employers of either players or umpires.

III

It was the custom of the time for the host clubs of individual grounds to select England Test sides against Australia. Lord Harris had declined the captaincy when Lancashire CCC staged the first 'Test' of 1884 because they proposed picking Crossland. Harris had, however, led the side at Lord's, when MCC picked the team, and won the only decided match of the series. In spite of the backstairs bickering it was all very friendly, with the Australian captain Billy Murdoch fielding substitute for England in the first game and catching one of his own team; England, up against it in the third, put on every man to bowl, including the Hon. Alfred Lyttleton, the wicket-keeper, who removed his pads and took 4 for 19 with slow underarmers; and Walter Read, batting at number ten, scored a century to save the follow-on. A – professional – sour note was struck, however, in a Players v. Australians match at Sheffield, when Arthur Shrewsbury and two of his Notts colleagues declined to play for the £10 fee offered by the Yorkshire committee.

The players' action was criticised by most of the press – 'every well-wisher of the sport will regret the action they have taken' – and, more to the point, seems to have backfired on Shrewsbury when he went with Shaw and Lillywhite on yet another visit to Australia. The whole team this time were not only professional but, with the exception of J. M. Read of Surrey, northern. According to Shaw and Shrewsbury they were a happy family and not over-indulgent: 'Experience had tamed the wild spirits of one or two ... who had visited the Land of the Golden Fleece and of bountiful hospitality on previous occasions.' But there was nothing but trouble ahead. In one representative match, closely contested, Billy Barnes, a rumbustious fellow from Sutton-in-Ashfield, who was not responsive to authority, particularly when drunk, refused to bowl in either innings when Shrewsbury asked him to. More seri-ously, Murdoch's team had not forgotten Sheffield, and were, as *Wisden* put it, 'animated by a feeling of bitter hostility towards Shaw and his party'. So the tour was punctuated by disputes, players' strikes and pained reaction from Australian dignitaries and .press at their 'unpatriotic conduct', sacrificing 'the cricketing honour of their nation to monetary considerations' and 'reducing cricket to a mere money-making matter'.

As a result the Melbourne Cricket Club decided the time had come for them to raise the social and moral tone by sponsoring the 1886 tour to the mother country. They were warmly welcomed by the upholders of rectitude in England. C. W. Alcock, for instance, began his article in his weekly maga-zine, *Cricket*, on a suitably patriotic note: 'This is the first Colonial team that has visited us since that other gallant body of Colonials was ranged beneath our flag in the Soudan.' The humiliating 'scuttling out', Kitchener's gallant, but late and unavailing, attempt at rescue and General Gordon's martyrdom, a poignant memory today, were then fresh in the mind, and Alcock must have been particularly pleased with the allusion. He went on to praise Melbourne CC's approach to the tour, 'organised on new and non-mercenary principles' – like those of *Cricket* magazine, no doubt – and then to moralise about the possible consequences: 'Their trip, let us hope, will be free from the usual dismal squabbles about gate-money, about amateur and professional rank, about the distinctions of "Mr" and "Esquire".'

This was hypocrisy of the most self-deluding kind. After all, the Australians had not created these thoroughly English distinctions, but merely drawn attention to their flimsy basis. MCC and their adherents would have put to the sword any vulgarian who tried to abolish this God-given demarca-tion. By the same token they did not want the Colonials – however useful on the battlefield – poking their noses into things they could not possibly know anything about. So when Melbourne CC tried to scupper a projected further

Shrewsbury, Shaw and Lillywhite tour of Australia that winter by sponsoring rivals of their own choosing, there was a great clamour in the papers about whether they had any right to do so. In desperation Major Wardill, the Liverpudlian secretary of Melbourne CC, appealed to MCC to select a team for them, but MCC declined to become involved, so he was obliged to leave the field clear for the mercenaries.

IV

The chief of these was now Arthur Shrewsbury, who was also the best batsman in England. It was customary at the time to qualify 'best' by adding 'professional' out of deference to W.G., of whom everyone, except Australians in general and Spofforth in particular, stood in awe. It has since become obligatory to quote in evidence W.G.'s reply when asked who he would choose to open the innings with him – 'Give me Arthur' – as if that settled the matter. Without entering into pointless controversy we may simply note that Shrewsbury had a better average than W.G. against Australia and that for the next decade he was as good as any batsman in English county cricket. This was only gradually becoming a meaningful concept.

The county secretaries had, for the first time, begun to meet in a body in 1882. Their first difficulty was deciding who should be eligible to join the magic circle. Since every county could play anyone they liked there was no logical reason for excluding anyone, and any county club with a fixture against one of the original nine seems to have been invited to meetings. However, successful and conservative clubs like Notts were not keen on expanding and they frequently clashed with liberals and thrusting newcomers. The terms 'first-class', 'second-class' and 'minor' counties were beginning to be used: the English love of hierarchy was strong. On the other hand, the English like their hierarchies, especially those with social overtones, to be self-evident rather than explicit, so Darwinism, otherwise highly unpopular in the best circles, held sway.

Newcomers with varied pedigrees began to press their claims. Somerset, with a long history of superior club cricket, notably in Bath, had formed a county club in 1875, at a meeting in Devon (!), on condition that there should be no county ground. Their I Zingari-like resolve had melted by 1886, when they took a lease on the Athletic Ground in Taunton. Captained by E. Sainsbury of Bath and assisted by Blues like W. N. Roe and E. W. Bastard, a fine left-arm slow bowler, they abounded in amateur talent. Their want of professionals showed, however, in 1884, when, bereft of Bastard, they allowed Hampshire to put on 645 against them, and the following year, when only nine gentlemen turned up, even Bastard could not save them.

Hampshire themselves, eager to recover ancient glories, had been aroused from torpor in the 1860s by the patronage of the cynosure, Sir Frederick

Bathurst, and the chairmanship of Mr Thomas Chamberlayne, one of the few untitled presidents of MCC. They were further uplifted in the 1870s by the leadership of the four-Blue athlete Clement Booth and later by the batting of F. E. Lacey, about to become secretary of MCC, and E. G. Wynyard, foremost of many young military men. With a new ground in the great commercial centre of Southampton, a stiffening of decent professionals, and enthusiastic secretaries in, first, Col. James Fellowes of the Royal Engineers, founder of both the Dorset Dumplings and the Hampshire Hogs, and then the celebrated Dr (later Sir Henry) Russell Bencraft, they were well placed for elevation.

So too were Leicestershire, whose president in 1886 was the young but already legendary Nathaniel George Curzon, MP, a future Viscount and Viceroy of India. More relevantly they had as vice-president the Mayor of Leicester, Charles Marriott, who had been the county's leading batsman for some years and was a member of MCC. Having evolved from the unruly urban contests of the late eighteenth century (Chapter Four) and the fashionable ones of the early nineteenth (Chapter Five) with the aid of a good supply of hunting parsons who played cricket in the summer, Leicestershire also had some good professionals, including the outstanding bowler Pougher, a stalwart of the Lord's ground staff.

Essex, too, had good credentials, though not much heard of since they had played Middlesex in 1787, inaugurating Lord's first ground. Nowadays they were basically a gentleman's club side at semi-rural Leyton. They had powerful leadership in the Cambridge men, C. E. Green, a great benefactor, H .G. Owen and the recruit from Middlesex, A. P. Lucas, with staunch professional support from Lancastrian James Burns and local boy Henry Pickett. By contrast, Warwickshire's driving force was William Ansell, who claimed to have wrested control from 'a few gentlemen in and around Warwick': the new powers, though boasting a title or two, were mostly products of the Industrial Revolution, and of Birmingham, the centre of a sprawling conurbation second only to London's. They took advantage of the relaxation of the Limited Liabilities Act (at a time when commercial expertise was superseding industrial know-how) to float a Cricket Ground Company, headed by Sir Thomas Martineau, whose prospectus promised investors a fair return for their money, subject to the overriding aim of bringing first-class cricket to Edgbaston.

Warwickshire's brash assault on recognised values was actively opposed: otherwise there seemed no way of deciding between the claimants. Indeed the county secretaries' first action was a negative one: Derbyshire, after repeated criticism in the sporting press, were demoted in 1887 on the grounds that they had only won one match in four years. The press, in fact, now seemed to be deciding such policy as there was by publishing primitive 'league tables' and talking of a 'championship'. This infuriated purists like Fred Gale, the

'Old Buffer', and he wrote a long piece protesting at their impertinence. *The Times* in a leading article set out the charge: 'Cricket reporters are on their trial. Their offence is that they have introduced a classification of counties into major and minor, or first-class and second-class.' Its answer was that the press were merely meeting public demand:

> It would be healthier if there were more love of cricket for its own sake and less excitement about 'results' ... But the emulative spirit of our countrymen will not have it so ... the intense spirit of competition which is the chief feature of modern cricket precipitates itself in the worship of success.

The counties, split between *dirigistes* and people who just wanted to be left alone, set up a sub-committee – Kent, Middlesex, Surrey, Sussex and Gloucestershire – who came up with the idea of a County Cricket Council to regulate such matters. The prime mover was, of course, Lord Harris, who chaired the chaotic proceedings of this ephemeral body. A sub-committee (same membership) was asked to produce a report. It proposed an elaborate scheme of three divisions, with promotion and relegation, but this was rubbished by the full meeting of the council. Similar things were still happening over a hundred years later, and will always happen when the vested interests of unregulated, self-appointed bodies collide. On this occasion the clash was so violent that in 1890 the County Cricket Council was adjourned *sine die* on the casting vote of the chairman, M. J. Ellison of Yorkshire, not a great progressive.

In 1891, Derbyshire's vacant place was given, by some arcane process, to Somerset, but no other decisions proved possible. Mr Ellison tried in 1893 to get agreement on an egalitarian scheme: all counties would qualify if they played three-day matches 'out and home' with at least six other counties. This would do away with 'the very invidious distinctions which had existed for some years and would also abolish the hated word "championship"'. By 1894 the counties were obliged to ask MCC to arbitrate for them.

The result was a compromise. 'Cricketing counties shall be considered as belonging to the first-class or not' but without any further categories. But 'first-class' was to be determined, not according to results, but on the basis of playing an agreed number of three-day matches, home and away, with existing members of the fraternity, counties, MCC, universities, Australians, etc. This brought Derbyshire back and admitted Hampshire, Essex, Leicestershire and Warwickshire into the fold, and left MCC free to admit future claimants. On the other hand, MCC acknowledged the claims of 'championship' to the extent of adopting a system of points – one for a win, minus one for a loss. It was certainly not a league, such as the professional soccer clubs had set up in 1888, since the counties were still free to pick their own opponents. But it was a further slither down the slippery slope towards organised competition.

V

The irony was that all this was the creation not of Old Clarke or his dreaded successors, the ultra-professional Shaw and Shrewsbury, but of the gentlemen, ranks swollen by flocks of university men brought up on summers of three-day cricket, and the county members, who for a modest subscription and the price of a railway ticket could now enjoy all the cricket they wanted. Shrewsbury was in fact losing ground on the colonial branch of his enterprises. He did not make much profit out of the 1886-7 tour despite the absence of competitors, because the Melbourne crowds showed little interest in either the English professionals or their sanitised, non-mercenary but undistinguished opponents. And if the old animosities had gone, new ones arose. The second Test was enlivened by the bibulous Billy Barnes, who, after taking 6 for 28, got involved in a fight with the London-born Australian captain, Percy McDonnell, missed McDonnell, hit a wall and took little part in the rest of the tour. It says much for Shrewsbury's tenacity of purpose that he resolved to try again the following winter in spite of opposition from the Melbourne CC, who were busy, this time with the tacit support of MCC, trying to organise a tour by, of and for, gentlemen.

Knowing the crowd-pulling power of such an approach, Shrewsbury tried to counter-attack by signing amateurs of his own. He hooked only fish of moderate size: three from Sussex, C. A. Smith as captain,[3] G. Brann and W. Newham, and the footloose L. C. Docker. This was not enough to convince the Australian press, which referred to the 'professional team brought out by ... Shrewsbury', contrasting them with 'the English amateurs who are to visit Australia under the auspices of the Melbourne Club'. Melbourne had made much in their advance publicity of the slightly bluer blood of their own team. It was headed nominally by the Hon. M. B. Hawke, no less. In the event Hawke was prevented by the death of his father and consequent accession to the title from playing any part, but it still had the Anglo-Irish baronet Sir Timothy O'Brien and a couple of Varsity chaps. However, the captain, G. F. Vernon, his Middlesex colleague A. E. Stoddart, and Walter Read – who was said to have been paid £1,000 and still quibbled over expenses – were all what the newspapers were beginning to call 'shamateurs'.

Shrewsbury was considerably irked by all this, not from any desire to overthrow the established hierarchy, but because he realised the snob appeal of the amateur label and wanted to cash in on it himself. He wrote to Alfred Shaw bitterly complaining that Vernon's team were doing better business, even in Sydney: 'People think that they are all amateurs – "Gentlemen of England" – and that is the reason they get patronage.' He gave orders for similar billing for his own team. But nothing made much difference, as the two rival groups went round the country vying for custom. In the end they decided to cut their losses and join forces for a match against a Combined

Australian eleven, another of the improvised affairs later designated Test matches; but it was boycotted by the leading Victorian players and Shrewsbury's tour dwindled into financial failure.

This left him with a liquidity problem at the end of the tour, and his subsequent instructions to his partner Shaw illustrate a point made forcibly by Joe Darling, inveighing against English amateurs: 'the only difference was that most of these supposed "amateurs" got twice as much pay as the "professionals".' Shrewsbury was having to pay even his rather lightweight gentlemen £200 each. If funds were slow to come through, Shrewsbury told Shaw, 'you must make Newham and Brann wait until the others are paid ... Newham and Brann won't tell anyone they [have not been] paid, you can rely on that.' Shrewsbury hoped to refill his coffers from a football[4] tour he was trying to arrange in Australia after the cricket, and he had thought it would save him money if he could persuade a few of the cricketers to stay on. Smith and Brann had agreed, but then reneged, as the Rugby Football Union, having got wind of the project, seemed likely to declare it a professional venture. Shrewsbury's biggest worry, however, was that Andrew Stoddart – one of Vernon's 'amateurs' and a much better footballer than Smith or Brann – would pull out of the deal. He sent him a £50 retainer and Stoddart stayed on and in fact captained the side.

Unfortunately, far from baling out the cricket tour, which lost £2,400, the football venture lost a further £800. Since he had missed a season's cricket at home, and had turned down the offer of the Notts captaincy when Shaw lost the job, Shrewsbury's acute business sense seems to have led him astray for once. The captaincy decision was in itself significant, for after stopping the gap with the veteran wicket-keeper Mordecai Sherwin (also the Notts County goalkeeper), the Notts committee decided the time was ripe for an amateur, J. A. Dixon. Dixon, too, was a Notts County and England soccer player, but a forward – which had sociological connotations of its own – and an amateur when the FA was still powerful and the term still meant something. As it happened, he was not only a decent cricketer and a good captain, but, on the good authority of Peter Wynne-Thomas, 'a sagacious man of affairs, a faithful citizen, a philanthropist, a wise magistrate and a true friend'. And he was unlikely to join in the next players' strike.

Symbiotically, the end of the era for the Notts captaincy also saw the end of the entrepreneurial professional touring ventures. A light at the end of the tunnel appeared to glimmer when the Earl of Sheffield, who traditionally hosted visiting Australian tourists' opening matches, approached Shrewsbury about taking a subsidised tour out there in 1890–91. Shrewsbury sent him an itemised estimate of costs, based on £250 a man for twenty-one weeks – it came to £6,632! – and thought receipts would just about cover this. He warned his lordship about including amateurs, pointing out that Lord Harris's amateurs' expenses had been about twice those of the professionals.

W.G., now aged forty-three, was a special case: in 'purely pecuniary' terms his presence could add £2,000 or more to the takings: 'a young generation of cricketers has grown up since Dr Grace's last visit and many would flock to see him play who have only read of his great reputation.'

In the event Shrewsbury decided to stay at home to look after the business, but Shaw went as manager. W. G. Grace was captain, there were four other amateurs, including Stoddart, and it emerged afterwards that the costs had been almost double Shrewsbury's estimate. One of the reasons was that Grace had insisted on his wife and family being paid for too. Shrewsbury commented:

> If he hadn't taken Grace out Lord Sheffield would have been £3,000 better off ... and also had a better team. I told you what wine woud be drunk by the Amateurs. Grace himself would drink enough to swim a ship.

Lord Sheffield lost over £2,000 on the tour, and cancelled a projected second venture, preferring to cement Anglo–Australian friendship by founding the Sheffield Shield competition, and importing Billy Murdoch as captain of Sussex.

Shaw and Shrewsbury were finished with touring, and spent their winters looking after their sports-goods business, which was now facing competition from another great Notts batsman, young Billy Gunn, who had started his working life as an apprentice bat-maker. Neither Gunn nor any other professionals followed them as tour operators, however, and the shamateurs moved in. There was a promising new seam to be mined in South Africa, where cricket had been taken first by the army and was enthusiastically played by British settlers, who here and there tried to teach it to the Boers, though not of course to the native population. The first tourists, mostly amateur, were recruited by a Major Warton of the general staff in Cape Town on behalf of the Western Province Club, and led by C. A. Smith, who may not have made as much money as he had hoped, but liked the country so much that he stayed there. Three years later, in 1891–2, the ex-schoolmaster Walter Read took a team which included a couple of Australians, Billy Murdoch and J. J. Ferris, the great bowler, who afterwards played for Gloucestershire.[5] And after that, as we shall see, Lord Hawke moved in.

VI

The death of the entrepreneurial professional may have occurred in foreign fields, but the obsequies were conducted on the English county scene. The creators of the new rail-linked network of sylvan retreats and urban oases were not of a mind about everything: there was a 'North–South divide' with a transpontine London version, a corresponding ambivalence about gate-money, and a good deal of tut-tutting about 'some people's excessive concern with results'. But they had much in common – admiration for stylish amateurs, docile professionals and three-day cricket – and a lack of business acumen.

For men in charge of powerful and potentially lucrative organisations, they were remarkably unsuccessful. The very idea of a profit-maximising cartel would have been distasteful to these gentlemanly fellows. In an important sense this was a microcosmic reflection of the nation, which had reached a position of world leadership, but lacked the qualities needed to live with the logic of their position in a competitive age. The English upper classes valued too much their own comfort and dignity, they did not believe in regulation, they hated the machines that had brought them prosperity and despised the men who were expert in their use.

Life at the top had not proved too easy for Britain as she failed to keep up with the scientific and technological demands of the second phase of the Industrial Revolution. There was no lack of new British inventions, but the Germans and Americans were quicker to take them up, and better at technical education. Soon there was a whiff of recession. First agriculture, for so long the staple, was brought near to ruin by the free traders – as Disraeli had prophesied – and cheap food was imported from abroad in exchange for manufactured goods. Then, as foreign competition sharpened in manufacture, the balance of trade suffered. In 1870 Britain's exports had equalled those of the USA, Germany and France put together. In 1890 the level had dropped to three-quarters. The Fair Trade League began to clamour for protective measures and public works.

The agitation had much support amongst the middle classes, who felt themselves hardest hit by 'the Great Depression', as they melodramatically called the slight slackening in what had seemed an automatic advance. Happily there was no threat to the prevailing belief in the essential, not to say divine, benignity of market forces. The latest manifestation of providence, the limited liability company, proved a highly popular alternative to working for a living, not least amongst those burdened with no longer profitable land. 'Something in the city' became the thing to be. Agriculture was still bottom of the heap economically and the country was now thoroughly urbanised: three parts of the UK's 35 million population in the 1881 census lived in towns, some 7 million in Greater London. But the rural myth prevailed, its destiny in the hands of a few thousand great landowners and their urban counterparts, and the country became a place for gentrified townsfolk to spend their long weekends in leisure pursuits.

The rural myth was at its least amusing in Ireland, and 'the Irish Question' was beginning to dominate English politics. Gladstone's late conversion to Home Rule split the ruling Liberal Party, and let in Lord Salisbury's Tories, with the support of a new coalition of Liberal Unionists. Ireland was seen as an imperial 'Queen and country' issue. Victoria's Golden Jubilee in 1887 was also the year of 'Bloody Sunday', when riots arising from a protest meeting over Irish policy had to be put down by force. A. J. Balfour, Salisbury's nephew, was made Secretary for Ireland and tagged 'Bloody Balfour' for his suppression of riots there. And at home, the shadowy alliance of anarchists, Irish nationalists and Socialists sent shivers down the spines of all right-thinking folk, not least the landowners who headed the socialist demonology.

But there was no danger of class-oriented revolt. Most Britons, however humble, were proud of their heritage and thought inequality an inevitable consequence of freedom. And in any event, the industrial working class did not see itself as, or operate as, a homogeneous unit on Marxist lines, battling against oppression by the ruling class. The workers were as stratified as the rest of society: threats of industrial action came from specific groups aiming to do well for themselves. The London dock strike of 1889, which succeeded without violence, ushered in an era of collective bargaining that showed the British way of managing these things. The trade unions, following medieval traditions, were themselves hierarchical and jealous of their individual independence. The Trades Union Congress, founded in 1863, was destined to continue to be a talking-shop for years to come.

The unions were not yet politicised: they were certainly reluctant to back ventures like Keir Hardie's Independent Labour Party of 1893. But in what they saw as their main task they were highly successful. By the turn of the century Britain's skilled and semi-skilled workers were the best paid in Europe: the rates for skilled craftsmen in London went up to 36s. or 38s. a week, and foundrymen's wages even to £2 2s. This seriously overlapped with lower-middle-class clerical workers, elementary schoolteachers and the like. There were fluctuations: it was not a good time to be a miner, for instance. And at the bottom of the scale, farm workers were lucky to get 15s. But generally speaking the workers did well, for the lower prices brought by competition put up real wages by about 30 per cent in the last quarter of the century. Liberal economists made much of this; the business and professional class did even better and the inequalities increased.

In one respect there had been a great advance for the workers. Their economic level at last allowed them to think seriously about shorter hours rather than higher wages. The Factory Acts, which many employers had resisted on economic grounds, had proved beneficial to production. The Nine-Hour Day legislation of the 1870s was followed by the Eight-Hour Day in 1883; it was slow to take hold, but the Gasworkers' Union actually went on strike to secure its implementation and it gradually became the norm. Greater leisure meant more time for sport amongst the working classes in industrial areas, and at last they began to influence the way the sports developed. Inevitably, both for historical-social reasons and because, specifically, its higher form took up more time than more modern sports, cricket adapted itself relatively badly to the new phenomenon, and allowed the gap between its first-class élite and those who could only play in their spare time to become permanent and practically unbridgeable.

We have already noted the factors that installed the county clubs and the three-day game at the pinnacle, and the philosophical and organisational difficulties that beset the creation of any kind of competition even amongst the handful of clubs concerned. Below them were not only a score or so of 'minor' counties (ranging from those on the fringe of the inner circle, like Worcestershire and Northamptonshire, and counties marooned by industrial progress, like Norfolk and Cambridgeshire, to ultra-gentlemanly optimists in Montgomeryshire and Carmarthenshire), but also a hundred or so wandering clubs and regimental elevens and countless town, works and village teams. The only 'ladders of opportunity', apart from the privileged access from public school to university and old-boys' club, were fortuitous.

At a basic level there were no cricket fields in the industrial areas and conurbations on which the workers could spend their greater leisure. A letter to *The Times* in 1883 from a concerned clergyman made a constructive proposal:

> Everyone must allow that the game of cricket is more popular now among the working men of London than it was say five or ten years ago. Then on Saturday afternoons such a thing as an artisan in flannels was never to be seen; now there is not a more common sight ... The question is often asked where can he play? Every year the population increases by 50,000; consequently green fields are further and further from the scene of his labours ... It has occurred to me that some suitable fields ... should be secured at once, either by the aid of the state, under the strong plea of recreation for the masses, or better still by the representative club of the country, the Marylebone, and should be let to the working men's clubs at a fair rental.

It was, perhaps, a little soon for such socialistic schemes.

And further up the ladder there were other philosophical obstacles. In the northern and Midlands districts, where gate-money had corrupted soccer and rugby clubs, cricket clubs (often the summer half of the same clubs) tended to be looked at askance by the southern-oriented cricket establishment because they arrayed themselves in leagues in a vulgar competitive manner. This was sheer unredeemed snobbery. League competition had grown out of the popularity of cup-ties, as in soccer. The amateur soccer clubs could at least rationalise their opposition to leagues because they paved the way for professionalism. MCC, who had always employed professionals, had no such excuse. The first one in club cricket, the Heavy Woollen Cup, was introduced in 1873, the year in which MCC had tried unsuccessfully to launch its own. In 1887 the Lamb Trophy encouraged the competing clubs to form a Huddersfield Association, and after the Football League made its spectacular début the following year, cricket leagues sprang up in industrial districts, where both players and spectators responded to the idea of Saturday afternoon matches that could be played to a finish.

The Birmingham and District League and Bolton and District Association (1888) were followed by the North Staffordshire (1889), the [North-East] Lancashire (1890), the South-East [later Central] Lancashire (1892), and the Ribblesdale and Northern Leagues (1893). Within a few more years there came the Leeds and District, the Durham Senior and the Bradford Leagues (1902), and the sprawling and complex Yorkshire Cricket Council. These were essentially amateur combinations, but clubs were typically allowed one or more professionals. And therein, apparently, lay the offence, for hiring pros encouraged an undue emphasis on gate-money – and on winning.

Another related offence was being 'northern', for the leagues were quintessentially phenomena of the new industrial Britain. One-day cricket in the 'South' followed the pattern of a hierarchy of clubs playing traditional rivals, from village-green stuff, complete with local vicar, blacksmith and assorted straw-chewing yokels followed by supper and flagons of ale at the village inn, to fashionable suburban clubs like Hampstead, where Andrew Stoddart could be seen when Middlesex and England calls permitted. The compendious *Barclay's World of Cricket*, published as recently as 1986, by which time the cricket team of almost every hamlet in the land belonged to a league, still bears the ancient caste-marks. Thus its 'historical survey' of club cricket mentions no club further north than Bristol, whilst that dealing with league cricket up to 1964 ventures no further south than Birmingham, apart from a brief foray into Wales.

Geography was never a complete guide to the 'North–South divide'. There were gentlemen's clubs in the northern conurbations – like Liverpool CC, which had over 500 subscribing members in 1894 and despite expenditure of more than £1,500 still showed a profit of £282 on the year. (Similarly, the Liverpool Rugby Club was able to resist pressures to take on working-class players who needed 'broken-time' payments and so avoid the descent into professionalism.) And South Wales had both a semi-professional competition and perhaps the most overtly élitist club of all, the South Wales Hunts CC, open only to hunt subscribers and supporters and the landowners whose terrain they traversed in the winter. But the contrasting stereotypes were fairly well represented by, on the one hand, Wimbledon CC, which could afford to buy its ground in 1889 for over £3,600 and to go on improving its facilities during the next decade without getting into the red, and, on the other, the vast majority of northern cricket clubs, which had to rely on their footballing sections to bale them out. In 1886 the new Manchester paper *Athletic News* reckoned that it would be very hard 'to point to a cricket club which did not get into debt'.

The three-day game and midweek cricket did not exempt the counties from the socially based dilemmas of seeking gate-money or going bankrupt. Even before the Football League started and soccer clubs began to coin money, *Wisden* (1887) quoted an official of Derbyshire CC saying that Derby County FC 'often took more in one match than the Cricket Club did during a whole season'. Whether cricket, if it had developed at its highest level as a one-day league system, could ever have been as popular as soccer is debatable, but it would certainly have been more accessible to players and spectators of all classes. As it was, the leagues offered an alternative, part-time outlet for players. Amateurs needed little time off work; professionals could draw a fee for a Saturday game or perhaps an evening or two's coaching.

Co-operation between league and county clubs was rare, and more often they were regarded as rivals and intruders, not only in seducing Saturday crowds but in spoiling their monopoly position as employers. Anything more than a season's contract was a rarity, not only amongst the less affluent counties, but competition sometimes forced them into concessions. In 1898, Warwickshire, for instance, were obliged to yield to the repeated requests for a five-year contract from their leading batsman, Willy Quaife, imported with his elder brother from Sussex four years earlier, fearing that he would join a league club. In fact Quaife then stayed for another thirty years! There were indeed many more rumours of players going into the league than actual departures: it was mostly people at the end of their county careers who crossed the line.

The reason was in large measure the lure of a benefit match yielding several hundred pounds after a period of satisfactory service. Other factors had more to do with history and with social attitudes – the entrenched position MCC and the counties now held; the glamorous aura given to county cricket by the socially superior amateurs; and the powerful hold of the rural myth. Players as well as gentlemen liked the social tone of the county cricket in its impressive or rustic settings, the good wickets and the unhurried tempo: and the county professionals saw themselves as a cut above the part-timers in the league, and often indeed above the soccer pros.

The later Victorian years belonged to the lower middle classes rather than 'the workers'. In the 1892 election seventy-two Irish nationalists were elected compared with one Independent Labour member. The radical spirit that was perceptibly stirring the country was in the hands of the eighty-two-year-old Gladstone and his Liberals, who in turn were in thrall to the 'Celtic fringe'. When Gladstone retired the Queen chose as his successor the fifth Earl of Rosebery over the heads of his seniors, despite her personal dislike for this raffish race-horse owner, because he was sound on the Irish Question and the Empire. His main achievement in the sixteen months before the Liberals gave way to Lord Salisbury once more was to win the Derby twice.

The lower middle classes were also the target of the new popular newspapers like the *Evening News* (1894) and the *Daily Mail* (1896), both of which cost a halfpenny. The first popular Socialist weekly, the *Clarion*, started in 1891, owed much of its success to its leavening of sport and leisure activities, often treated humorously. Its founder, Robert Blatchford, was a keen cricketer and there were regular articles on the subject by him and other contributors. Although these quite often had a north-country flavour (the *Clarion* was Manchester-based) and tended to give extra attention to professional players, they were thoroughly traditional in their outlook, romanticising the working class and their quaint habits and speech comically rather than polemically.

Their most anarchical feature was to set aside the conventions of calling amateurs 'Mr' every time they appeared. Their thorough acceptance of the hierarchical status quo comes over well in a 1898 piece by Blatchford himself, moralising about a bumptious young club batsman from Boston-cum-Muddeep who found himself out of his depth when called up for Lancashire Colts against the County XI and blamed the umpire:

> That theer Humpire gev me t'wrong block. Aw said 'Give us middle and leg.'
> But awm main sure he gev me middle and hoff. Ah played t'ball with a bat
> straight as a rush, but it copped summat on t' ground, ran up my bat, hit me on
> t'bacca box and went i' me sticks.

What we may take from this, apart from the fact that Socialism has its own quota of snobs, is that the readers and writers of the *Clarion* were just as much addicted to county cricket as anyone else.

CHAPTER ELEVEN

Home and Colonial

IN 1894 THE Revd R. S. Holmes, the first historian of the county championship, confidently announced the demise of the old world:

> Twenty-five years ago the great matches of the season were North v. South and Gentlemen v. Players. The former have to all intents and purposes disappeared, whilst the latter no longer possess the charm they once did. It is by no means certain that in twenty years time the matches between the Amateurs and the Professionals will be held.

There were other innocents who, like Holmes, saw the new county allegiances as unifying factors that would render the old divisions obsolete, but there were more powerful forces that kept them – and Gentlemen v. Players – in being until 1962. The counties in fact were the perfect vehicle for amateur control and the perfect setting for the continued display of public-school and university talents in later, adult life.

'The crowds flock to county matches', Holmes went on. Even this was only partly true. Certainly, average gates were double those of ten years earlier, but most of the extra numbers came from big matches involving the leading counties. In 1892, 34,000 went to the first day of Surrey v. Notts, and 72,565 over all three, both records. Over 20,000 had been at the first day of Lancashire v. Kent at Old Trafford to see Jack Crossland bowl Lord Harris for a duck. Yorkshire drew a record 30,000 in a single day against Surrey at Leeds three years later. For the newcomers and the less populous counties it was a different story, and the gate-money option was not available even if they had wanted it.

II

Surrey were now the top county in every way. Their team, firmly led by John Shuter, retained all its established favourites, with the batting strengthened by the great Tom Hayward, out of the old Cambridgeshire stable, and the bowling by the best opening pair any county had yet produced – the swift and subtle Bill Lockwood and the majestic Tom Richardson. Organisationally, too, Surrey were the envy of lesser counties. The Oval never quite managed to become the national sports centre Alcock had envisaged, but the FA Cup Final was held there until 1892, when the problems of co-existence became too great. Alcock himself, a master diplomat, managed to combine secretary-ship of the FA with that of Surrey, and both with his various journalistic assignments, between 1872 and 1896.[1] By 1899 Surrey had over 4,000 members and an income of £13,593.

Yorkshire and Lancashire were almost as well placed financially: like Surrey they had good membership and also plenty of support at the turn-stiles. The Yorkshire team had been slow to respond to Lord Hawke's overtures and the old drinking problems resurfaced sporadically.[2] But the professionals replacing the old guard were more biddable: J. T. Brown, a fine opening bat of England quality, his opening partner 'Long John' Tunnicliffe, noted for his slip-catching and his sobriety, and the immortal George Hirst and Wilfred Rhodes, both model citizens as well as all-rounders of world-class. Schofield Haigh was a fastish bowler only just short of their quality and David Hunter an admirable wicket-keeper.

They were utterly dedicated to the county and to the policies of its leader. Hirst was a fastish left-arm bowler, who discovered how to swerve it in the air, and the sort of no-nonsense batsman who could make stacks of runs but was also the kind that everyone wanted to see occupying one end if things were going badly in a Test match. He had a touch of humour and kindliness in his make-up that helped him in his many years of service, first as player and then as revered county coach. Rhodes, highly serious even as a young man, was one of the most remarkable cricketers England has ever had. A great slow left-arm bowler, as good as there has ever been, he began as number eleven batsman for England, proved his worth in some notable tight corners, and when his bowling magic faded or was no longer so valued, made himself into an opening batsman for England good enough to share in a series of record-breaking partnerships with the young Jack Hobbs, and then in a marvellous late flowering became a match-winning bowler again.

Lord Hawke clearly felt that he was due most of the credit for the success of Wilfred Rhodes, whom he had brought into the team to replace Bobby Peel – sacked for drunkenness and its spectacular aftermath[3] – and in his autobi-ography he emphasises Rhodes's reverence for him. Hawke was slightly less successful with the splendid all-rounder Ted Wainwright, to whom the young Neville Cardus was later assistant at Shrewsbury School. In his autobi-ography Cardus told the story of going to find Ted in the local on his first day:

I introduced myself. 'I'm the assistant pro', I explained. 'Art thou?' he replied, 'well, have a drink with me.' I explained that I didn't drink – only ginger ale. 'Christ,' he said, 'tha'rt a reight bloody cricketer.'

In Hawke's Yorkshire regime Wainwright is remembered for a wonderful moment when self-preservation overcame his dedication to the cause. Albert Trott, the Middlesex Australian, hit one 'as high as Blackpool Tower'; Ted moved towards it, waited for what seemed an hour while the ball climbed into the clouds, then thought better of it. Lord Hawke rushed up: 'Why didn't you catch it, Wainwright?' 'Well, your Lordship, it were a bit 'igh, weren't it?' There was some fine tuning still to be done, clearly.

Hawke was not as bright as his idol, Lord Harris, and so less skilful in concealing his ineffable self-satisfaction. His autobiography, which must be one of the least modest works ever compiled,[4] is full of comments like 'I believe I have done more than anyone else to raise the standard and self-respect of the splendid paid section of first-class cricketers.' He took particular pride in the personal incentives he had introduced:

> the mark system ... was entirely my own idea ... I gave marks according to my view of the importance to the side of what was done. Not only did I reward good batting and really excellent bowling ... but I also allocated marks for fine wicket-keeping and smart fielding.

His usual award was 2s. 6d. and his limit five shillings. It must have taken a certain temperament to play alongside a captain who was not only baronial, literally as well as figuratively, but doled out alms, or the promise of them, on the spot. It may have been disconcerting for opponents, too, to find out what their dismissal merited. Sir Pelham Warner, subtler at concealing immodesty than Hawke, recalled in his autobiography, *Long Innings*, that once, when caught at slip by Tunnicliffe, 'as I walked away I heard Lord Hawke say, "Ten shillings for that one, John"'.

Reinforcement of Hawke's attempts to infuse a nobler spirit into his men came in 1890 with the arrival of a young Harrovian embarking on the first of his four years acquiring Blues at Cambridge. This was the Hon. F. S. (later Sir Stanley) Jackson, a magnificent all-round cricketer, captain of Cambridge and later of England, but having more to do with the rest of his life than to devote it exclusively to cricket and so never became captain of Yorkshire. Jackson was another hard man, and a martinet so far as professionals were concerned. Joe Darling – 'I have heard some English captains speak to their professionals like dogs' – tells a story which shows Jackson pulling rank on 'that fine little English professional, J. T. Brown' when the Australians were playing Yorkshire: 'The amateur called Brown for an impossible run, and Brown said, "No, sir."' He was told to run whenever he was called, without hesitation. A little while later Jackson called Brown again for a short single: Brown ran as instructed, and to the Australians' delight Jackson had run himself out.[5] Jackson was also listed by Darling as one of the amateurs of whom the umpires were afraid and who did not scruple to take advantage of the situation.

Lancashire, already out of favour at Lord's, became the odd men out in the 1890s. They had a fine team, usually second and once first in the championship, good crowds and healthy membership, but a sort of collective bloody-mindedness meant that they continued to employ bowlers with dubious actions, both veteran Alec Watson and the new man Arthur Mold. This apart, Mold and the eccentric genius Johnny Briggs, another import from Sutton-in-Ashfield, made them a powerful bowling side. In batting they had the dependable Albert Ward, a refugee from Yorkshire, and later the admirable and immensely popular J. T. Tyldesley, the supreme professional. Tyldesley had all the strokes and cut like a whiplash: C. B. Fry wrote of him, 'He threw the bat at the ball without letting go of the handle.' The most exciting batsman, though, was Hornby's successor, another strong-willed, individualistic amateur. Young Archie MacLaren, Harrovian son of Lancashire's honorary treasurer, something big in cotton, came straight into the side from school in 1890, and made a century against Sussex. He was an imperious batsman, all grace and style, but as a captain he was dictatorial, and as a cricketing politician he was both maverick and easily discouraged by not getting his own way, a bad combination.

III

But all the serious ills of county cricket could, and would, be attributed to professionalism. Hornby and MacLaren lacked the grooming that four years acquiring Blues at Oxbridge would have given them, and they were connected with trade, but one – or one's brother or cousin – had been at school with them. In his *Cricket of Today and Yesterday*, P. C. Standing, a turn-of-century commentator on the state of the game, argued that, though standards had fallen in the 1890s, club and county cricket was in better standing because of 'the greater percentage of "good men" available'. These good men, on further analysis, turned out to be amateurs. This had a beneficial effect, not because amateurs came cheaper, but because they did not go on strike:

> The sordid side of what should be simply a splendid sport is to be deprecated by everyone having the interests of the game at heart. We cannot rest satisfied if it is to degenerate into a mere gate-money affair.

The particular evils of gate-money affairs were rarely precisely spelled out – they didn't need to be. Gate-money was what had led to soccer clubs from nasty industrial towns forming a Football League in 1888 and to rugger clubs in similar locations breaking away from the Rugby Union in 1895. One effect was to let in a lot of yahoos who thought that for sixpence or a shilling they were entitled to express an opinion; the other was to exalt mere hirelings far above their station. 'Professionalism, *pur et simple*, nobody has a right to shy at,' declared P.C. Standing, 'but it is of all things essential to regulate the relations between those who pay to play and those who are paid to play.' This imperative may no longer seem so categorical today in any event, but such a statement of the difference between gentlemen and players was manifestly ridiculous even then. The high-toned *Badminton Magazine* had pin-pointed the problem in 1896: 'For frank and open professionalism there may be a good deal to be said, but nothing can make the "shamateur" attractive.'

Yet the ultimate 'shamateur', W. G. Grace, MCC, was a public idol. In 1891, just before embarking on his lucrative trip with Lord Sheffield, he had struck a chord with all right-thinking persons when he expressed fears that cricket might become 'too much of a business, like football'. Now, in 1895, enjoying a remarkable revival of form at the age of forty-seven he turned it to commercial advantage by inspiring a testimonial fund that produced the astonishing amount of £9,703. Only one professional had yet enjoyed as much as £2,000 from a benefit (ironically, the disgraced Bobby Peel in 1894). Richard Barlow and George Ulyett had managed only £1,100, George Lohmann £1000, and the average even for internationals like Bobby Abel, Tom Emmett and Arthur Shrewsbury was little more than £600.

The professionals' feelings may be imagined, but it grated even on some of W.G.'s admirers amongst the amateurs. A. G. Steel, struggling to write a congratulatory piece on W.G.'s Indian summer for *Wisden*, began with a gentlemanly disclaimer:

> Yielding to none in admiration of the 'hero' of a hundred hundreds, and to none in love for the game in which he is so proficient, I am bound to say I was not altogether pleased with the *Daily Telegraph* testimonial.

Neither was the editor of the *Daily Telegraph*, according to his assistant:

> 'The greatest cricketer ever, unquestionably,' declared Sir John Le Sage ... 'But,' he added with a roguish twinkle in his gimlet eye, 'he was perhaps the most handsomely paid of any public servant ... And believe me ... Grace so carefully counted the number of shillings as they were acknowledged in the columns of the paper, that he knew, to the last bob, what would be handed over to him.'

The Times, on the other hand, produced an ingenious defence. The testimonial, it argued, marked the end of outworn inhibitions:

Fifty or even thirty years ago the British middle class, speaking generally, was still half-consciously ruled by a survival of the old Puritan idea that amusements as such were morally wrong.

Now, however, the 'popular love of national games, and especially cricket' had grown to 'a positive passion thanks to the publicity given by the sporting press', so it was entirely natural that the country would want to honour its great sporting hero in 'the practical English' way. Fair enough, perhaps, were it not for the English sanctimony about gentlemen and players, but the conclusion was so tongue in cheek as to be really hard to swallow: the writer hoped the testimonial would encourage W.G. 'not to regret that he sacrificed, during the years of his prime, his profession to the national game, and was content to be, instead of a busy country doctor, the greatest cricketer in the world'.

Max Beerbohm subscribed to the testimonial, 'not,' he said, 'in support of cricket but as an earnest protest against golf'. Max's wonderful caricature of the great man[6] shows his huge, bearded figure dwarfing not only tiny bat but also the surrounding terrain, and it bears the inscription, 'Dear old W.G. – to the left is the grandstand; to the right the funeral of one of his patients.' Such licensed jesters were few, however, and the very number of contributors at a shilling (5p) a time indicates a most generous and warm-hearted response. In his last article before his death in 1973 Sir Compton Mackenzie recalled the tremendous impression W.G.'s renascence had made:

> W. G. Grace was in his forty-eighth year and he had taken considerable pains to get himself into the best physical condition possible. He was by far the heaviest player taking part in the great matches and he was in his thirty-first season in first-class cricket. Moreover he played many long innings without a mistake: 288 against Somerset at Bristol in five hours, twenty minutes; it was his hundredth century; 257 against Kent at Gravesend, and The Champion was on the field during every ball of the game.

The testimonial was a privilege:

> Schoolboys all over the country were invited to contribute. I can still recall from eighty years ago our determination not to let our pocket-money of sixpence per week be given to cigarettes until we had the necessary shilling for WG.

IV

By contrast, the decision of the Yorkshire committee that autumn to pay two pounds a week from September to April to their ten first-team professionals shook county cricket to its foundations. As S. H. Pardon, the editor of

Wisden, commented, it 'excited a feeling of anxiety, not to say alarm', for manifestly 'only clubs with a large amount of money ... [would] be able to act with such liberality'. Lord Hawke, in this respect at least, could justify the praise he heaped on himself for raising the standards of the professional cricketer – and at the same time keeping a tighter control over what they got up to in the winter, including, as we shall see, touring abroad for the wrong sort of people. Winter pay was not new: as Pardon pointed out, Surrey had been paying some of their players – 'in a less public way' – for some time past. He clearly thought too much publicity a bad thing: it could 'breed dissatisfaction in counties ... where such a winter wage ... is out of the question'.

Pardon gave only qualified support to the claims of the professionals:

> The earnings of the players have certainly not risen in proportion to the immensely increased popularity of cricket during the last twenty years, but to represent the average professional as an ill-treated or down-trodden individual is, I think, a gross exaggeration.

He was writing in the context of a players' strike before the Oval Test of 1896, when Lohmann, Abel, Richardson, and Hayward of Surrey (the selectors) and Billy Gunn of Notts wrote a letter demanding a fee of £20 for the match, compared with the £10 fee for the two previous tests at Lord's and Old Trafford. The *Wisden* match account tells admiringly of the Surrey committee's firm handling of the situation, 'taking steps to secure the best possible substitutes for the revolting players'. However, after three days Abel, Richardson and Hayward backed down and asked for mercy, and, controversially, were reinstated.[7]

This did not quite end the matter. The incident had provoked all manner of recriminatory comment in the press, and the expenses of the amateurs, particularly Grace and Andrew Stoddart, were cited as an undesirable anomaly. Stoddart withdrew from the team, but W.G. brazened it out. He was fortunate – as he always seemed to be – in that it fell to Surrey to make a statement giving the reports 'the most unqualified contradiction'. During many years, Alcock stated, when W.G. had played in three-day matches at the Oval, he had had only the standard £10 expenses. He could have specified how many years – seventeen – for after the 1879 scandal even W.G. would not have dared try it on with Surrey again.

S. H. Pardon, summing up the position in his *Wisden* piece, agreed that there were 'no doubt abuses', but he quoted 'a famous cricketer – a county captain and quite behind the scenes' – as saying that he did not know 'more than half a dozen' amateurs who made money out of the game. He concluded with a suitably ridiculous excuse for 'the Champion':

> Mr W. G. Grace's position has for years, as everyone knows, been an anomalous

one, but 'nice customs curtsey to great kings' and the work he has done in popularising cricket outweighs a hundredfold every other consideration.

Grace was in all conscience becoming hard to bear. In 1893 there had been a great row at Gloucestershire. As *Wisden* recorded, 'It was quite an open secret that a spirit of mutiny prevailed' and at one point W.G. resigned the captaincy, only to withdraw his resignation in the autumn before the committee got round to appointing a successor. After a few rather more cheerful years following his renascence he finally overreached himself, declaring his intention to accept the £600-a-year post of cricket manager at the Crystal Palace, which was being revived as a leisure centre. He saw no reason why this should not be combined with the captaincy of Gloucestershire and was quite put out when the committee worms turned. As a result this extraordinary fifty-year-old pulled up stumps and left Gloucestershire altogether, and for four more years captained a freelance outfit called London County, which bore a remarkable resemblance to the old United South of England XI.

V

If W.G. in his declining years did nothing for the amateurs' claims to financial probity, his standards of sportsmanship did not improve either. In fact he grew wilier and, in the words of an admiring old pro, 'too clever to cheat'. In 1893 he pulled off perhaps his finest confidence trick when, by body language alone, he persuaded the young Cambridge University and Notts batsman Charles Wright to toss him the ball back, then appealed for handling the ball and got him out. Joe Darling, who first visited England in 1896, described the Australians' wariness: 'We were all told not to trust the old man as he was out to win every time and was a great bluffer.' Darling recalled a friendly match in 1896 when he survived a close call for a run-out from W.G., who portentously rounded on the umpire. As it happened, however, this was Bob Thoms, 'about the only umpire in England who was not afraid of Grace or anyone else', and he told W.G. to mind his own business. It had caused a great hullabaloo when a New South Wales umpire had been so upset by a remark W.G. made during a match on Lord Sheffield's tour that he had refused to stand.

When he created what amounted to his own personal empire at Crystal Palace, W.G. was inevitably harder than ever for umpires to handle. The journalist F. B. Wilson – one of the new public-school and university types – described what it was like bowling to him in these affairs:

> He missed the ball entirely ... but hooked it round to short leg with his foot and ran down the wicket shouting, 'Out if I hadn't hit it, well bowled, out if I hadn't hit it.' I had shouted, so had the wicket-keeper, and the umpire's hand was up. But he put it down again and signalled 'a hit'.

As Wilson explained, the Old Man should have been out even if he had hit it: by running after the ball had struck his leg he had hit the ball twice other than to guard his wicket. However, 'No umpire in the world would give him out under either count.'

The combination of imperious amateurs, insecure umpires and obsolescent laws made for plenty of incident and a gradual revision of 'not cricket'. John Shuter, who was later to write a high-minded chapter on 'Playing the Game' for the prestigious Badminton Library volume on cricket, shocked the purists in 1887 with the first of a series of ungentlemanly, not to say caddish, breaches of the laws. At the time it was not lawful to declare an innings closed, so Shuter, captaining Surrey against Nottinghamshire, gave his batsmen instructions to get themselves out, not merely by lofting catches but by hitting their own wickets or standing outside the crease to get run out. Wishing to avoid such unseemliness, MCC reacted remarkably swiftly, and two years later the law was changed to allow declarations – on the third day.

The next alarming episode took place at Lord's itself in front of the fashionable crowds watching the second day of the Varsity match of 1893. The law said that if you gained a first-innings lead of 80 your opponents had to 'follow on'. Now when this had first come in, in 1854, the pitches were so poor that 80 was an enormous deficit, but latterly it had become much more likely that tired bowlers would come in for punishment in a second consecutive innings. So Oxford's last-wicket batsmen tried to get themselves out three runs short of having to let Cambridge follow on, and the Cambridge captain, none other than the upright F. S. Jackson, ordered his bowlers to bowl wides to the boundary in order to stop them. This caused fierce argument, drawing attention, *inter alia*, to the inadequacy of the law. MCC, seizing upon the least relevant point, increased the required margin to 120 – and in 1896 even more shocking scenes took place.

The miscreant this time was Frank Mitchell, again the Cambridge captain and a Yorkshireman, but a less straight-laced version of Jackson. His pre-emptive action in ordering his bowlers to bowl no-balls to prevent Oxford claiming a 'follow-on' was greeted with 'a great shout of "Cricket!", "Play the game!", "Shame!" and other cries'. 'If the honourable traditions of cricket are to be preserved,' wrote *The Times*'s correspondent, 'there must be no more tactics such as those which were employed ... yesterday, of all places at Lord's and in such a match as Oxford v Cambridge.' 'Is it cricket,' he asked, 'to tamper with the natural course of a match?' But for all the righteous indignation MCC did nothing until 1900, when they extended the privilege of declaring to after lunch on the second day, increased the required deficit for a follow-on to 150, and, grasping the point at last, allowed the team in front to decide whether to enforce it.

VI

Frank Mitchell was emblematic of the latest wave of amateurs coming into county cricket: four years a Blue at cricket, three at rugger, international caps at both, a member of the University Volunteers, introduced to South Africa on a Lord Hawke tour, and described as a stockbroker in his early career. He was a journalist and wrote books on cricket and rugger. He served in the Boer War, settled in South Africa, for whom he played cricket, then served in the First World War before returning to England. There were other career patterns but this was not untypical. The idea of service abroad was one of the duties of Empire, but it could also be pleasurable and profitable.

It was inevitable that cricket, the noble, manly, quintessentially English game that Andrew Lang proclaimed as 'a liberal education in itself [that] demands temper and justice and perseverance', would be seen by empire-builders as part of the necessary civilising process they were bestowing on untamed lands and their uninstructed peoples. Lord Harris, who believed that cricket was a gift of God and that he had been chosen to pass on the authorised version to less fortunate folk, whether in Lancashire or New South Wales, saw no reason why it should not be equally beneficial to the teeming millions of the Orient. As Under-Secretary for India in Lord Salisbury's government in 1885 he articulated the imperial mission:

> England in her supreme confidence, in an admiration for her own free institu-
> tions, had undertaken to educate oriental people on western lines, to imbue
> them with western modes of thought, and to encourage them to admire and to
> strive at western systems of government.

In 1890 Harris was called to follow the family tradition of colonial service and became Governor of Bombay. At a farewell dinner he told the guests: 'I have done my best to promote the noble game in this country – I hope not unsuccessfully – and I intend to extend my patronage to the promotion of cricket in India.' His labours amongst the citizens of Bombay, some of whom were resistant to westernisation, including cricket, are outside the scope of this book, but Harris was more than satisfied with his own achievement, maintaining throughout his life that cricket had 'done more to consolidate the Empire than any other influence'.

Consolidating the Empire was a political imperative and a psychological strength, buttressing British self-esteem and unifying loyal subjects of the Queen regardless of class. It was less clear whether it was an economic aid or a burden. Another delight revealed to the world in Lord Hawke's auto-biography is a set of doggerel verses about the enigma of India that he felt should be preserved for posterity:

A land that we've conquered and have to hold
Though it costs us millions of lives and gold,
Shall we call her the jewel of England's fame?
Or throw our curse at her vampire's name?
But whether we bless her or damn her, or deride her,
We are bound by our honour to stand fast beside her,
The Empire's India.

Hawke's entire service to his fellow-men, at home or abroad, was delivered through cricket, which he felt it his duty to play all the year round. He made nine international trips before the First World War, apart from lesser tours with Yorkshire. After his inglorious Australian experience he went with G. F. Vernon to India and Ceylon in 1888–9, playing mostly against expatriate whites, but also fulfilling the ambitions of a Bombay Parsees Club, only one rung down from the exclusive European Club. The Parsees won.[8] Hawke went back at Lord Harris's request three years later following a similar programme, but also playing a slightly racially mixed All-India team.

Another imperial duty for Lord Hawke was a tour of South Africa in the winter of 1895–6. Although sanctioned by MCC, and led by one of its luminaries, it was funded by Douglas Logan, one of the growing breed of recent millionaires out there. Africa was the fashionable place for all imperialists, active or armchair, a cockpit for contending European powers, offering control of the trade routes to India both north and south and the promise of all manner of mineral wealth in between. The expatriate Cecil Rhodes, having frantically acquired untold riches and an Oxford education, was now embarked on fulfilling his dream of a British axis down the length of the continent. As Premier of Cape Colony he tried to organise a rising against the Boers in Transvaal by British 'Outlanders', and news broke of his henchman Jameson's raid as Hawke and his team were in Cape Town playing a match. They could not meet Rhodes, drowning his sorrows privately, but Hawke, Sir Timothy O'Brien and Charles Wright went to dine with his brother Frank and the other prisoners in jail to cheer them up, and took £98 off them at poker.

Hawke afterwards claimed that he had declined to call on Paul Kruger, the Boer President, but according to C. B. Fry, a member of the team, they did visit him and Hawke tried to butter him up, but neither he nor anyone else could get much out of the old man. This was a convivial tour, much enlivened by the Australian-born fast bowler Sammy Woods of Cambridge University and Somerset. It was only slightly marred by the Jameson business, and not at all by concern for the native inhabitants. The three 'Test' matches played testified to the South African advance and were also, Fry wrote in his autobiography *Life Worth Living*, contested in good spirit: 'Everyone who has ever been to the Cape wants to return. The space and the crystal air are recalls to delight.' South Africa's material assets were an added attraction that greatly aided her claims to recognition in the cricket world.

VII

The colonies were not the only places with racial problems. Whilst Lord Harris had been in India encouraging cricket, a temporarily dispossessed Indian prince, K. S. Ranjitsinjhi, had been emerging as a batsman of note in England. At Cambridge University, where his colour hampered his progress and he played much of his cricket for local teams on Parker's Piece, he hired as his own personal coaches and net bowlers the England stars Lockwood, Richardson, Hearne and Hayward, and practised assiduously, eventually winning a Blue in his final year, 1893. He found a congenial slot in Sussex under Billy Murdoch and within two years was the most exciting batting prospect in the country. In 1896 he was not picked for the first Test against Australia at Lord's because Lord Harris, returning to the corridors of power at Lord's, questioned his qualification for England. His Lordship had many supporters in this, and the MCC secretary actually wrote to Ranjitsinjhi explaining the matter of principle involved. However, the maverick Sir Home Gordon afterwards told how a fellow MCC member had threatened to get him expelled 'for having the disgusting degeneracy to praise a dirty black'. And Lancashire, whose principle was that anything Lord Harris said was wrong, had no hesitation in choosing Ranji for the second Test at Old Trafford, where he duly made 62 and 154 not out.

Ranji thereafter spent his time – and money – to good effect, making friends and influencing people. This did not include Lord Harris and his acolyte Hawke. But he accompanied the buccaneering Stoddart and MacLaren to Australia the following winter and made a wonderful century in his first Test innings there. (The team was thoroughly beaten, however, and Ranji was ridiculed along with the other stars for the excuses they made. Stoddart had already earned on his 1894–5 tour a reputation for being a better winner than a loser. This time MacLaren took the prize for claiming that a fly in the eye had caused him to get out in the fourth Test, but Ranji was derided also for explaining, 'When I say we had no luck I would instance Briggs' downfall to a very poor ball ... it was ill-fortune for him that a man should have been standing on the precise spot where it fell.') He did better for himself by winning the good opinion of W.G., not least in helping to swell the gates at Crystal Palace by turning out for his London Counties outfit.

Another who made the same judicious move was Ranji's protégé, friend and amanuensis, C. B. Fry. The pair also collaborated in shameless flattery of the Old Man. Fry, a classical scholar who was also a fine all-round athlete, a poetry-lover and a born leader, was the epitome of all that was best in the Oxford scheme of things. Yet he avoided stereotypical excellence and conventional priggishness through a sense of mischief and some taste for irony. An extrovert

Children playing with hockey-stick-shaped bats and two-stump wickets, trundling the ball along the ground. From a decorative border, The Arms of Shrewsbury, 1739. (*MCC*)

Cricket at the fashionable Artillery Ground, Finsbury (1743) looks very similar. (*Norman Barrett Collection*)

Fifteen-year-old Lewis Cage in 1768 has a stylish curved bat but still uses two-stump wickets. (*MCC*)

John Frederick Saville, third Duke of Dorset, one of the most celebrated patrons and a leading player of the late eighteenth century. (*MCC*)

Sir Horatio Mann, a rival patron but an indifferent performer, was an addict better known for amiability than shrewdness. (*MCC*)

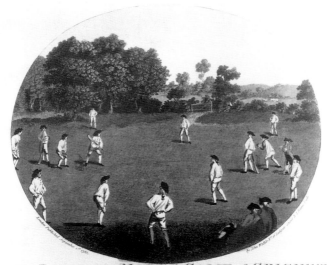

The LAWS of the NOBLE GAME of CRICKET,
as Established at the Star and Garter Pall-Mall by a Committee of Noblemen & Gentlemen.

THE STRIKER

Early laws were revised by 'a committee' of noblemen and gentlemen at the Star and Garter tavern in 1774. (*MCC*)

The Revd Lord Frederick Beauclerk looks as though butter would not melt in his mouth, but was a hard competitor, noted for his crafty ways. (*MCC*)

Tom Walker of Hambledon, known as 'Old Everlasting', was a tough professional who so frustrated Beauclerk that he dashed his hat on the ground and called Walker 'a confounded old beast'. (*MCC*)

Fuller Pilch, the greatest batsman of the 1830s, was noted for his forward defensive play, but his stance suggests that he kept his (unprotected) legs well out of the way. (*MCC*)

William Clarke's All-England XI (1847) brought together many of the best professionals and 'shamateurs' in the country.
From left to right: Guy, Parr, Martingell, A. Mynn, W. Denison, Dean, Clarke, N. Felix, O.C. Pell, Hillyer, Lillywhite, Dorrington, Pilch and Sewell. (*MCC*)

Alfred Mynn, 'the Lion of Kent' was a great schoolboys' hero. (*MCC*)

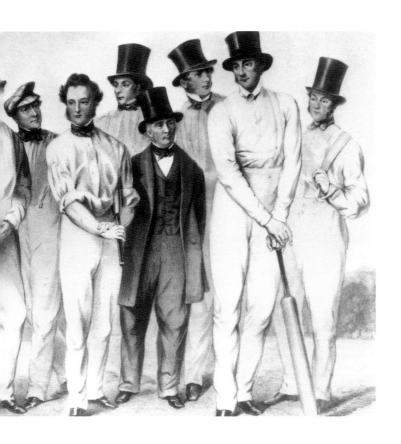

William Lillywhite, 'the nonpareil'; despite his portly form and top hat, he was a formidable early exponent of the new round-arm bowling. (*MCC*)

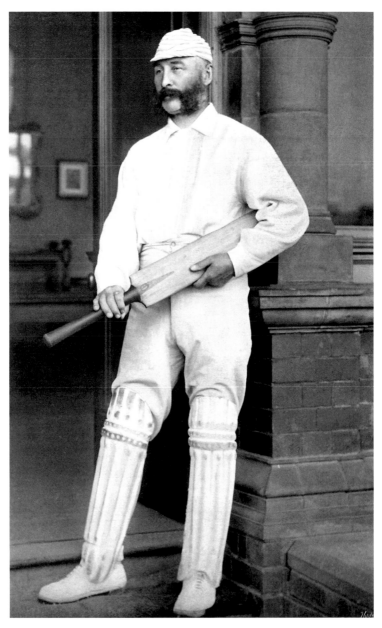

E.M. Grace foreshadowed his brother, W. G., as a leading amateur cricketer and made a great deal of money from the game. He was also known for his unorthodox tactics. (*Norman Barrett Collection*)

who affected a monocle and was given to impromptu monologues, he drew admiring circles around him. An out-and-out believer in the gentlemanly honour code, he ignored orthodox canons of batsmanship, like E. M. Grace, and was a fast bowler with an action that shocked spectators at the Varsity match and had him frequently no-balled. An Epicurean cigar-smoker who nevertheless kept himself fit, a Corinthian footballer and Blackheath rugger player who also played full-back for Southampton in the FA Cup final, the list of paradoxes goes on. The ultimate one was that he had so many talents, so many friends in high places and so obviously enjoyed the limelight, yet devoted much of his life to running an educational charity, training boys for entry to the navy.

Fry's most lucrative talent was for journalism. He had begun as a schoolmaster, but his expensive tastes required something more and he wrote widely for the popular press, whilst focusing mainly on two regular jobs – athletics editor of the *Champion*, a boy's weekly, then editor of *C. B. Fry's Magazine*. This enabled Fry to apply his keen analytical mind to a variety of topics – he particularly enjoyed composing answers to correspondents. He also wrote some perceptive and highly literate treatises about cricket. Perhaps the best were two written with the Middlesex batsman and innovatory photographer, G. W. Beldam,[9] in which magnificent action photographs of the great players of the age are accompanied by Fry's perceptive and incredibly detailed comments, sometimes reminiscent of Sherlock Holmes elucidating esoteric mysteries to poor old Watson. His most famous work was, however, as a ghost for Ranjitsinjhi.

The Jubilee Book of Cricket was suitably titled to catch the market for imperial things like cricket. The fervour of Ranji's devotion to the Empire had not been diminished by the snubs at Cambridge and Lord's, and he dedicated his book 'by her gracious permission to Her Majesty, The Queen Empress', commending cricket to her as one of the blessings of 'her happy occupation of the throne'. The other happy occupant of a throne, that of cricket itself, was W.G., recently made captain of England at the age of forty-eight. Ranji (and Fry) paid him gracious tribute, in a famous passage which seems to combine the effusiveness of one author with the analytical thought processes and confidence of the other, packaged in their joint diplomatic skills:

Any cricketer who thinks for a moment can see the enormous change WG introduced into the game. I hold him to be not only the finest player *born or unborn* [my italics], but the maker of modern batting. He turned the old one-stringed instrument into a many-chorded lyre. And, in addition, he made his execution equal to his invention. All of us now have the instrument, but we lack his execution. It is not that we do not know, but that we cannot perform.

That 'born or unborn' might have embarrassed a lesser man, but not Ranji. Sir George 'Gubby' Allen told a story about being taken to tea with Ranji and

Fry as a boy and listening entranced to the flow of conversation. When it temporarily ceased he ventured to ask. 'Who was the greatest batsman of all time?' After a long pause Ranji eventually broke silence. 'I think, Charles,' he said primly, 'that I was better than you on a soft wicket.' He was an extraordinarily good batsman, with a distinctive wristy style. Countless others testified to Ranji's unique qualities: Gilbert Jessop, the fastest scorer of the day, called him 'the most brilliant figure during cricket's most brilliant period'. In truth, the Sussex members of the day were fortunate to be able to make the comparison between him and Fry for so many seasons after Billy Murdoch – and Lord Sheffield – brought them there to help him build up a side that would put the county back on the map.

VIII

Lords Harris and Hawke, meanwhile, were welcoming a recruit of their own. Hawke's next imperial assignment took him to the West Indies, Harris's birthplace. The first tour there, all-amateur, led by the Middlesex batsman and Teddington hockey player R. S. Lucas, had been warmly welcomed by the upper reaches of the highly stratified (by colour) cricket-playing community. The following winter, 1896–7, two similar groups set sail, one led by the amiable but virtually non-playing MCC member and future MP (Sir) Arthur Priestley, the other by the ubiquitous Hawke. They got in each other's way (through, says the wonderfully peppery Major Rowland Bowen, 'the stubborn and ill-mannered mulishness amounting almost to insufferable arrogance on the part of Lord Hawke'). The colonists remained pathetically grateful for this show of favour. Bidding Priestley's team farewell, the Solicitor-General of Barbados said:

> Mr Priestley has referred to the sympathy which the West Indies colonies have shown to them, but it is something more than sympathy that we feel. We feel we are more brothers than friends. [Hear. Hear.] This strong filial feeling is only the natural outcome of the relationship which exists between us and the Mother Country. We are sons of Old England.

Apart from his mulishness, the significant thing about Hawke's trip was that it was the first overseas venture of P. F. Warner, the ultimate establishment man, equally facile with bat, pen and political manoeuvre and a travelling salesman for cricket. Warner had been born in Trinidad, where his father had been Attorney-General, and, like Lord Harris, whom he revered, he was a fervent imperialist, though, unlike Harris, he did little about it except play cricket. He was educated at Rugby, where he was coached by Tom Emmett (Fry, who obviously did not care much for him, described him as 'an imperturbably accomplished school batsman'), and Oxford, where he got a Blue in 1895. He was intended for the law, but although he was eventually called to the Bar in 1900, he never practised. Outside cricket he dabbled in the universal pool, the Stock Exchange. But for a quarter of a century he spent his summers playing for Middlesex and most of his winters touring as first player and then administrator, skilfully combining this – and Test selection – with journalism.

He had already begun his journalistic career in 1897 with a series of articles for the *Sportsman* about the West Indies tour, and by 1900 was writing the first of his many books of reportage and reminiscence, emblematically called *Cricket In Many Climes*. Warner's claims for cricket began modestly enough: it was, he wrote,

> extending its influence wherever the English language is spoken, and it is even said by diplomats and politicians that its friendly intercourse does much to strengthen the amity of nations, and to make for international understanding.

However, within a few years he was unashamedly waving around Thomas Hughes's aphorism, already one of the most shameless clichés of cricket writing, and embellishing it with a more recent one: 'Cricket has become more than a game. It is an institution, a passion, one might almost say a religion.'

Whilst Warner was being groomed for the role of 'pavilion magnate', as Fry put it, Ranji and Fry had their innings. They were, for a decade, the most influential and fashionable names in cricket, but as neither was a luminary of MCC they had little political influence, and both had other things to do with their lives. For a time, however, they gave Harris and Hawke a run for their money. There was no difference between them on essentials such as the re-establishment of the feudal system, but they occupied slightly different places in its elaborating modern version.

Fry, the neophyte, was so steeped in the attitudes of the English gentleman, so contemptuous of what he called 'the merchant-minded', so jealous of his amateur status that he bristled when Sir Rufus Isaacs, a famous lawyer, tried to pay him a compliment, saying: 'I wish I were as distinguished in my profession as you are in yours.' Fry commented: 'Sir Rufus prided himself on his diplomatic gifts, but that is the one and only time I have been called a professional cricketer.' His description of the prudential conduct of England's two leading professionals in the first match of the Australian tour at Sheffield Park in 1896 is redolent of the public-school virility cult.

This was the day when the formidable Ernest Jones, on his first appearance, was making the ball fly on a dodgy wicket – the time when Jones sent one through W.G.'s beard, causing him to squeak, falsetto, 'What – what – what!', whereupon the Australian captain Harry Trott said, 'Steady, Jonah!' and Jones said, 'Sorry, Doctor, she slipped.' Jones took 7 for 84, including W.G., F. S. Jackson, Ranjitsinjhi and Fry, but Fry's account refers only to amateur heroism – Jackson got a cracked rib; W.G.'s chest was black and blue; 'Ranji flicked Jones's fastest ball off his nose' – before accusing the professionals, Shrewsbury and Gunn, of getting out on purpose:

> When Arthur Shrewsbury got to that end, having watched the first and before the catch was held he had folded his bat under his right arm-pit and marched off. Then the 6 feet 3 inches of William Gunn walked delicately to the wicket. His first ball from Jones whizzed past where his head had just been. William withdrew from the line of the next ball and deliberately tipped it into the slips, and he too had pouched his bat and was stepping off to the pavilion before the catch was surely caught.

For this dereliction of duty, Fry says, Shrewsbury was left out of the Test team three years later (by which time Fry had got himself on to the selection committee) and, he adds, 'We nearly left out William Gunn, too ...'

Installing Fry in a seat of power was one of the unexpected consequences of Lord Harris's opposition to Ranji's playing for England. As soon as the dust had settled, Lord Hawke, Harris's ally, had put a proposal before the county secretaries to abolish the system of separate selection committees – an obvious move since they proposed to have five Test matches in future – and got agreement to a Board of Control set up and controlled by MCC, with a sub-committee of Test selectors, of which Hawke was made chairman. At the first meeting in 1899 Hawke duly opposed the inclusion of Ranjitsinjhi, by then the outstanding English batsman. But he found himself implacably opposed by W.G., already chosen as England captain, who insisted on including not only Ranji but Fry, whom W.G., indeed, had already 'co-opted' on to the selection committee! As Fry wrote in *Life Worth Living*,

> Lord Hawke ... did not favour me as a batsman, nor Ranjitsinjhi – was it as a bowler? He gave way to W. G., saying that, if the Old Man wished it, let him have Fry and Ranji for the first match, but it would be the only one they would play in.

They – perhaps fortunately – lasted the whole series, and, as Fry commented, 'We afterwards together made a surprising number of runs against Yorkshire.'

By an equally bizarre process the England captaincy changed hands:

> The hour was the hour of luncheon. I was a few minutes late. The moment I entered the door WG said, 'Here's Charles. Now Charles, before you sit down, we want you to answer this question, yes or no. Do you think that Archie MacLaren ought to play in the next Test match?'

Fry said yes, and found that the committee had been discussing whether W.G. should stand down on grounds of corpulence. 'That settles it,' said the great man – and in came MacLaren, not only to open the innings but as captain. This curious decision appears not even to have been discussed: and there was at least one captain of distinction in the team already. Fry says, 'I do not believe that [the selectors] realised in bringing him in ... they were going over the head of F. S. Jackson.' In truth the selectors, with Lord Hawke in nominal control, do not seem to have realised much, and MacLaren doubtless added more liveliness than logic to their deliberations.

IX

By now the disagreeable face of imperialism was showing itself in Africa. Kruger's success in foiling the Jameson raid had evoked a congratulatory telegram from Kaiser Wilhelm of Germany, convincing thereby a large section of the British public that Rhodes was in the right of it, and that both the Boers and their German allies (who inconveniently occupied Tanganyika) were going to have to be stopped sooner or later. But the Germans were not the only or most immediate problem. The French, elbowed out of Suez, held large tracts of North and West Africa and an eastern foothold which they aimed to link. This ambition clashed directly with the British drive south, liberating the Nile valley. As Victoria's Diamond Jubilee celebrations echoed tumultuously round the world General Kitchener was avenging Gordon's death, slowly and remorselessly. First Dongola, then Berbera, then the defeat of the Dervishes at Atbar, the annihilation of the Mahdi's armies at Omdurman and finally the recapture of Khartoum brought exultation; but it also brought the possibility of a showdown with the French ever closer. Kitchener held his nerve, the French, with troubles at home, backed down – and Britain had a new hero.

It was a sign of the times that the most powerful figure in Lord Salisbury's government at the century's end was the Colonial Secretary, Joseph Chamberlain. By this time defending the Empire, and the British way of life, had become synonymous with public-school cricket and its values. The best-known expositor of this theme was Henry Newbolt, a deeply Christian lawyer with a talent for patriotic verse in rhythms like drumbeats. His *Vitaï Lampada* (1898) was quoted for many years as serious inspiration for the young and as reassurance for ageing cricketers that they had not spent their lives in vain. It may not carry the same ring of conviction in today's more cynical times, but it may be worth exhuming, to try to catch the flavour of an age of Empire. Newbolt begins with a school cricket match:

> There's a breathless hush in the Close tonight,
> Ten to make and the match to win,
> A bumping pitch and a blinding light,
> An hour to play, and the last man in.

But it's clearly more than a game; it's a ritual undertaken in the right spirit by high-minded chaps:

> And it's not for the sake of a ribboned coat,
> Or the selfish hope of a season's fame
> But his Captain's hand on his shoulder smote.

Then the talismanic incantation designed to stiffen number eleven's sinews: 'Play up! Play up! and play the game!' The spine-chilling sequel, invoking images of Kitchener's triumph, makes its point graphically:

> The sand of the desert is sodden red,
> Red with the wreck of a square that broke:
> The Gatling's jammed and the Colonel's dead,
> And the regiment blind with dust and smoke.
> The river of death has brimmed his banks
> And England's far and honour a name,
> But the voice of a schoolboy rallies the ranks:
> 'Play up! play up! and play the game.'

The sentiments, colourful, bracing and shocking by turns, were those that sustained the flower of British youth as they bore the White Man's Burden into the remote corners of empire. Kipling, however, thought it odd that Kitchener, having crushed the Sudanese, was now raising funds to build a school for the élite of Khartoum in which they would, *inter alia*, learn cricket. He imagined the reaction of a Muslim schoolmaster serving with the Bengal infantry in the Sudan:

> How is this reason (which is their reason) to judge a scholar's worth,
> By casting a ball at three straight sticks and defending the same with a fourth?
> But this they do (which is doubtless a spell) and other matters more strange,
> Until by the operation of years, the hearts of their scholars change.

The confidence of the nation in their ju-ju was unshaken. When Britain went to war with the Boers the following year the only question seemed to be whether it was quite cricket to attack such a small opponent. It turned out not to be so easy, cricket or not, and the struggle gave plenty of time for reflection on the nation's preparedness or lack of it. Without troops from the other colonies the Mother Country would have fared disastrously. Kipling, a serious-minded imperialist, disgusted at the lack of response to the call of duty from the upper classes who had left the task to a 'remnant', called, in his poem 'The Islanders', for national service to be taken as seriously 'as it were almost cricket'. He did not believe, it seemed, that making ten runs on a bumping pitch in a blinding light was a sufficient preparation for the sterner challenges of life.

Some cricketers, of course, had tried to prove him wrong. Shining examples at the very top were Lord Harris, aged fifty, who served as assistant adjutant-general with the Imperial Yeomanry, and the thirty-year-old F. S. Jackson, who saw active service with the Royal Lancasters. And there were regular soldiers like Major R. M. Poore, later the linchpin of Hampshire, already in South Africa. But the great majority stayed aloof like the non-cricketers. Kipling was withering about the 'witless learning' of the public schools and Oxbridge, and about the hunting set, but the shaft that went deepest into the midriffs of the sporting types was his crack about them contenting their souls 'with the flannelled fools at the wicket or the muddied oafs at the goals'. P. F. Warner, who was a part-time member of the fashionable Inns of Court Regiment but not a combatant, met Kipling in Cape Town soon after the Boer War in the company of a rugger-playing soldier who ventured to ask whether the poet had not perhaps been too hard on the sportsmen. Kipling allowed the possibility but added, 'You have to hit an Englishman more than once on the jaw before he will take a thing seriously.'

CHAPTER TWELVE

Flannelled Foolery

EVEN WHEN THE BOER WAR eventually ended there were stark truths to be faced. Imperialist Britain had very few friends in a hostile, fiercely competitive world. Nervous of a Russian thrust in the Far East, she formed an alliance with Japan, but she also sought an accommodation with Russia's ally and her own historic enemy, France. It was either that or a pact with Germany, who, with the excitable and aggressive Kaiser Wilhelm at the helm, was mounting a strong industrial challenge, building a vast fleet and apparently spoiling for a fight. When things were still in the balance, Edward VII, whose only intellectual accomplishment was to speak French and whose personal dislike for his nephew Wilhelm found an echo in his subjects' hearts, made an official visit to Paris in May 1903, largely on his own initiative. He was a big success and in his wake the Unionist government, now led by A. J. Balfour, concluded the celebrated 'Entente Cordiale', thenceforth the cornerstone of British foreign policy.

Domestically the Unionists reacted constructively to the Boer fiasco. They had been shaken by the revelation of the poor physical and educational standards of the recruits, and 'National Efficiency' became the watchword. Balfour, an intellectual aristocrat, was the architect of the great 1902 Education Act, which extended and improved elementary education and offered a chance to the brightest to transfer to local-authority secondary, technical, or even grammar schools. Influential intellectuals and philanthropists were giving serious and sympathetic attention to the plight of the poor, and early sociological studies attempted to measure and publicise the effects of urban and industrial sprawl, against a defined poverty level. Doubts about the validity of Victorian belief in progress began to intensify. The new and remarkable advances that the upper classes could now enjoy – electric light, telephones, motor cars, gramophones – contrasted violently with the appalling housing conditions in city slums and remote rural villages.

Numerically the greatest problems were in the towns, which now held 80 per cent of the population. London alone had 7 million (compared for example with 5 million in the whole of Scotland and 4 million in ravaged Ireland), and there and in the other conurbations more and more of the countryside was gobbled up. Three-quarters of the land was owned by a mere 5,000 people, some of whom drew over £100,000 a year in unearned income. As a noted economist explained, half the nation's wealth belonged to some 5 million people and the other half had to be shared amongst the remaining 39 million. Amongst earners a tiny élite got £5,000 a year whilst the average adult male industrial worker earned £70 a year. (Almost a third of the workers were women, paid much less than men.) Attempts to rectify these anomalies were still left to the *realpolitik* of encounters between employers and the trade unions, which persistently creamed off layers at the top of the problem.

Regardless of how the wealth was distributed, the Unionists, in seeking to improve the worsening trade position, were impaled on an economic policy that sought to turn the Empire to material advantage: in return for preferential tariffs from the more advanced, i.e. white, colonies, the government made no treaties with foreign countries that would undermine imperial trade. This had less appeal to the widening British electorate than cheap imports of food and mass-produced clothing, and so in 1906 the Liberals once again came in on a landslide of enthusiasm for free trade. They included two strange bedfellows, a seceding Unionist, Winston Churchill, descendant of the Duke of Marlborough and recently a heroic war correspondent in South Africa; and a fiery, demagogic Welsh lawyer, Lloyd George, a notorious pro-Boer. And alongside them were fifty-three Labour members, proudly carrying the hopes of the working class.

II

The Edwardian era owes much of its reputation as a lost age of antediluvian splendour to its self-indulgent monarch, whom Lord Northcliffe, the newspaper magnate, famously described as 'the best king we ever had – on the racecourse'. It was a good time for lotus-eating, without a doubt. In first-class cricket, that is to say, it was a good time to be an amateur, preferably a batsman. For Archie MacLaren, the ultimate Edwardian cricketer, it was a splendid time, though as captain of Lancashire he was suddenly beset by bowling problems. Johnny Briggs and Arthur Mold had long been Lancashire's mainstays. Now poor Briggs, who had a strange disorder, apparently of a rare, epileptic type, was finally stricken irrecoverably and died in an asylum in the winter of 1901. And Mold, whose action, though suspect, had gone unchallenged throughout his career, suddenly became the centre of controversy.

There had arisen, of all things, a crusading umpire. He was not English, but Australian. James Phillips had come to England in the 1890s, and like many more illustrious colonials had qualified for Middlesex. Turning to umpiring as the next best thing, he immediately made an impact. C. B. Fry, who as an amateur had been allowed to get away with throwing by the impressionable English umpires, was spectacularly exposed by Phillips, and never forgave him. In his most patronising vein Fry wrote of Phillips, 'He was quite honest, but was ambitious to achieve the reputation of a "strong" umpire. His other ambition was to qualify as a mining engineer and he used to go about with a Hall and Knight's Algebra in his pocket.'

Another fast bowler with a dodgy action who thought umpires were for professionals was Charles Kortright of Essex, an amateur with a private income who revelled in his reputation as 'the fastest of them all'. He was the subject of one of Norman Gale's 'Cricket Songs':

> Who is Kortright, what is he
> That Lang doth so commend him?
> Bowly, fierce, and fast is he;
> The heavens such pace did lend him
> That he might admirèd be.
>
> Fast he is, but is he fair?
> For throwing is unkindness.
> Those to libel him who dare
> Do only prove their blindness;
> And, being kicked, retract it there.

His iron-clad assumptions allowed Kortright to try to expose Arthur Mold, and he told MacLaren what he proposed to do. In the middle of his bowling spell he stopped and 'perpetrated a bare-faced throw – to prove that the umpire would not notice it!'

Phillips, meanwhile, had convinced at least some English amateurs that he was indeed a 'strong umpire' and not an Australian upstart. Andrew Stoddart took him as the English umpire on the 1897–8 tour, when he proved his credentials by no-balling Ernest Jones, the beard-piercer. Jim Phillips's deeds seem to have given heart to his English colleagues and next season Fry was no-balled by three other umpires as well as Phillips, and one or two less prominent figures were also called.

But things did not come to a head until 1900. First Fry was called again – by Billy West, an amateur turned professional, turned umpire and also a champion boxer, and so not to be trifled with. At any rate, Fry afterwards bowled a little slower and with a perfectly fair action. Then came the climax, when Phillips no-balled Arthur Mold so decisively that he was taken off and bowled no more in the match. (*Wisden* commented that Mold was 'the luckiest of men to have gone through nearly a dozen seasons without being no-balled'.) Later in the season Phillips also called E. J. Tyler, a slow left-armer, to show that it was not just speed that was the problem.

In December the county captains met – as they now did annually – and recommended disbarring serious offenders, suspending others for a period, and warning others. This was rejected by MCC, who said they approved of the principle involved but wanted to strengthen the umpires' hands by not actually suspending anyone, a characteristically ambivalent position. The inevitable happened. MacLaren, who had defended Mold in the press, selected him for a match in which Phillips was umpiring. When Mold was put on he was no-balled sixteen times, and though he was allowed to bowl in the second innings without challenge, never played for the county again.

That September Lord Harris sent a letter of Olympian length, style and self-satisfaction to *The Times* protesting MCC's reluctance to do anything to diminish umpires' authority or to act as a referee but suggesting that they be asked to do just that – advised by the county captains. In December MCC officially approved a version of this, and, with a pistol held to recalcitrant heads, the honour code was given a further lease of life. And that, anticlimactically, was it. There was a scare in 1908 when the professional Ralph Whitehead, playing for – guess who? – was no-balled four times on his first appearance, but Phillips had retired by then, and Whitehead seems to have persuaded the umpire, T. Brown, that it was a temporary aberration. This was an isolated incident and no more cases surfaced until after two world wars.

III

Meanwhile the world had been made safe for Edwardian batsmen to go about their lawful business of smiting sixes and fours. Generations of cricket chroniclers have searched Roget for appropriately aureate adjectives to describe the splendour of the batting, delivered with grace and style by gentlemen with several initials before their names. L. C. H. and R. C. N. Palairet, openers for Oxford University and Somerset, perhaps best exemplified the requisite qualities and nomenclature, although every self-respecting county had two or three amateurs in the cavalier mode.

In Worcestershire, who joined the championship circle in 1899, the Lyttleton family handed over the batting gloves to another remarkable family, the Fosters, seven brothers, all of whom played for the county. H.K. was captain at the start, giving way to the remarkable R.E. for a year in 1901, the only full season he could devote to county cricket. R.E. was another of the astonishingly gifted young Oxbridge types who played for England at both soccer and cricket. The very number of these raises the question of whether technically standards were quite so high as they subsequently became. R. E. Foster, however, may well have been one of a much smaller élite who would have been great players in any age. He made a record score of 287 against Australia at Sydney in 1903–4; he coped skilfully with the swerve and the googly, the great innovations of the day; and he was good to watch as well as efficient. The other Fosters, all of whom had two or more initials and three of whom between them captained the side for quarter of a century, were perhaps not quite of this epic quality, but contributed enough for the county to earn the nickname of Fostershire.

The championship they entered was now dominated by Yorkshire, who won the title three times in succession from 1900 and were never out of the first three until 1909. They did not entirely conform to the dashing image of the era: only the new batsman David Denton could set the pulses racing for spectators who were not, as Yorkshire's tended to be, primarily concerned with winning. But they were efficient, they had wonderful bowling, and they worked as a team – which is why it didn't matter that Hawke, who had created the team, was a below-average performer. Hawke told the *Manchester Guardian* in 1908, when he had been captain for twenty years: 'I am no advocate of wholly professional sides. Yorkshire has always played amateurs and to my mind they are the moral backbone of a county team. Once you do away with them you will inevitably create an eleven which will only play for the gates.' A fine text, but two amateurs were Yorkshire's normal maximum.

At the other extreme were Middlesex, who usually had only three professionals – the mainstay of the bowling, J. T. Hearne, the highly competent swing bowler J. T. Rawlin, and the former Australian captain Harry Trott, a splendid all-rounder. They had been led since the 1880s by A. J. Webbe, listed in the Harrovian Register as 'of no profession', and he was followed by the fearsome Scottish rugger international and wicket-keeper Gregor Magregor. The rest – G. W. Beldam, C. M. Wells, P. F. Warner, the remarkable B. J. T. Bosanquet, who devised the googly, his pupil R. O. Schwarz – were amateurs, gifted but not always available, and they astonished everyone by winning the title in 1903.

By contrast, Surrey, who had reached a peak towards the end of the nineties, winning the championship under K. J. Key, then went into relative decline. They had plenty of batting talent – Tom Hayward opening the innings with first Abel, then the young Jack Hobbs, the Master in the making; followed by Hayes and Holland (the plethora of aspirates being a cruel joke of the Almighty, so the superior folk at Lord's claimed) and Andy Ducat, an England soccer player, and later Andy Sandham; there was a great wicket-keeper, Herbert Strudwick; and for a few years there were still Richardson and Lockwood followed by some better than average replacements like Walter Lees, Tom Rushby and the wholehearted J. W. Hitch ('Billitch') among the bowlers.

But Surrey had begun to have leadership problems not long after the turn of the century. For a while prospects seemed brighter under Lord Dalmeny, the wayward son and heir of the Earl of Rosebery, the former Prime Minister. Dalmeny was a true Edwardian dasher at the crease and much admired by the sporting press, at least until he became involved in dubious practices on the racecourse. If he had put his whole mind to it he might have done well as a captain in a Hawke-ish sort of way, but he had also become a parliamentary candidate to please his father and, somewhat to his surprise, was elected in the Liberal landslide of 1906. Then the clash of interests led to wisecracks such as that of the gossip columnist who wrote that during one match 'he had to hunt about for a substitute to field for him as he was anxious to speak and vote for the Second Reading of the Coal Mines Eight Hour Bill'.

His successor, the diminutive H. D. G. 'Shrimp' Leveson Gower (pronounced Looson Gore and often hyphenated), was already what Fry called a 'pavilion magnate'. He was a four-year Oxford Blue, became a stockbroker and spent the rest of his life in cricket. He had become a MCC committee man in his twenties and by 1908 was a Test selector. Fry, making a joke about 'Shrimp's size, said he had a 'tall reputation' as a captain, but for Surrey he seems to have fallen somewhat short in attendance. This indirectly caused Surrey to lose their brilliant young all-rounder, J. N. Crawford, who played for the county as a schoolboy and for England at nineteen. Crawford was made acting captain against the Australians in 1909, but quarrelled with the committee when they wouldn't pick two players charged with insubordination, and took off for Australia himself. One of the professionals, Rushby, was consigned to outer darkness, that is to say, signed for Accrington in the Lancashire League, but later made his peace and returned to the fold.

Nottinghamshire seemed a long way from their past greatness, but they were never easy to beat and actually won the championship in 1907. They were also a good deal less cautious under Dixon and his successor, A. O. Jones, a Cambridge Blue and a rugger player, who made plenty of runs, opening the innings with young James Iremonger, a Notts Forest and England soccer player, for whom Arthur Shrewsbury had moved down the order. Shrewsbury had a wonderful season in 1902, playing 33 innings at an average of 50, and according to *Wisden* 'seemed, as it were, to renew his youth', but within a few months he had committed suicide, apparently under the delusion that he had an incurable disease. He had been a great player, but the new men were a lot more fun.

There was Iremonger, a fine all-rounder; the first Joe Hardstaff, known as 'Hotstuff', another Forest footballer; and two new Gunns, John and young George, to carry on the tradition when William finally retired. George was a classical batsman, but quirky, somewhat too whimsical to fit the Roundhead part fate had allotted him. Life was sterner for bowlers, but Notts had one who made life more amusing for everyone except opposing batsmen and la-di-da amateurs. This was Tom Wass, who opened the bowling and stuck at it on some unhelpful wickets. He was a miner, and a very hard man who, he said himself, 'feared nowt'. In the winter he kept himself fit by 20-mile walks, often following the hounds on foot. In summer he bowled fast leg-cutters. All year round he drank beer in quantity, and kept himself to himself unless provoked.

The result was a strange caricature of the neo-feudal professional created by the new county system. When he had first come to play for Notts, the captain had gone to pick him up at the station, to find him accompanied by a huge sheep dog. According to wicket-keeper Tom Oates,

> 'What,' says skipper, 'tha can't bring that wi' thee to t' ground, tha knows.'
> 'Then,' says Tom, 'if t'dog can't coom, Tom woan't coom.'

Wass was known as 'Topsy' to his friends, but when a distinguished amateur so addressed him he growled, 'Tom Wass is my name. I gi' thee mister and I'll 'av mister from thee, if tha must talk.' Wass was one of the earliest examples of a type known as rough diamonds, good enough technically to play for England, but not quite polished enough.

There was great rejoicing amongst the highly polished when Kent at last won the championship in 1906, not least because they did so at high speed. Their scoring rate was 80 runs an hour, consistently, as if from conviction rather than fluctuating with the conditions. According to an admiring pundit, Major Philip Trevor of the *Daily Telegraph*, 'Their men discarded a cricket maxim, the expediency of which had so far gone unchallenged: "First make the game safe and having done so, begin to try to win."' Kent started trying to win from the start. Their batting was mainly amateur, led by C. J. Burnup, a Cambridge cricket and soccer Blue, and the glamorous Kenneth Hutchings, but this was the first season of the professional, Frank Woolley, arguably the best English left-hand bat ever, and a tidy spin bowler. He was a product of a remarkable outfit, the Tonbridge nursery set up in 1897 to produce young cricketers for the Kent side. As its coach Capt. W. McCanlis wrote in 1906,

> This, like other institutions, is the outcome of necessity. Kent for many years had been essentially an amateur side, doing great things at times, when at full strength in the latter end of the season ... A good side in all matches was required.

As well as coaching, the young players were given a chance to play with local clubs, unusual in the south, where club professionals were often not permitted. So, in due course, a stream of fine players – Woolley, Colin 'Charley' Blythe, a great left-arm bowler, Fielder, Humphreys, Seymour, Hardinge, Hubble – passed through the nursery. The result appeared to be a triumph for neo-feudalism, a largely professional side imbued with the amateur spirit.

Lancashire's batting was even more splendid than Kent's. Tyldesley got better and better, solid polished steel to follow the golden amateurs. MacLaren had already, in 1895, made the record score of 424: now in 1903 he and his opening partner, the graceful R. H. Spooner, made 368 before tea against Gloucestershire. The team were interesting sociologically. Reggie

Spooner, of Marlborough, who played in ten Tests, was also a rugger international, whilst Jack Sharp, a fine long-serving professional who played in three Tests, was a soccer player for Everton and England. (He was a highly successful businessman, in sports equipment, and he was able after the war to turn amateur and captain Lancashire.)

Another unusual character was the fast bowler Walter Brearley, of Bolton, an amateur whose vowel sounds had remained uncorrupted by social aspirations and whose temper suited his whirlwind style. He told Cardus of a Roses match at Sheffield when, after bowling most of the day and having innumerable lbw appeals turned down, George Hirst hit a short one over the ropes:

> The crowd, sarcastic-like, shouts, 'Ow's that, Maister Brearley?' and next ball he hits me again over the ropes, and crowd shouts 'Ow's that?' again; so I knocks his middle stump flying in two, and Ah runs down pitch and picks up broken halves of wicket and Ah brandishes 'em at crowd. And then Ah runs off field and comes back wi' six new stumps and gives 'em to umpire and says, 'Here, take these, you'll need all bloody lot before Ah've done.' And he needed four on 'em, Ah can tell you.

Brearley's aggression was not reserved for opposing batsmen. In 1906 he fell out with the committee, and refused to play for Lancashire for most of that season and the whole of 1907. He was actually playing for Cheshire in the Minor Counties competition when he was selected for England that year.

Lancashire were never far from the top and won the championship for the second time in 1904. In the middle of their struggle that season, the *Manchester Guardian*, in a leading article, took a detached and rather cool look at the state of cricket:

> The less aggressive form the Lancashire team has been recently showing is partly, no doubt, due to over-work. The weather and the exigencies of the championship have allowed little respite. It is of course too late to suggest that originally cricket was a game, and that the element of grim toil is a little out of place. The obvious reply is that the championship is here to stay ... But can nothing be done?

It went on to complain about the system in which each county had to play at least seven others home and away, and to plead for a reduction by Lancashire, who chose to play all fourteen other counties – 'We shall never, we hope, forget that the game is more than the championship.'

The *Guardian* concluded by supporting Northamptonshire's application to become first-class, facetiously suggesting that so many be admitted that it would become logistically impossible for them all to play each other. *Wisden* put forward an equally irrelevant, not to say reactionary argument. It was, so the great Pardon reckoned, a very good step and one calculated to increase the harmony of county cricket. If the second-class teams realise that if they show sufficiently marked superiority over their rivals promotion will follow as a matter of course we shall hear no more of proposals to adopt the system of the Football League.

That despised but highly successful organisation had formed a Second Division and introduced promotion and relegation in 1893.

In fact Northamptonshire's superiority in Minor Counties competition had been almost entirely due to one man, George Thompson, an all-rounder good enough to be picked for the Players in 1900 and for An England XI against the 1902 Australian tourists, taking 8 for 88 and earning selection for Lord Hawke's tour of New Zealand. The rest were mainly amateurs, one of whom naturally acted as captain, but Thompson remained the major force that rendered them, by perseverance and building up a settled team, capable of beating Yorkshire in 1911 and running them close for the championship in 1912. Whether this demonstrated the inferiority of the Football League's system is another matter.

IV

What kind of people watched the county championship? Obviously for the most part – certainly on working days – those for whom it had been created, the members, the players and their families, clergymen, actors, writers and the like. But we should be careful not to draw too hasty conclusions from this: the evidence of huge Bank Holiday crowds suggests that in those days, when all sporting entertainment was live, many of the working class would have gone more often if it wasn't for their work. A piece in the *Clarion* in 1905 featured a philosophical character, Brother Eli, who spoke with a grotesque Lancashire accent and carried to the Roses match a couple of bricks ('Med by British labour on t' eight 'ours a day principle') to stand on so that he could see: others less well equipped 'wandered disconsolately around, vainly trying to find a chink to gaze through'. When Spooner – 'Mister Spoonah' – was out, 'Eli almost wept. "It met ha' bin mi own brother," he explained tearfully.'

Another working-class habitué of Edwardian Old Trafford similarly afflicted was the young Neville Cardus, who confessed in his autobiography that as a lad he cared so much for cricket that he sometimes could not bear to watch it:

> I closed my eyes and prayed that God would make George Hirst drop down dead before bowling the next ball. I loved Spooner so much that I dared not watch him make stroke.

An unathletic, short-sighted boy utterly uninterested in any other sport, Cardus presents another curious aspect of cricket's appeal: he found that you didn't have to be athletic to enjoy playing it. He discovered this not at school but on waste land playing with other urchins. Thirteen-year-old Cardus's formal education ended in 1902 after a mere four years at a 'Board School'. 'There were no playing fields attached to this establishment,' he wrote, 'only a playground made of asphalt.' Yet he gradually discovered a talent for bowling, developed it in a Sunday School league, and was able eventually to get a post as assistant professional at Shrewsbury School.

His inspiration for doing this was as unlikely as the rest of his highly improbable life – a brief glimpse of MacLaren batting before the game was rained off:

> This ... thrilled my blood, for it gave shape and reality to things I had till then only felt and dreamed about of romance ... From MacLaren to Wagner and the romantic gesture would henceforward be a sure and natural transition.

Yet, as he lay on the grass watching his heroes, even he noticed a fly in the golden-age ointment – easy runs on easy pitches can get very boring: 'It was the custom of Old Trafford crowds in those days to while away tedium by the singing of part-songs – plagal, I think – whereat they would applaud themselves.' They also – less amusingly – chanted 'left, right, left, right' in time with the steps of policemen patrolling the boundary edge.

It was fielding on the boundary in a county match at Old Trafford that C. B. Fry received another assault on his amateur dignity. A spectator, he recalled,

> spent the whole of Lancashire's first innings telling me, 'Fra, Fra, you bluidy amateurs is no good.' Then I made a lot of runs, and he spent the whole of the second Lancashire innings in saying, 'Fra, Fra, th'art nowt but a bluidy professional thysel'.

The question of 'shamateurism' was also being aired more formally. In 1903 the Hon. R. H. Lyttleton, contributing a chapter on 'Amateur and professional' to the cricket volume of the *Country Life* series on sport, began by complaining that such was the commercialisation of the game that merely defining the terms was nowadays almost impossible, more so in cricket than any other game: the boundary line had become almost obliterated.

Lyttleton blamed several things for this: the Australians being allowed to call their players 'Mr' or 'Esq.' when they were actually professionals; the lengthening of the season so that cricket was now a full-time occupation; and in county cricket competition and gate-money:

> The winning of matches being the golden key to financial prosperity, the Committees have been driven to adopt a system of paying the amateurs money and what thirty years ago was done in one or two instances is now a matter of universal practice.

Expenses, sinecure posts of club secretary, winter jobs and 'complimentary' matches were now the norm. When MCC had recently been asked to manage a tour to Australia they could not afford the fees asked by the amateurs.

There was no need, Lyttleton argued, for impoverished amateurs to adopt such underhand methods; they should turn professional. The modern professional, though still recruited from 'the shop, from the factory, from the pit and from the slum', could now look towards a better and more secure income – some had earned as much as £2000 from a benefit match, and they could augment their incomes by endorsements of equipment, or by keeping a shop or a public house. The 'dress and deportment' of the pros made it difficult to tell them from the amateurs.

> The calling of a professional is in every way an honourable and good one. What puzzles many of us is that, this being the case, so many should adopt the profession but deny the name.

The reason, of course, was in the very 'Mr' and 'Esq.' labels that Lyttleton felt should be reserved for amateurs. A more cogent critique of the system appeared three years later in A. E. Knight's splendid *The Complete Cricketer*, which C. B. Fry reckoned was the best book on cricket he had ever read. Albert Knight was a professional batsman with Leicestershire who had played three times for England on the 1903–4 Australian tour. He was deeply religious, and his somewhat ostentatious habit of praying for success produced many stories, particularly in county cricket, where the pros were in the habit of lodging with each other at away matches as an economy measure. One of the better ones concerns a match with Yorkshire when he stayed with the lay preacher John Tunnicliffe, who, when asked how the visit had gone, said ruefully that he had been 'out-petitioned'. Walter Brearley called on MCC to ban Knight's praying at the wicket as an unfair practice.

But Knight's book is a masterpiece of its kind, stuffed full of learned observations in weighty prose.[1] This is how Knight conveyed his belief that university and public-school influence on cricket was reactionary:

> Matthew Arnold, musing over the beautiful city which did not appreciate his interpretation of the Faith of the Centuries, wrote of Oxford as 'the home of lost causes and forsaken beliefs, of unpopular names and impossible loyalties'. If this were true of theologies, that Oxford bent not her knee to the passing Zeitgeist, but set aloft her lonely light amid the mists of Tubingen criticism, she may do the same for sport.

He acknowledged the virtues of amateurism, but politely deplored MCC's influence in 'the maintenance of distinctions which in county cricket have no true validity'.

Then, like a revolutionary removing his kid gloves, he came to the nub:

Many an 'amateur', so termed, playing in county cricket, is more heavily remu-
nerated than an accredited 'professional'. The distinction once had a valid
foundation, based essentially on differences of wealth and social station. The
reason for that distinction has quite disappeared.

The 'exclusive "Mr" or "Esquire"' should be abolished: true gentlemen, he
reckoned, 'disliked these miserable and most hateful labels and distinctions
which sicken honest people by their unfairness'.

Lord Harris, now the treasurer and acknowledged guru of the MCC, who
fancied himself a true gentleman and prided himself on his honesty and fair-
ness, was far from sickened by the distinctions. Writing in response to an
invitation from *The Times* in 1909, he expounded the establishment position
with the riveting clarity of a closed mind and one-way vision:

> The real distinction is not whether A receives £5 or £2 for playing in a match,
> not whether B receives £200 and his expenses or £50 and his expenses for
> representing England on a tour; but does he make his livelihood out of playing
> the game ...

This last clause took him on to dangerous ground, so he quickly defined it to
suit his own argument: 'does he engage himself day in and day out to play
from May 1 to August 31? If he does he is a professional, and knows he is a
professional.' And so with remorseless, if not entirely convincing logic, to the
purpose of his rationale: 'and he recognises as convenient, and bows to those
social regulations which distinguish the amateur and professional at cricket.'
These he thought were so normal and commonplace as to be scarcely worth
mentioning: 'little more than this, that the rule of the ground should be
observed; and that the guests should accept the arrangements made by their
hosts.'

What he meant by this specious nonsense was that there were sometimes
separate dressing-rooms for amateurs and professionals and separate gates for
them to proceed from there to the wicket. 'From old practice,' he went on,
'the prefix "Mr" or the affix "Esq." is still used: but no one lays any particular store by them.' And after a good deal more disingenuous guff of the same
sort he summed up with astonishing gall:

> Therefore after two centuries of comradeship on the field *amateurs and profes-
> sionals have agreed* [my italics] that in the republic of cricket there is no need to
> encourage disputations on the definition of an amateur.

Finally he commended these principles, based on 'the wisdom of experience',
to newer sports like football and athletics, currently having trouble with the
problem.

V

One of the many points to which Harris did not address himself was Lyttleton's claim that MCC could not afford to pay the amateurs' asking rate for a tour of Australia. This was the tour of 1901–2, when the leadership fell into the hands of the piratical Archie MacLaren. One of the key members of his team was Gilbert Jessop, the sensational young all-rounder who had stepped into W.G.'s shoes at Gloucestershire. He was a good example of the sort of 'shamateur' Lyttleton had complained of, as well as of the degenerative effect of the games cult on university admissions.

Jessop was unacademic. He had left his private school when his clergyman father died and worked as a teacher, starting to play for Gloucestershire in his vacations in 1894 when he was twenty. Two years later he was admitted to Cambridge, assisted by a clergy scholarship: he joined in the summer term, and so was able to play for the university for four seasons in his three years' residence before leaving without a degree. He won his first cap for England in 1899, his final year, then after a cricket tour of America he spent a short time working for the amateurs' friend, the Stock Exchange. He had also continued to play for Gloucestershire and when W.G. left he replaced him as captain, suitably recompensed for loss of earnings, in the summer of 1901.

In these early years Jessop was a fast bowler, and he had opened, not very well, for England in his first Test. He had so electrified his fellow-students when he first went up to Cambridge that they had composed a class-conscious limerick in his honour – and that of the virility cult:

> There was a young fresher called Jessop
> Who was pitching 'em less up and less up,
> Till one of the pros
> Got a blow on the nose
> And said, 'In a helmet I'll dress up.'

He was also the swiftest cover-point – with the strongest throw – that anyone could remember. But above all he was a great attacking batsman. As his great admirer 'A Country Vicar' wrote: 'He was a mighty hitter. Not a blind slogger however, who smites wildly at everything ... He was dashing, daring to a degree, seemingly reckless. But behind it all was the cool, calculating brain of the super-batsman.' He was a destroyer in county cricket. In 1897 at Harrogate he had carted the Yorkshire bowling for 101 out of 118 in forty-five minutes.

But his finest hour was in the final Test of 1902, when with the Ashes lost and another defeat seeming inevitable, he strode out with England, needing 263 to win, on 48 for 5. A stocky figure, long-armed, stooping very low over the bat – they called him 'the Croucher' – but 'it was the crouch of the panther – ready to spring – waiting for the precise moment to make his attack'. As the newspaper poet put it,

> The Croucher at the wicket took his stand
> And crashed the Cornstalk trundlers to the ropes.

Jessop made 104 out of 139 in seventy-odd minutes. There were 76 runs yet to be made when he was out. It was the Yorkshire professionals, George Hirst, who made 58 not out and Wilfred Rhodes, last man, joining him with fifteen still to get, who saw them through.[2] But it was still Jessop's match, and it confirmed his status as a national hero.

Alas, he did not feel able to accept MCC's invitation to go on the official 'expenses only' tour in 1903–4: he wrote about it for the *Daily Mail* instead. He also put it about that he might not be able to afford to captain Gloucestershire the following season, telling the *Daily Express* that it depended whether the county could support him in his business interests. He afterwards announced that his problems had been solved and that he would be able to play cricket as much as he liked. He had, it seems, been offered a £500-a-year job as a director of a tobacco firm, but unfortunately it fell through because of a takeover, so he turned increasingly to journalism – which was well paid and need not, for a celebrity, involve any actual writing, but was not thought highly of by the purists at Lord's, both for its contravention of the 1878 edict 'that no gentleman ought to make a profit by his service in the cricket field' and because of the impropriety of commenting on games in which one took part, criticising MCC and so forth.

There was not much MCC could do about it, though, except not select journalists, which they could hardly do since so many amateurs were involved in it. Fry, the first, was thought very shocking, especially when he started writing regularly for the *Daily Express* when it started up in 1900 as Sir Arthur Pearson's response to the highly successful *Daily Mail* of Alfred Harmsworth (Viscount Northcliffe) at the cheaper end of the market. Now everyone was at it. *Punch* satirised the situation in 1904 in a cartoon of a match in which all the participants were busy scribbling as they played.[3]

The most assiduous and influential of the player-scribblers was P. F. Warner, who began writing a weekly article for the highly superior *Westminster Gazette* in 1903. He was in fact MCC's choice to lead the tour to Australia that winter in place of the maverick MacLaren, and for the rest of his career as player, selector and tour manager earned his living from his writing. Not all of it was above the counter. He reported for *The Times*, which did not name its writers, on matches in which he himself was engaged, referring to himself as 'Mr Warner' to complete the deception. Other unethically anonymous amateurs were H. D. G. Leveson-Gower and G. V. J. Weigall, of Cambridge and Kent.

VI

MacLaren, though not yet a journalist, had been early in the literary field (1896) with a slim volume on how to play cricket; he also endorsed bats and other equipment. This apart, his taking out the 1901–2 team to Australia did not please the luminaries at Lord's. They gave him no help in assembling his team, and Lord Hawke invoked his seigneurial rights over Yorkshire players – stemming from the winter pay deal – to refuse permission for George Hirst and Wilfred Rhodes to tour so as to conserve their energies for Yorkshire's next championship season. This brought into the frame one of the few men ever to tangle with MacLaren and come out on top, the arch-professional Sydney Barnes, who had just signed for Lancashire.

Barnes, then a twenty-one-year-old fast bowler, had been asked in 1894 to join the ground staff of his native Staffordshire, a hitherto undistinguished cricketing county, but found the terms unattractive. Instead he went to Rishton in the Lancashire League, a lucrative way of supplementing his income. He was invited to play for Warwickshire in a game or two, but was not made very welcome by the other pros – snobbish about the League but also jealous of the money he was getting there. He played two or three more games for Warwickshire, but on the next occasion he was invited to play by telegram one morning and when he returned home that night found another message, 'Do not come. An amateur is playing.'

So he stayed in the League, first with Rishton, then with Burnley, dropping his pace and experimenting with spin, until he was discovered by Lancashire's scouts. He played several games in 1901, taking six wickets in the final match of the season. There had been talk of his signing for the following season, but Barnes was not sure – he thought it a great deal of hard work for relatively little money. He was playing for Burnley the following Saturday when MacLaren, by then in desperate straits for another bowler, sent him a telegram that caused a sensation when taken out to him on the field. The offer was for a tour followed by a season's contract with Lancashire. This represented steady employment to Barnes, for whom job security was always a prime consideration. He therefore accepted, though not without misgivings.

Barnes's bowling was a sensation in Australia. His first Test wicket was that of Victor Trumper, the most admired batsman in either country, and after 5–65 in the first innings and a more modest showing in the second, he shot to eternal fame by taking 6–42 and 7–121 in the next Test, getting both Trumper and Clem Hill twice. But the sixty-four overs he had to bowl were more than he had bargained for. He brought no starry-eyed public-school enthusiasm to the task – and he very definitely did not respond to MacLaren's metaphorically smiting him on the shoulder and urging him to play the game.

For Barnes it was hard work, both physically and mentally: he thought batsmen out. He was dedicated, but in his own way. He tried his best to get batsmen out, but he expected due consideration and due reward for the exercise of his arts. A knee injury in the third Test put him out of the match and England on the skids. He played in no more Tests on the tour, which turned into a disaster. Towards the end, when the team was crossing to New Zealand by boat, a storm blew up and they feared for their lives: and in the middle of it, MacLaren was heard to mutter, 'Well, there's one consolation. If we go down that bugger Barnes will go down with us.'

They survived, and returned to face the contracted season with Lancashire together. Barnes's in-and-out performances and proneness to injury led *Wisden* to suggest that he gave up too easily. MacLaren was busy for most of the season leading England in the Test series: Barnes was chosen for the third Test and took 6–49, but was dropped for the next. (This was the occasion when Fred Tate, a decent Sussex stock bowler, was chosen for his only Test, dropped a vital catch and got out with four to make to win the match.) In the euphoria of the famous face-saving victory of the final Test, and Hirst and Rhodes's part in it, Barnes slipped out of the reckoning.

He signed again for Lancashire in 1903, hoping for selection for the 1903–4 tour. He bowled his boots off that season, taking 131 wickets at 16.85 apiece, but this was the year when MCC finally decided they must take over regardless of the quality of the teams they could afford. The compliant P. F. Warner was chosen as captain when F. S. Jackson was unavailable, and neither the contentious MacLaren nor Barnes were invited. (If the intention of choosing Warner was to raise the moral tone, it was not entirely successful. In the second Test Warner, having won the toss and decided to bat, changed his team to include an extra batsman.[4]) At the end of the season, when picked for the Players v. Gentlemen match, the weary Barnes could bowl only one over before retiring. *The Times* thought it unfair that he should claim a fee and then not perform.

Barnes for his part thought it unfair that he should only be paid the same as team-mates who did much less work. Lancashire's standard fees were £3 a week in summer and £1 in winter, whereas Church in the Lancashire League offered him £8 a match for playing on Saturdays only. So he tried to bargain with Lancashire, delaying signing for the following season as long as he could, and longer than MacLaren liked. He was warned that if he didn't sign he would be dropped for the last match and so would not be paid. Barnes still refused to sign but turned up for the match, changed and ready to play: MacLaren had to order him back to the dressing-room. Barnes's distinctly non-feudal behaviour aroused, like Milton's Satan, 'a dismal universal hiss', and he went back, this time for good, to the leagues and Staffordshire.

Yet, however much the high-minded might expostulate, when it came to the pinch Barnes was too good to ignore completely, and – again at the last minute – he was picked again for the 1907–8 Australian tour. He bowled more overs than anyone else on either side, and his courageous batting helped England to avoid a whitewash. He was even chosen for Tests at home in 1909, the last three only, but still got through more work than anyone else – and kept his stranglehold on the great Trumper. He was thirty-eight before he was chosen other than as a replacement, for the 1911–12 Australia tour, by this time the acknowledged master, able eventually to sort out even the most opinionated of captains (J. W. H. T. Douglas) sufficiently for England to recover the Ashes. When the South Africans came to centre stage – pushed prematurely by wealthy local politicians – he exposed their limitations, both in the soggy Triangular Tournament of 1912 and in the following winter's tour. On this, however, he unfortunately lapsed into anti-feudal attitudes: he was unplayable until the final Test, for which he became unavailable when the promised financial sponsorship did not materialise. Douglas, an Olympic boxer, had to throw in the towel.

CHAPTER THIRTEEN

End of an Era

THE CONVENTIONAL WISDOM of cricket chroniclers, and the hackneyed description 'golden age', suggest an untroubled era suddenly and irredeemably shattered by the rude intrusion of harsh alien values. Yet the values – competitive and aggressive – that led to the First World War were, let us be clear, very much a part, both of the British make-up and of the upper reaches of their 'national game'. Seen from mullioned public-school windows, cricket was an emblem of ancient virtues, amalgamating the virility cult, the honour code and the defence of King and Empire, with concepts like fair play, the straight bat, playing the game and so forth as added charms against malevolent non-cricketing foreigners. When the Gatling jammed there was always cricket.

Patriotic duty apart, cricket's gilded pre-war age was not viewed with quite such an uncritical gaze by those living at the time. In part this was the inevitable fate of any treasured institution – things ain't what they used to be and never have been, particularly the things folk remember doing in the perpetual sunshine of their extreme youth. Cricket, in particular, had been plagued by nostalgia since people first began to think it worth writing about. John Nyren and his ghost reckoned the game had been ruined by allowing round-arm bowling.

In 1907 E. V. Lucas produced a new edition of Nyren, with an admiring commentary, and a year later contributed a piece to *The Times* welcoming a revival of the Hambledon club and a commemorative game against Jessop and an All-England XI:

Any step that can bring sentiment again into first-class cricket is to be welcomed: for a hard utilitarianism and commercialisation have far too long controlled it.

What was intended as 'an occasional pastime, marked by geniality and rapture' had become 'a more or less mechanical trade'. Its 'glorious uncertainty' would always save it from 'the worst depths of professional mechanism' but 'a three-day match to-day can be a scene of little joy and little enthusiasm'.

Consciously or not, this echoed Mary Mitford's dismay at seeing her first county match:

> There they stood ... silent, solemn, slow ... making a business of the thing ... instead of the glee, the fun, the shouts, the laughter, the glorious confusion of the country game.

But was village cricket still what it was? Fred Gale had long since laid down the ground rules:

> There ought to be at least two or three old fogeys who ... declare there never were such days as when Squire A or Squire B ... were alive; there must be an inn where cricketers have met within the memory of all the oldest inhabitants; I prefer a green where the stocks are still standing, and I would rather not play at all if there is no parish beadle.

In the 'golden age' it all depended which village. Siegfried Sassoon's chapter on 'The Flower Show Match'[1] is part of a fictionalised evocation of the era, unsentimental yet appealing, and all the more effective for the contrast of its sequel in the trenches. In this superior village in Kent, where the teas cost half a crown, the ground is well kept, the lower orders are respectful, and there are versions of all the stereotypes: the public-schoolboy on vacation and the wheelwright's son; the groom and the prosperous saddler; the umpire who says 'hout'; the ponderous, taciturn, good-natured yokel; the 'stalwart, fierce-browed farmer'. The visiting wicket-keeper is a highly unpopular parson who used to play for MCC, lets everyone know it, and is not to be trusted. One of his habits is 'genially engaging the batsman in conversation' to distract his attention:

> The pestered batsman rounded on the rather foxy-faced clergyman with, 'I bin playing cricket nigh on thirty years, and parson or no parson, I take the liberty of telling you to hold your blasted gab.'

On the other hand, a Berkshire clergyman, in an article for *The Times* in 1907, refuted the notion that every English village had

> a spacious village green where squire's sons, parson's sons, farmers' sons, village lads, the blacksmith, the carpenter and the wheelwright play on terms of equality while others look on with critical eyes.

This might be true of first-class counties, but it was 'a fond delusion' in other places. Of fifteen villages in his locality only one had a village green. Nor had he found it easy to start a club to play 'the national game': when the effort had been made and young members had been issued with their 'tackle' louts had dispossessed them, and the farmer had taken a crop of hay off the ground as well as a large rent.

Another article the following year commented sadly on the pathetic attempts of the working-class youngsters playing in London parks. It was not so much a shortage of space (although more could be done to open up some of the Royal parks): London County Council had provided 442 reserved grounds that season for some 10,000 players in some 30,000 matches as well as countless thousands on unreserved pitches. What they lacked was tuition. The author paid tribute to the work of the university and public-school missions working with the poor of the East End and to the several cricketers he knew who devoted 'an hour or two of their spare time every week to the pleasant and profitable task of coaching'. He went on to urge much more – 'no investment of one's leisure returns higher interest' – and to assert, 'Cricket is unquestionably the best antidote to Hooliganism.'

No one had yet suggested that Hooligans be taught cricket at school – unless their parents could afford the fees, that is. Luckily it was perfectly possible for good cricketers to burst forth from a Board School background. The greatest batsman of his time, Jack Hobbs, was already leaving school for a seven-and- six-a-week job at the age, thirteen, when the gilded amateurs were starting at their public schools. But his father was a net bowler at Fenner's – and, even more to the point, he was Jack Hobbs. Still, if cricket was the great character-builder everyone said it was, it is a pity that it was not prescribed for more of the population. In practice, it was soccer that got such attention as the elementary schools could offer. St Matthew's C. of E. School, Cambridge, where Hobbs went, had goal posts painted on the schoolyard wall. It was logistically more practical, and there was also a closer resemblance between the juvenile version and its first-class model.

II

At the other extreme, even country-house cricket, popularly supposed to be at its zenith in those spacious prelapsarian days, was causing concern to some contemporaries. As early as 1903 Henry Leveson-Gower, himself a pillar of the Scarborough Festival, detected signs of decline, though of fifty-six days' cricket played by I Zingari twenty-one had been at country houses. The problem was not shortage of venues, but a dearth of players of the requisite calibre and social standing. This he attributed to the increasing number who now had to work for their living – even if only on the Stock Exchange. But also county cricket was taking up more time, and the leading amateurs, particularly if they played for a club as well, had not many weekends free.

Not many, let us hope, were like the celebrated A. J. Raffles, gentleman cracksman. His creator certainly thought not:

> Old Raffles may or may not have been an exceptional criminal, but as a cricketer
> I dare swear he was unique. Himself a dangerous bat, a brilliant field, and
> perhaps the very finest slow bowler of his decade, he took incredibly little inter-
> est in the game at large ... He professed to have lost all enthusiasm for the
> game and to keep it up only from the lowest motives.
>
> 'Cricket,' said Raffles, '... is good enough sport until you discover a better
> ... What's the satisfaction of taking a man's wicket when you want his spoons?
> Still, if you can bowl a bit your low cunning won't get rusty, and always looking
> for the weak spot's just the kind of mental exercise one wants ...

After which Raffles, who played for I Zingari and the Gentlemen, takes
advantage of a vulgarly expressed invitation to Lord Amersteth's cricketing
house-party – 'Nothing riles me more than being asked about for my cricket
as though I were a pro myself' – to steal Lady Melrose's jewels from under
the nose of detectives and a professional burglar.

E. W. Hornung's parody of Sherlock Holmes and of cricket (made more
pointed by Raffles's Dr Watson, who is an old-school admirer, hopeless at
cricket himself, called Bunny) was a deliberate and highly successful
gimmick, designed not only to cash in on the vogue for crime stories amongst
the otherwise respectable middle classes, but also to tease his brother-in-law,
Conan Doyle. It was a salutary contrast to the sentimental and self-deluding
orthodoxy of such as Edward Cracroft Lefroy, who wrote to a friend: 'There
is something idyllic about the pastime ... The whole edifice of Christian
virtues could be raised on a basis of good cricket,' and whose sonnets seek to
illustrate the point. Thus he exalts the honest violence of fast bowling in
which 'the mid-stump [takes] three somersaults in air' over the subterfuge of
spin – 'In knavish hands a most unkindly knack'. For, he assures us,

> ... no guile shelters under this boy's black
> Crisp hair, frank eyes, and honest English skin.

Hornung was not trying to make fun of cricket. On the contrary, he
believed deeply in its character-moulding powers, and was apt to quote
Newbolt and the *Punch* verses:

> For it isn't the winning that makes a man
> But it's playing the game on the good old plan,
> As hard and straight as a mortal can –
> In fact it is playing the game.

But his Great Umpire was, if not pagan, a distinctly Old Testament deity.
Both he and Doyle were amongst the numerous enthusiastic literary crick-

eters, and members of the MCC, the difference being that Doyle was pretty good at the game, whereas Hornung, though as unflinching in the face of fast bowling as the next man, was asthmatic and extremely short-sighted. Doyle had been a regular member of the Allahakbarries, a light-hearted literary and artistic cricket team founded in the 1890s by James Barrie, the future author of the astringent *The Admirable Crichton* and the ultra-whimsical *Peter Pan*.

Doyle, whom Barrie described as '... a grand bowler. Knows a batsman's weakness by the colour of the mud on his boots', was in fact so good in his prime that he had to be excluded from some of the more convivial fixtures. Otherwise Barrie found it a 'depressing rule' that 'the more distinguished as authors his men were the worse they played'. No one knew in advance whether A. E. W. Mason, a fast bowler, 'was more likely to send the bails flying or hit square leg in the stomach'; Augustine Birrell smashed Barrie's bat 'and instead of grieving called out gloriously, "Fetch me some more bats."'; 'E. V. Lucas had (unfortunately) a style'; Jerome K. Jerome was listed as 'subsidised crowd'. Other regulars were Owen Seaman, editor of *Punch*, and Bernard Partridge, its celebrated cartoonist.

The Allahakbarries' most distinguished cricketer, without a doubt, was the young and extravagantly named Hesketh Vernon Hesketh-Prichard, a Scottish connection of Conan Doyle, who thought highly of him as a fast bowler and recommended him to both London County and Hampshire, for whom he played off and on until the war. Part of the off was the 1901 season, from which he absented himself in order to present his book *Through the Heart of Patagonia* to an expectant public. He had a great triumph, with both bat and ball, in 1904 for Gentlemen v. Players, when one account read: 'Cricket such as this raises the national pastime to a higher standard, in which nerve and brains co-operate with mere physical and mechanical attributes.'

He later toured the West Indies, now a regular port of call for imperial ambassadors following the example of the indefatigable P. F. Warner; and his finest hour was when MCC asked him to lead a tour of America, where his speeches and his sportsmanship were greatly admired, especially in the Philadelphia stronghold. (This, as gentlemanly a cricketing community as you could hope to find, including imported English coaches, sent three teams to England between 1893 and 1908, featuring the legendary in-swing bowler J. Barton King, who was as good as any in the world.)

A noted explorer, whose other works included one on life in Haiti, and later a gallant soldier, with an expertise that led to yet another book, *Sniping in France*, Hesketh-Prichard's literary acclaim, nevertheless, did not quite match that of his cricket, and he has to be seen as an obverse illustration of Barrie's maxim. C. B. Fry's view of why so many creative artists – Galsworthy, John Drinkwater, Clifford Bax, who introduced his brother Sir Arnold as 'a very useful bowler', Hugh Walpole, Ben Travers, for example – were so interested in the theory of cricket but not good at putting it into practice was that they had too much imagination, a distinct disadvantage in a cricketer. It certainly enhanced the game's reputation to have so many romantics and wordsmiths as propagandists for it. The best of these writers, the ones that have worn best, are those in whom the sense of humour is uppermost.

For instance, A. A. Milne, turning out a weekly piece for *Punch*, mostly prose and a lot of it expendable, could produce a set of amiable verses, 'An Average Man', that begin:

> Of Tomkins as a natural cricketer
> It frequently has been remarked – that IF
> He'd had more opportunities of bowling
> And rather more encouragement in batting;
> And IF his averages so disclosed,
> Batting and Bowling, had been interchanged;
> And IF the field as usually set
> Contained some post (at the pavilion end)
> Whose presence rather than a pair of hands
> Was called for, then, before the season finished,
> Tomkins would certainly have played for Kent.

P. G. Wodehouse, the Master, was a cricketer at Dulwich College, capable of opening the bowling with N. A. Knox and, on one famous occasion, against Tonbridge, bagging seven wickets, including that of K. L. Hutchings, to Knox's one. In his riper years Wodehouse found golf funnier, but before the First World War he wrote many better-than-average school stories and other novels in which cricket plays a part. The best-known is *Mike* (1909), the first in which the irrepressible Psmith appears. Psmith, said to have been based on Rupert D'Oyley Carte, knows where to draw the line: 'The last time I played in a village cricket match,' said Psmith, 'I was caught at point by a man in braces. It would have been madness to have risked another such shock to the system.'[2] Barrie's own offering on the subject – 'A rural cricket match in buttercup time with boys at play, seen and heard through the trees; it is surely the loveliest scene in England and the most disarming sound' – is itself disarming, but he spills over into mawkish excess: 'From the ranks of the unseen dead, forever passing along our country lanes on their eternal journey, the Englishman falls out for a moment to look over the gate of the cricket field and smile.'

III

The ranks of the unseen dead were soon to be unnaturally swollen. Already the war-clouds were gathering and the country was torn between ignoring them and investing heavily in naval rearmament, a costly business that inflated the budget of 1909, already blown up by the cost of social reform. The Liberal Government, led by the ambivalent Herbert Asquith, now had Lloyd George as its Chancellor of the Exchequer, and his tax proposals – an increase in death duties, income tax up to 1*s*. 2*d*. (6p) and supertax on incomes over £3,000 a year – and the proposed old-age pension of 5*s*. (25p) a week were denounced by the Liberal Lord Rosebery as 'not Liberalism but Socialism, the negation of faith, of family, of property, of monarchy, of Empire'. The House of Lords, prodded out of its customary well-bred lethargy, rejected the Budget and precipitated a constitutional crisis, the more serious because the Lords were also the bastion against Irish Home Rule. It took two general elections and Asquith's threat to create 500 new and radical peers, reluctantly backed by the inexperienced George V, to overcome the Lords' resistance and replace their veto by delaying powers.

Irish politics were always on the edge of violence and now private armies were on the march in Ulster and the south, and fears mounted that Home Rule would bring serious trouble into which Germany could poke her nose. The suffragette movement, only slightly less alarmingly, had also developed an activist wing that, having discovered the publicity value of disruption, was playing cat and mouse with the police. A bomb damaged Lloyd George's house, there were two attempts to set fire to the Wimbledon stands and Emily Davison killed herself under the hoofs of the king's horse in the 1913 Derby.

Politics was gradually becoming less of an aristocratic game. The electorate was slowly extending, and every male householder now had a vote. But even this limited progress for the common man was greater than his snail-like social and economic advance. 2.5 per cent of the population had 65 per cent of the national wealth, and only one in nine earned the £160 a year at which they had to pay income tax. Industrial wages for men averaged £75 a year, agricultural £40, women's work £30. Male clerical and skilled industrial workers might get £100. The next layer of this stratified society was two-fold: a salaried class, averaging £340 a year, with a few judges and the like earning up to £5,000; and a comparable hierarchy of the self-employed – lawyers, doctors, farmers and shopkeepers – and gentlemen of independent means.

At the pinnacle sat the really rich, the landowners, financiers, top industrialists and businessmen. Social class was not determined solely by money, of course, and capitalism and industrialisation had been absorbed into, rather than changed, the underlying social structure, based on birth and breeding. The result was a nation of whom some 2 per cent were unmistakably upper class, about 80 per cent lower class, and the remainder a *mélange* of overlapping and contending middle classes. In a society fast losing its interest in religion two underlying concepts were firmly accepted: that the rich man in his castle and the poor man at his gate were both put there by divine decree; and that God, having made the country, would not live in the man-made town if He could help it, especially at weekends.

There was talk in the papers – especially Lord Northcliffe's *Daily Mail* and his new acquisition *The Times* – of the German menace, but it was easily dismissed as scaremongering for party political purposes. In particular, little was done about the industrial threat Germany headed: after all, Britain's share of world trade was still, at 30 per cent, the biggest. But it was shrinking with protective tariffs all around. Yet the notion of a controlled economy was alien – another source of dislike of the jackbooted Germans who were masters of state intervention – and when times grew hard it was every firm for itself. Exports of coal brought in quick returns but provided cheap fuel for foreign manufacturers; exports of textile machinery to Asia undermined Lancashire's cotton trade.

Even more damaging than this, industry had low social status, even amongst its own leaders, who sent their children to public schools and Oxbridge, where jokes were made about 'rude mechanicals'. A cultured life of a not too demanding nature, was what increasing numbers of the burgeoning middle classes wanted: the twenty years between 1891 and 1911 had brought a sharp increase in the number of actors, authors, editors and journalists and a drop in the number of engineers. Even more people, without aesthetic pretensions, merely sought to make money as unlaboriously as possible: the number of stockbrokers rose by 220 per cent. Industry was stagnating, through neglect of technology, gentrification, an accompanying anti-industrial culture and seduction by the lure of the easy money of capital investment.

The short-sightedness of employers was matched by a profound conservatism amongst the workers. Skilled men sought to maintain their privileged position, embedded in the centuries-old, craft-based apprenticeship system against the inroads of the factory system, which enlisted the semi-skilled and unskilled, even women. Trade unions saw their role as maintaining their members' jobs, according to established custom and practice, by slowing the pace of production if necessary. The Trades Disputes Act, passed by the Liberals in their initial euphoria, had given unions exemption from being sued for damages, and now, in the heightened political tension, they began to assert themselves. Industrial unrest began in 1910. An attack by disgruntled miners on the pit-head at Tonypandy in South Wales caused the Home Secretary, Churchill, to send in the army; there were disorderly strikes by seamen, London carmen and dockers, and at the Liverpool docks two strikers were killed by restraining troops.

The strikes continued through 1911, creating an atmosphere of tension in which Lloyd George's National Insurance Bill, a contributory sickness benefit scheme, seemed like a Marxist plot, and the Shops Act, providing a weekly half-holiday – an idlers' charter – also intensified party strife, bringing in an aggressive new Tory leader, Bonar Law, who spoke of the need for 'direct action' in support of beleaguered employers. All this aroused great interest amongst international revolutionaries, not least Lenin, who was most disappointed when the miners settled for a guaranteed minimum wage: dockers tried to repeat their previous success, but aroused so much public hostility that they had to give in.

By contrast, one professed Socialist thought there had 'never been a period as good for a young man to live in'. Giving up his £1 a week job in marine insurance for a £2 10s. a week summer engagement as assistant cricket professional, young Neville Cardus went to live 'among the toffs' at Shrewsbury School and found it 'a heaven down here below'. And he was thereafter, as they say in Ireland, 'on a pig's back'. Cricket itself, at this and every other time, was an ideal dream-world for those seeking escape from reality. And the edifice that was its finest glory, county cricket, was creaking at the joints, like the lumbaginous Archie MacLaren.

IV

A major cause of the malaise was the increased number of drawn matches. These had almost doubled from the 20-odd per cent of the 1890s, reflecting, alas, not a greater proportion of keenly fought contests but the greater supremacy of bat over ball, assisted by the British climate. Three days was a long time to watch a stalemate, wet or fine. There was much talk of brightening things up, but every suggestion of change was rejected.

The century had begun with a proposal to alter the lbw law with the intention of making life marginally easier for bowlers by preventing excessive pad play. The Hon. Alfred Lyttleton, no less, had proposed the motion in a lengthy MCC debate, because 'the present cricket [was] somewhat dull'. Other old stagers deplored the deliberate use of pads, which once had been thought unethical and unsporting. But P. F. Warner, a pad-player, though professing complete objectivity, argued against it:

> I assure you I have the best interests of the game at heart, and as I have played all over the world I think I am entitled to an opinion. This has been the finest game in the world for many generations, and so I ask you to beware how you tamper with the present laws.

The proposal was carried by 253 to 188, a majority of 65, but short of the two-thirds required, so things stayed as they were.

Two years later a proposal to widen the wickets slightly was similarly rejected. And when in 1911 the great F. R. Spofforth, long resident in England, proposed that two runs be awarded to the fielding side for every maiden over bowled, the pontifical S. H. Pardon rebuked him with all *Wisden*'s biblical force:

> Never, I should think, has such an absurd suggestion been put forward by a first-rate expert ... Cricket does not stand need of alteration ... It must not be tampered with to please people who think that it can have the concentrated excitement of an hour-and-a-half's football.

Actually, the great excitement of the season, real whizz-bang stuff, took place before only a handful of spectators at Hove, scene of Ranji, Fry and company's triumphs – on a Saturday, thought then to be the best day for the last day of a match. This particular match looked like subsiding into an easy victory for Sussex when Ted Alletson, the ultimate one-game wonder, did his stuff. Batting at number eight for Notts he transformed a 9-run lead at fifty minutes before lunch into one of 236 forty minutes after.

There are no accurate accounts, and it all happened too quickly for even the scorers to keep up, but according to one eye-witness, Alletson was 47 at lunch, took ten minutes to complete his 50, scored another 50 in the next fifteen minutes and then 'proceeded to treat the bowlers in a more ferocious manner', adding 89 in the next fifteen. Time was wasted in finding replacement balls for those he hit out of the ground and in digging one out of the soft wood of the pavilion in which it became embedded. Alletson hit eight sixes, twenty-three fours and only seventeen singles. Alletson, who had been in and out of the team, had not previously been known as a hitter, and now seemed not to believe what he had done. For a game or two he fitfully swung the bat, but by the season's end he had withdrawn into his shell, and the skipper, A. O. Jones, complained to a fellow-amateur, 'The man can't be normal. I've told him that I'll play him in every match all through the season even if he makes recurrent cyphers, as long as he'll hit, but he just won't do it.'[3]

Falling gates had been a matter of concern to the more cerebral for some years now, and it began to seem obvious that merely stylish, attractive or even hard-hitting batting was no more than icing on a cake that to be palatable needed winning as a main ingredient. In 1905 Lord Harris, anticipating Kent's triumph the following year, told the prestigious *Badminton Magazine* that 'nothing is more popular than success, and a successful eleven will draw much better than an unsuccessful one'. It was not quite so simple, however. Yorkshire, who had won the championship in 1905, had covered their expenses in only two of the matches. They played thirty games a year compared with other counties' average of twenty-four. Ostensibly they did this in order to help out the weaker counties by bringing them bigger gates, but as *Wisden* suggested it had more to do with improving their win–loss ratio.

This was all very well if they did win but it was ruinous if they didn't deliver the goods. When they dropped from the heights to a humble eighth in 1910 the crowds stayed away, or, as *Wisden* put it, 'the comparative ill-success of the Yorkshire team brought about a regrettable apathy on the part of the public ...' And, conversely, the team with the fewest financial worries in the abnormally dry but financially disastrous season of 1911 was Warwickshire, who, to everyone's astonishment, jumped from fourteenth place to win the championship. *Wisden* did not like this much either:

> From the moment the team began to win matches, people flocked to the Edgbaston ground in such numbers as to relieve the Committee of all anxiety about money. Such sudden enthusiasm suggests rather too much the spirit of Association football ... One can only hope that the Birmingham public, having at last taken up county cricket in real earnest, will support their eleven in bad seasons as well as good ones.

Warwickshire were led by a twenty-two year old, Frank Foster, the latest, and one of the least credible, of the 'golden age' amateurs, capable of scoring 305 in four hours and twenty minutes in the last season before the war, of developing 'leg-theory bowling' and of helping Barnes rout the South Africans in two series.[4] Yorkshire, by contrast, were just leaving the Stone Age: Lord Hawke retired in 1910, at fifty, having been captain for twenty-seven years. His spirit remained, however, for he became president, and ensured that successive captains were amateurs, usually even worse performers than he. Under his immediate successor, the future Sir Everard Radcliffe, the bad spell continued, but even under Sir Archibald White, the next undistinguished leader, the core of professionalism – essentially the great Hirst and Rhodes – was enough to take them to first, second and fourth.

These were great years for the adventurous David Denton, and there were developing stars like the curiously Christian-named Major Booth and Alonzo Drake, and the new young opener Percy Holmes, who looked like being a bit of a dasher, but all were imbued with the characteristic Yorkshire philosophy, which was about winning. Wilfred Rhodes is usually credited with coining its pithiest expression, but it must have already been a dressing-room platitude when Wilfred rebuked a careless recruit with the stern reminder, 'We don't play cricket for fun, you know.' Yorkshire folk enjoyed this sort of joke against themselves – especially when they were winning championships – as they also did in the context of the wonderfully tense 'Roses' matches.

A great new young all-rounder, Roy Kilner, from the deep south of Barnsley, caught the spirit of it when he said he thought umpires were a 'super-flu-ous luxury' who only 'got in t' way': 'What we want in Yorksheer and Lancasheer is fair do's – no umpires and honest cheatin' all round in accoordance wi' the laws.' He said the 'Roses' games were like no other: 't' two teams say good morning to each other before t' match and then all we say for t' rest o' t' game is "How's that?"' A spectator version of the joke concerns a pinstripe-suited chap at Headingley who ventures a well-modulated comment on some aspect of the play: a flat-capped local says, 'Are tha from

Yorksheer?' 'No, I'm not.' 'Are tha from Lancasheer?' 'No.' 'Then what the 'ell's it got to do wi' thee?'

V

It was a ridiculous sort of championship, of course, in which counties were only required to play a minimum of fourteen matches and could choose their own opponents, inhibited from choosing only rabbits by the ties of history and the claims of the turnstile. In 1911, in an attempt to inject some reason into the situation, Lancashire proposed a two-division scheme (a first division of eleven, with the rest joining the leading Minor Counties to form the second, with promotion and relegation of one club) but this got nowhere, and naturally caused a lot of ill-feeling.

Lord Hawke was said to have followed his master Lord Harris in opposing this, but the following year Yorkshire joined Lancashire in a cloak-and-dagger bid to try to restrict the championship to eleven clubs, dropping the counties with the smallest crowd-appeal – Derbyshire, Essex, Northamptonshire, Somerset and Worcester. When it came into the open Northants made a counter-proposal, for a continued sixteen-strong championship, each playing everyone home and away in two-day matches, with an interchange of the bottom two with the top two of the Minor Counties. The ensuing debate engendered more heat than light, and was shelved when Harris made clear that MCC would countenance no change that didn't have the support of the vast majority of counties. It was agreed not make any changes until after 1917.

The whole thing must often have seemed academic to the stragglers in this caucus race. Derbyshire had looked like going under completely in 1910, which was cold and wet, and Lancashire as well as Yorkshire had lost heavily. In *Wisden*'s view Somerset had the 'best excuse for giving up the fight as hopeless, the supply of talent being so inadequate'. The great Sammy Woods was spent at last, the splendid professional Len Braund was past his best and the young amateur spin-bowler J. C. White was scarcely fledged. The vigorous rugby international John Daniell had more spirit and acumen than actual talent. They kept going somehow. Gloucester, too, in spite of the magnetic attraction of Jessop, and the solid support of some developing professionals like Alf Dipper and Charles Parker, were almost always in the bottom half of the table, and slithered perilously near to bankruptcy.

In *Wisden*, Pardon sketched the dilemma: county cricket was much more expensive than it used to be, what with winter pay and bonuses for professionals; probably too much was played, but there was

an obvious danger in cutting down programmes. With the busy agents of the Lancashire League always on the look-out for talent, committees cannot hope to

retain their professionals unless they ensure them a large amount of remunera-
tive employment.

He offered only one rather feeble suggestion:

> Annual subscriptions cannot very well be increased, but a good many people
> would, I should fancy, if the situation were brought clearly home to them, be
> willing to pay two guineas a year instead of one.

C. B. Fry, who saw cricket as 'a cult and a philosophy inexplicable to the
profanum vulgus', warned of 'the mob rule of spectators with little knowledge
of the game'. P. F. Warner more diplomatically explained the off-hand attitude of most county clubs towards the gate-money customers in *Badminton
Magazine* in 1912: 'County clubs naturally like to make ends meet, but they
are not possessed with an unholy idea that profit is everything and that the
game is nothing.'

Warner, we should note, was rapidly becoming the central figure in cricket,
doubly influential because of his extensive writing about the game. His
philosophy was proclaimed by the gaudy Harlequins cap, the élitist badge by
which Oxford men liked to be known, that he invariably wore – in bed, some
said – and by his encyclopaedic knowledge of every facet of the history and
current statistics of the game. The captaincy of Middlesex from 1908 gave
him a regular seat in the inner circle of MCC and, of course, greater prominence at Lord's. He improved his batting and leadership skills by assiduous
attention to detail and devoted his whole working life with the same astonishing single-mindedness to cricket, cricket politics and cricket writing.

The amiable 'Plum' was always available and it was an irony that when in
1911–12 he accepted MCC's invitation to tour Australia, after it was turned
down by C. B. Fry, he should fall ill and be obliged to hand over the reins to
the belligerent J. W. H. T. Douglas, who had a great triumph. Warner made
the most of the enforced rest by writing a book about the tour with a heartfelt
tribute to MCC in its regenerate role as Empire-builder:

> ... whither should the Empire turn for guidance but to the club which has
> grown up with the game, which has fostered it, and which has endeavoured to
> preserve its best traditions? And it is the wish of every true cricketer that the
> MCC should so continue to conduct its affairs that it may always remain not
> only the trustee but the mother of cricket.

But it was the reluctant mother of cricket's other unwanted child that
needed attention, particularly financial, now. In 1911–12 Middlesex, of
course, had less expenses than other counties through sharing Lord's with
MCC, and a healthy and well-heeled membership. But Worcestershire had
never made a profit since being admitted to the championship, and neither

Northants nor Gloucester would have been able to compete if there had been a 1915 season.

Even counties with good membership and a healthy attitude to gate-money, like Notts and Lancashire, were stretched, largely because of ambitious development schemes conceived in palmier days. There was a very heated annual meeting at Old Trafford in 1913, after their most unsuccessful season for a long time. The atmosphere had been soured by the captain, A. H. Hornby (son of old 'Monkey'), complaining about the committee in an inter-view with the *Manchester Guardian*, and in particular about a proposal to reduce the fixture list. A special sub-committee was appointed and after much deliberation an amicable solution was found, which involved Lords Derby and Ellesmere and the newspaper magnate Edward Hulton promising increased subscriptions for three years and a county-wide appeal for funds.

In those days, of course, clubs playing each other kept the whole profit from home games; occasionally a couple of the less fashionable counties might agree to aggregate the two fixtures, especially when one leg occurred at holiday times, but this never involved a whale and a minnow, so it contributed little to the sort of redistribution that might have made the cham-pionship a healthier cartel. Nor were there transfer fees, as in the despised Football League, to reduce the inequalities. Only the Test matches made any contribution to the general weal: gross receipts were shared with the tourists, and then after the host club had taken 20 per cent of the moiety (less expenses) plus stand receipts the remainder was shared amongst the counties and MCC. This, compared with their financial needs, was chicken-feed, but it helped reconcile some of the pundits to these colonial invasions, now distressingly frequent.

VI

The diehards were not convinced. Apart from the Australians' uncouth disre-gard for such valuable traditions as the distinction between Gentlemen and Players, their visits had long been thought by purists a distraction from the regular religious devotion that was due to 'the county'. The Triangular Tournament of 1912 was *a fortiori* thought 'likely to furnish a surfeit of unhealthy excitement, which would defeat the purpose of wholesome cricket among those who have its best interests at heart.'

The Times was gloomy about the prospects as the 1914 season began. It acknowledged that the fundamentals were still in place:

> Cricket as a game can never die while we have our public schools and our universities. It will be our national game for many years because the men who have played it and supported it [at these places] will wish their sons to do the same.

But after that there was a problem:

> Unfortunately at the present moment there does not seem to be the same 'county spirit' as there used to be. Perhaps it is owing to the fact that people have to work more than they did 20 years ago.

Perhaps it was, indeed.

It may be too melodramatic to say that county cricket was in crisis when the war came, yet only because its financial problems were not new but were built into the system and had been there since the beginning. By 1914 pressure to turn what was intended as a gentleman's pastime into a business had exposed the weaknesses of the system. The war did not cure them, but it put them on ice for a while, offering a theoretical opportunity for a fresh start in a new age. This was not taken – washed away, as we shall see, in post-war sport-hunger and waves of nostalgia – but it would be wrong to regard the war as a tiresome interruption of a highly successful enterprise, still less as the destroyer of a golden age.

The present generation's understanding of the Great War, as it used to be called, does not go much beyond the impression that it started suddenly on a Bank Holiday, that everybody thought it would be all over before Christmas and that they were proved horribly wrong by the subsequent four years of carnage in the trenches. What is generally forgotten is how popular the decision to go to war was. All the pent-up jingoism of the long years of European peace came bursting out: cheering crowds gathered in Trafalgar Square and Whitehall, waving Union Jacks and singing patriotic songs, or booed and hissed outside the German Embassy.

Beyond all this the cause was just. It was manifestly right that Britain should not rest secure under the navy's protective scarf but should stand by her allies and stop the Kaiser's bullying. It was, in H. G. Wells's phrase, 'the war that will end war'. Britain had no standing army, nor did she feel the need of one. Kitchener, the hero of Khartoum, was made War Minister and immediately undertook a recruiting campaign: volunteers flooded in faster than they could be trained or equipped. Kipling's poem spelled out the message:

> For all we have and are,
> For all our children's fate,
> Stand up and take the war,
> The Hun is at the gate!

And the rush to the colours was led by the sport-mad aristocracy he had excoriated a dozen years earlier. It was as if they knew their hour had sounded. This was a chance for a beleaguered class to show their worth to the nation, to fight for all they held dear. Now was the time to turn to the sterner game of war.

CHAPTER FOURTEEN

'Turn the Dark Clouds Inside Out'

KIPLING'S OWN SON, a keen footballer, was amongst the starry-eyed youngsters who left their public schools to serve the cause in fulfilment of their Newboltian destiny.[1] E. W. Hornung's son Oscar, captain of games at Eton, also joined up and wrote home from training camp expressing eagerness 'to have a plug at those blighters over the water'. To his uncle Conan Doyle he wrote perceptively: 'I am waiting to go off any night now – I am longing to go – it is a chance for us chaps, isn't it? It is the one good thing the war has done – to give public-school fellows a chance – they are the one class who are enjoying themselves in this war.' From the trenches he wrote comparing it 'to putting your left leg to the ball at cricket' or playing in a house match, '– only the odds are not so much against us here and we've more to back us up.' His father wrote some poignant verses the following spring, beginning:

> No Lord's this year: no silken lawns on which
> A dignified and dainty throng meanders.
> The Schools take guard upon a fierier pitch
> Somewhere in Flanders.

By early autumn Oscar was killed, leading his platoon.[2]

First-class cricketers in plenty also rushed to the colours, especially from the hunting set, like Lord Dalmeny and the young Hon. Lionel Tennyson, who recalled packing in 'feverish haste, so anxious was I not to run any chance of missing the war'. Reservists and regular soldiers naturally hastened to join their regiments: both captains, Sir Archie White and A. H. Hornby, together with Lancashire's Reggie Spooner withdrew from the Bank Holiday 'Roses' match. *The Times* stopped printing the cricket scores, but most counties continued their championship programme – Yorkshire played as many as seven more games – and W.G.'s stern letter to the *Sportsman* on August 27, declaring it not fitting

that able-bodied men should be playing day by day and pleasure-seekers look
on. There are so many who are young and able and are still hanging back. I
should like to see all first-class cricketers of a suitable age set a good example ...

still found a few deaf ears.

The 1915 championship was not officially abandoned until January and
that spring, with the casualty lists mounting, Surrey, whose ground had
already been commandeered by the military authorities, issued a statement
that

owing to the war, the cricket will be considerably interfered with in the coming
season. The County Championship will not take place, but in the event of the
war coming to an early conclusion it is hoped that some matches may be played
in July and August.

It was fortunate for the cricketing authorities that they eventually decided to
suspend operations. The amateur Rugby Union had responded at once to the
call, clubs were enlisting *en masse* and their gallant heroes were soon making
the headlines – Adrian Stoop, the England captain, winning a string of
medals; Edgar Mobbs, overage but raising his own sportsman's company and
setting the fashion for punting a rugger ball ahead of the attack; and most
telling of all, the golden boy Ronald Poulton-Palmer, killed by a sniper's
bullet.

Cricket's image was restored somewhat when MacLaren and Jessop, both in
their forties, were commissioned to assist in the recruiting drive, at which they
proved highly successful. 'Plum' Warner also got himself a war job, first at the
Inns of Court OTC then at the War Office as a staff captain, interviewing potential officers. And while Col. F. S. Jackson, a combatant soldier, was busy setting
up the 2/7th West Yorkshire Regiment and Sir Archie White was hunting for
Turks with the Royal Horse Artillery, Lord Hawke was making it clear to
Yorkshire professionals that 'a strict condition of their continued engagement'
would be participation in war-work. Kent also encouraged enlistment by
supplementing volunteers' services pay. The full force of public anger was
turned on the Football Association in a fierce newspaper debate before the
League programme dwindled away after the 1915 Cup Final. Racing also
deflected some of the moral indignation, as the turf authorities used all their
influence and ingenuity to resist inroads on their sport.

The least morally indignant were the servicemen themselves. All ranks
liked something to bet on, and soccer was the ordinary soldier's game, the
stuff of romanticised accounts of Christmas truces on the Western Front. But
cricket's wavering claim to be the 'national game' would have been questioned
by the very middle classes who supported it most strongly if the counties had
attempted to continue. The best-known front-line cricket story, the poet

Robert Graves's bizarre account in *Goodbye to All That*, involved no Germans and no English private soldiers either:

> 24 June, 1915, Versailles. This afternoon we had a cricket match, officers v. sergeants, in an enclosure between some houses out of observation from the enemy. Our front line is three-quarters of a mile away. I made top score, 24; the bat was a bit of a rafter, the ball a piece of rag tied with string; and the wicket a parrot-cage with the clean, dry corpse of a parrot inside. Machine gun fire broke up the match.

II

On the Home Front, meanwhile, the pavilions and administrative buildings at Lord's and various county grounds were soon being put to use accommodating army units and military hospitals. MCC staff gave up their spare time to making hay nets for horses, the essential military transport. There was still room for a few schools matches, one Lord's game, reported in *The Times*, attracting off-duty soldiers as spectators. MCC also played a fair number of schools matches – public schools, of course – and the schools themselves filled the gaps in their fixture lists left by clubs no longer operating by widening their social horizons. Nothing melodramatic from the outsider's viewpoint, perhaps, but Winchester 'who had for sixty years played only one other school – Eton – now arranged matches with Charterhouse, Wellington and Bradfield'. A fair number of regimental games were played at Lord's and at the Oval, whilst Crystal Palace staged a match between the Royal Naval Depot and the Sportsmen's Battalion, which included 'Patsy' Hendren of Middlesex and Hayes and Sandham of Surrey. Otherwise it was a barren scene for cricket-lovers. Its bleakness was exemplified in April 1915 by the suicide of Andrew Stoddart, for whom middle age, loss of purpose and gloom about the war had proved too much, and in November by the death of W.G., which seemed depressingly emblematic of the end of an era.

Club cricket, the staple of the south of England, virtually disappeared in any organised sense, though one or two clubs tried to carry on for a time against a rising tide of moral disapproval as the war news worsened. An additional worry was the mounting pressure to put playing fields to more utilitarian purposes, such as vegetable growing. In 1915 the sports journalist E. A. C. Thomson called a meeting of leading club cricketers to discuss ways of fending off the threat, and out of this grew the London Club Cricket Conference, with the aim, expressed at its first AGM in 1916, of fostering amateur cricket 'on non-competitive lines'. This article of faith, which lasted until after the Second World War, was stoutly maintained as conference membership spread beyond London throughout the south, and helped to widen the gap between the two sides of the great divide.

League cricket, meanwhile, had been torn between trying to carry on as usual, assisting the morale of munitions workers and others in vital reserved occupations who proliferated in the north, and incurring odium for indulging in 'unpatriotic' and frivolous activities at a time of national peril. Most scaled down their operations and ceased to employ professionals, at least officially. The notable exception was the Bradford League, which flourished as never before. The ball started rolling when the Saltaire club signed Sydney Barnes and drew enormous gates: others followed suit. The *Yorkshire Post* thought this 'out of harmony with the spirit of the times, directly opposed to the serious interests of the nation, and a melancholy response to the dominating and inexorable call'. But there was another inexorable call, that of the pound sterling, and soon every club was at it. Indeed the restrictions on numbers of professionals were lifted: Keighley had so many that some had to play in the second team. Most of the well-known players were northerners like Schofield Haigh, George Gunn, Cecil Parkin, Percy Holmes, Tom Wass, Ernest Tyldesley, the young Herbert Sutcliffe (playing as A. N. Other, apparently to conceal his movements from his CO) or exiles like Bill Hitch, but there were also illustrious southerners like J. W. Hearne, Charles Parker, Frank Woolley, and even the model professional, Jack Hobbs, who, with a wife and four children to support, worked in a munitions factory until he joined up in 1916.

That year saw the Easter Rising in Dublin as well as the depressing naval Battle of Jutland and the disaster of the Somme. By November the British army had lost 420,000 men. Conscription had been introduced, alarming Cardus, who did not approve of the war. His eyesight saved him the necessity of military service, and he drifted until he found a haven at the *Manchester Guardian*. Conscientious objectors were given a much harder time. Mrs Emmeline Pankhurst had taken her Women's Social and Political Union along the constructive and politically shrewd path of patriotic endeavour, and her members handed out white feathers on suspicion and carried placards that read 'Intern them all'. The war news got no better – amongst cricketers, the legendary Kenneth Hutchings and the promising Major Booth and Percy Jeeves were killed in action – but the public became inured to it and, seeing it was going to be a long haul, looked for some respite.

Warner, on sick leave and light duties, hit upon the idea of services charity matches at Lord's, involving Dominions teams and such English players as could be spared from their units, ranging from Private Hendren and Corporal J. T. Tyldesley to Lt-Col. J. W. H. T. Douglas. Two were held in 1917 – one of which was the last public appearance of Sergeant Colin Blythe before he was killed in action – and a further two in 1918, one of which was attended by the king. In 1917 *Wisden*, emboldened by Warner's experiment, flew a kite for the resumption of county cricket, citing a shift in public opinion since 1915, when the Surrey secretary had told him that he was going to put up the nets for members, but doubted if any would use them, fearing ribald remarks from 'men in tramcars'. County cricket, after all, unlike racing and the dreaded soccer, had voluntarily suspended operations, and now, with professional boxing and even billiards in full swing, it seemed 'as legitimate as any other recreation'. Perhaps it was, but, morality apart – and the bloodbath of Passchendaele was a reminder of the real world – logistically it was a non-starter.

Warner, nevertheless, was indefatigable in devising, and playing in, the one-day, and even two-day, substitutes that proliferated in the second half of the war: various charities and a lot of active servicemen's morale profited thereby. Apart from Lord's, other southern grounds, like Leyton, were active and as many as 119 services and schools games were played at Canterbury in 1917. The less time-consuming and frankly more popular soccer was now resuming in modified, regional fashion with plenty of under-the-counter payments for professionals in the North and in Scotland, so it was inevitable that in the hot summers of 1917 and 1918 professional cricket would prove irresistible to the sport-starved public. The leagues mainly benefited, but in 1917 a Yorkshire County XII played two-day games against both the Bradford League and a reinstated Yorkshire Council, when, amongst others, the young Maurice Leyland was tried out. The formula was repeated in 1918, and various other holiday games were played, at places like Scarborough and Harrogate. 'Exhibition' matches were played at the Oval and Folkestone as well as at Lord's.

In a further game [recorded H. S. Altham] between a representative schools side and an eleven raised by Captain Warner, Lord Harris delighted everyone by batting for half an hour when many half his age had been cheaply dismissed.

By this time, too, things were better organised behind the Western Front. The soldier whose job it was, during the intervals of actual fighting, 'to reconnoitre an area suitable for cricket, ask the farmer for permission to play, agree a rent and hire or borrow a roller' recalled it as a democratic business – 'On the field there was one rank only – acting private' – but the illustration he gives of this is the audacious shout of 'Run like hell!' from Captain F. H. Bateman-Champlain to his batting partner Major-General Sir Victor Couper, as if it were the bumpkin Lamborn addressing the Duke of Dorset. The only team selection problem was who to leave out: 'The universities, Eton, the counties and the big leagues were represented.' The impression is of a party for officers and a few of their batmen, still an essential requisite for every serving gentleman.

There is also the atmosphere of an old-boys' outing in Altham's account of the cricket at Etaples, 'where the old Essex player Charles McGahey looked after some very respectable matting wickets'. Amongst those playing in one match were 'Johnny Douglas, Nigel Haig, Dick Twining, Harry Longman, Donald Knight and poor Reggie Schwarz[3]'. They were all public-school men, three of them Etonians. A skewed sample of the population, perhaps, but then so was the sample that risked and lost their lives in the war. Britain lost nearly three-quarters of a million men, most of them very young indeed. A generation had been cut down and of them the finest – the first to volunteer, the fittest physically and the best educated. They were also the most privileged: one in five of titled families and of Oxford and Cambridge and public-school men gave their lives. A bigger proportion of officers than men were killed and of the most vulnerable category – junior officers, 35 per cent of whom died – most were public-school men.

Those who succeeded them were, almost by definition, less secure in their convictions and though some were rebellious and cynical none sought to change society through cricket or sought to change cricket itself. It was part of the England, Home and Beauty that we had fought for. And happily the structures were still in place and in better repair than anyone would have predicted or dared to hope. Indeed most county clubs benefited financially from the war, which had rescued them from the desperate straits they were in. The basic reason was simple: wage bills had shrunk (for instance, Surrey's ground staff went down from twenty-five to four), but a sizeable proportion of members had been persuaded to carry on paying their subscriptions as a sort of investment in hope for the future. Since the counties were supporting the war it seemed a patriotic duty.

The pattern was fairly constant regardless of playing standards. Warwickshire, who had been doing particularly well since their championship success, had lost £714 in 1914–15 because of the loss of gates in August, but by the following year they were back in credit, thanks to subscriptions of £1,105 and very limited outgoings. The income from subscriptions fell to £600 but this was still enough to cover expenses. Equally, Worcestershire, which had been facing closure, managed to make a modest profit in 1916–18, thanks to subscription income and additional appeals. Derbyshire, Hampshire, Leicestershire and Somerset cleared off most of their debts. Gloucestershire baled themselves out by selling their Bristol ground to Fry's for £10,000. Sussex improved their position marginally. Bigger clubs like Nottinghamshire and Lancashire that had overreached themselves with expensive development programmes emerged relatively unscathed: Lancashire's paid-up members stayed above 1,100 compared with 1,600 in 1914, whilst Notts, helped by a special appeal from the Duke of Portland, reduced their debts from £5,400 to £672. Yorkshire received over £5,500 in subscriptions during the war and the other 'Big Six' clubs, Surrey, Middlesex and Kent, kept their heads well above the water. Essex and Northamptonshire were the worst hit, but altogether it was a brighter picture and not one to encourage thoughts of radical change.

III

MCC were scarcely the organisation to encourage radicalism. Indeed they had more than a little difficulty in determining and contacting their membership. The worthy secretary, still F. E. Lacey, did his best, but it was 1922 before he felt able to tell the world what the score was. Meanwhile, the counties, still numbering sixteen,[4] had been considering all sorts of innovations, from shortening the boundaries and penalising teams for allowing maiden overs to limiting the number of professionals and excluding left-handers to enliven the proceedings. All were resisted and the general conclusion was that as little as possible should be changed for the 1919 season.

The editor of *Wisden*, commenting afterwards on the outcome, was confident that no more would be heard of such misguided schemes, adding:

> It is only right here to pay tribute to the steadfast confidence of Lord Harris. In the darkest days of the war he expressed his conviction that when peace came back cricket would have all its own charm for the English people. Everything he said was amply justified last summer.

And so it appeared. Despite admission charges being doubled to take account of the entertainments tax – introduced as a wartime measure – and the greatly increased cost of everything, gates had soared.

The only mistake seemed to have been in agreeing to an experiment with two-day matches, proposed by Warwickshire. The idea was to take advantage of the continued wartime 'daylight saving' scheme to play longer hours, thus attracting more after-work spectators and making it practical for more people to see entire games. The diehards were against it – MCC did not introduce it for their own matches, Gentlemen v. Players and Oxford v. Cambridge – and on the improved wickets in a dry season many matches were left drawn, so it was quickly abandoned. *Wisden* was delighted at this, remarking sarcastically that it 'overlooked the needs of the human stomach'. And once more conservatism seemed to be vindicated, for the crowds increased again in 1920.

It was in fact the sort of boom that comes after an artificial restriction of supply, and as wartime conditions relaxed and the euphoric, escapist mood took hold, the enormously increased demand for entertainment benefited all sports. The manpower shortage and the munitions drive had pushed wage levels up and most returning troops found little difficulty in finding jobs. By 1920 the cost of living was up by 75 per cent but the average wage-level – now £150 a year in industry, £120 in agriculture – had more than kept pace, whilst the standard working week was generally down to forty-eight hours. The return to peace was punctuated by strikes, the cost of repaying the war debt was going to be horrendous, the pressure to end wartime restrictions was irresistible, controls vanished almost overnight, the value of the pound plummeted – but in the short term there was plenty of money in circulation and everybody wanted a good time.

Revolutionary events in Russia had caused great alarm: Kipling warned against premature peace-making:

> God rest you, peaceful gentlemen, let nothing you dismay,
> But – leave your sports a little while – the dead are borne this way.

At first troops were sent to support the White Russian forces, but it seemed one sacrifice too many. Yet when they were withdrawn the fear of Bolshevism spreading to Britain – intensified by strikes and minor mutinies amongst troops waiting to be repatriated – was etched in the consciousness of the more entrenched of the establishment, not least, as we shall see, the steadfast Lord Harris. Lloyd George and his Government took constructive steps to counteract communistic tendencies: a mixture of gratitude for services rendered, electoral prudence and nervousness led to strong support for a spate of welfare legislation. The 1918 Education Act provided free compulsory schooling to the age of fourteen. Local authorities were required to draw up schemes for low-cost housing. The Unemployment Insurance Act of 1920 offered a modest contributory benefits scheme. They all suffered, in the event, for lack of money: but at least they had been thought about.

The fundamental problems of cricket remained unsolved because largely unaddressed. Overall the attendance figures were impressive. Yorkshire, the strongest county, which had had some 100,000 paying customers in 1914, had over 112,000 in 1919, nearly 200,000 in 1920 and 284,000 in 1921. At first the expansion was general: for example, Essex, threatened with extinction in 1914, attracted an estimated 80,000 in 1920, comparable to the very best years of the golden age, and reached 115,000 in 1921. But thereafter the old distinctions between rich and poor, never removed, were intensified. Whereas 7–8,000 had been a good gate at Lord's or the Oval before the war, now it was 20,000 and could go up to 30,000. Lancashire and Yorkshire also did well: a 'Roses' match at Sheffield drew 45,000. A more lasting, less volatile improvement in county finances came through increased membership: Yorkshire had reached 2,100 by 1920 and a massive 7,000 by 1924.

In the euphoric expansionist mood Glamorgan were accorded first-class status in 1921. *Wisden* bleakly recorded at the season's end that their promotion had not been justified by results: indeed it was only in 1924 that 'the county at last did something to justify its promotion' – five wins in the season. They played eight amateurs, selected from a range of variable quality, the best a young fast bowler called J. C. Clay who soon, in steadier mode, emerged as captain. They were assisted by the lucky accident of being number seventeen, the odd men out, and so were given the prestigious fixture of the current touring team on the August Bank Holiday weekend when everyone else played traditional opponents.

Everywhere it was the needs of the members, the desire for wall-to-wall cricket regardless of quality, that prevailed. In August 1919 *The Times*, in a leading article of concentrated nostalgic clichés, had summarised the case for reinstating the game in all its pre-war amplitude: the 'average Englishman' was a 'leisurely being', cricket was 'played in mean, dark streets where the wicket is a lamp-post ... on all our village greens and commons ... at all our schools, great and small' (poetic licence this last bit) and it was not understood by foreigners. Inevitably the writer put in a special plea for country-house cricket and the Canterbury week, with its 'house-parties at all the great houses in the neighbourhood', and ended, 'Its revival is a sign that all is well with our great game.'

Only one cloud disfigured the orthodox horizon – what *Wisden* called 'the menace of the Lancashire and Yorkshire Leagues'. The veteran Sidney Pardon made league cricket sound immoral, offering the pros better pay than they were getting from the counties: 'The temptation of more money for less work is very strong.' The novice Cardus also declared his hand, exuding equal measures of aesthetic disapproval and social snobbery in a report for the *Manchester Guardian* of a match between Oldham and Rochdale: 'The game was typical of league cricket through and through. For most people on the ground all that mattered apparently was cricket as a contest; there seemed little insistence on the game's artistic or spectacular charms,' adding, in a serious libel, 'Bad strokes were cheered just as lustily as good strokes.'

IV

As part of its contribution to post-war regeneration *The Times* had commissioned a long series of 'Cricket Reminiscences'. These were supplied by the facile pen of P. F. Warner, who shamelessly concluded the first one, under a cloak of anonymity,

> In that match 20 years ago Mr P. F. Warner played a faultless innings of 150, and only a few days ago he scored another century on his favourite ground.

Remarkably, Warner was still playing, aged forty-six. More remarkably still, in the following season he led Middlesex to their first championship since 1903. R. C. Robertson-Glasgow, the young Oxford and Somerset bowler, a man of unusual intelligence and wide interests, described his first encounter with him:

> Here he was in the flesh, bald as an ostrich-egg under his Harlequin cap, slight, small-boned, pale of face, and with nothing but cricket in his conversation.

W. G. Grace. This irreverent drawing by Max Beerbohm satirised W. G.'s domination of the game. The original caption read: 'Portrait of dear old W.G. – to the left is the Grand Stand; to the right the funeral of one of his patients.' (*MCC*)

Sir Pelham Warner. A pillar of the cricket establishment, on and off the field, Warner was also a prolific journalist. (*MCC*)

Arthur Shrewsbury, the greatest professional batsman of the era. When W.G. was asked who he would choose to open the innings with him, he allegedly replied: 'Give me Arthur.' (*MCC*)

STARS OF THE LATE VICTORIAN AND EDWARDIAN 'GOLDEN AGE'

(All photographs Norman Barrett Collection)

A. C. MacLaren

T. W. Hayward

K. S. Ranjitsinhji

C. B. Fry

The Hon. F. S. Jackson

G. L. Jessop

W. Rhodes

A. A. Lilley

B. J. T. Bosanquet

S. F. Barnes

T. Richardson

Hobbs and Sutcliffe, England's greatest opening partnership. (*MCC*)

Denis Compton, not only a great batsman, but an entertaining one. He had a fan club of film star proportions and was widely known as 'the Brylcreem boy'.
(*Norman Barrett Collection*)

A. V. Bedser, England's opening bowler in the decade following the war. He later became Chairman of the Selectors, and 'the first bowler to be knighted since Sir Francis Drake.' (*Hulton Getty*)

F. J. Titmus. As Fred Titmus walked to the wicket in an early game for Middlesex in 1949, a loudspeaker announced a correction to the printed score cards: '"F. J. Titmus" should read "Titmus, F. J."'. (*Hulton Getty*)

E. R. Dexter, whose imperious style and attacking batsmanship suggested a return of the Golden Age. 'Lord Ted' was less admired as a Chairman of Selectors. (*Hulton Getty*)

Middlesex were not, on paper, a particularly strong side. They had a few other Harlequins, Free Foresters and I Zingari caps – notably those of all-rounder Nigel Haig, hard-hitting F. T. Mann, and G. T. S. Stevens, who had sensationally played for the Gentlemen the previous year while still a school-boy – and first-rate professionals like Hearne, Hendren and the solid Harry Lee, and they had a willing new fast bowler in Jack Durston. But they lacked strength in depth and thus were greatly helped by the ludicrous arrangements that allowed them to play only twenty matches in the season, compared with Sussex, who played thirty. (Derbyshire played only eighteen, losing seven-teen, the other being rained off.) They squeezed home with a last-match, last-minute victory over Surrey, Jack Hobbs and all.

This was Warner's finest hour, but by no means his last. No sooner had he hung up his boots than he was splashing learned cricketing ink about, less anonymously than before. He was now the regular correspondent of the *Morning Post*, the stoutest pillar of respectability, and in 1921 he started his own periodical, the *Cricketer*, which was a sort of sporting equivalent. Its first issue made it clear that this was to be no alternative or rabble-rousing sheet: 'Cricket,' it announced, 'as Tom Brown has told us in the best of all school stories, is an institution and the habeas corpus of every boy of British birth.' It hoped to appeal specially to boys 'learning to play the game, in every sense of the word'.

The second carried a gushing review of Lord Harris's autobiography, which included a restatement of his pre-war views on the value of the distinc-tion between gentlemen and players and of conventions like calling the amateurs 'Mr' and the pros by surname only. Warner not only approved of this but put it into practice in his magazine in so thorough a fashion as to make its accounts of matches indigestible, as in this description of an historic over in the Nottingham Test of 1905:

Mr Noble and Mr Hill looked set for the day when Colonel Jackson went on to bowl. Off his first ball Mr Noble was caught at the wicket by Lilley; the fourth bowled Mr Hill; and the sixth saw Mr Darling taken high up at slip by Mr Bosanquet.

Warner introduced his regular contributors with the same punctilious concern to let it be known which dressing-room they came from:

Mr MacLaren, who will make a special feature of School Cricket ...; Mr Jessop ... the greatest genius that cricket has produced, Mr Knight ... one of the younger set [he was 35 and a war-veteran]; Mr Altham of Repton, Oxford and Hampshire ...; Mr G. N. Foster ... one of the great cricketing family; and Mr F. B. Wilson, a former captain of the Cambridge XI.

By the third issue, though, the surge of editorial power seems to have gone to his head to the extent of a long and detailed criticism of MCC for not fore-seeing and catering properly for the great crowds at the Lord's Test match – 'It is not pleasant to see women fainting in a crowd, and the authorities at Lord's cannot escape criticism' – and so forth, concluding with the injunction: 'The interest in cricket to-day is greater than it has ever been and the MCC must, in their own interests, move with the times.' The spluttering from the Long Room could be heard across at the Oval and for three days the offending publication was ordered off the shelves at Lord's: Warner there-after made ample amends for his unfortunate lapse.

The *Cricketer* had no more wish to move with the times than MCC, unless they could somehow have been put into reverse. But in fact, despite all the fond backward glances, post-war conditions powerfully accelerated the pace of social change, and blurred social divisions – munitions millionaires acquired peerages and ex-officers sold motor cars. Women had shown that they could do many jobs that were formerly masculine preserves, from medi-cine to driving, and hundreds of thousands of them, moving into factory work, had acquired a taste for the independence given by money of their own. There was a dramatic decline in the numbers going into domestic service. Women's war service had been recognised by giving them a vote – but only after thirty, by which time they might have acquired sufficient gravitas for the task. Many more people paid income tax, now risen to 6s. (30p) in the pound, and salary earners were now 22 per cent of the working population. The professions were in greater demand as living standards and welfare advanced, and administrators, clerks and shorthand typists proliferated as the tentacles of government, specialisation and bureaucracy continued to spread.

The better sort, and particularly the landed gentry, felt themselves hardest hit by the war, and even before that by Lloyd George. He had used wartime controls to keep rents down, and now in his post-war reconstruction the patrician landlords had been elbowed out. (One million acres were sold, mostly in parcels for owner-occupation: taxation and death duties were blamed, but land values were high as those enriched by the war moved up the social ladder. Many opulent new golf courses began to appear. So selling land had its compensations.) Still, no one could deny that he had got things moving in the war – including even generals' brains – as nobody else could have done. In doing so he had split the Liberal Party, and his wartime coali-tion had lost the support of the Labour Party.

He was elected in the 'Khaki Election' of 1918 with the support of the Tories, now rampant and triumphalist, who could otherwise have won every English seat. Labour's fifty-nine members became the official opposition. Parliamentary arithmetic was simplified by the refusal of Sinn Fein, who swept the board in southern Ireland, to take their seats. Their decision to set up their own assembly, however, kept Ireland at the centre of Westminster affairs. One way and another Lloyd George had his work cut out. But the

Empire was intact, and Britain had emerged from the war as the acknowledged leader of the western world, despite her war debts, which her American
allies seemed unsportingly keen on being repaid.

V

MCC and the *Cricketer*, that is to say Harris and Warner, both played their
part in preserving this natural order of things. Warner was first to show
awareness of the new Russian menace. England, under J. W. H. T. Douglas,
had just been trounced 5–0 on the first post-war tour of Australia, and when
Warwick Armstrong's tourists arrived the following year, complete with the
ultra-fast Gregory and McDonald, there was an inordinate delay in appointing a captain. In fact there was such a dearth of (axiomatically) amateur talent
that the fifty-year-old Fry was being canvassed. Warner made a ponderous
joke of the delay, assuring his readers that it was not

> a brilliant Bolshevik move on the part of the players ... to choose their own
> captain and play under him, or else loot the pavilion – any pavilion – seize the
> till, confiscate any portable property and burn the buildings.

Eventually the selectors settled for retaining Douglas for the first two
Tests. This cannot have been easy for them, for what Douglas lacked in
brains or cricketing ability he made up in aggression and a win-at-all costs
attitude that jarred on the nobler minds around headquarters. As captain of
Essex, a position his detractors said he owed to the fact that his father held the
lease on the Leyton ground, he was described by the old Etonian publisher,
gossipy journalist and cricket fanatic Sir Home Gordon as 'not only bad but
brutal, almost incredible in his ruthlessness'. Douglas's wartime experiences
had not mellowed him and he had several contretemps with the Australians,
the most notable of which puts ball-tampering in its true historical perspective. In his entertaining autobiography *10 for 66 and all that* the great
leg-spinner Arthur Mailey admitted (from the safe distance of 1958) that he
kept powdered resin in his pockets and that he surreptitiously lifted the seam
for Gregory and McDonald. Douglas discovered this and threatened to report
him – until Mailey pointed out that Douglas's own thumbnail was worn down
to the flesh.

(Another malefactor on that tour was the idiosyncratic Rockley Wilson,
who after captaining Cambridge and playing a few games for Yorkshire
around the turn of the century had devoted himself to coaching at
Winchester, emerging rarely. As a forty-one year old he had done well in the
August holidays of 1920, had caught desperate selectorial eyes and been
chosen for that winter's tour of Australia. Unfortunately, he had offended
both the Australians and MCC by criticising the umpires in the *Daily Express*,

giving rise to a celebrated sequel. Holding forth in the Long Room, Wilson broke off in full flight to raise his hat and greet Lord Harris, who frostily made a minimal movement towards his outstretched hand. 'Lucky to get a touch, really,' Wilson told his friends.)

The search for some new amateur leader having failed, the selectors turned back to Douglas, who was unable to provide the requisite magic, losing two more Tests. The reins were then handed over to the Hon. Lionel Tennyson, a hard-hitting batsman and even more forceful character, who set an example of courage in defeat, but not much else, as in all thirty players were tried in the five-match series. S. H. Pardon was withering about the selectors and very gloomy indeed about the state of English cricket:

> During all the years I have edited *Wisden* there has never been a season so disheartening ... England was not merely beaten but overwhelmed.

There were legitimate excuses for the performance – Hobbs and Hearne were injured or sick, for instance – but not much excuse for the hand-to-mouth amateurism of the selectors and their old-boy network, or for the rigidity and self-satisfaction of the county system, which had produced too few good young players and had taken three years to find this out.

The situation was not helped by MCC, reluctant and utterly unsuitable guardians of the game's fortunes, whose concern appeared to be with the arrangement of the deck-chairs rather than the icebergs piercing the vessel's hull. Worse was alleged in 1922, when Lord Harris, whose relentless pursuit of wrongdoers in the matter of residential qualifications was renowned, was accused of using his position at MCC to influence decisions in favour of his own county of Kent. There were two current instances. One concerned Mr Alfred Jeacocke, a leading amateur who was playing for Surrey, although, Kent claimed, his house was actually in Kent and only the other half of the street was in Surrey. The other case was that of a young professional, one W. R. Hammond, who because his soldier father had been stationed there, had been born in Kent, but had gone to school in Gloucestershire, who wanted him to play for them.

Harris's response appeared in the *Cricketer* under the remarkable heading 'EFFECTS OF BOLSHEVISM'. This was not a report on events in Russia but a denial of the foul slanders against him. 'The Kent Committee,' he began,

> does not conceive it to be its duty to hunt about the country for cases on suspicion, but where it knows the facts it does think itself bound in loyalty to its comrades the first-class counties, to ask for an enquiry through the Committee of the MCC.

It was not true that Kent had invited Jeacocke to leave Surrey and play for them instead. Hammond's case was more complicated:

> We know that he was born in Kent and that his *bona fide* residence was with his mother in Hampshire. His occasional residence at school in Gloucestershire was no qualification, for the counties had specifically barred such residence.

It was not only Gloucestershire partisans who felt that this self-righteousness, which delayed Hammond's progress by a year, was misplaced. Lord Deerhurst, president of Worcestershire, meeting Harris in the Long Room, was heard to say icily, 'May I congratulate Your Lordship on having buggered the career of another young cricketer.' But Harris had made clear what was at stake by his magisterial summary of the situation: 'Bolshevism is rampant and seeks to abolish all rules and this year cricket has not escaped its attack.' Extraordinarily, too, the flag-waving MacLaren, in a book subtitled *A Straight Talk To Young Players*, warned them against 'innovation', that is, unorthodox play and neglect of basic techniques, which he believed had led to England's thrashing by the Australians in 1921. The innovator, he declared, was 'the Bolshevist of the cricketing world' and it was 'about time that he was suppressed'.[5]

An irreverent visitor to the Oval in 1924 made fun of the revolutionary threat:

> On Monday we had several bad shocks to our sense of the solemnities of cricket. For example, we saw Fender, the Surrey captain, lead the 'gentlemen' members of his team to the professionals' quarters and bring his team out ... in a body, just for all the world as though they were all flesh and blood ... We felt that Bolshevism had invaded our sanctuary at last.

Warner, however, took it all with deadly seriousness. He was outraged when Cecil Parkin, Lancashire's effervescent off-spinner, wrote an article criticising the current England captain, the dashing A. E. R. Gilligan, of Cambridge University and Sussex. Gilligan (with his opening partner, Maurice Tate) had just routed the visiting South Africans in the first innings, but had let them off the hook in the second, Parkin reckoned, by not making proper use of him, a humiliating experience. 'I feel I should not be fair to myself,' he wrote, 'if I accepted an invitation to play in a future Test match.' ('Not that I expect to receive one,' he added, astutely.) Warner used the columns of the *Cricketer* to demand an apology from Parkin and action from Lancashire. Parkin was not one for apologies – he is said to have remarked to the fiery Douglas, a previous captain who opened the bowling, 'You bowl 'em in for an hour or so, then I'll bowl 'em out' – and Warner prophesied that 'the cricket world [would] regard him as the first cricketing Bolshevik and [would] have none of him'.

To his chagrin, the ensuing correspondence did not quite produce unanimous condemnation. Six Lancastrians complained of southern bias amongst the selectors. Worse, a Balliol man gave his view that the preference of Gilligan over Percy Fender, the Surrey captain, was due to petty jealousies between Lord's and the Oval and the public-school snobbishness 'current at the self-constituted headquarters of cricket'. Warner was highly indignant: 'We are pained and grieved that an Oxonian should be responsible for such biased ignorance and such wrong-headed and fantastic ideas.' The magic circle tightened to repel the attack. In the 1924–5 *Cricketer Annual* Lord Hawke disposed of the whole age-old North–South debate in less than a page, giving his personal assurance, backed up by a quotation from Lord Harris, that there was no prejudice: the main problem was a shortage of amateurs in the North, which led to a lack of enterprise. The climate also produced wet wickets and notable variations of temperament.

It was at that winter's Yorkshire county dinner that Hawke, perhaps tired and emotional, responded to the Bolshevik Parkin's suggestion in the *Weekly Dispatch* that Jack Hobbs should be made captain of the national side: 'Pray Heaven no professional may ever captain England!' he cried out. In a country that had experienced its first Labour government without civilisation collapsing this was a bit thick. Warner did the best he could in his defence, pointing out Hawke's great services to the pros and attempting (not very successfully) to explain it away: 'What no doubt Lord Hawke meant was that it will be a bad day for England when no amateur is fit to play for England.' This assumed, of course, that any amateur selected would take precedence over all professionals, but it sounded marginally better.

In any event, Warner put the blame squarely on Parkin 'pirouetting into the limelight'. He was at pains to assure his readers that he considered Parkin's remarks offensive, not because he was a professional – unthinkable – but because they were 'entirely contrary to the spirit of the best of games'. That settled, he pointed out that captaincy carried responsibilities off the field as well as on and 'these were better shouldered by an amateur than by a professional'. Poor Parkin, who had spent most of his early career in the leagues, was obliged to return. Lancashire, whose president, Sir Edwin Stockton, persuaded the *Weekly Dispatch* to print no more of his scurrilous articles, sacked him in 1926.

CHAPTER FIFTEEN

The Warner Tendency

BOLSHEVIKS WERE LURKING AROUND the political scene also, and it was a major task of the rising Labour Party to dissociate itself from such extremists, whether in Russia or in the tiny British Communist Party. Lloyd George had run into trouble over Ireland, offending both sides, and, once the post-war boom had evaporated, the recession had brought wage cuts and a series of strikes, and had set back welfare plans. The Tories took over, but internal dissension and the death of their leader, Bonar Law, left things in the hands of the ultimate party man, Stanley Baldwin. Faced with a growing problem of unemployment, Baldwin called an election to secure a mandate for protectionist measures, but failed, and in 1924 Ramsay MacDonald was invited to form Britain's first Labour Government.

The experiment with Socialism was brief and unsocialistic: the government brought in subsidies for council-house building and waved a flag for secondary education for all, but they clashed bitterly with the trade unions, threatening them with the wartime Emergency Powers Act to put down a wave of strikes. This show of responsible government won some support among the middle classes. So did Labour's enthusiastic support of new-style imperialism expressed in the highly successful British Empire Exhibition. But MacDonald was a dyed-in-the-wool pacifist and a strong supporter of the League of Nations, and his advocacy of reconciliation with the Germans was not popular. What finally cooked his goose, though, was the 'Red' scare: a deal with the Russians over their war debts precipitated an election, and the forged 'Zinoviev letter', supposedly Moscow urging British Communists to stir up a revolution, did the rest. The Tories got a huge majority, but Labour also got more votes than before, the Liberals were squeezed and the main battle-lines for the future were drawn.

There was a similar dichotomy in social and cultural life as Britain wavered on the brink of the modern world: Einstein versus Newton; Freud versus guilt; Marie Stopes versus the Church; the Jazz Age versus John Reith's BBC;

Eliot versus Yeats; Walton versus Elgar; the motor car versus the horse; Bloomsbury versus convention; gin versus sherry; the Prince of Wales versus George V; D. H. Lawrence versus Galsworthy; and many other movements and counter-movements stirred the surface of British teacups. But in spite of the widespread addiction to drink, gambling and tobacco, the nation maintained an outward appearance of respectability – even the football fans wore collars and ties – kept sex under wraps, and cared what the neighbours thought. And cricketers, amateur and professional, saw themselves as upholders of tradition rather than iconoclasts.

II

Nevertheless, the Parkin episode indicated the gulf between the polite, neo-feudal assumptions of MCC and the brash modernities of post-war Britain. The dream-world of county cricket, built in the image of a leisured class that no longer existed in sufficient numbers to pay for its pleasures, could not survive without taking on board alien values that it hated and tried to destroy. A notable feature of the 1920s was the shift of cricketing strength to the North. In part this indicated the sterner competitive edge required for survival in the post-war world; in part the infrastructure of local leagues in which young players could cut their teeth. After Middlesex's two victories in 1920 and 1921 no southern county won the championship until after the Second World War. Since the administrative, political and social power remained firmly in the south-east this made for even greater difficulties and resentments.

Yet the saga still had many years to run, for reasons not easy to explain. Why did the fortress of English first-class cricket remain inviolate when it was so manifestly in need of reform? The German Rudolf Kircher, who in 1928 wrote an admiring book about the British games cult, noted that if Englishmen were asked what was the most typical national game they said cricket, not because it was the most popular, but because it was 'preeminently English'. He was amazed to find great crowds at Lord's for matches lasting 'no less than three whole days', adding that: 'Anyone who is neither an Englishman nor a cricketer finds this slow-motion film tedious after half-an-hour.'

There was, of course, an element in Lord's matches that had more to do with fashion and the social round than cricket. At the Eton and Harrow match, as at Ascot, Henley or the newer-fangled Wimbledon, the best people went because it was the done thing. A. P. Herbert poked gentle, rather snobbish, rather xenophobic British fun at it in the now-respectable *Punch* of 1923:

> I love Lord's. I love Eton and Harrow. I love the sunny green, the happy crowds, the coaches, the frocks, the pretty ladies, the grey top-hats, the

cultured talk ... I love to feel that this is England, this is the national game, a manly, dangerous game, and I think with pity of the effeminate dagoes who can only play pelota, basket-ball and lawn-tennis.

As for the actual match,

> The wicket was 'plumb', the batting orthodox, and if there is anything more boring than orthodox batting on a 'plumb' wicket I suppose it is professional billiards.[1]

Conversely, in serious cricket circles spectators' views were not considered important. After the miseries of 1921 a contributor to the *Cricketer* grumbled that too much was made of what 'the crowd' thought: 'the crowd which so often applauds the wrong thing, and, time after time, exhibits complete ignorance of the laws and usages of the game'. This view may have been emotionally satisfying to élitists, but it was not one likely to relieve the chronic financial problems of the strugglers in the county championship. Fred Root, of Worcestershire, who had played in the leagues in 1919–20 while qualifying, and then returned at the end of his county career, wrote of the Lancashire League: 'Crowds are large and the knowledge of the people who make up those crowds is quite exceptional.'

It caused a great stir when in 1921 the fast bowler Ted McDonald signed for Nelson, a struggling Lancashire League club, while he was over with the victorious Australians. He, too, it turned out, was qualifying for a county – Lancashire – but meanwhile it proved a great boost not only to Nelson but to attendances wherever he went. Nevertheless, whether from financial caution in uncertain times or shortage of available stars, the other clubs were not yet ready to follow Nelson's lead. Although Nelson, when McDonald left in 1925, signed the South African tourist J. M. Blanckenberg as a replacement, they were still unique.

Few leading English professionals wanted to follow the example of Sydney Barnes, who was still playing in the leagues. Jack Hobbs, writing in 1924, was uncomplimentary:

> The standard of play is on the whole not very high; a side may have a couple of good bowlers and two or three decent batsmen, but the teams are no better than those fielded by good class clubs in London.

Hobbs was, of course, writing about the Bradford League in wartime, and he was in any event very much an establishment man by temperament – essentially a non-industrial southern working-class type who just happened to be the best batsman in the world.

But the very different, brash northerner Cecil Parkin also made similar comments based on his own extensive experience of the two spheres: 'League cricket is not in the same street as county cricket: it is not the same game.' Some of the differences would appear to be an advantage to bowlers: 'From the bowler's point of view ... it is ten times easier to get wickets in the league ... For one thing the pitches are not perfect ...'. Yet for the eighteen-year-old pit-boy Harold Larwood, recruited to Nottinghamshire as a probationer in 1923, the glamour of the first-class game weighed far more than the prospect of toiling on heavily marled wickets. His heroes, Joe Hardstaff, 'Dodge' Whysall and Sam Staples, had all worked at local pits, and Trent Bridge was like a cathedral to a curate. As for Lord's, that was 'the Holy of Holies'.

For batsmen, around whom the game was constructed, the county game was a professional necessity. As Cecil Parkin said,

> the pace league cricket is played at gives a batsman little or no chance of playing himself in ... A league club has no use for the batsman who, like the county cricketer, can only score from loose bowling.

Hobbs, too, had pointed out the disadvantages for batsmen – 'The average duration of play is from 2.30 until 7.' The question remains whether there was not room for compromise between four-and-a-half hours and three days. And had paying customers at the turnstiles been the only consideration no doubt some accommodation would have been arranged. Yet in fact the gap was to grow wider, as the money-spinning Test matches came more and more into the reckoning and the counties were given a further lease of life.

III

Reconciliation between crowd-pleasing and fulfilling the self-sufficient aims of the first-class game was, ironically, easier in the North, where winning was acknowledged to be the main purpose of cricket at this level: spectators accepted a certain amount of boredom as part of the deal. Perhaps Old Trafford members were more fastidious about what strokes they applauded than the folk who watched Haslingden or Rochdale, but they certainly needed powers of endurance, especially in 'Roses' matches, in which not losing was of paramount importance.

On these occasions, it was said, if Lancashire won the toss and were batting, the senior pro, Harry Makepeace, would say, 'Now, lads, it's a grand wicket, no fours before lunch,' and Charlie Hallows and Frank Watson, who opened, needed no such admonitions. Yorkshire had uncharacteristically brisk openers in Holmes and Sutcliffe, but even they were careful not to risk the lash of Wilfred Rhodes's tongue by cutting too early in the day – 'It never were a business stroke' – and if they failed, the next man in was Edgar Oldroyd, who had raised obduracy to an art independent of outward events.

And the bowling, now headed by Abe Waddington and the bleakly hostile George Macaulay, operated under Rhodes's guiding principle – 'Give 'em nowt.'

Viewed from St John's Wood, ethnic inferiority began at Watford, so the inter-war years, in which Middlesex's two championships in 1920 and 1921 were the South's sole successes, were laid waste by an undifferentiated northern mass, but there were perceptible differences. Yorkshire members, and Yorkshire crowds in general, and even the non-cricketing general Yorkshire public, were at one with their team in believing that it was their mission to secure the Holy Grail and to protect it in perfect purity from infidel hands. They had won the championship in 1919, and then, after Middlesex's rude intervention, won it again in 1922, 1923, 1924 and 1925. It had come to seem part of the natural order of things, and it was a trying time when Lancashire prevailed in 1926, 1927 and 1928, an impious assault led by Macdonald, who took over 400 wickets.

Yorkshire, all of whose players were native-born, naturally looked askance at this colonial importation: Emmott Robinson, a quintessential Eboracian, made a point of referring to him as 'a Tas-maaa-nian' to emphasise the diabolical liberty being taken. Emmott had come into the side after the war at the age of thirty-six and stayed twelve years before retiring. It is hard to resist the feeling that the supremacy of inter-war batsmen must have been increased not only by the plumb wickets but by the long-toothed nature of the fielders. Emmott, however, was a renowned cover-point, and made up in will to win what he lacked in youthful pace.

Neville Cardus, whose imaginative flights of nostalgia-laden prose were now in vogue, developed also a compensating comic strain in the ancient tradition of 'Bring on the clowns': north-country professionals, being readiest to hand and least reticent, were his favourite subjects, and Emmott Robinson was foremost among them. This is how he saw him:

> He had shrewd eyes, a hatchet face and grey hairs, most of them representing appeals that had gone against him for leg-before-wicket. I imagine that he was created one day by God scooping up the nearest acre of Yorkshire soil at hand, then breathing into it saying, 'Now lad, tha's called Emmott Robinson and tha can go on with new ball at t' pavilion end.' ... He had no time for the flashing bat school, 'brighter cricket' and all such nonsense. He dismissed it with one good word: 'Swash-buckle,' he called it.

Emmott hadn't much time for the wearers of fancy caps, either, a characteristic shared by most Yorkshire folk, and illustrated in a story they like to tell about themselves. Emmott was on duty in a warm-up game against one of the universities. An elegant young fellow came in, elaborately took guard, surveyed the field and carefully adjusted gloves, cravat and gaily coloured cap. Emmott, unimpressed, shuffled up to the wicket, turned his arm over and clean bowled him. As he passed Emmott on his way out the young man said, 'Jolly good ball, sir!' and Emmott replied, 'Aye, lad: it were wasted on thee.'[2]

After the semi-retirement of the fifty-year-old George Hirst in 1921, Robinson became a sort of deputy-sage to Wilfred Rhodes, who was in charge at Yorkshire whatever amateur was officially captain. As Wilfred matured – he went on until 1930, when he was fifty-three – and the captains came and went, the stories multiplied. A favourite one had it that Emmott, encountering the current incumbent taking a stroll around the ground during the luncheon interval, quietly said to him. 'You'd better come in now, sir. Wilfred's declared.' And Bill Bowes, of the incoming generation, revealed in Rhodes's obituary that when he once asked him about 'a famous England captain', 'Was he good?' Rhodes replied, 'Yes, Bill, very good. He allus did as he wor told.'

At the head of that incoming generation was Herbert Sutcliffe. He developed from the 'debonair and powerful' strokemaker R. C. Robertson-Glasgow played against in 1919 to the serene and commanding figure who formed with Hobbs the most famous opening partnership England ever had, and with Holmes a record-breaking one for Yorkshire. Sutcliffe, the orphaned son of a publican, was not your average working man, for he had left the army with a commission and he brought the qualities that had got him there to bear on his life as a professional cricketer. He was always immaculately turned out, carrying a small suitcase as well as his cricket bag so that his flannels could keep their creases. His glossy black hair was always well groomed, never ruffled, and he batted in the same imperturbable way.

As Robertson-Glasgow said of Sutcliffe in his maturity:

He sets himself the highest available standards of batting and deportment. His physical discipline equals his mental, shown in the cool clear eye and the muscularity of frame. If he is bowled he appears to regard the event less as a human miscalculation than as some temporary, and reprehensible, lapse of natural laws.

Others were less generous. Another Oxford man, I. A. R. Peebles, a protégé of P. F. Warner at Middlesex, whilst praising Sutcliffe's batting, was clearly affronted by his pretensions:

He emerged from the First World War an officer, convinced that he could take his place in any society, and to this end took pains to acquire the accents of Mayfair and Oxford. This attracted a certain amount of ridicule, which might have disconcerted a lesser man, but, his mind made up, he was not to be deflected.

Cardus, who already in 1923 was bemoaning the demise of the cricketer-artist of the golden age and the arrival of canny utilitarianism, also took exception to Sutcliffe's speaking not 'with the accents of Yorkshire but of Teddington'. He saw the advent of the likes of Sutcliffe and Hammond with their Savile Row suits as the sign of the imminent collapse of the old feudal order. 'The county cricketer,' he wrote, 'has in certain instances become a man of bourgeois profession.' This he clearly resented, and perhaps, as he implied, so did some of the old hands in the Yorkshire dressing-room. But to at least one of the younger men, Bill Bowes, himself a grammar-school boy – a type more frequently to be found in the professional ranks as the educational reforms began to take hold – Sutcliffe was a hero:

> There was something in his walk, his carriage that compelled attention. Here was no ordinary man ... And professionalism was very important to him.

In a graphic description of what was going on, Sutcliffe himself told Bowes:

> Lord Hawke lifted professional cricket from there to there [raising his hand from knee to shoulder level] and even Lord Hawke always wanted it back again.

He could never get it back, of course. George Hirst and Wilfred Rhodes were content on retirement to coach at public schools[3] in the old fashion, whereas Sutcliffe became so successful that he sent his own son to a public school. But Cardus's complaints that feudal civilisation was collapsing were misguided (as well as mean-spirited). Sutcliffe, Hammond and the like were not trying to overthrow the establishment, but to join it.

IV

The Bolshevik menace had, in any event, been held at bay on the wider political scene. With the Tories back in power there was a feeling that the Empire was in safer hands, and the flow of cheap imports helped strengthen the sentiment that bound these distant parts to the mother country. But in fact the imperial tide had already turned: the family was growing up, with the usual results. In 1926 the increasing maturity of the (white) Dominions was recognised by making their Parliaments accountable only to the Crown, a largely symbolic relationship, and developing and managing the smaller colonies and mandated territories became the main task of the vast army of young men deployed around the globe cultivating a proper sporting spirit. In India the old Raj remained in place, despite warning signals.

But the tide seemed to be turning in other ways, mostly to British advantage. Emigration had halved. The population growth had slowed, probably assisted by birth control and women's marginally greater independence, and better nutrition and medical advances brought a general improvement in health. The 1918 Education Act, seeking to learn the lessons of the war, had authorised local authorities to provide 'facilities for social and physical training', but money had been scarce and priority in state education had gone elsewhere than playing fields. Public-school boys played games; elementary-school lads did drill and played their cricket and football in the multitude of Sunday School and similar leagues and competitions. By the late 1920s, however, there were signs of progress.

It began, as these things tended to do, from top down, amongst the lower middle classes. Overlapping the upper forms of the elementary schools were secondary grammar schools, church and local authority, provided or subsidised by the state. They charged modest fees, but as a condition of subsidy had to offer at least 25 per cent 'free places' to children from the elementary schools. Increasing numbers in these schools stayed on to fifteen or sixteen, and a few went on to universities, particularly the new provincial ones. The Hadow Report of 1926 recommended that all pupils should transfer at eleven to secondary schools, either the existing grammar schools or new technical or 'modern' schools. This won all-party support and was gradually implemented as funds allowed.

These fluctuated, but by the mid-1920s were becoming more plentiful as industry picked up. Pre-war production levels had already been reached in spite of shorter working hours and went on improving. Jobs were again becoming easier to find, and though prices were twice pre-war levels wages were three times as high. Income-tax was reduced to 4s. (20p) in the pound. Promising new industries – motor vehicles, light engineering, electricity – were developing, particularly in the South.

The trouble came from the old heavy industries, now facing decline. They were not helped by the Government's success in restoring the value of the pound back to parity with the gold standard, a hallowed mark of respectability but ruinous in its effect on the export market. Baldwin thought the solution was to reduce wages to make the older industries more competitive. The price of coal affected them all. The million-strong mining industry, which had done wonders in the war, but was now kept going by government subsidy, had been allowed a wage increase by the Labour Government and now found the market flooded by cheap East European coal. Hence the General Strike of 1926, backed by railway, gas, electricity, engineering and printing workers for nine muscle-flexing days, with miners struggling on alone for six more months before being forced to go back to work, accepting longer hours and lower wages.

Industrially and economically the recovery was swift, with new legislation to prevent a recurrence and voluntary consultative machinery aimed at improving relations between the two sides of industry. The Unions had burned their fingers; Communist Party membership fell still further. Production reached record heights in 1928 and the cost of living fell by 15 per cent. Industry was helped by a de-rating scheme, and unemployment fell. Local authority welfare services – public assistance and housing schemes – were standardised and improved. The euphoric mood even led to a lowering of the voting age for women from thirty to twenty-one. Sun-bathing, camping, rambling, the slimming vogue, flimsy clothes, the 'talkies', 'the dogs' and the BBC Dance Orchestra (leader Jack Payne) were further signs that Britain was beginning to enjoy itself.

V

For P. F. Warner 1926 was not the year of the General Strike, but the year in which he achieved another ambition: becoming chairman of selectors. As he was still daily plying his trade as a journalist it was, as he put it, 'urged in certain quarters that a member of the committee should not be allowed to write'. He, naturally, did not agree. His views, set out – at some length – in his book, *Cricket Between Two Wars*, seem to boil down to saying that there could be a problem, but not if the writer concerned was P. F. Warner:

> A Test Match to-day is an Imperial event. Almost every ball is broadcast to the uttermost ends of the earth, but you must get the right men to do the chronicling – men who are imbued with a genuine love of the game and a respect for its traditions.

The Board of Control did indeed impose a ban after Warner's disastrous spell of office and 'sacking', and this prevented his early return. Meanwhile the gentlemanly honour code, in which Warner so fervently believed, became even more frayed at the edges.

The context was one in which England had won only one of her last fifteen Test matches against Australia, but true believers had taken hope from the marginally better performance on the latest tour under A. E. R. Gilligan. Gilligan himself had little to do with it, the decisive factors being Macdonald's absence for Australia, and the blossoming of Maurice Tate, the supreme medium-pacer, for England. And as George Hirst had sensibly said, in his retirement speech in 1921, 'Cricket goes in cycles. Australia, within a few years, will meet the same treatment as England suffered this year.'

However, MCC and Warner were convinced that inspirational amateur leadership could hurry things along.[4]

Their first choice was A. W. Carr, an old-fashioned blood-and-thunder, huntin' type, who had led Nottinghamshire, still a good side, shrewdly and forcefully since the war. Warner, Carr afterwards noted, expressed complete confidence in him, a gesture that modern soccer managers have come to fear from their chairmen, but in those innocent days was taken at face value. The first Test was washed out after fifty minutes, but Carr was soon in doubt about Warner's sincerity, for as he wrote in his bitter account, *Cricket With the Lid Off*, 'I never really had a free hand. I was constantly being advised to do this or that.' In particular he is very clear that the controversial decision to declare in the second Test, with England 475 for 3 in reply to Australia's 383, was not his: 'P. F. Warner told me to declare the innings closed.' Warner's version, in his book, was neatly exculpatory:

> Carr was criticised for his action, but he knew what the critics did not know, that neither Bardsley nor Taylor was able to bat.

The match, in the event, was drawn, and Carr was reprieved. He got in trouble again in the third Test. The weather had been wet and Carr decided to put the Australians in. He took advice, listened to the groundsman, and, he adds, 'certainly Warner was determined in that opinion'. The plan misfired. Bardsley was out early, and Macartney should have been, but Carr, having set a trap for him, dropped an easy catch and Macartney went on to make 151 of Australia's 494. England managed to draw, but Carr's judgement was blasted by experts gifted with hindsight.[5] However, the *Daily Express* demanded to know on behalf of the public whether 'the captain of England was exercising his unfettered judgement or was carrying out a policy dictated by the Selection Committee'. Warner's account again has no mention of his own role, but makes an elaborate defence of the decision.

In the fourth Test, again ruined by rain, Carr was afflicted by tonsillitis, and Hobbs took over as captain – proving, said Warner, 'a good leader, the side working happily under him'. It was no surprise – except to Carr – that he was replaced as captain for the final Test, but the manner of it infuriated him. He was still seething nine years later when he came to write his angry memoirs, surprising stuff from an Old Etonian, and saying little for the amateur spirit that imbued the corridors of power. In essence Carr complained that Warner stabbed him in the back without warning and then wrote him a long and hypocritical letter full of things like, 'I believe I feel it almost as much as you do', 'take it in the grand manner' and 'your giving up your place will give you an even greater hold, if such is possible, on the affections of the cricket world'.

Warner's choice to replace him was A. P. F. Chapman, a young Kent player of whom the conventional descriptions by his admirers were 'debonair', 'golden boy', 'charismatic', 'colourful', 'gay' (old-style), a 'free-hitting batsman', a 'magnificent fielder', but whose captaincy was admitted to be 'not of the intellectual or subtle school'. But this was the match in which, famously, forty-nine-year-old Wilfred Rhodes was brought back; he not only bowled magnificently but presumably did the thinking for Chapman, who 'did as he wor told': England won back the Ashes and the national honour was saved. Ironically, although the country was elated, and MCC rewarded

Warner with the captaincy of an all-amateur tour of the West Indies, the Board of Control were not impressed by his selectorial work and threw him and his committee out. Warner made a great show of 'no hurt feelings', but he noted 'the opinion of many' that he 'had had something of a raw deal'.

Many others were mystified as to why Chapman had been brought in over the heads of vastly more experienced and talented professionals. But none of the establishment shared that view: even Carr was not in favour of Hobbs. Actually it seems highly unlikely that Hobbs would have accepted, even if asked, for he was too humble and too circumspect to step out of his allotted place. According to Bill Bowes, however, Sutcliffe believed strongly that Hobbs should have been captain. Sutcliffe himself does not appear to have had captaincy aspirations, not only out of disdain for 'shamateurism', which would have been a possible route to the England job, but perhaps because he did not want to take on anything that would interfere with his batting and his business interests.

Certainly there was a curious episode early in 1928, when, on tour in South Africa, he received an oddly phrased but friendly letter from F. C. Toone, the secretary of Yorkshire, currently seeking a replacement for Major Lupton. It read:

> Dear Herbert, At the Committee meeting yesterday you were appointed Captain without your status being altered. It is hoped that this will be agreeable to you and that you will accept the same and will be happy and successful in your new and honoured position.

Sutcliffe replied by cable, not to Toone but to Lord Hawke: 'Official invitation received yesterday. Great honour. Regret to decline. Willing to play under any captain elected.' And so William Worsley, later Sir William, distinguished socially but under-engined as a cricketer, took the helm.

VI

MCC, for their part, appointed various amateur England captains over the next few years as the Imperial circle widened. Captain R. T. Stanyforth, who had played no county matches, was perhaps the most unusual, but A. H. H. Gilligan, whose chief claim seems to have been that he was A. E. R.'s brother, and the Hon. F. S. G. Calthorpe were both men who only played in Tests as captain. The professional stars – who now included Geary, Hammond, Larwood and Leyland as well as the established Woolley, Hobbs, Sutcliffe, Tate and Hendren – carried the burden, whoever commanded them.

South Africa, West Indies, New Zealand and, later, India were for the most part easy victims. Australia was the real test – and also the source of repeated post-war humiliations. The 1926 victory had brought back some of the old arrogance and whereas the Australians were reported as 'even in the moment of defeat ... generously glad of it' and 'good for the game "at home"', England could stop pretending for a while. There was no longer any need to cultivate the unnatural art of losing gracefully, and instead there grew a determination not to let the advantage slip. *The Times* published a semi-jocular but penetrating leading article 'On being a good hater', asking, 'Do they not begin to say "May the best man win" when they have lost their stomach for the fight and are tolerably sure that their own side is going to be beaten?'

This was inspired by the 1927 Eton v. Harrow match and it was from the vast reserves of aristocratic aggression, now restored after wartime losses, that revival was fuelled. As if to remind the nation how and why she had won the war and where it was being carried on, in 1928 Sir Henry Newbolt issued a new version of his old battle-cry:

> Our countrymen of England who winter here at ease
> And send abroad their cricketers to fight across the seas

adding, however, a prudential rider,

> They long to win the rubber, but inwardly they know
> The game's the game: howe'er the luck may go.

The fiction was exposed by Chapman's troops in Australia that winter. By then the custom was to play six-, seven- or even eight-day matches in the hope of getting a finish on the bone-hard pitches, on which mammoth scores were compiled. A twenty-year-old Australian called Donald Bradman described his first experience of Test cricket under the gay and debonair Chapman: 'England, though leading by nearly 400, went in again and left us over 700 to attempt in our last innings with two men out of action.' One can see how that sort of thing might leave an impression on a fresh young mind, and if Bradman had been a reader of Newbolt hitherto he chucked the book away. He was also irked by the rather lofty comments of P. G. H. Fender, the Surrey captain, covering the tour for the press. In his column and a subsequent book Fender had criticised him as brilliant but unsound and 'unwilling to learn'.

There was an even less chivalrous amateur amongst Chapman's men, Douglas Jardine. Born in 1900, Jardine had been just too young to serve in the war and was all the more aggressive for it. Sired in Bombay of a cricketing lawyer father, he was steeped in the traditions of Lord Harris, whose views on colonial development and colonials and whose treatment at the hands of Australians he had learned and absorbed at his parent's knee. Brought up and schooled at Oxford, Winchester and Oxford again, Jardine was a steely, less ambivalent version of Warner, Harlequin cap and all. His own, sour experience of Australians began in 1921 when he was left on 96 not out by Warwick

Armstrong's insistence on a two-day game in order to give them a rest day before the Tests.

Jardine apart, there was still strong antipathy to Australians in English amateur circles over their role and status in the ludicrous 'Gentlemen and Players' conventions. The superior newspapers still punctiliously wrote things like: 'Larwood, Tate, Geary and Mr Stevens all bowled well. Larwood, in particular, rendered valuable service by getting rid of Mr Woodfull and Mr Macartney.' And in the mid-1930s A. W. Carr was indignant that although to them 'cricket was more or less a matter of £.s.d.', Australians 'were made a great fuss of and given privileges denied to our own professionals', adding, to show how broad-minded he was:

> I know plenty of professionals whom I would delight to have as guests in my own home, but I am afraid I cannot say the same thing about many of the Australians I have met.

Similarly, Jack Fingleton, Test batsman and political correspondent, wrote that in 1928.

> Jardine's flannels had barely emerged from their first laundering before he made up his mind that he liked neither Australia nor the average Australian.

He reckoned that Jardine, with his Harlequin cap and silk cravat, aloof air and stately walk, was God's gift to barrackers: 'Where's your butler to carry your bat?' they yelled as he came in, and when he swatted flies someone called out, 'Don't kill 'em, they're the only friends you've got!' Jardine's own supercilious summary was:

> To take the most charitable view of the position the behaviour of Australian crowds at its best, when judged by the standards accepted by the rest of the world, is not naturally good.

As to barrackers,

> Here was Democracy arrogating to itself the right to demand in full a pound of flesh for which it had paid the princely sum of a shilling or two at the gate.

Yet this was the man chosen eighteen months ahead of time as captain for the 1932–3 Australian tour.

VII

Democracy, outside MCC circles, was coming more into the picture in England. With both the Liberal and Conservative parties split over economic policy, Ramsay MacDonald found himself in office – though again heading a minority Labour government powerless to practise Socialism. However, by now pacifism was more fashionable, with Churchill, the only senior politician warning of the dangers of 'world disarmament', crying in the wilderness. MacDonald's starry-eyed support for the League of Nations, his wooing of the United States and his loosening of the ties of Empire – again with only Churchill dissenting – were widely supported. This last policy was a hit-and-miss affair. The 1931 Statute of Westminster, proposing a Commonwealth of freely co-operating nations, did not bring unity. The Irish Free State used it as a loophole to escape and the Boers to develop apartheid. Mahatma Gandhi was brought from prison to confer in London but proved unshakeable. Even in the white Dominions, where it worked best, the old ties of blood and sentiment had to contend with economic self-determination.

One of them soon had to contend with Jardine. When he heard of his appointment, Rockley Wilson, who remembered Jardine vividly as captain of Winchester, said, 'Well, we shall win the Ashes, but we may lose a Dominion.' But Warner, reinstated as chairman of selectors, and Lord Hawke, chairman of MCC cricket committee, who joined them, were not in the habit of exercising their minds on such profundities. They were, in any case, not the initiators of events, but simply caught up in things they only dimly understood – victims of the *Zeitgeist*, as Albert Knight might have charitably observed.

At one level the advent of the Bradman era signalled the coming-of-age of a nation, inspired by a new hero, shaking off colonial shackles by, literally, beating their old masters at their own game; but this was a young hero of quite exceptional analytical powers, with the post-war social aplomb of the commercially successful. MCC, at the receiving end of this assault, reacted predictably, deploying its professional troops under a patrician leader – post-war variety – in defence of the established caste system. After Chapman's tour, when Hobbs, Sutcliffe and above all the magnificent Hammond had ground their opponents into the dust, it was Australia's turn in 1930. Where Hammond had scored two double centuries in successive Tests, Bradman followed his first double hundred with an astonishing 334 not out.

Warner was appointed early in 1931 for the precise purpose of picking a squad to win back the Ashes in 1932–3. Chapman was abandoned and the hard man Jardine was appointed captain at once for the 'warm-up' Tests in 1931 and 1932 against India, and joined the selectors. There were also two Test trial matches before the Australian trip – all of this indicating remarkable care. The selectors were anxious, on Warner's own account, to have 'the right type of bowlers for Australia', but his only amplification is to say that Verity, the Yorkshire slow left-armer, was to be the 'end-holder'. He afterwards tried to give the impression that the way his fast bowlers bowled – at the batsmen's body – came as an unpleasant surprise to him, but he was undoubtedly fully aware of what they were capable when choosing them. Larwood and his left-armed partner Voce were known to practise what was euphemistically known as 'leg theory' for their hairy-chested skipper, A. W. Carr. As for Bill Bowes, on 22 August Warner, writing for the *Morning Post*, sanctimoniously declared,

> Bowes bowled with five men on the onside, and sent down several very short-pitched balls which repeatedly bounced head high and more. Now that is not bowling, indeed it is not cricket, and if all the fast bowlers were to adopt his methods MCC would be compelled to step in and penalise the bowler who bowled the ball less than half-way up the pitch.

Yet shortly afterwards Bowes was added to the touring party.

Warner had certainly known all about Jardine, writing approvingly, 'The coming tour appeared to him in the light of a crusade.' And the main purpose of Jardine's intimidatory tactics was to try to nullify the threat of Bradman. His plan had been formulated years earlier:

> Though I did not take part in the Oval Test match of 1930 I have been told that Bradman's innings, impressive though it was in the number of runs scored, was far from convincing on the leg stump.

Bradman had scored 232, but Percy Fender, Jardine's friend and predecessor as captain at Surrey, had not been impressed. He had certainly had plenty of time to study him close-up, for Bradman, stung by Fender's strictures in 1928–9, had already scored a very rapid 252 not out in the Surrey match. The guru's pronouncement was that he was vulnerable to short-pitched stuff on the line of the leg stump.

Jardine visited F. R. Foster to discuss the 'leg-theory' field settings he had used on Warner's 1911–12 tour: Foster subsequently apologised to friends in Australia, writing, 'I am sorry my experience and advice were put to such an unworthy use.' And, famously, Jardine held a clandestine meeting with Larwood and Voce, chaperoned by Carr, in the Piccadilly Hotel, to be sure they knew exactly what he had in mind. In these less innocent days of helmets and body-armour it all sounds rather small beer, but it was real cloak-and-dagger stuff. More to the point, it was a calculated breach of the existing conventions by the MCC and their gentlemanly representatives, using the hired hands to do the actual deed. And Warner, who was tour manager as well as chairman of selectors, did nothing to try to stop it in the preliminary games, though the Australian press had made much of the 'battery' of fast bowlers. Of the game against an Australian XI when Bradman had been made to look distinctly fallible, Larwood afterwards wrote:

> The Australian XI batsmen in that match got the full force of Bowes, Voce,

Allen and myself. Even Allen made the ball get up, but one paper described him
as medium-paced compared with me.

Bradman himself escaped injury, through illness in the first Test, a placid
pitch in the second and fancy footwork in the third, when matters came to a
head. *Wisden* described this Test as 'probably the most unpleasant ever
played'. Ironically, the actual physical injuries were caused when the intimidatory field placings were not being used. In the worst episode Woodfull was
batting with Bradman at the other end. Larwood sent one inches from
Woodfull's head. The next struck him over the heart. 'Well bowled, Harold!'
cried Jardine – for Bradman's benefit. Then, as Woodfull shakily resumed,
Jardine stopped Larwood in his run-up and ostentatiously moved the slip
fielders over to the leg side. The ploy worked: Bradman ducked out of the
way of a couple and then put up a simple catch.

As soon as Woodfull himself was out, Warner went round to the Australian
dressing room, presumably hoping for an amicable chat over tea and cucum-
ber sandwiches, but found to his astonishment that the Australian captain was
in quite an angry mood, tersely commenting, 'I don't want to see you, Mr
Warner. There are two teams out there. One is trying to play cricket, the
other is not.' Warner was also surprised and angry when the story was leaked
to the newspapers, tried to organise a rumour that Woodfull had apologised
and was really chagrined when Woodfull denied it. His peace mission did not
please his own team either. Jardine was livid, and the team issued a statement
pledging their full support to their captain.

The storm spilled out of the teacup on the day after the Woodfull incident
when Bertie Oldfield, the Australian wicket-keeper and late-order batsman,
slashed at a rising ball from Larwood and was laid out with a fractured skull.
The Times's report, under the headlines 'ENGLAND'S LEAD' and 'FINE
INNINGS BY PONSFORD', did include a brief reference to the injury,
adding, 'The indignant crowd abused Larwood and Jardine, and continued
their wild shouting when England opened their innings.' The Australian
Smith's Weekly was more forthright. Under the headings '"It's Not Cricket" –
But Woodfull Always Plays the Game' and 'Jardine answerable for Larwood's
bowling tactics', its report began:

> Today the man who plays cricket in a fine sportsmanlike way that nobody in the
> world can excel is W. M. WOODFULL, captain of the Australian Eleven. He
> took his knock over the heart from savage bowling. He played his innings and
> he scored runs. Then he told Manager 'Plum' Warner, plainly and simply, what
> he thought of the bowling tactics of the English Eleven ... All the honors are
> with him and none are with Warner or Jardine.

The paper had urged the Australian Board of Control (ABC) to protest to
the MCC and they lost no time in doing so. After first seeking the help of

Warner and his assistant Palairet and being told there was nothing they could do, they sent a cable stating:

> Body-line bowling has assumed such proportions as to menace the best interests of the game, making protection of the body by the batsman the main consideration. This is causing intensely bitter feeling between the players as well as injury. In our opinion it is unsportsmanlike. Unless stopped at once, it is likely to upset the friendly relations existing between Australia and England.

In those pre-television days, with the most meagre of press coverage (only the three London evening papers had sent men out there) and with communications generally both sketchy and slow – there was no airmail, seamail took about three weeks, telephoning was a complex and uncertain art – sending such a cable was to begin a dialogue of the deaf. The assumption at Lord's was, of course, that 'our men' were being slandered and that the Australians, who had been good at dishing it out when Gregory and Macdonald were playing, did not like it when the roles were reversed.

Percy Fender, at home in London, had rushed into print next day with a long piece in the *Daily Telegraph* headed 'THIS "BODY-LINE" BOWLING IS NEW ONLY IN NAME'. Condemning the Australians' 'acrimonious bickering' he harked back to his old claim that the Australians had a weakness on the leg stump, and added, 'Why Jardine's determination to play on this weakness should cause "intensely bitter feeling between the players" one can only speculate.' Fender dismissed the complaint that it was dangerous – it was just that the Australians couldn't play it. Neville Cardus told readers of the *Observer* that a statue should be erected to Larwood for ridding the game of its 'fatty degeneracy'.

The Times produced a long-winded and opaque leader, of the 'on the one hand this, on the other hand that' variety but containing a defining sentence:

> It is inconceivable that a cricketer of JARDINE's standing, chosen by the MCC to captain an English side, would ever dream of allowing or ordering the bowlers under his command to practise any system of attack that, in the time-honoured English phrase, is not cricket.

With this self-evident truth in mind MCC drew themselves up to their full collective height to send a cutting reply, beginning,

> We, Marylebone Cricket Club, deplore your cable. We deprecate your opinion that there has been unsportsmanlike play. We have fullest confidence in captain, team and managers.

They went on to call the ABC's bluff, suggesting that if things had really become intolerable then they would reluctantly agree to cancel the rest of the tour.

ABC, under pressure from their own government lest poisoned relations should affect trade – agricultural prices were already at rock bottom – replied in less confrontational terms and concluded by saying that cancellation was not contemplated, but still did not apologise. MCC were not satisfied that the slur had been expunged, and despite cautionary words from J. H. Thomas, the convivial proletarian Dominions Secretary, who was anxious not to put at risk the recently concluded imperial trade agreements, MCC stood on their dignity (perhaps emboldened by the thought that their incoming president was Lord Hailsham, the Secretary for War) and in reply delicately indicated that resumption required retraction. Biting the bullet, ABC, who could scarcely have persuaded Brisbane to cancel their Test match because of events in Adelaide, cabled, 'We do not consider the sportsmanship of your team to be in question,' and the series staggered on.

One of the more fatuous comments that helped the British public to reach the conclusion that the Australians were squealers was the view of a neutral. The great South African batsman, Herby Taylor, told *The Times* that the Australian protests were absurd and that there was no danger if the batsman played forward. Woodfull and company, no doubt grateful for such opinions, took the added precaution of wearing cork chest protectors in the fourth Test, but Larwood was again the decisive factor in a ten-day marathon that won the Ashes for England. The courage of the little Lancashire batsman Eddie Paynter in leaving his hospital bed to play a vital innings was a more agreeable theme than the stridencies of body-line, especially since the view seemed to be hardening that Jardine and his men were the innocent parties, forced to endure intolerable barracking.

One congratulatory editorial declared that: 'Jardine as captain and Larwood as a decisive moral force have played under very trying conditions.' The Ashes won, Jardine still continued to use his great 'moral force' lest dropping it be construed as an admission that it was in any way an unusual, let alone illegal, tactic. As a result both McCabe and Bradman were hit. The New Zealand-born cartoonist (Sir) David Low of the *Evening Standard*, creator of Colonel Blimp, summed up the series with a picture of a batsman in a full suit of armour surrounded by a ring of leg-side fielders saying to each other, 'The feller's a cad, sir,' ''Tisn't cricket, sir' and 'Play the game, sir!'[6] Amongst the Englishmen saddened by the episode was Sir Arthur Quiller-Couch, who offered verses 'For Old Cricketers':

> The batsmen stands to hide his wicket,
> The bowler at his body aims:
> Tho' these perfect the 'art' of Cricket,
> Do they improve the best of games?

The game we played with zest, and after,
Homeward thro' meadows scented warm,
Rehearsed, re-played with generous laughter,
Victor and vanquished – arm-in-arm.

CHAPTER SIXTEEN

Reconciliation

RAMSAY MACDONALD'S effusive congratulations to the MCC team on winning the Ashes were no doubt intensified by relief: he had enough worries without the secession of a Dominion. The Labour Government had not lasted long, washed away in the wake of the Wall Street collapse of November 1929, which badly hit British exports to the USA and the many countries dependent on American finance. Unemployment rose to 2.5 million, as cotton exports fell away, steel output halved, and shipbuilding, already reduced, fell to less than half its immediate post-war level. Not all industries were affected: for the fortunate ones wages and employment stayed stable, and, since American and German industry were even harder hit, the price of imported goods fell. The working classes were themselves sharply divided between the employed and those on 'the dole'.

Faced with the choice of high taxation, reneging on repayment of the national debt or cuts in public expenditure, the government broke up in disorder. His local party threw MacDonald out when he agreed to head a 'National Government' coalition with Baldwin, and embarked on fierce economies – raising income tax, reducing state salaries and wages, and even cutting the dole money. There was trouble with the unions and a strike in the armed forces; foreign investors got cold feet; the value of the pound fell by 30 per cent. After an election in which 'National Labour' denounced Labour's manifesto as 'Bolshevism gone mad', MacDonald and Baldwin resumed their double-act with a strongly conservative supporting cast.

II

The slump was selective in its effects, hitting the older industrial areas more than elsewhere, and intensifying the competition amongst sporting authorities for the working classes' diminishing spare cash. It blew a chill wind over the cricket grounds of the northern leagues, and there was gloomy talk of economies. Since the wages bill was the main item of expenditure and the single professional had the lion's share of that, their choice was a simple one. Stories about the high wages on offer – Fred Root of Worcestershire had been offered £600 for the season in 1927 – were no longer so frequent. But Nelson, whose earlier experiment with Ted McDonald had caused a sensation, sprang another surprise and in the process demonstrated how to survive in a recession.

After McDonald the club had returned to obscurity and were drifting onto the rocks financially. In 1929 they decided to buy their way out of trouble by engaging the West Indian Test player, Learie Constantine, for a fee said to be £750, and probably over the nine seasons he played for them exceeding £1000 a year. These were unbelievable sums, regardless of the recession, when a cotton worker, if employed, could expect about £100. Among sportsmen even the soccer players were restricted to maxima of £8 a week in season, £6 in summer, and in county cricket only Yorkshire came close to those standards. Nelson's gamble paid off. 1929 was a fine summer with much exciting cricket, and they went on to win the league title – they won it seven times and came second twice before Constantine left in 1937. By this time the worst of the recession was over and so were Nelson's financial worries.

And this time other clubs took the plunge, too: nearly all the Lancashire League clubs, many of the Central Lancashire and a few in the more conservative Bradford and Staffordshire leagues were stirred into emulation. Constantine himself (later Lord Constantine) has told the story of his time with Nelson. It was a rewarding and an educational experience both for the Trinidadian solicitor's clerk and his new fellow-citizens, as he took up lodgings with a club official in this small, rather dingy town called after a railway halt at the Lord Nelson public house. In the small towns of pre-war Britain, with limited experience of black immigrants, racism was not yet a major issue, more an ignorant assumption of white superiority, and Constantine soon became a very special kind of hero to Nelson, who christened him 'Connie'. A favourite story of 1929 was of the Lancashire schoolmistress asking a pupil when Ramsay MacDonald had previously been Prime Minister. 'Don't know, Miss,' he said, 'but I know he were t' pro for Nelson before Connie.'

The curious phenomenon of overseas stars playing alongside local boys was also a feature of the northern Rugby League clubs, the difference being that all the other cricketers were amateurs. The mixture worked well and the crowds did not feel their local identity diminished by their imported carpetbaggers. Success was what did it, but being a great entertainer like Constantine helped, too. Not everyone liked the trend. Sydney Barnes remarked sourly, 'They now look for clowns, not cricketers.' But it was indicative of the concern shown for the paying customers. As Constantine wrote admiringly in 1933:

Usually these matches are played on Saturdays, beginning at two and ending at seven ... The mills finish work on Saturdays at 10.50 so that everyone has time to get home, do a little shopping, have lunch and get down to cricket ... Sometimes a league match is played on a week-day because shop assistants are at work on Saturday afternoons. In Nelson these matches are played on the Tuesday half-holiday, in East Lancashire on the Thursday half- holiday, and so on. These week-day matches begin at 3 o'clock ...

Compare this with the immutable hours of county cricket designed around the meal-times of the leisured.

Consider also the nature of the game being played, through the eyes of C. L. R. James, Constantine's friend, who saw him in a 1932 duel with Ted McDonald, recently retired from Lancashire and returned to the League: 'This is a big match, with far more spectators and more tension than two-thirds of the first-class county matches played in a season'. And consider how a West Indian dealt with the time constraints:

Constantine takes a long stride with his left foot across the wicket and, leaning well forward, glances McDonald from outside the off-stump ... These strokes were characteristic of Constantine's batting in the league. That is the way he transferred the liabilities of one-day cricket into assets. Assets for cricket of all days, one as well as five if that last-named monstrosity continues.[1]

Another who compared the leagues favourably with county cricket was Fred Root. Root was no Bolshevik – on the contrary, he was a member of the executive of the Dudley Conservative Association – but as soon as he was safely retired from Worcestershire he wrote a book of unusual frankness about the cricket scene. His admiration for Todmorden, to whom he went in 1933, began the day he arrived:

Cricket was in full swing and as many people were on the ground to cast a critical eye over my doings at the nets as would have been reckoned a good county match 'gate' at Worcester.

Nor was this merely passive interest:

Practice is efficiently organised and wonderfully popular. There are no fewer than six full nets at Todmorden every available evening.

Constantine found the same at Nelson: 'It is nothing surprising to have thirty or forty people practising and hundreds of people looking on ...'. Root positively rhapsodised over the community involvement:

Everybody seems to be a member of their Lancashire League club. They would rather miss joining the Co-op than the cricket club, and when bad times make money scarce, their sacrifices to enable them to pay their annual subscription are almost pitiful.

And again the involvement was active. Everybody helped with the rolling and weeding: 'Cotton manufacturers rub shoulders with their own weavers, and the "ground staff" is democratic to a degree.'

III

Fred Root's disenchantment with county cricket was partly financial. With Worcestershire, a struggling county, he had averaged less than £300 a year, out of which hotel bills, taxi fares, flannels and cricket-equipment bills, insurance and massage fees had to be paid. In the Depression years, furthermore, the pros were asked to take a 10 per cent cut. The management circularised the other clubs, and Root 'was informed that at least four counties paid less than Worcestershire and several other counties paid the same rate'. Yorkshire were obviously the plutocrats of the county scene. Remarking on the odd circumstance that Yorkshire players rarely became umpires when they retired, Root suggested that this was because they didn't need to.

Benefit matches were the lure that kept many county cricketers in the game and helped ensure their loyalty and good conduct, especially after the extraordinary judgment of the House of Lords in Seymour v. Reed in 1927 which exempted them from tax.[2] Here again Yorkshire were the best county: Roy Kilner's record £4,000 in 1927 was mouth-watering. However, it remained a record until after the war. Meanwhile only six other cricketers got more than £2,500, again much dependent on the county. In the 1930s Yorkshire handed over £3,600-odd to Maurice Leyland whilst Gloucestershire managed £2,500 for Walter Hammond and Nottinghamshire £2,000 for Harold Larwood ('a national hero,' thought Root, 'or he ought to be'). Root himself staggered the Worcestershire committee by asking £500 in 1929: they countered with £250 and only agreed his price when he began talking about league cricket. Even so, he had to take it in instalments.

Benefits were notoriously chancy affairs, the weather being the chief problem. Players were, of course, responsible for the expenses of their match, whether it was rained off or not. It was possible to insure against loss, but since premiums were based on average 'gates' they could be prohibitive, particularly in one of the poorer counties. Hence the favourite dressing-room story of the player who, when asked if he would like a second benefit, replies, 'No, thanks. I can't afford it.' Fred Root told it about Dick Burrows, in his own club. A real-life victim was A. W. Shipman of Leicestershire, who in 1934 lost £60 on his benefit because of poor attendances.

It had been a disastrous season generally for Leicestershire. As *Wisden* commented sadly, the public demanded brighter cricket and their desire was certainly complied with, but even so the 'gates' were extremely disappointing ... During the season a suggestion was made that Leicestershire should merge with Lincolnshire, but *naturally* [my italics] nothing came of the proposal.

They were reprieved when 'a few county enthusiasts' cleared off their debts of over £5,000, and the club carried on, hoping for better things – the prevailing philosophy of the times. Their plight demonstrated, however, that 'brighter cricket' in itself was not enough to attract the general public – if indeed anything could overcome the inherent flaws in the county championship. As Fred Root summarised the problem:

> The majority of supporters of sporting events do not claim expert knowledge. What they want for their money is something exciting, something competitive ... Win or lose ...

Another of the weaknesses he criticised was the great and apparently chronic and immutable variation in the playing strength of the counties, cemented as they were to their privileged roundabout. There were good years amongst the bad between the wars but the weaker clubs found it no easier to break into profitability – certainly not by winning championships. Nottinghamshire (1929) briefly broke the stranglehold of Lancashire (1930; 1934) and Yorkshire (1931–3; 1937–9), but only Derbyshire (1936) succeeded in doing so from outside the Edwardian 'Big Six'.

Derbyshire's feat, coming from bottom place in 1920, with a tiny staff and perpetual financial worries, was a tribute to what could be achieved by a tightly knit, home-grown group, utterly professional and typically graduating from the local leagues. The attraction of escaping from factories and mines increased during the Depression years. The first great exemplar of the saying 'Whistle down a pit in Derbyshire and up comes a fast bowler', Wilf Copson, began his cricket at the age of seventeen in spells of unemployment during and after the General Strike. But the prevailing conditions produced a splendid crop of all kinds of professional talent – the combative leg-spinner Tommy Mitchell; prolific batsmen Denis Smith and Stan Worthington; and all-rounders George Pope and Leslie Townsend – led in classical fashion by dedicated amateurs from the public schools.

But Derbyshire were soon to be overshadowed, like everyone else, by Yorkshire, who were champions for the rest of the decade. Sutcliffe was there still, but opening with the newest Pudsey product, young Len Hutton; followed by the rock-solid Wilf Barber and Cyril Turner; and Maurice Leyland, the best left-hander since (or perhaps including) Frank Woolley; the larger-than-life wicket-keeper/batsman, Arthur Wood, unlucky to coexist with Kent's magnificent Leslie Ames; and bowlers of every kind: Bill Bowes and Frank Smailes to open, Ellis Robinson for off-spin and Hedley Verity, as good a left-arm spinner in his own way and time as Wilfred Rhodes in his. They were led by an amateur, Brian Sellars, son of a well-known industrialist, an old player and committee man. Sellars made up for his technical deficiencies by a somewhat uncouth charisma that seemed to bring the best out of the syndicalist professionals who, realising that they were keepers of the Holy Grail, dedicated themselves first and foremost to winning. The important Emmott Robinson role was now filled, less quirkily perhaps, by Arthur Mitchell, a fine but ultra-defensive batsman.

Cardus told one of the best of the many Arthur Mitchell stories, ringing true of everyone involved even if, as may be suspected, it is an invention. Meeting Cardus, in the company of the more genial Maurice Leyland, Arthur confessed, 'I don't like thy writing, Mester Cardus; it's too fancy.' Maurice quickly interposed, 'Well, that's more than anybody could say about thy batting, Arthur.' Another classic is Mitchell's comment to the young Hutton – or whoever – who, after taking a brilliant catch close in, lay full-length holding the ball aloft enjoying the plaudits of the crowd: 'Gerrup, lad. Tha's makin' an exhibition of thysen.'

One of the devices Root proposed for levelling up playing strengths was some form of transfer system. This 'cattle-market' was currently causing great controversy in soccer, in which as much as £11,000 had recently changed hands for a single player. MCC, needless to say, did not favour such vulgar goings-on, and they certainly did not think Root's supporting arguments relevant to the gentlemanly game they presided over. His idea was to liberate star players who fell out with their clubs to try their luck elsewhere instead of being put out of work: he gave as examples two spin bowlers, Kent's 'Tich' Freeman and Lancashire's Dick Tyldesley – and himself. He felt himself an indirect victim of the body-line 'bunkum' in which Larwood's 'tragedy' had been brought about by 'narrow-minded, ignorant critics' and 'chicken-hearted, inept batsmen'. He had been bowling 'leg-theory' for years – and indeed had claims to have invented it – to the mild disapproval of Lord's but to Worcestershire's satisfaction, only to find it suddenly under a dark cloud and himself asked to bowl off-spinners round the wicket.

IV

The reason for Root's contretemps was the change of front amongst the English establishment about body-line when, with the Ashes safely won, they actually saw what their representatives had been inflicting on the Australians. This change was very gradual. At first, as the cablegrams from the ABC continued, MCC became more convinced that the Australians had got above themselves. This became crystal-clear when in April 1933, MCC were told not merely that the ABC thought an amendment to the laws was needed, outlawing deliveries intended to intimidate or injure batsmen, but that they had drafted one and intended to apply it in the new season.

This *lèse-majesté*, or damned impertinence, evoked an appropriately dignified brush-off. MCC dismissed the 'proposed' new law as impractical (it would give far too much power to the umpires) and moved swiftly on to what they thought to be the real cause of the unpleasantness in the recent series:

> Barracking has, unfortunately, always been indulged in by spectators in Australia to a degree quite unknown in this country. During the late tour, however, it would appear to have exceeded all previous experience, and on occasion to have been thoroughly objectionable.

Then, after complaining that the Australian authorities had done nothing to stop it, they went on to suggest that unless things altered it was 'difficult to see how the continuance of representative matches can serve the best interests of the game'.

But their moral position was already compromised. First, there had been dissidents amongst the amateurs on the tour, who had not liked Jardine or his attitude. They ranged in degrees of opposition from the Nawab of Pataudi to R. E. S. Wyatt. Wyatt, Jardine's vice-captain, had led the side, using the body-line attack to devastating effect, in the pre-Test rehearsal against an Australian XI, but later appears to have changed his view. The 'Noob', one of the anglicised Indian aristocrats[3] who played for England in those days, had scored a century in the first Test, failed in the second and been dropped for the rest of the series. He had also, however, failed another important test, refusing to field in Jardine's leg trap: 'I see His Highness is a conscientious objector,' Jardine had remarked mockingly.

In between Pataudi and Wyatt was the Australian-born Etonian G. O. B. 'Gubby' Allen, a Warner protégé, who had declined to bowl body-line himself, but fielded very effectively to it when required. In a letter to his father from Australia Allen had written, 'Douglas Jardine is loathed ... he is a perfect swine and I can think of no words fit for Mummy to see when I describe him.' As for Larwood and Voce, they were 'swollen-headed, gutless, uneducated miners'. Allen had not returned with the rest of the team; when he appeared at Lord's in due course, he was discussing the tour with the MCC secretary William Findlay and Findlay said that he refused to believe that any Englishman could ever bowl at a batsman. Allen reputedly replied, 'If that's what you think, the sooner you find out what really happened the better.' MCC did in fact set up an enquiry to look into what had taken place, but there was not much danger of its reaching any conclusions markedly different from those of Findlay and Jardine.[4]

Its chairman was the hawkish Lord Hailsham, who at a celebratory banquet for the team said, 'Jardine is probably the best captain in the world to-day and

his gallant band of sportsmen have worthily upheld England's reputation.'
Jardine had come home to cheering crowds and he behaved with becoming
modesty. His first official utterance was in an article in the *Nottingham
Evening News*. It began, 'To me, I confess the term body-line is meaningless,'
and continued in the sort of style that might have been adopted by a visiting
Martian anthropologist who had fallen foul of a tribe of malevolent cannibals.
He was reappointed captain for the forthcoming tests against the West Indies.

By contrast, his loyal henchman, Larwood, who suffered from the twin
disadvantages of being a professional and being naïve, did not fare so well. He
had not assisted his cause by a bitter interview given to the *Sunday Express*
almost as soon as he got off the boat, beginning, 'Now I can speak. For
months I have been muzzled because of my agreement with the Marylebone
club', and going on to accuse Bradman of 'being too frightened. Yes, frightened is the word ...', of setting himself up as a superstar and much else in
that vein, and roundly condemning the crowds for 'not knowing what sportsmanship meant'. He also disclosed that the body-line plan had been
prearranged. There followed a ghosted book in the same vein, by the time of
whose publication the need for diplomacy, especially from professionals, was
becoming apparent. Fortunately for Warner and his fellow-selectors,
Larwood had returned lame from the tour, so they were not obliged to
consider him for selection.

Nevertheless, MCC had the chance to see body-line in action that summer.
First the West Indians' two fast bowlers, Constantine and Martindale, had
given some of the England batsmen what Warner called 'a taste of their own
medicine'. Jardine, who was nothing if not courageous, took it without flinch-
ing, but there were mutterings about some of the professionals. Hammond's
ardour had been cooled – as indeed whose wouldn't? – by a crack on the chin
which obliged him to leave the field for a while. Even more shocking was the
sight of body-line tactics in the Varsity match. The chief perpetrator was
Kenneth Farnes, an exceptionally tall – and fast – Essex and England player
who, having tried his hand at being a bank clerk, had gone to teacher-training
college in Cambridge. Several Oxford men were hit, one being bowled off his
jaw, the other breaking his wicket as he recoiled from a blow on the neck. As
Warner primly put it, 'the Cambridge tactics certainly did not meet with
general approval'.

But then later in the year, Jardine's extraordinary, stiff-necked and unrepentant book came out, bristling with righteous indignation at the insult the
ABC had offered 'the Premier Club' and notable for a long and detailed
history of Australian crowd disorder, beginning with 1879, when Lord Harris
(who behaved 'awfully well') had to be rescued from the mob by 'Monkey'
Hornby. This fulsome praise for MCC and its recently deceased patron saint
made it very difficult for Jardine's critics – notably Warner – to unseat him,
and he was made captain for the next winter's tour of India.

Warner had been frantically trying to square the circle since his return from Australia, basking in the reflected glory of the Ashes victory whilst at the same time trying to reoccupy the moral high ground, reminding everyone of his disapproval of body-line. He had a hard time of it, for though he explained the difference between leg-theory and body-line carefully to the readers of his new employers, the *Daily Telegraph*, their previous correspondent, Thomas Moult, a cricket poet and nostalgia merchant, was decidedly hawkish, as was their editorial stance. When Warner gave evidence to MCC's enquiry, furthermore, they told him that he 'had got the wrong perspective'. Jardine and, at his own humbler level, Larwood, were also sickened by Warner's tightrope-walking.

But the tide was slowly turning against them. The cablegrams continued to flow back and forth, but by October 1933 MCC were saying that they agreed 'and always have agreed that any form of bowling which is obviously a direct attack ... upon the batsman would be an offence against the spirit of the game', and in November they and the advisory County Cricket Committee and the Board of Control for Test matches, with the county captains in attendance, adopted this as a guiding principle. The Australians, not unnaturally, sought something firmer, either legislation or an undertaking that body-line would not be used against them again. MCC, under increasing government pressure, had voted by only eight votes to five to invite them back in 1934 and could not bring themselves to go beyond an assurance that if the Australians came the Tests would be played in the same spirit as in the past. The ABC tried one more time, but on finding the MCC immovable, backed down. It was only by a small majority, with several members protesting that they hadn't been given time to vote, but the financial and political realities were what counted, both to the cricket authorities and their governments.

Warner had a good political contact in his old friend Sir Alexander Hore-Ruthven, Governor of South Australia, who had a hot line to Jimmy Thomas and the Cabinet. They had been anxious lest the projected tour be cancelled and were now even more anxious that there should be no unpleasantness when they came. The *New Statesman* printed a set of verses satirising what was going on:

> Dimly one can see the process – say that British exports fall:
> 'If you'll give us further preference, Larwood shall not bowl at all.'
> While if meat should be in question, then experience suggests
> An increased Australian quota in return for four-day Tests.

On the other hand,

> If a Test match should be cancelled we shall tax at higher rate
> All Australia has to send us, to recoup the vanished 'gate'.

In January 1934 Warner, who could see his prospects of a knighthood diminishing rapidly, confessed his misgivings to Hore-Ruthven. Larwood was no problem:

> The real trouble is Jardine. Is he to be captain? At present I say 'No' unless he makes a most generous public gesture of friendliness and then I am not sure I would trust him. He is a queer fellow. When he sees a cricket ground with an Australian on it he goes mad! He rose to his present position on my shoulders, and of his attitude to me I do not care to speak. It is hoped he may retire at the end of the Indian tour but in many quarters here – where they do not know the truth – he is a bit of a hero.

Hore-Ruthven's advice was forthright:

> If you want the game to be played in the proper spirit and the whole controversy buried once and for all, keep Jardine out of the picture on any plea you can find. I know the difficulties of not appearing to let him down, but the question is so vital that some excuse must be found for leaving him out.

The honour code was crumbling by the minute. Warner, deciding that discretion was the better part of valour, resigned from the selection committee. This turned out to be a mistake. He had fled the field too soon. In April, holidaying in India after the tour, Jardine sent a telegram, published in the *Evening Standard*, announcing that he had 'neither the intention nor the desire to play cricket against Australia this summer'.

V

The absence of the demon king did not, however, provide a happy ending. *Wisden*'s melancholy post-mortem began,

> No matter the angle from which it may be viewed it is next to impossible to regard the cricket season of 1934 as other than unpleasant.

This, the editor emphasised, did not refer to losing the Ashes, sad as that was, but 'the whole atmosphere of cricket in England was utterly foreign to the great traditions of the game'. Much of his criticism was directed at the press, for retailing tittle-tattle and creating an atmosphere of suspicion, but he also confessed that he thought the cricket authorities would do better if they were a little more open about their policies.

But burying body-line had been necessarily a stealthy affair. Even with Jardine gone there remained Larwood and Voce. Larwood in particular had said some nasty things about the Australians and showed no sign of repentance. They sent a powerful emissary to try to persuade him to apologise, Sir

Julien Cahn, the former president of Nottinghamshire. Cahn, the scion of a furniture empire, was an absurdly pretentious fellow who had bought his way into Midlands hunting circles, scandalising traditionalists, and who owned two private cricket grounds where he indulged his fantasies like some latter-day Sir Horace Mann. When he took part in the country-house matches for which he was celebrated a butler pumped up his inflatable fielding pads. In the inter-war years such philanthropists, however ludicrous, were doubly valuable for their scarcity value, and he bore messages in the form of nods and winks from both MCC and the Dominions Office when he took Larwood aside at one of his festival games and told him what was required if he wanted to resume his Test career. Larwood indignantly refused in the memorable words, 'I'm an Englishman – I will never apologise.'

The way back had been made no easier for Larwood by the sudden change that now seemed to have come over most of his old team-mates. He was particularly scornful of Hammond's volte-face, for 'Wally' had been one of the strongest supporters of the campaign against Bradman. And he was not helped by the intransigent attitude of Arthur Carr, his county captain, to Australians, or his contempt for Warner and the two-faced men of MCC. Carr's declared view was that he naturally opposed 'direct attack' bowling and that neither Larwood nor Voce practised it. 'Consequently,' said *Wisden*, 'it was not in the least surprising that ... Voce and Larwood felt they were justified in continuing to bowl ... fast, bumping leg-theory deliveries, with the leg-side packed with fieldsmen.'

The first occasion to attract notice was Nottinghamshire's match against their historic enemies, Lancashire, whose president, T. A. Higson, was a long-serving selector of no great repute. According to Carr, Lancashire, inspired by Higson on behalf of MCC, were intent on making a protest against the Notts bowlers even before the match began: so they seem to have decided to give them something to complain about.[5] The Lancashire captain, P. T. Eckersley, and his heir-apparent, W. H. L. Lister, were the principal victims, but George Duckworth, their wicket-keeper, a veteran of the 1932–3 tour, was hit about the body and made the most of it. Duckworth, noted for his vociferous appeals, was a staunch loyalist, almost as likely to quote Rupert Brooke as the *Pigeon Fancier's Gazette*, and he had been a convinced believer in body-line, even giving lectures on the subject. He now changed his tune, to Warner's glee and Larwood's disgust.

Larwood, trying to save face in case he wasn't chosen for England and unwilling to play if he was to be emasculated, made it easy for Higson and his fellow-selectors, by telling the Notts officials that he wasn't fully fit before the first Test, and even easier before the second by telling the readers of the *Sunday Dispatch* that he had decided not to play against the Australians because Woodfull had not withdrawn his old 'not cricket' remark. Thereafter he was in the wilderness along with his equally resentful captain, Carr. The last significant act of the drama took place in August, when the tourists came to play Notts. Carr and Larwood had withdrawn themselves from the arena, but Voce took 8 for 66 in the Australians' first innings and was setting about them again in the second when bad light stopped play.

The Australian management complained to the Notts honorary secretary, Dr Gould, a medical man, and to MCC. The acting captain, the veteran professional Ben Lilley, was said to have reported that Voce had been in pain two days earlier and on this pretext Dr Gould examined Voce and pronounced him unfit to play. The England selectors also took the opportunity to pass him by, and in spite of England playing three fast bowlers, Bowes, Allen and the very, very fast left-armer E. W. 'Nobby' Clark, Australia scored 700-odd in the first innings, won the Test match and regained the Ashes.

The reverberations continued in Nottinghamshire, and after a match against Middlesex at Lord's – again with Carr absent, but vocal off-stage in support of his bowlers – more complaints were made and the committee once more apologised. As Larwood put it, 'Middlesex was also Plum Warner's club: he was one of the first to squeal ... Warner raised no objections when the Australians had to face body-line!' Nottinghamshire was torn apart over the issue, bitter recriminations began, and Carr was relieved of the captaincy. This provoked further protests, public meetings and so forth, and the committee resigned *en bloc*. The row eventually subsided: the final stages are recorded in detail in Carr's *Cricket with the Lid Off*. Remarkably, in 1935, after all that had gone on, he was still able to complain that Australians did not seem to appreciate that cricket was 'a game not a mixture of war and all-in wrestling'.

VI

The increasingly local nature of the dispute helped MCC to distance themselves from the problem, whilst at the same time reluctantly reaching the conclusion that, if gentlemen couldn't reach agreements, legislation was after all required. Before the 1935 season they declared illegal 'persistent and systematic bowling of fast, short-pitched balls at the batsman *standing clear of his wicket*' (a strange proviso) and issued appropriate instructions to umpires about dealing with offenders.[6] They also addressed one of the causes. As Larwood – or his ghost – wrote:

> Cricket is a batsman's game ... When somebody says, 'It's a perfect wicket' they mean perfect for the batsman, not the bowler ... The fast bowler ... tries to batter his way through the batsman's defence ... Purely defensive batting reduces the speed bowler to panting futility. That is why he must drop a few short.

Apart from perfect wickets an additional source of frustration was the lbw law, which permitted unbridled use of pads to any ball that pitched a fraction wide. Now at last, after much consultation, MCC took the plunge and permitted a trial of a new rule, under which the batsman could be out if hit on part of his body on an imaginary line between wicket and wicket, even if the ball pitched outside the off-stump.

Several prominent batsmen were strongly opposed to the experiment, which followed various other modest attempts to redress the imbalance between bat and ball[7] – a slight reduction in the circumference of the ball, intended to make it easier to manipulate; a slight increase in the size of the wickets – not to mention the 'do-it-yourself' body-line assault. Herbert Sutcliffe was a determined opponent of lbw, a threat to the style of bat-and-pad play he had perfected. But by no means all the objectors were professionals: indeed two of the most eloquent were R. E. S. Wyatt, the new England captain, and the dashing E. R. T. Holmes, the captain of Surrey.

A few xenophobic churls blamed the new rule for South Africa's Test win at Lord's, but most were agreeably surprised at the outcome. The editor of *Wisden* was immensely cheered, commenting:

> The fight between bat and ball became more equal than it had been for many seasons … The experiment brought great gains to cricket. Definite results in results in the 234 County Championship matches numbered 171 as against 134 in 1934 … Only seven batsmen … had aggregates reaching 2,000 as compared with nineteen a year before. Strangely enough Wyatt, Holmes and Sutcliffe, of those who did not like the experiment, made considerably more runs than in 1934.

The bright new dawn matched the changes coming over the country. The depths of the crisis had been reached as the body-line series was enacted, with unemployment reaching three million; but by 1934, Neville Chamberlain, the Chancellor of the Exchequer, was pronouncing the recession almost over and reducing income tax, and a year later production was soaring and the cost of living plummeting, and unemployment was shrinking to the Celtic fringes and a few northern 'black spots'. They were heedless times. It was the era of cinemas, Radio Luxembourg, cigarette cards, football pools, hiking, Fred Perry and Henry Cotton, baby cars, Monopoly, Gordon Richards, the Silver Jubilee, Mosley's Blackshirts, Benny Lynch and Tommy Farr, the Lambeth Walk, the Rector of Stiffkey, ribbon development, the Spanish Civil War, Stanley Baldwin, and Princesses Elizabeth and Margaret Rose.

There were alarming developments, though, and Hitler and Mussolini were now among the range of topics – the weather, motor cars, gardening, golf handicaps and so forth – permitted in discussions on the 8.22. But at least Britain seemed to have drawn back from the brink and there was a new wave of imperial fervour, following the death of the old king and the unfortunate seduction of Edward VIII by 'that American woman'. The Government of India Act had staved off the dissolution of the Raj, and in 1936 a Test team came to England, led by the Maharajkumar of Vizianagram, India's equivalent of Sir Julien Cahn: having presented gold watches to opposing captains and sent home his best player, Lala Amarnath, 'Vizzy' was given a knighthood and a lot of friendly full-tosses. With Warner returned to the selectors (but not to team management) the 1936–7 Australian tour, led by 'Gubby' Allen, was a diplomatic and financial success. Record crowds saw Bradman get the better of Hammond in their personal contest, with Australia winning the Tests 3–2. And Warner got his knighthood.

The dominance and great popularity of Test cricket was in marked contrast to the domestic scene. A committee of enquiry in 1937 reported that the counties collectively were losing £27,000 annually and the clamour for brighter cricket grew. Fred Root was scornful of the various 'petty and puerile efforts' made to ginger up county cricket – Saturday starts, later starts, smaller balls, bigger wickets, seven balls to the over, covering wickets (optional), banning 'trial' balls – and pointed out the real difficulty, that the county championship, the only competition, was governed by conditions so unequal and so peculiar that it was not a competition at all. 'Why not an English Cup for cricket?' he asked.

Frank Woolley, too, an adornment of the golden age, raised another fundamental matter when he retired at last in 1938:

> It is amazing how the public steadfastly refuse to attend the third day of a match, when so often the last day produces the best and most exciting cricket ... I am fully aware that in 1919 ... two-day games proved a failure, but then we played three matches a week. I think if the counties played matches of two days' duration with a day's rest in between for travelling, it would be a step towards better cricket.

And he added another simple truth that still plagues first-class cricket: 'We have been suffering from a surfeit of cricket. There are too many match days and the players get jaded.'

It was not only professionals that questioned the inflexibility of the system. B. H. Lyon, the Gloucestershire captain, was a fervent advocate of 'brighter' cricket who staged exhibition games under simplified rules, and his brother, M. D. Lyon, of Somerset, wrote trenchantly about 'the crisis in first-class cricket'. He told how, when he asked a girlfriend to come with him to Lord's, she said, 'Come to a cricket match? I'd rather go to the dentist.' Amongst his remedies were a knockout competition, and three-day matches in which no more than three or three-and-a-half hours were allocated to each innings. But no one who mattered wanted any changes.

VII

It was commonly suggested – and still sometimes is – that many of the evils of the inter-war years were the result of increased professionalism. Thus as early as 1931 the *littérateur* and country cricket enthusiast, Sir John Squire,[8] introducing Cardus's *Cricket*, felt able to say,

> That the first-class game is not so amusing as it was is generally admitted. It stands to reason that cricket dominated by amateurs must be livelier than cricket in which professionals ... set the tone

– a questionable assumption bolted on to the equally dubious implication that amateurs no longer called the tune. Witness Fred Root – 'Many times I have been ordered by my captain to bowl negatively ... Not only in county matches, but in a Test match.' And Jardine himself, explaining a slow innings by Sutcliffe in Australia – 'He was playing under instructions... mine and mine alone.'

Squire also begged the question of the 'shamateur', by then less the exception than the rule. Root recalled a time when Worcestershire advertised for a 'secretary' to strengthen not the accountancy but the playing staff. 'Among the number of applicants were several leading amateurs of the day. One of them asked that he be paid £1000 a year ... and so the game goes on, full of make-believe; and yet everybody intimately connected with cricket knows all about it.' Root was particularly scornful about the nonsenses of the Gentlemen v. Players conventions, the latest absurdity of which had the Australian, Alan Fairfax, playing for the Gentlemen against the Players between professional engagements for Accrington in the Lancashire League.

The prejudice against professional captains was kept in repair by the various 'shamateur' fictions. Worcestershire had, in 1933, actually appointed as their secretary and captain the stylish batsman C. F. Walters, who had left Glamorgan for the purpose. (Glamorgan already had as their captain and secretary the charismatic Maurice Turnbull, England cricketer and Welsh rugby international, who, said his successor, 'converted a stumbling and shame-faced bankrupt into a respectable member of society, with a bank-balance of £1000'). Leicestershire, who had dwindled to the depths under a succession of amateurs, made a dramatic recovery after shocking the purists by appointing Ewart Astill, their veteran all-rounder, as captain in 1935. But the New Zealander C. S. Dempster, attracted to Leicestershire by a mixture of business and Sir Julien Cahn, for whose eleven he played, was busily qualifying in the Lancashire League and took over as captain the following year.

This is not to suggest that the amateur county captains of the thirties did not include some excellent ones – such as the admirable R. W. V. Robins of Middlesex, innovative, intelligent and dedicated, Maurice Turnbull or Beverley Lyon – but as a species they had too much power for their own good: over their humble professionals, over the umpires and over their committees. As C. B. Fry put it, 'There is no one in England to dictate to an amateur cricketer what he should do or what he should not do.' Jardine had already demonstrated that, and there could be extraordinary lapses into bad manners such as that of E. R. T. Holmes in Hendren's last match for Middlesex in 1937, when an appeal for bad light was allowed in bright sunshine in order to bring an amateur squabble to an end.[9]

There was even less to be said for the prejudice given voice by what Root called 'a cricket big-wig' against a professional captain for England. The particular big-wig, Lord Hawke, passed on in 1938, but his influence lingered on in the Long Room and in bar-parlours throughout the land. Hawke's death coincided with a milestone in the history of double standards in the national game – the conversion of Hammond (W. R.) to W. R. Hammond and his subsequent elevation to the pinnacle. Hammond, for all his dashing batsmanship, good looks and the faultless tailoring to which Cardus took such exception, was a strange, rootless individual, chronically insecure. Son of a soldier who rose from the ranks in an unfashionable regiment, Hammond spent much of his childhood abroad, and, as we have seen, his start in county cricket was hampered by complications over his residential qualifications. And once he did get going, a long and serious illness, caused by blood-poisoning after a mosquito-bite, put him out of action for over a year. Both his social mix – a Cirencester Grammar School boy but without the family background or money to take him on to university – and his star status set him apart from the ordinary run of professionals and led him to seek the company of the amateurs. He married the daughter of a Bingley wool merchant in 1929, but was no Sutcliffe in the management of his financial, business or domestic affairs, and eventually failed in all three.

By 1938, however, he felt able – and perhaps impelled – to turn amateur and was duly awarded the accolade. Fourteen years later, disillusioned and driven to write 'revelations' (*Cricket's Secret History*) that promised more than his inhibited nature or the straight-laced times could ever fulfil, he wrote forlornly,

> Apparently it is only the nominal status, not the man or his characteristics, to which exception is taken. I can say this because I captained England, after most of a cricket life-time as a professional. I was the same man as before, or perhaps I even had a slightly declining skill by that time. But because I changed my label all was well.

Hammond was a confused man at a confusing time. Chamberlain, who had done well in domestic politics, was Prime Minister, 'an old man craving peace in a nation destined for war'. Hitler annexed Austria but was still thought open to reason. Nevertheless ARP and 'keeping fit' became national duties:

the Physical Training and Recreation Act conferred government recognition and money on the long-standing problem of urban youth, and the National Fitness Council began the thankless task of co-ordinating the work of a myriad voluntary bodies. There was, belatedly, a little flurry of social legislation – a maximum forty-eight-hour week, holidays with pay for some 11 million of the working population, the principle of free tripartite secondary education for all. Public opinion polls became a factor in politics, and – the surest sign yet of incipient democracy- the Amateur Rowing Association at last lifted its ban on manual workers and a Metropolitan Police crew was allowed to compete at Henley.

In his film *The Lady Vanishes* Alfred Hitchcock, before seeking refuge in Hollywood, neatly captured the mood of the moment, showing a couple of cricket fanatics stranded in crisis-torn Europe, and foiling the schemes of murderous spies and traitors by their phlegmatic efforts to get back home for the Test match. The upper-class image of cricket did it no harm – quite the contrary. Imitation 'Oxford', after all, was the industrial patois of all early British screen idols; only comedians and villains spoke with regional accents. And so the great wave of publicity for sport that came with wireless was presented in impeccable English. At first the tempo of cricket was deemed more suited to 'eye-witness accounts' rather than 'running commentary' and it was only with Howard Marshall, a Harlequins rugger player and Oxford Authentics cricketer, that the BBC found its first 'voice of cricket'.

This augmented greatly the wider circles of cricket followers who might never, for one reason or another, go to first-class matches, but who took an interest in their county's performances, or those of particular stars, usually, of course, the batsmen. Times were changing, at a pace accelerated by the sudden phenomenon of body-line – the great pillars of the game like Hobbs, Sutcliffe, Woolley, 'Patsy' Hendren were gone, and only Hammond, Leyland and the supreme wicket-keeper/batsman, Leslie Ames, of the really great early post-war generation remained at or near the peak both of form and of popularity. Hammond was the master-batsman, the supreme stylist, but Bradman had overthrown our champion in statistical terms, and, with Larwood out of the reckoning, seemed invincible.

Yet the cycle was already turning, assisted by an influx of talent into the professional ranks. The complex social factors involved in this included the uncertainties and insecurities of the employment situation, and the enhanced image of the professional (given a rosy colouring by the glamour of Sutcliffe and Hammond), and a more general, if slight, diminution of subservience exemplified by the custom of calling the amateur captain 'skipper' rather than 'sir'. (It wasn't quite the post-war workman's semi-derisory 'Squire' – cricketers weren't like that – but it was a tiny slither down the path to democracy.) And things were happening in the education system, both in the general raising of standards and in the encouragement given to working-class children, particularly boys, to share in the national preoccupation with games.

It was not unknown now for stronger-minded cricketers from the better schools to turn professional: Charles Barnett of Gloucestershire and England had been, like his father before him, at Wycliffe – and he eventually finished up in the Lancashire League. All sorts of school below the most socially superior looked for the reflected glory that came from producing an England or even a county professional. Mr Fred Scott, the headmaster of Bracondale School in Norwich, had a concrete wicket laid in order to assist the development of the young Bill Edrich, second and greatest of four cricketing brothers. He played for Norfolk at sixteen, joined Lord's ground staff, qualified for Middlesex at twenty-one and won his first England cap a year later. Down in Somerset, another farmer's son, young Harold Gimblett, a schoolboy prodigy in club cricket, made the fastest century of the season on his county début in 1935.

Urban elementary schools usually had poorer facilities, tending to lack grass. Denis Compton, another Middlesex prodigy, went to Bell Lane School in Hendon, which was notably short of the stuff, and after hours he and his older brother Leslie played in the street. Their father was a club cricketer, however, and by the age of twelve young Denis was playing alongside him. London schools were also particularly well served by various competitions, and that same year Denis played for North London Schools v. South London Schools at Lord's: two years later he got a place on the Lord's ground staff after scoring a century for a London Elementary Schools XI. MCC members got some good bowling practice – and Lord's some cheap manual labour – out of the deal, but such apprenticeships were recognised as good for the character for those who had not had the privilege of fagging at a public school.

Suddenly, from all quarters, there was a host of young professional talent pressing for England selection. The tensions between the media-fed concept of entertainment value and the more sombre realities – averages, patience, learning from mistakes, reluctance to lose – reached a new peak just before the Second World War. The two great young players who managed to satisfy both criteria, Len Hutton of Yorkshire and Denis Compton of Middlesex, represented the head and the heart, the north and the south of the Englishness of cricket – and indeed of England. Both scored lots of runs in those years. Denis Compton – also an Arsenal footballer in that team's glory days – won most praise for the livelier cricketing virtues, but it was Hutton who, in the final Test of 1938, broke Bradman's record score as England, under Hammond's approving gaze, ground the Australians into the Oval dust. England made 903 for 7, beating Australia by an innings with Bradman unable to bat through injury.

Hutton's innings was a record of the less agreeable kind, lasting over thirteen hours. In this particular match, though no time limits had been set, only four days were needed. Howard Marshall, whose deep, rich voice had borne the tidings over the airwaves with suitably episcopal dignity, was not in fact too impressed by the spectacle. His report in the *Daily Telegraph* concluded,

> While we may reasonably be pleased at England's mastery, I cannot believe that any true lover of cricket will be easy in his mind about the conditions in which it was achieved.

His misgivings were not widely shared, either in Yorkshire, for whom it was all part of the glory of what seemed like permanent possession of the Holy Grail, or for dear old 'Plum' Warner, chairman of the selectors, whose account stops just short of gloating.

There was worse, or more ridiculous, to come before Hitler intervened. The final 'timeless Test' of that winter's South African tour was still unfinished after ten days when the England team had to leave to catch the boat home. It was not, admittedly, as bad as persisting with body-line bowling, but it was nevertheless a somewhat peculiar direction for the custodians of a 'national game' to take, rather like presenting a group of folk-singers with a performance of Wagner's *Ring* cycle as an instructional aid. It was the end of that particular road.

PART IV

Modern Times

CHAPTER SEVENTEEN

Shaken, not Stirred

THERE HAD BEEN MUCH TALK in the 1930s, not all of it in jest, about the unfortunate circumstance that the Germans did not play cricket. So it was entirely fitting that Sir Home Gordon should begin his inspirational article in the *Cricketer* for September 1939 with a suitable metaphor – 'England has now begun the grim Test match against Germany' – and should express his war aims in another: '. . . we do not wish merely to win the ashes of civilisation. We want to win a lasting peace with honour and prosperity to us all.'

The cricket season was almost over when war was declared, and the championship was already settled. The West Indian tourists had already gone home, leaving seven matches unplayed, and the few remaining county games were cancelled at once, with none of the unfortunate disposition to linger over it as in 1914. But, of course, it was all very different. No one had any illusions about 'this little lot': everyone was going to be in it, not just Tommy Atkins. There had been early indications in the last months of peace: the air-raid shelters, sandbags and barrage balloons; the issue of gas-masks; and since June the heart-rending sight of thousands of schoolchildren, with their teachers, flocking to the railway stations as part of the government's planned evacuation.

Then, on the very morning war was declared, the air-raid sirens wailed and a chill clutched the stoutest hearts. Fortunately, it was a false alarm, but as people stumbled about in the blackout that gloomy winter there were many road accidents, and the first catch-phrase of the war was the ARP Warden's thunderous cry, 'Put that light out!' Another contrast with the First World War was the unhurried pace at which the war machine was assembled. There was no mad rush of volunteers without equipment for them; conscription, with exemption for 'reserved' occupations, proceeded according to plan throughout the 'phoney war', when German preparation for the blitzkrieg was mistaken for incapacity. The RAF were kept from bombing Germany for fear of reprisals, but the Luftwaffe bombed cruisers on the Clyde, and U-boats wrought havoc.

Industrially, too, the picture was bleak. By the spring of 1940 there were still a million unemployed; yet the munitions work force had increased by only 10 per cent. Unions opposed dilution of labour by the unskilled and the better-off grumbled at income tax at 7*s.* 6*d.* (37.5p) in the pound. The main thing that preserved industrial peace and social harmony was food rationing, nervously introduced after an opinion poll showed that the public wanted it, and when the government, to stave off a wage claim, brought in food subsidies, allowing prices that made rations affordable to the poor, much of the population began to be better fed than ever before.

During that first winter the importance of maintaining morale was borne in on everyone. The blackout was modified, cinemas and dance-halls flourished, and the wireless brought cheer to the fireside: *ITMA* took the steam out of wartime restrictions and pomposity and featured a ludicrously incompetent German spy, Funf, while as many as six million listened in to the bizarre 'Lord Haw-haw'.[1] More actively, a National Youth Committee was set up to foster the efforts of local authorities and voluntary bodies in all manner of recreational activities for the young. The Central Council of Physical Training and Recreation, an alliance of voluntary sports bodies, one of whose key members was Stanley Rous, secretary of the FA, also placed themselves at the government's disposal.

The FA, still sensitive about 1914, had laid plans at the time of the Munich crisis for an immediate cessation of all professional soccer, and they duly suspended league activity. After a few days, however, friendly matches were allowed, except in a few sensitive areas: at first maximum crowd size was specified, but this proved superfluous, as there was no great interest in friendlies or in the regional leagues that followed. Almost all league clubs took part, but their teams gradually disintegrated as their players joined, or were called, up. These recruits were by no means all bound for the sharp end of the war. The Army Physical Training Corps, advised by the FA, was vastly expanded both in size and concept – sport as well as drill and gymnastics had a central place. The RAF, too, invested heavily in 'recreative welfare' and soon both services had an array of sergeant PTIs and a fair sprinkling of officers. Most were professional sportsmen, chiefly soccer players, but including some famous cricketers, notably Sergeants Hutton and Compton.

Equally important, the value of sport was recognised on the Home Front, too. In 1940 a Mass Observation survey commented, 'Sports like football have an absolutely major effect on the morale of people,' which may not today seem an earth-shattering discovery, but was certainly a departure from previous thinking on the subject of how to win wars. Significantly, soccer was now the model, especially as the Football Association was adding civic virtue to its manifest populist claims to the title of 'national sport'. But cricket had its own emblematic part to play. Major H. S. Altham, in the 1940 *Wisden*, described the 'sobering experience' of a visit to Lord's the previous December:

there were sandbags everywhere, and the Long Room was stripped and bare, with its treasures safely stored beneath ground, but ... one felt that somehow it would take more than totalitarian war to put an end to cricket.

II

More tangibly, Altham also reported 'a general feeling that the game can and should be kept going wherever possible'. With conscription in force, he added, 'there is no room for the charge of skrimshanking': where it could be played without interfering with the war effort it could 'only be good for the national morale'. He might have added, too, that not only Britain but also her great Empire was at war: the choice had been made for India and the colonies, but the Dominions – even South Africa, after an election – had come in of their own accord. And cricket was supremely the imperial game. MCC, with their secretary Col. R. S. Rait-Kerr gone to war, persuaded their man of empire, Sir Pelham Warner, to become acting secretary for the duration, and he took the opportunity to stage, amongst the array of domestic reminders of former glories such as the Varsity match,[2] many charity and morale-boosting efforts and services games, including Commonwealth-oriented ventures.

London, in this different kind of war, was much the leading centre, despite the loss of the Oval on what might loosely be called war service. It was commandeered in 1939 and modified for use as a prisoner-of-war camp, a role for which it had been selected, some said, because of its architectural style. Wire cages, divided by posts set in concrete blocks, were constructed on the playing area – awaiting prisoners who never came. Similarly, though the Long Room was stripped for action and Lord's was prepared for both enemy attack and War Office requisition, it was spared both.[3] Not only did MCC teams play the usual list of public schools but Lord's staged many representative games, in which most of the pre-war stars and some new discoveries raised money for charity.

Of the regular wartime sides the two best-known were the British Empire XI and the London Counties XI, which both started in 1940. The British Empire XI, thought up by Warner himself, was a loose-limbed assembly, mostly English county players but leavened by resident colonials – the West Indian Dr C. B. Clarke was the mainstay. The London Counties XI was started by Desmond Donnelly, then in the RAF, but later a prominent Labour MP and journalist. Both teams played one-day charity games in London and the south-east, with forays further afield. Of the matches staged at Lord's during the summer of 1940, whilst the Battle of Britain raged, the best remembered was that between these two, when Frank Woolley came out of retirement and played against Denis Compton.

The profits made for charity were real enough, but the main purpose was to sustain the morale – of the players as well as of the people who came to watch. Other prominent sides came from the services, and Civil Defence organisations – ARP, fire service, police – which all had their own teams, national and local. So increasingly did the Dominions services, as between Dunkirk and the invasion Britain became a vast training camp and air-base. Some of the more sought-after and available players, conspicuously Denis Compton, fought under many colours.

Altham had been careful to qualify his remarks by adding, 'Of course anything like county cricket is out of the question.' Aside from the proprieties it simply was not practical to stage a wartime championship. In the same 1940 *Wisden*, Robertson-Glasgow had reminded enthusiasts that three-day cricket, even in peacetime, 'was scarcely maintaining the public interest except in matches between the few best, or the locally rivalrous, teams'. His solution was to improvise as many one-day games as possible in the spirit of pre-scientific, village cricket: 'Many would delight to see again a few Edwardian drives and a late Victorian pull or two.'

(In fact not only 'pre-scientific' club and village cricket remained on show, sometimes in straitened circumstances, sometimes enhanced by the vagaries of military postings and the prevalence of reserved occupations: the 'northern' leagues flourished, albeit with fewer exotic stars than in peacetime. There were now scores of these organisations, ranging geographically from Northumberland to South Wales and Monmouthshire, and in degrees of amateurism from the Merseyside and District to the star-studded Lancashire combinations, but all providing the spice of competitive cricket on a part-time basis.)

Most counties, in a mixture of prudence and more flamboyant virtues, had reached for the mothballs at the outset. Yorkshire, under Col. Sir Stanley Jackson's leadership, again proclaimed the dual policy of war service for all players and asking their members to continue paying their subscriptions as an investment in the future. Similarly, Surrey's circular letter to members began by quoting their 1915 appeal, and Kent announced a policy of no official matches, supplementing staff's wartime earnings and appealing to members to keep up payments. Generally speaking, such appeals worked best in the more prosperous counties, but Somerset, all of whose players were in some form of national service and who ended all contracts in 1942, had some 800 members' faithful and largely cricketless support throughout the war.

Nottinghamshire, by contrast, though many players were in the forces or on other war-work, saw it as their duty to follow MCC's example and give their members something for their money. They played six matches at Trent Bridge in 1940, mostly friendlies against other counties, and were rewarded not only by pleasant days for members, but some new discoveries, like R. T. Simpson, then a young policeman. They even showed a surplus of £43 in 1940, but the ground was showing signs of neglect and there was an overdraft of £525. Most counties managed to maintain a surplus, ranging from Yorkshire, who, at the height of the war, declared 'satisfaction with the financial position ... £1242 [having] been received in subscriptions and donations', to Worcestershire, whose surplus 'grew slightly to about £200', and Leicestershire, who were saved from disaster by a seven-year covenant of £50 from Sir Julien Cahn.

The 'phoney war' encouraged talk of starting a county competition, relying on the superannuated, the medically exempt and home-based servicemen with time to spare. There were lots of wild and woolly suggestions. Lancashire, who produced a carefully thought-out scheme for a regionalised version, including Minor Counties, were somewhat aggrieved when MCC declined to take the matter further. However, Lancashire's own enthusiasm was dampened somewhat when Old Trafford was bombed, and the committee eschewed all official cricket thereafter, devoting members' subscriptions to a war-damage fund.

III

The war had brought horrors at sea, but the land war was turning into something of a bore, encouraging lunacies like the popular song 'We're going to hang out the washing on the Siegfried Line' and Chamberlain saying Hitler had 'missed the bus'. Then came the blitzkrieg – Norway, Holland, Belgium and France lost and Britain standing alone and under siege. It was a turning-point not only in the war, but in the social and political life of Britain. There was no outward change: a refugee from France, travelling by train to London, observed that 'all along the line young men in flannels were playing cricket in the sunshine on beautifully tended fields shaded by oaks and poplar trees'. But the Battle of Britain and the threat of invasion sharpened perceptions dramatically, and, even as the old patrician Churchill took the helm, there were the beginnings of a first, faintly stirring democratic spirit, and the Labour Party – Attlee, Bevin, Morrison – took a full share in the conduct of the war in a truly national government.

Hence the paradox that in the middle of the greatest war in history, Britons from the various classes that had been pitchforked into it together were thinking already of the sort of society they wanted after it was all over. One dramatic change was already happening in industry, where the sense of purpose bred teamwork existentially, but the two spectacular and unprecedented pieces of planning were the Beveridge Report, which laid the basis for the post-war welfare state, and the Butler Education Act, inspired by the revelations of the evacuation of slum children into the countryside, which was actually passed in 1944 while the war was still on.

No doubt similar motives prompted the representatives of MCC and the counties when they appointed a select committee in 1943 to produce a plan for post-war cricket. There was a notable difference, however, in that these plans were for the élite county game, and the committee members were made up, almost to a man, of the élite game's élite. Since many of them were in the services, the point can be illustrated by listing the ranks of the committee's core, all England or county amateur captains: Col. Sir Stanley Jackson (chairman), Lt. Col. G. O. B. Allen, Group Capt. A. J. Holmes, Major E. R. T. Holmes, Major R. Howard, Squadron-Leader R. W. V. Robins, Major A. B. Sellars, Capt. M. J. Turnbull, Flying Officer R. E. S. Wyatt and, later, Squadron-Leader W. R. Hammond.

(Gentlemen and players no longer became respectively officers and other ranks quite so automatically as in the Great War; distinction as a professional sportsman could assist promotion, if only as a PTI. Outside this specialism, too, things were more flexible: amongst the Yorkshire players commissioned were not only the amateurs Sellars and Yardley, but the professionals Bowes, Leyland and Verity. In the more meritocratic RAF anything was possible, the most spectacular examples being Edrich, W. J. and Ames, L. E. G. who became Squadron-Leaders. Even so, the general pattern in all services was for the division between amateurs and professional cricketers to be reflected in that between commissioned and non-commissioned officers. Thus it was Lt. Col. S. C. Griffiths, Flt. Lt. R. T. Simpson and Lt. T. E. Bailey, but Sergeants D. Brookes, T. G. Evans, L. G. Berry. G. Cox, C. Washbrook, Flt Sgts A. V. and E. Bedser, L. Cpl. L. H. Compton, and so forth. In particular, public-school boys – to the disgust of the *Daily Mirror* – had an inside track throughout the war, and at the beginning the well-connected could get red-carpet treatment.[4])

There were more immediate matters needing attention than plans for cricket, and the active-service members of the committee did well to spare time for meetings. Maurice Turnbull did not live to see the plans become reality, for he was killed in classic infantryman's fashion by a sniper's bullet in Normandy in 1944. He was the third English Test player to give his life. The first, Kenneth Farnes, had died in a flying accident in 1941; then two years later Hedley Verity was killed leading his infantry platoon in Sicily. All would have agreed with Warner, defending the citadel as the German bombers roared overhead,

> I had the feeling that if Goebbels had been able to broadcast that the war had stopped cricket at Lord's it would have been valuable propaganda for the Germans.

Goebbels had no chance. In 1943 no fewer than forty-seven matches, including a few representative two-day games, were watched by over 200,000 spectators. The following year was disrupted by bad weather and 'doodle-bugs' so the numbers were down, but as admission charges were doubled, from 6*d*. to 1*s*. (2.5p to 5p), charities benefited by a record amount. Lord's apart, a tremendous amount of public cricket was played by the services, not only the armed forces, but also the various Civil Defence organisations, for whom county professionals like Harold Gimblett, Joe Hulme, John and James Langridge, J. H. Parks and Frank Lee were in regular action. Woolwich Garrison fielded a regular team, and Blackpool Services, who headed the Ribblesdale League, were capable of beating every other team in the North when stars like J. F. Crapp, W. Cornford, G. Cox , W. H. H. Andrews, R. J. Partridge and E. P. Robinson were available. The Royal Australian Air Force (RAAF) was in England in such strength that it could run a regular side of much more than county standard.

Most of the counties also felt able to play a game or two, to try to maintain contact with their players and to discover new talent. Northants attempted none until 1943, when they blossomed forth with a dozen games, mostly against the likes of British Empire XI but including one against Leicestershire. Notts, who had lost money in the early war years trying to keep the flag flying, were rewarded in 1943 when many defaulting members resumed subscribing. Sussex, for whom Sir Home Gordon had volunteered to act as honorary secretary, trebled their number of games and even staged a three-day representative match, South of England against the RAAF. Surrey concentrated on encouraging young talent all over the county: their Colts developed quite a following, as did some of the clubs to whom they farmed out their young players. One of them, Epsom CC, which played charity matches against all the representative sides, was accorded four pages of *Wisden*'s 300-odd, more than any of the counties.

IV

Epsom sprang from the Club Cricket Conference tradition, which set its face against what it called 'competitive cricket', sullied as it was by the quest for cups and points and even money. Ironically, however, league cricket, for all its northern vulgarity and pre-war status in *Wisden* as a despised enemy of county cricket, was accorded seven pages. These did not, however, devote a paragraph each to, say, the Bolton, Northern, Saddleworth and District, Lancashire and Cheshire, Durham Senior, Yorkshire, Huddersfield, Leeds and District, Bassetlaw, and North Staffordshire, or the Yorkshire Council or the North Wales Cricket Association. Instead they gave results and averages from the three or four leagues that employed star professionals, presumably for the nostalgic resonances of the familiar names to be found there.

As in the First World War the Bradford League, which stayed unashamedly professional, overshadowed all the others, calling on a galaxy of talent – George Cox, Eddie Paynter, C. B. Harris, George and Alf Pope, L. F. Townsend, Tom Goddard from English counties, Martindale,

Constantine and Clarke of the West Indies as well as many Yorkshire veterans like Wilf Barber and future prospects such as Alec Coxon and Arthur Booth. The Birmingham League drew its county players more narrowly from its own region. Eric Hollies and Joe Mayer of Warwickshire were the leading lights.

The Lancashire League also took on a more home-spun look by suspending professionalism. But it was nevertheless able to maintain good standards - after all, in spite of the publicity given to the overseas stars, even the strongest leagues had always been essentially amateur. By contrast the Central Lancashire League, although technically suspending professionalism, relaxed its regulations to allow guest appearances from players engaged in work of national importance, with the result that there were actually more paid players than ever. John Kay, the chronicler of early league cricket, who was playing for Middleton as an amateur at the time, recalled one match in which their opponents, Crompton, fielded nine players with Test or county experience. But having an assortment of out-of-practice pros was no guarantee of success: Crompton lost as many matches as they won.

Thus in both Club Cricket Conference and league territory more people had easy access to cricket of higher standard than ever before. This process was further accelerated when local councils and voluntary groups, answering the call for 'holidays at home' in the later war years, featured cricket competitions and exhibition matches as part of their programme of attractions. And of course, in the atmosphere of make-your-own entertainment engendered by wartime conditions, more adults than ever before played the game, in the services or for factory, office or colliery, or were sought to fill the spaces left in town or village teams by those called up.

Yet by far the biggest section of the wartime *Wisden* – almost a quarter of the whole – was the section devoted to the public schools. This was a reassuring sight for the devotee and a splendid antidote to wartime gloom, for it offered not only continuity of tradition but an occasional hint of decorous democratic progress, such as the success of W. H. H. Sutcliffe of Rydal School, son of Sutcliffe, H., educated in a less grand Pudsey establishment. This subtle mixture of nostalgia and hope for the future reflected a more general public mood. Yearning for the good old days, memories enhanced by the softening magic of time, was deepened by tantalising glimpses of the great stars in local leagues or big charity games. The wartime newspapers, insofar as their meagre newsprint allocation allowed, kept their readers informed about the doings of pre-war heroes. Hutton's arm, broken in a gymnasium in 1941, caused much anxiety, especially in Yorkshire, and his progress when invalided out, he played in the Bradford League , was studied as closely as the war news.

Sports coverage was, of course, a central feature of the home news in special forces newspapers like *Reveille*, which, despite an occasional mild enquiry 'about how much actual military duty [Service players] do in a week', thought cricket, like soccer, 'a shining example of providing entertainment for war-workers'. The momentum increased in the second half of the war with the great accumulation of servicemen in the south of England over the long period of preparation for the Normandy landings. commonwealth fighting men, notably the Royal Australian Air Force, with squadrons permanently stationed in Britain, provided the opposition to the England teams in one-day internationals in 1943 and 1944 and in the six spectacular three-day 'Victory Tests' that stretched through August 1945, arranged even before the Japanese surrender precipitated by Hiroshima.

V

It was hardly to be expected that Sir Stanley Jackson's committee would propose a radically different future for first-class cricket after the war. Their report, published in March 1944, was full of stirring rhetoric, calling for attacking play and 'a dynamic attitude to the game' and urging the resumption of county cricket at the earliest possible moment. But it rejected two-day county matches, Sunday cricket, time-limit and over-limit cricket or indeed any radical changes. It proposed a uniform number of games (twenty-six), which, as well as making more sense of the championship, would have left space for a knock-out competition, but it set its face against anything other than three-day matches, and although the press got very excited about the prospect of a cricket cup, the idea was dropped. Its major innovation was to allow a new ball after fifty-five overs. Even this dubious contribution to brighter cricket was conditional: 'It is anticipated that in the first season the supply of balls may be insufficient for this, but possibly a used one in better condition may be substituted.'

One of the pretexts for abandoning the idea of a midweek knock-out competition was concern lest the government, in its anxiety to assist industrial recovery and the export drive, might intend to clamp down on midweek sport. To some extent this was paranoia, encouraged by the election in 1945, by a huge majority, of a Labour government. Not only had the great warleader, Churchill, been unceremoniously rejected, but when at the first meeting of Parliament the Tories had greeted his arrival with 'For he's a jolly good fellow', government supporters had out-sung them with 'The Red Flag'. Their election programme had centred on the nationalisation of key industries – railways, coal, electricity and gas supply – and on the implementation of the wartime Beveridge plan for national insurance and free medical treatment, and they had a strong mandate to carry it out.

The transformation was duly implemented, though the result was some way short of the Marxist hell the diehards predicted. This was partly because the class structure did not change in its fundamentals: Attlee's government was well stocked with the products of Oxford and Cambridge (institutions as yet little touched by democracy), who also made up three-quarters of the administrative class of the Civil Service and provided, along with fellow-travellers such as retired generals, many of the managers the nationalised industries and other new bureaucracies required. The government were certainly deeply anxious not to inhibit the export drive by encouraging absenteeism, and floated the idea of trying to ban midweek soccer, but this was received so badly that they were forced to backtrack.

Cricket supporters were not so numerous or so occupationally oriented that their absence was deemed likely to imperil industrial production. The diversion had been enough, however, to fend off the threat of dangerous experiments at crowd-pleasing. The Victory Tests had given plausibility to the view that the same cavalier spirit would be displayed in the county championship, and great confidence was expressed in the county captains to bring this about. Shortly after the 1946 season began the five surviving Worcestershire Fosters wrote to *The Times* congratulating all concerned on the 'sporting results' achieved so far. By July, however, MCC felt impelled to issue a stern warning about the contrived declarations that were bringing about such conclusions.

The old regime was back in force, reactionary as ever, and now, furthermore, apparently as intent on performing what it conceived as its duty to the game as the Labour government were on nationalisation. The difference was that MCC was still what it had always been, a private club, and an élitist one at that. So the arrangements it made for what was supposed to be the national summer game were not likely to show the same democratic concern as Aneurin Bevan for the National Health Service. Col. Rait-Kerr, restored to civilian life, brought military precision to a painstaking and prolonged revision of the laws, which were buttressed by all manner of ancillary regulations and rendered even less penetrable to the unschooled mind by copious explanatory notes. The deckchairs on the *Titanic* were now arranged in a manner befitting a great institution.

The aims of those who clamoured for reform – making the first-class game accessible to more people, both as potential players and as spectators – had always had to contend with the environmental and time factors that cut it off from the clumsy frolickings of the average performer. *The Times*, in a lyrical piece hailing the start of the 1946 cricket season, noted the gulf between concept and actuality for many people:

> Cricket is a religion on which they have been brought up and to which they
> adhere even though they seldom attend the celebrations.

The gulf, as in Christian observance itself, was to go on widening, and for much the same reason – fear that making the product too readily accessible would cheapen and denature it.

Yet at first the format of first-class cricket did not much matter, so great was the hunger for entertainment in the immediate aftermath of the war. Even a wet summer, indifferent standards and the increased prominence of swing and seam bowlers encouraged by the fifty-five-overs new-ball regulation, did not keep the crowds away. The Oxford and Cambridge match attracted 12,000 on the Saturday and 10,000 on the Monday. However, Gentlemen v. Players was less reassuring to traditionalists, both in its attendance and in its one-sidedness. Its old-world charm was wearing thin, and nothing was more revealing of MCC's unfitness for its task in the post-war world than the pertinacity with which it clung to the distinction.

Much was made of the slight relaxations in its discriminatory practices. Some counties no longer required their professionals to herd together in a poky little dressing-room while the amateurs, or even a single amateur, rattled around in one twice the size. It seemed like the storming of the Bastille when, in the match between MCC and Middlesex, the amateur dressing-rooms at Lord's were put to communal use. However, Lord's score-cards continued to put amateurs' initials before the surname and professionals' after. (This, explained Col. Rait-Kerr's daughter Diana[5] in the third updating of the club's official history, was at the insistence of members but 'out of interest rather than snobbery'.) Hence, the début of one sixteen-year-old future international was marked, as he proceeded to the wicket, by a loudspeaker announcement apologising for an error on the printed score-cards: '"F. J. Titmus" should read "Titmus, F. J".'

Professionals made a more substantial social advance with the appointment of the pre-war stalwart, Leslie Berry, as captain of Leicestershire. (This was for the entirely pragmatic reason that 'no amateur was available', a sorry state that lasted two seasons until Leicestershire recruited a Mr S. J. Symington, whose only experience of first-class cricket was this season as captain. They then felt able to afford to appoint C. H. Palmer, a Worcestershire 'amateur', as secretary and captain.) Warwickshire, meanwhile, had arrived, somewhat hesitantly, at professional captaincy in 1948,[6] appointing Tom Dollery, a minor-public-school product. Dollery's achievement in building up a side that won the championship – beating Yorkshire by a street – in 1951 could not be ignored. Warwickshire had also broken new ground – and made themselves solvent – by raising money through lotteries and other extra-curricular activities, and thus could lay claim to being the first modern county cricket club. This, needless to say, was not universally regarded as a compliment at the time: genteel poverty was to be preferred.

VI

Test matches had become essential to cricket's economy. This apart, there was a upsurge of warmth towards the Empire, whose bonds had been strengthened by the collective wartime effort against totalitarian oppression. It was becoming clear that not only the temporary ally, the Soviet Union, but the abiding one, the USA, strongly disapproved of this anachronistic arrangement, and that both would encourage its centrifugal nationalist movements. But as these alien forces grew, the imperialist tendency became more active. In January 1946 the Imperial Cricket Conference – really MCC's Colonial Branch – drew up a seven-year programme of Test matches for the enlarged magic circle, which now included India, West Indies and New Zealand as well as the original three members. India were the first post-war visitors, rising above the mounting political crisis at home and the grave shortage of equipment and clothing in rationed[7] and straitened Britain, to bring the last team before partition. As the Nawab of Pataudi, a pre-war Oxford man, led a united team, including Abdul Hafeez Kardar, soon to go up to Oxford, traditionalists could shut their eyes and imagine that the fairy-tale would continue.

A more realistic portent was the successful Test debut of A. V. Bedser, a young Surrey professional in the Maurice Tate mould, who was to be the mainstay of the English attack for many years. Bedser was a great, if unspectacular bowler. Unfortunately he was also a model for many lesser players, who were able to imitate his basic in-swing if not his subtle variations. This tedious tendency was encouraged by the succession of changes brought in to offset the dominance of the batsmen – the slightly smaller ball, the 1935 lbw law, the fifty-five-over new-ball rule, and most of all the balls with enlarged seams introduced in the 1950s. And, Bedser apart, there was not, in the early pre-war years, much else of Test-match promise, save the intriguing but unpredictable leg-spin of Kent's Douglas Wright.

Nevertheless, England's 1946–7 touring team, full of accomplished batsmen, were confidently looking forward to meeting Australia and re-establishing pre-war supremacy. Things did not go quite according to plan. Hammond, feeling his age, his arthritis and his personal troubles, was more brooding and introverted than ever. He had been aloof with the Australian press and skittish at an official welcoming dinner. Then came the first Test, when, after Australia had lost two early wickets, an uneasy-looking Bradman appeared to edge a ball to Jack Ikin at second slip. Ikin threw it up in triumph. The batsman did not move and after a while Ikin appealed, but was refused.

Bradman afterwards wrote, 'In my opinion the ball touched the bottom of my bat before touching the ground and therefore it was not a catch.' Hammond, however, was incensed, believing that Bradman, knowing he was out, should have 'walked' without waiting for the umpire's decision. At the end of the over, as he walked past the batsman, he said tersely, 'That's a bloody fine way to start a series.' Bradman went on to make 187 out of Australia's 645. Australia won the match by an innings and in due course the series, whilst poor Hammond went on in smouldering resentment, unable to match Bradman either with the bat or in captaincy.

This particular refinement of 'not cricket' – 'walking' – had been developed in the English county game by the gentlemanly captains who, in true Duke of Richmond spirit, set their honour code above the authority of the humble umpires. It was never so widespread in Australia – or for that matter in the northern leagues – where different social conventions applied. Under either convention it can be assumed as more likely to take place when a batsman has just made a century than after he has made three successive ducks. It has, in fact, a slightly unreal 'holier than thou' aura, and may be thought less of a realistic proposition than the basic tenet of the code: not expressing dissent, either orally or by body language, however disappointing or seemingly unfair the umpire's decision.

In this context the comments of the English journalist E. W. Swanton, reporting on the tour for the *Daily Telegraph*, are worth studying. He deplored the emerging tendency in the English press to criticise umpires' decisions, which breached 'the tradition in all sport that the findings of the umpire or referee are final and binding', adding dryly that 'cricketers are apt to claim, with not too conspicuous modesty, that specially noble virtues are inherent in and derivable from cricket'. At Melbourne, he reckoned, things had got to such a pitch 'that the question of the hour is not whether England can win or save the match, but whether Edrich or Compton was or was not lbw'. As the press box at Melbourne was beyond mid-wicket and third man, he pointed out that the only 'evidence' on which journalists could base a contrary judgement was 'the gestures or demeanour of players on the field'. And unfortunately, he continued, 'both Edrich and Compton, in the heat of the moment, were unable to avoid giving the impression of being surprised when given out'.

VII

Edrich and Compton were doubtless better pleased with the umpiring on their return home, for the following season they starred in one of the greatest episodes of modern cricket mythology. Compton made 3,816 and Edrich 3,519 runs in the sun-baked summer of 1947, bringing Middlesex the championship after years of Yorkshire domination, and apparently heralding the long-awaited era of brighter cricket. Ms Rait-Kerr hailed the 'remarkable spirit of revival' that brought thousands to stand in queues to watch county matches. On big days Lord's had posters put up at Underground stations warning that the gates were closed. Middlesex, charging 1*s*. 6*d*. (7.5p) admission, from which entertainment duty was deducted, still made a record profit of over £5,000 on the season. South Africa, not yet in the grip of the Afrikaner Nationalist party and its fervent application of apartheid, sent an attractive team that shared the sunshine and Compton and Edrich's plundering: they gave half their share of the gates of the Old Trafford and Oval Tests to help with rebuilding the grounds after war damage, and still took home £10,000 profit.

The editor of *Wisden* took the opportunity to moralise about the county championship:

> In every way the season of 1947 bears comparison with any year within living memory. Attendances which rose beyond those known in the past, with obvious appreciation by ever-increasing multitudes, clearly demonstrated the great hold the game takes on spectators once they are aware that both sides and every individual mean to expend all their energies striving for a definite result.

For although such a dry summer and such heavy scoring on batsmen's wickets might have been expected to produce many more draws, some three-quarters of matches were won outright.

Swanton, however, was less sanguine in the *Daily Telegraph*. First he complained about the decline in moral tone, noting that

> there were undoubtedly more decisions, relative to the matches played, which batsman or bowler begged leave to doubt this last English summer than on MCC's tour in Australia.

This apart, something needed to be done, he reckoned, to 'ensure a general state of prosperity independent of the artificial stimulus of "records" and heat waves'. His own proposals included competitions on 'the league or cup principle ... to stimulate a zest and enthusiasm dampened by the war and present conditions'.

These conditions included the stark austerity that continued as the government struggled to restore the crippled economy. War debts amounted to £3 billion, capital had been reduced by £2 billion and overseas investments by £1 billion. As patriots saw it, Britain's wartime sacrifices counted for nothing, and the Socialist government were in the grip of Wall Street, obliged to seek a dollar loan and agonisingly trying to conserve foreign currency. The Marshall Plan, offering aid for European recovery, was in the offing, but meanwhile belts had to be tightened. Literally: the first casualty was the Food Minister, overcome by the complexity of his task. No one was starving: indeed children, with statutory issues of orange juice, halibut-liver oil and milk were better nourished than ever before, but the depressingly long list of rationed foods – meat, tea, sugar, biscuits, sweets, cooking fat – got longer for a time when bad harvests threatened a shortage of bread.

Morale was worse than during the war, especially after 1947, which began with the worst freeze on record, killing a third of the country's hill sheep and tens of thousands of cattle, followed by floods that drowned over half a million acres of arable land and destroyed 80,000 tons of potatoes and 70,000 acres of wheat. There was an acute housing shortage, intensified by the wartime baby boom. The new National Coal Board, taking over a shambles and only slowly getting a grip, did not reach pre-war production levels until 1950: in 1947 coal was so short that the government exhorted people to limit baths to 5 inches of water. Petrol rationing continued despite the small number of cars (barely up to the pre-war total of 2 million by 1948). Cigarettes went up in price from 2*s.* 4*d.* (11.7p) to 3*s.* 4*d.* (16.7p) for twenty and drink was more heavily taxed than ever before. Shortages brought inflated prices – deeply resented – and 'spivs' who headed the swift decline in personal morality. This was usually justified as reaction to apparently sense-less and ever-proliferating bureaucracy or as protest against unrelenting and baffling deprivation – 'You wouldn't think we'd won the war, would you?'

It is easy to see how the warming rays of the sun and the flashing of Compton's bat brought a deceptive 'feel-good factor' into cricket for a while, especially amongst the well-to-do, who, as ever, found ways of softening the harshness of life. Diana Rait-Kerr's official history is again revealing. Describing the 1947 Eton v. Harrow match, she wrote: 'The ground was crowded with elegant and lovely debs profiting from the luncheon interval to parade the New Look.' Now the New Look was still, as far as the government and its Chancellor, the austere Sir Stafford Cripps, were concerned a deeply unpatriotic frivolity. The vogue introduced by the new fashion house of Christian Dior in Paris a year earlier was being boycotted by British designers at Cripps's request because it required more cloth than the standard just-below-the-knee length article. (Clothes were strictly rationed and even the Royal Wedding was fairly plain as these things go.) These good intentions were undermined by the arrival of wicked New Look Parisian garments in chic London shops, and the fashion spread like a plague through high society.

By spring 1948 officialdom yielded. The President of the Board of Trade, Harold Wilson, announced philosophically, 'We cannot dictate to women the length of their skirts.' Once started, the New Look became a liberating symbol, a cloud no bigger than a woman's hand that indicated a strong desire for an end to austerity and an impatience with the old pace of things. It became a potent sales gimmick in furniture, cars, houses, even pens, as the now ubiquitous disposable ball-point hit the market at a price about the same as that of a cheap suit.

In 1947–8 MCC sent a team to the West Indies, short of some obvious stars and led by the forty-five-year-old 'Gubby' Allen. They proved accident-prone, and most of the younger players failed to come up to expectations: MCC appointed a sub-committee to advise on what seemed to be going wrong. The tour apart, continued national service and full employment with high wages were discouraging new players from coming in to replace the old pre-war ones, who were wearing out. The report referred to 'post-war reaction' and diet deficiency and recalled the Findlay report of 1937, which had warned against too much cricket. MCC's response was to cancel a projected tour of India and to propose fewer tours generally.

All of this was in the context of a high-minded policy of not seeking a profit from these overseas ventures. MCC, for all the post-war boom, was short of money. Essentially this was because of the absurdly low subscriptions: it was thought a big step when they were put up from £3 to £4 a year for new members after 1946. (The counties offered a comparable bargain: Yorkshire's subscription had gone up to £2 in 1945.) Thus MCC's surplus of £12,000 in 1948 concealed an actual trading deficit. Revenue had increased by 70 per cent since 1945 but expenditure, reflecting rising prices and wages, had gone up by 105 per cent. The waiting lists were opened up and the membership was increased to 8,000 by 1950.

No cricket-lover was thinking about money matters in the summer of 1948, however, except insofar as the clicking turnstiles consoled them for the devastation wrought by the incomparable Australian team. Lindwall and Miller, the spearhead of the attack, were the decisive factor, and Bradman, the old master, brought his Test career to a fitting conclusion. He had already swept his old tit-for-tat adversary Hammond from the stage: now he showed up the clear weaknesses in the philosophy of amateur captaincy. N. W. D. Yardley, also the Yorkshire skipper, was a fine cricketer and a thoroughly nice chap, but scarcely a man of steel or a master-tactician. Nor did the selectors do much for the amateur principle by their evident lack of clear policy.

The consolation for MCC and the county treasurers lay in the record attendances and profits. 132,000 saw the Lord's Test, which grossed receipts of £43,000. Even more attended Old Trafford, in spite of poor weather, while at Headingley the 158,000 attendance was a record for any match in England. Perhaps the whole tour – and the paradoxical state of the first-class game – was best epitomised by the tourists' match against Essex early in the season, scheduled for three days but over in two. Australia made 721 on the Saturday, a record score for a single day, then on the Monday twice bowled Essex out cheaply. But both attendance figures – 32,000 – and receipts – £3,482 – were ground records.

Confusing signals, too, came from the championship victory of Glamorgan, who won by making shrewd use of their limited talents and by fine fielding. They were aggressively led by the pre-war rugger international Wilf Wooller, an opinionated fellow who combined blimpishness with Welsh national fervour, and their tactics depended heavily on tight bowling to a leg-side field. Wooller was also an energetic – and vocal – county secretary, and the team's success helped put their finances on a very sound footing. It was good, too, for the health of the championship to see the title being more widely shared. But pessimists feared that Glamorgan's victory meant that the standard had plummeted.

CHAPTER EIGHTEEN

Winds of Change

IN THE INTENSE ATMOSPHERE of national crisis that always invests British sporting defeats, constructive discussion tends to be stifled because of the assumption that the divine order of things has been arbitrarily and malevolently tampered with, and because quick fixes are demanded by the custodians of the national weal in the media. After the 1948 débâcle there were, amid the usual wand-waving solutions, some glimmerings of recognition that the way to start improving the Test team was to provide better opportunities, facilities and coaching for the youngsters coming into the game. MCC announced an enquiry into youth cricket. The public schools and most of the local-authority grammar schools had splendid facilities, but things were very different for the 80 per cent who didn't 'pass the scholarship' and the idea was to start doing something about it.

The enquiry was the brain-child of 'Gubby' Allen, who had bluntly asked a startled and unsuspecting meeting of the general committee, 'What has MCC ever done to help the boys of this country as a whole over their cricket?' Its chairman was Harry Altham, the former Winchester housemaster and highly regarded cricket historian, whom Allen also successfully supported for the key post of treasurer of MCC – against the banker backed by his former patron Warner. The committee of enquiry also included some of the less hidebound MCC luminaries as well as representatives of regional club cricket associations and of voluntary organisations like the Central Council for Physical Recreation and the National Playing Fields Association.

There was a fresh breeze, if not exactly a wind of change blowing in and around the corridors of power. HRH the Duke of Edinburgh turned out to be a cricketer (as well as a tiger-shooter, yachtsman, carriage-driver and polo-player) and was opportunistically elected president of MCC in 1949. His presence, and his genuine interest in outdoor pursuits for the young, bred at Gordonstoun, gave a fillip to the charitable agencies that were Britain's alternative to state intervention. He was also president of his father-in-law's creation, the National Playing Fields Association (NPFA), and later the Duke of Edinburgh's Award Scheme. And he was the natural 'Twelfth Man' for the Lord's Taverners, a convivial collection of cricket-loving habitués of the hostelry at the ground, mostly actors, broadcasters and television personalities. This, starting from small beginnings in 1950, became a big-scale organiser of charitable events, mostly on Sundays, raising hundreds of thousands of pounds each year for the NPFA and, later, for the disabled.

In this optimistic spirit of charity the offspring of MCC's committee of enquiry, the Youth Cricket Association, chaired by Altham, put forth a steady stream of proposals for coaching schemes, training the coaches and so forth. Wearing his MCC treasurer's hat, Altham could find little money for such matters, but a one-off grant of £15,000 was eventually found to launch a central organisation, with the counties supporting its regional offshoots. It began with a three-day conference at which the notion of group coaching was unleashed on a sceptical world.

Group coaching, like cheap mass-produced footwear, was probably better than nothing. Apart from its assumption of an ideal mode suited to all physical peculiarities, however, it was a bit like learning to swim on dry land, and there was not much transferability of skills practised *en masse* in village halls or school yards to actual contests. Furthermore, the bible of this movement, the painstakingly produced *MCC Cricket Coaching Book*, was based on the assumption that before any thought could be given to attack, defence had to be thoroughly mastered. This, even if tenable as a theory, made for a joyless regime in the 'give 'em nowt' mode. Nevertheless some attention was at last being paid to the needs of the disadvantaged majority, and some 15,000 aspiring coaches attended courses in the twenty years before the Youth Cricket Association was disbanded.

At the same time as the coaching scheme, another venture began. Building on the pioneering pre-war endeavours of progressive education authorities like London, the English Schools Cricket Association (ESCA) ought to piece together a network of competitions at various age-levels. From the start, when six counties were represented, it gradually grew to cover the whole country. Harry Altham was its first president and he did his best to increase contact between this offshoot of the state education system and the public schools: the pinnacle came to be the two-day games at Lord's – MCC Schools v. NAYC, and ESCA v. the President's XI. It was all very reassuring that democracy was evolving without getting too far out of hand.

II

The springs of democracy in Britain have been as much associated with capitalist competition as with Socialist egalitarianism, and so it was to prove in cricket. There was no chance of, and no wish for, government intervention in sport, so the levelling-up process was limited by the extent to which the 1944 Act was achieving its far-reaching objectives, notably secondary education for all. A speedier way of bringing on young cricketers from humble backgrounds was the top-down process of the marketplace. First-class cricket was, albeit still somewhat shamefacedly, a money-making business, and there were clearly rewards already for the talented. 1948 was a landmark in the matter of benefits. The astute Cyril Washbrook persuaded the Lancashire Club to allow him the Australia match, which put £4,000-odd into the total of £14,000 raised by his season of highly organised fund-raising events and merchandising. And the sound but undistinguished county player, Laurie Gray, broke the Middlesex record with £6,000.

(Even the immensely popular and highly marketable Denis Compton, who was soon earning £1,500 a year as the 'Brylcreem Boy', could not quite match Washbrook's benefit, and £14,000 remained a record until inflation made a nonsense of comparisons in the later 1970s. We should perhaps multiply the figures of 1950 by about twenty to get some idea of today's relative values.)

Money was not the main consideration for youngsters thinking about careers. 'When you are in your teens you take up professional cricket because you love the game,' wrote one post-war Middlesex recruit, Fred Titmus:

> It is only later, when you have been playing a few years, that finance enters into it. I forget what I earned when I started in 1949 but I think it was £2 10s a week. It would have been all the same if it had been thirty bob.

Young lads might not have been concerned about such mundane matters but parents and headmasters tended to take a different view. The glittering prizes of Washbrook, Compton and the like were not sufficient to reconcile the head of a grammar school to losing a scholarship boy before taking School Certificate.

> I was determined to be a professional cricketer. My parents had no objection. My headmaster at William Ellis had... In his view it was a waste of time to play cricket or football for a living ...

But young Titmus didn't like school anyway, so he left at fifteen and worked in a solicitor's office until he was taken on the Middlesex ground staff. Titmus's near contemporary at Middlesex, Don Bennett, had passed his Higher School Certificate before taking the plunge, but he gave up a chance of going to university to do so. A few years later their colleague Ron Hooker was prudently studying for a degree in electrical engineering during the winter against the time when his cricketing days were over.

The counties were already competing for staff in a seller's market. They were soon, as the range of post-war leisure activities increased, to be competing for customers at the turnstile. Cyril Washbrook, in his candid autobiography *Cricket: the Silver Lining*, was outspoken in his criticism of six-days-a-week county cricket, proposing a basic pattern of one championship match a week over the weekend, including Sundays, except for August, the accepted holiday month. This thoughtful proposal, anticipating the more leisured, more affluent and less Sabbatarian society to come, had no hope of acceptance. Sunday, protected by Puritan tradition and by laws that restricted commercial activities, was left free for charitable exhibition matches of short duration and minimal seriousness.

III

Saturday, too, was still relatively free of the counter-attractions that came with greater prosperity and the universal motor car. So league cricket was well placed to take advantage of the post-war boom. Lancashire, Washbrook territory, took the lead, and Australians were the early star attractions. Nelson, true to its reputation, landed Lindwall himself. In the nature of things, specific fees were not generally made known, being properly thought a matter between the player and the tax-man, but the clubs sought to enhance the value of their purchases by publicising the general scale of the operation; thus Lindwall cost Nelson 'a four-figure fee' plus £400 to bring him and his wife from Brisbane for the season.

Playing cricket in England was a useful winter activity for Australians, and, as well as Lindwall, Alley (Blackpool), Freer (Rishton), Pettiford (Nelson), Fothergill (Enfield), Manning (Colne), Ken Archer (Accrington), McCool and Dooland (East Lancashire) were among those recruited. Some went on to be pillars of county cricket, following the lead of Ken Grieves (Lancashire) and George Tribe and 'Jock' Livingstone (Northants). These model professionals were accepted – except by ethnic purists like Yorkshire and those concerned about building up the Test team – as part of the English scene, and they certainly did much to brighten cricket.

In the leagues themselves, however, something of the original community spirit seemed to have been lost in favour of a more commercial one. The small industrial towns still had no difficulty in adopting exotic stars as local heroes, but the new men were not always conscious of the need to foster the essentially amateur traditions of the northern leagues. Charles Barnett had signed for Rochdale in 1949 – again for a reputed £1,000 a year – and had been a noted success, not least in helping to bring on local talent. He was greatly taken, as Fred Root had been, by the social and sporting possibilities of this type of cricket. And at the club's annual dinner he took the opportunity to slam the new-style carpet-bagging stars, who did no coaching but concerned themselves solely with their own performances and jacking up their own fees. Young players, Barnett warned, were becoming mere cannon-fodder; and he predicted a decline in public interest if there were no change in policy. At the time his outburst was given a mixed reception, but as the clubs ceased to attract and bring on good young amateurs and the matches became gladiatorial contests, the crowds began to dwindle away. It was the beginning of a process, whose effects are nowadays all too obvious, in which excessive commercialism, particularly when practised by well-meaning amateurs, can defeat its own object.

The post-war boom had not long to run in first-class cricket either. By 1951 the secretary of MCC, Col. Rait-Kerr, was writing an article for *Wisden* which began, starkly, 'Many people are highly critical of modern cricket and asking if all is well with it.' Attendances at county matches had dropped from 2.2 million in 1947 to 1.8 million, and this coincided with the steady increase in the number of drawn matches, from an average of 25 per cent in 1938, 1939 and 1946 to around 50 per cent in 1951. Test-match run rates in easy batting conditions had dropped as low as 40 runs an hour, and 50 was thought satisfactory. Could the game survive 'the emphasis on security, first and last?', he asked. Unfortunately Rait-Kerr offered few thoughts about what to do about it, other than that 'committees should encourage their captains and players in the belief that cricket must be "eager, quick and full of action"'. This was the formula offered by A. G. Steel in 1901, in the middle of the great golden age, when there was a similar percentage of draws.

IV

MCC's policy, as distinct from its rhetoric, did not always help to enliven the game. In 1949, seeking to separate sheep from goats, it had allocated only three-day Test matches to the New Zealanders. The result was four drawn games as the tourists proved their point. Five days were allotted to the West Indies tourists of 1950, who had different points to prove. Aside from demonstrating that Test cricket that was manifestly enjoyed by the players was more enjoyable to watch, this was the Test match in which Britain began to have the first glimmerings of what it meant to be a multi-ethnic society. West Indians had come in droves to find work, often of the menial kind scorned by the natives, and, displaying great knowledge of the game they loved, took great delight in the success of their countrymen.

Alas, not everyone enjoyed the sounds of the calypso at Lord's, serenading 'those two little pals of mine, Ramadhin and Valentine', nor the rapturous reception of 'the three Ws'. It all helped to set the turnstiles clicking, but, racism and snobbery apart, there was mounting depression over the failure of the national team to approach its pre-war mastery. Winning, at whatever speed, mattered deeply, especially as the end of empire drew nearer. It all added to the exasperation of increasing numbers of people at the Labour government's sternly moralistic policies. The export drive was working, but rationing and restrictions continued – clothes until 1949, food and restaurant prices (maximum 5s.) until 1950, petrol until 1951. The apparatus of the welfare state, some felt, was not only costly but sapped initiative. Nationalisation, too, was a divisive issue, and when the beady eyes of the doctrinaire turned to the steel industry, it proved a fatal mistake for a party reduced to a wafer-thin majority. Soon the Tories, led by seventy-seven-year-old Winston Churchill, were back in power, and freedom was the watchword.

In 1952 Neville Cardus followed Rait-Kerr's *Wisden* piece with another, pretentiously headed *A Call for Culture* and subtitled 'Safety-first can ruin cricket'. He saw slow play as the legacy of the departed Socialists:

> The pressure of the spirit of the age hinders freedom and individuality. Life in this country is rationed. Can we blame Bloggs of Blankshire if in a four-hour innings he lets us know that his strokes are rationed?

Indeed, he deplored most things in the modern game:

> Too much is said to-day of the material setting and organisation of cricket; of schools and coaching.

And:

> The tendency to put emphasis on cricket as competition, an affair of match-winning and percentages, is dangerous and if it is not checked the game may easily, as a three-day matter, become obsolete after another decade.

Cardus's remedy appeared to be a greater nobility of soul amongst cricketers. He had many disciples, yearning for the good old days when Archie MacLaren held sway: Douglas Jardine was not so much discussed publicly, but in smoke-filled corners his name and successful tactics were often recalled nostalgically as the new, professional-dominated era unfolded. It was Tom Dollery's 1951 success with Warwickshire (a vulgar crowd who held raffles and things to make money) that really set their teeth on edge. And there was worse to come: MCC, who had steadfastly upheld Lord Hawke's philosophy as long as halfway-credible amateurs were available, suddenly gave in and the very next season appointed the ultra-professional Hutton as England captain. It was reasonable to pick the likes of F. G. Mann and F. R. Brown, especially against the lesser international sides, and Freddy Brown had even won a Test against Australia in 1950–1 (once the Ashes had been settled). But N. D. Howard, the young Lancashire captain, and D. B. Carr, still being groomed to lead Derbyshire, stretched credibility to the limits.

Hutton had been the backbone of England's batting since the war, apart from a brief spell in 1948 when the selectors lost their heads.[1] There was a favourite story in Yorkshire illustrating his importance to the scheme of things. Two neighbours, Alf and Jim, had gone off to the match in time for the first ball, but had forgotten the sandwiches. Alf went home to fetch them, but came back ashen-faced, saying

> 'Hey, Ah've got bad news for thee. Thi house is burnt down, thi wife's run off
> wi' t' lodger and left thi kids out i't' street crying their eyes out.'
> 'Aye, and Ah've bad news for thee. 'Utton's out.'

Batting apart, Hutton was also a shrewd and thoughtful professional, from whom his county captain, Norman Yardley, and Freddy Brown, his England skipper, regularly sought advice. But he was no swashbuckler, and his shrewdness was salted with what southerners thought an excess of Yorkshireness. This had come to light in the Oval Test of 1938, when after England had scored over 900 and the Australians, beset by injuries, were struggling feebly in reply, he was so anxious to prevent W. A. Brown taking a single at the end of an over that he kicked the ball over the boundary. The umpires took a poor view and awarded Brown five – the original single plus the four contributed by Hutton. And as recently as 1951 against South Africa he had been given out for the rare and unchivalrous offence of obstructing the field: in his concern to stop a ball ballooning from his bat onto the wicket he had stopped the fielder making a catch.

His gravest fault, however, was being a professional, and the selectors (Yardley, Brown, R. E. S. Wyatt and Leslie Ames) came in for grave criticism, especially Yardley, who as Yorkshire captain was thought doubly treacherous to the cause. Leslie Ames, too, the first professional to be a selector in his own right, had, it was recalled, chosen to remain a professional in spite of his high wartime rank – unlike good old Bill Edrich – so was obviously some kind of doctrinaire Marxist. Poor Hutton himself came in for the worst of it, for it was borne in upon him that he was a stop-gap. Trailing clouds of pre-war subservience, he inevitably felt at a disadvantage when dealing with illustrious amateurs in the committee room and over-anxious about the impression he made. A more diffident version of Herbert Sutcliffe, he made an earnest attempt to adjust his vowel sounds in the fashion of those inhibited times, but with much less aplomb. And the pressure on him to win – and winning was what Britain increasingly craved as her status in the world came under threat – was increased by the malevolence of the worst of the reactionaries, who manifestly wanted him to fail.

Even those who welcomed the appointment seemed less than wholehearted. In the *Daily Telegraph* E. W. Swanton, already developing an archiepiscopal tendency, adverted to Hutton's estimable modesty and his knowledge of the game, but ended facetiously: 'If our new captain ever errs from an excess of adventure, there is at least one critic who will observe with the most sympathetic eye.' And in *The Times* Geoffrey Green concluded sternly:

> In an age of so-called equal opportunity for all, the professional player has at last attained his fullest stature, and it is now up to Hutton to prove not only himself *but also his colleagues* [my italics] worthy of the new principle which has been established.

V

Fortunately there followed years of enough success to hold the vultures at bay, though the Archbishop of Canterbury must have lived in dread of an urgent message asking him to second the Revd D. S. Sheppard, the former Cambridge University batsman, from his clerical duties. Sheppard was one of a group of Cambridge amateurs, beginning with the ex-serviceman T. E. Bailey and culminating in the greatest batsman of his era, P. B. H. May, that gladdened MCC hearts and stirred hopes of an amateur revival. Two other promising Cambridge batsmen, J. G. Dewes and G. H. G. Doggart, had been tried somewhat too early in hope of a miracle. Dewes, indeed, had been flung into the arena against Lindwall and Miller in 1948. Both, as genuine amateurs increasingly tended to do, had left the scene prematurely, but the slightly younger Sheppard, who may have coveted, if not his neighbour's ox or ass, the England captaincy, was the purists' choice for it, and seemed not yet to be totally impervious to persuasion.[2] Hence Hutton's stop-gap feeling.

He had an easy initiation against a weak Indian side, who did not relish the tearaway bowling of the young Fred Trueman, from Hutton's own Yorkshire. Trueman was still learning his craft and, rather more slowly, how to behave. He was an early cricketing example of a post-war phenomenon, the brash and undisciplined youth tolerated for his talent – the anti-hero. Most fast bowlers are temperamental and a good many are rough, but 'Fiery Fred', as his county captain Norman Yardley christened him, was a rare example of the species. He turned into a record-breaking bowler, hard-working, exciting, shrewd and aesthetically pleasing. The advent of ball-by-ball television coverage made him an immensely popular public figure, and when he retired his rudimentary sense of humour, prodigious memory and forthright views made him a radio favourite. These same qualities, however, made him less popular on the county-cricket circuit, where he was dreaded off the field like the Ancient Mariner.

Young Richard Hutton, Leonard's son, university-educated and from a cooler generation than Trueman, was reputedly the only man ever to halt his flow. Fred, by then an elder statesman, was holding forth as usual when young Richard took advantage of a momentary pause, for breath or pipe-filling, to ask, deadpan, 'Would you say you were a modest man, Fred?'[3] At first the senior Hutton, burdened by the generation gap, found it harder to contain Trueman. National service delayed Trueman's appearance in the Ashes series of 1953 until the final Test. He did well enough, but the vital contribution was that of Laker and Lock of Surrey on their home pitch, which – surprise, surprise! – was taking spin. Lindsay Hassett, the Australian captain, conceded gracefully with a droll little speech, and when Walter Robins of MCC congratulated him on it, he said, 'Yes, I think it was pretty good considering Lockie threw us out.'

Indeed, the Australians had had to put up with a good deal – dour batting, and time-wasting at critical moments. Hutton's caution, under the weight of England's expectation, held full sway. Bailey, the Cambridge 'amateur' who unashamedly made a living from cricket, also had a pragmatic attitude to how the game should be played. In the fourth Test, when England looked like losing, the Australians were hurrying to get in one last over before lunch. It was twenty-nine-and-a-half minutes past one when the two batsmen met in mid-pitch. Jim Laker recalled the scene:

> 'It's a lovely day,' remarked Trevor 'and we haven't a chance of an appeal against the light. But I can't say I feel like another over before lunch.'

So he appealed, and by the time the umpires met to confer, there was no time left.

And on the final day, with Australia chasing 177 in 115 minutes, Bailey's slowness in bowling his overs, and his mode of attack wide of the leg stump with six men on the on-side, ensured that they didn't get them. This sort of thing was not without precedent – indeed Warwick Armstrong had done something like it in 1921 – but it wasn't very good for the game either, and, as E. W. Swanton put it, 'Our method of forcing a draw rankled a bit.' The tactic, for which of course Hutton was ultimately responsible, led eventually to prescription of the number of leg-side fielders allowed.

Even the heroic, match-saving stand between Bailey and Willie Watson, the Yorkshire left-hander, at Lord's in the second Test was, to say the least, slow. As Peter West, the BBC commentator, wrote in his book of the tour *The Fight for the Ashes*:

> There is one thing about which we cannot delude ourselves ... the side which played the more attractive cricket lost the Ashes.

Statistics, which were slowly becoming appreciated as potentially much more than mere number-crunching, exploded the long-held belief that the faster-scoring side always prevailed.

All of which seemed to confuse mightily the editor of *Wisden* with regard to the debate started by Rait-Kerr and Cardus about the ills of county cricket. In

1954 he questioned the desirability of the 100-guinea cash prizes that were to be offered by a business firm for individual performances, particularly the prize for the fastest hundred. He went on:

> The comparatively small crowd who paid for admission on the fifth day of the Lord's Test last June sat enthralled while they watched the dour batting of Watson and Bailey against the might of Australia.

And the missing spectators, he might have added, were glued to their radios or television sets.

VI

Hutton's unromantic approach had ensured England's return to the top of the Test-match tree, but others were now jostling for a place in the upper branches. And as Coronation year and the ascent of Everest brought much talk of a new Elizabethan era, the forthcoming tour of the Caribbean assumed unusual importance for the national prestige. The new Queen recognised the importance of cricket to the nation – and the changing times – by awarding a knighthood to Jack Hobbs. MCC, though riddled with anxiety about sending a team abroad under a professional captain, could not withhold the post from the victor of the Oval. Hutton's team was a powerful one: Hutton, Bailey, May, Compton, Graveney, Watson, Evans (sub. R. T. Spooner) Laker, Lock (or J. H. Wardle), Trueman and Statham. However, it included some whom it would not have been wise to take on a Sunday-school outing, and MCC added to the problems by sending as player-manager the amiable but unassertive Charles Palmer, the Leicester captain and secretary.

The celebrated West Indian writer C. L. R. James commented stiffly:

> The 1953–54 MCC team was actively disliked. This was not due merely to unsportsmanlike behaviour by individuals. There is evidence to show that the team had given the impression that it was not merely playing cricket but was out to establish the prestige of Britain, and by that, of the local whites.

There was not a great deal of fraternising between the teams off the field; colour apart, it was not a thing Hutton encouraged. West Indian umpires were not at that time always of a high standard, but England won no friends by asking for one of them to be replaced. The crowds took an early dislike to the belligerent Trueman, who had been taught not to show sympathy when he hit batsmen and who was demonstrative in his dissent when frustrated. Lock's action was suspect and Trevor Bailey's leg-theory tactics were not appreciated.

Throughout the tour there were off-the-field incidents, mostly centring on Trueman, who was the sort of chap about whom stories are told and repeated

with embellishments, largely because of his boisterously know-it-all
demeanour. The apocryphal one of his having called out, 'Pass t' salt, Gunga
Din,' to a local dignitary in Barbados clung to him throughout his career, for
it seemed the sort of thing he might have said. Similarly, when a society
matron complained to the Governor of being insulted by a tall, dark-haired
cricketer at a yacht-club dance Trueman was, erroneously but at once,
assumed to be the one.[4] Fred alone had his good-conduct bonus docked at the
end of the tour.

On top of all this depressing social blundering the team became involved in
the unruliest crowd behaviour since the days when the Duke of Richmond's
team had the shirts ripped off their backs by the mob at Richmond. The
rioting, intimidation of umpires and bottle-throwing have been well docu-
mented and are more to do with the development of West Indian nationalism
than with English cricket, but it can be said that Hutton maintained the sort
of stiff upper lip Lord Harris would have approved. He had not yet won as
many MCC hearts as matches, however, and when he fell ill in 1954 the
groundswell of support for Sheppard, backed by sections of the press, began
again. Hutton survived, even after presiding over the humiliation of losing to
unconsidered Pakistan for the first time.

He went on to retain the Ashes in Australia, minus the banished Trueman
but plus the lightning-fast Frank Tyson, who combined so effectively with
Statham as to keep the veteran Alec Bedser out of the team. The one thing
that was not lightning fast was the over-rate, and England were roundly
booed for their performance on New Year's Day when they took the whole
five hours to bowl fifty-four overs. Yet they were successful, which was what
mattered by then, even to MCC. Hutton became the first playing professional
to achieve honorary membership,[5] and his knighthood in 1956 signalled his
retirement from the game, hastened by the stress of his lonely pioneering
journey through the class barrier.

1956 marked the 150th anniversary of the Gentlemen v. Players fixture.
Rain dampened already limp proceedings. Some thought this a fitting context
for an outmoded ritual. Yet others saw a revival of amateurism as the only
hope for the future of the game. These included not only MCC dinosaurs but
the Marxist C. L. R. James, who attributed the growth of England's ultra-
defensive cricket to the insidious effects of the welfare state yet argued
eloquently for the removal of capitalist shackles. But in fact the only amateurs
who stayed long in the game made their living from it, either as county secretaries or assistant secretaries – like Bailey, Palmer, E. D. R. Eagar of
Hampshire, Wilfred Wooller of Glamorgan and M. J. K. Smith of
Warwickshire – or as ornaments of firms that found it helpful to have famous
young men on their payroll. The difference from before the war was that the
'shamateur' had to play like a professional if he wanted to succeed. Both May
and the young Oxford batsman, M. C. Cowdrey, modelled themselves on

Hutton and could not have worked harder at their cricket had it been their only hope of earning a living.

It was not as yet a munificent living. The Test matches were keeping the counties afloat. Over half a million saw the 1953 series, bringing in over £200,000. Television, which MCC had embraced from the start, brought in some extra revenue, but encouraged people to stay at home watching the Tests rather than their local counties in the flesh. County cricket had become a national monument rather than a popular modern attraction, and the decision of the Chancellor of the Exchequer, R. A. Butler, to exempt cricket from entertainment tax (ahead of other sports), though greeted with ribaldry, was generally welcomed. However, it helped preserve the obsolete pattern – and incidentally continued to provide the leisured classes and geriatrics who made up the bulk of county membership with a great bargain – Yorkshire's subscriptions did not go up to £3 until 1958.[6]

VII

Whilst the guardians of cricket were making clucking noises over what things were coming to, a change had occurred in the real world. Churchill's re-election in 1955 had bred hopes of a recovery of pre-war glory, but he was too old – and too interested in Europe – to go along with the imperialist flag-wavers. His heir apparent, Anthony Eden, grown impatient with waiting, blew his chance when it did come and his high-handed approach to Egypt in 1956, attempting to liberate the Suez Canal from the nationalist leader Colonel Nasser, assumed a pre-war power for Britain that had in fact passed to the USA, who unceremoniously scotched the plan. Eden's successor, Harold Macmillan, proved adept in swallowing the bitter pill with nonchalance, and the following year he offered the consolatory catch-phrase, couched in suitably American idiom – 'most of our people have never had it so good' – that was to signal a new and ambivalent era. It was enough to bring a third successive election victory for the Tories in 1959.

The political debate in the early 1960s, whilst ostensibly about philosophical issues, really centred on this. Industrial production stagnated and Britain was losing trade to foreign competition: was the cause the Tories' neglect of technology or the sloth bred by full employment? Harold Wilson's promised white-hot technological revolution was a fine slogan to throw at the old-fashioned Tory leader, Sir Alec Douglas-Home, but automation threatened jobs. The car workers satirised in the 1959 film *I'm All Right, Jack* were the new working-class élite and the chief source of militant shop stewards. The vehicles they produced were almost as a big an annoyance to the middle classes as the militants were, for many of the new owners were working class, which seemed to be pushing democracy too far.

Class tensions were much in evidence, as wage-earners now often got more pay than salaried staff. (The average for weekly wage-earners in 1964, though only two-thirds of that of monthly paid salaried staff, was actually higher than that of weekly paid white-collar workers.) They were readier to spend it, too, on the new status symbols: 80 per cent of homes had television sets. In the disastrous inflationary spiral that followed, the government's attempts to help the balance of payments and keep the cost of industrial production down by 'pay pauses', besides being ineffective, were also perceived as class-based. The average wage, £8 a week in 1951, went up to £20 by 1964: the cost of living had almost doubled but this still left an average wage increase of 30 per cent in real terms. Teenagers had become sought after, both as workers and as a market, and their juvenile version of the class war, between the stylish Mods and the leather-jacketed Rockers, regularly spilled over into weekend violence.

MCC showed no sign of adjusting to this new and dangerous age, but their recognition that something was amiss was reflected in a string of reports. The first, in 1956, was by another committee led by H. S. Altham. Attendances (in what was admittedly a wet summer) had fallen by another half a million and were now only half what they had been ten years before, so they sought to speed things up – by shortening boundaries, limiting the number of leg-side fielders, penalising time-wasting and urging faster pitches. The counties accepted these, but turned down a scheme for limiting first-innings overs in favour of a bonus scheme for fast scoring, which was by far the most effective proposal – certainly for Surrey, who won the championship by a wide margin in 1957. Since this was the sixth of Surrey's seven consecutive championships, however, the scheme, by widening the margin of their superiority, did nothing to spice up the competition, which is generally regarded as the first essential in such a situation. And a wet summer in 1958 contributed to the loss of another half a million spectators.

As first-class cricket began, rather incompetently, to see itself as an industry, many aspects of the general industrial malaise began to creep in, both 'I'm All Right, Jack' and 'Parkinson's Law'. And suddenly the feudal calm seemed to be disrupted by a rash of prospective anti-heroes, unruly and outspoken young fellows with no respect for their elders, and an awareness of rights that was reminiscent of old Sydney Barnes at his most Bolshevistic. Yorkshire, which had the most conservative traditions, found it hardest to cope with the new era. Unlike other counties, most of whom now saw overseas stars as the answer to falling gates, they admitted no foreigners, which meant anyone born outside Yorkshire, and they persisted with amateur captains despite a long and unaccustomed run of failure to win the championship. They had many good young players of talent – Close, Illingworth, Lowson, Appleyard, Trueman, Wardle – but they included some awkward customers and collectively were too much for either the benign Yardley or his successor, W. H. H. Sutcliffe, at whom facetious Yorkshire crowds were wont to shout, 'Fetch thi Dad.'

The senior professional, Willie Watson, underestimated in Yorkshire as he was by the England selectors, bravely and sensibly took the opportunity offered by the forward-looking Leicestershire committee to take over as captain when the shamateur Palmer retired. Yorkshire's committee, who felt alone in an increasingly alien world – betrayed by those who left and by their seducers, undermined by those who stayed – settled for being 'masters in their own house'. They appointed as their captain a thirty-nine-year-old amateur, J. R. Burnet, of modest cricketing talent but an experienced leader of the Second XI, who set about restoring discipline.

The crisis came when Wardle, a gifted left-arm bowler and a crowd-pleaser but also a chronically insubordinate malcontent, was dismissed for some critical articles in the *Daily Mail*.[7] The committee's invocation of Hawkeish principle had the unexpected bonus of securing the championship again within two seasons. Burnet, job done, then retired, whereupon the committee abruptly changed tack by appointing the veteran professional Vic Wilson. This, too, proved successful, and after two more championships in three years Yorkshire were ready to embark on the altogether more difficult task of attempting to solve their leadership problems by turning poachers into gamekeepers, starting with the erstwhile boy-wonder, Brian Close.

The climate of unrest was not, of course, confined only to Yorkshire. Everywhere relationships changed as the old feudal barriers came down, and urban values spread to remote corners of the country, assisted by television. (The coming of TV – with two channels competing after 1954 – also spurred the newspapers into counter-attractions. In particular, news, which got there first electronically, began to take second place to gossip and the doings, and thoughts, of 'personalities', jazzed up by ghost-writers and sub-editors. Advertising, too, greatly increased its scope and power as ITV jingles penetrated every household and school playground.) Umpires reported players for poor behaviour. Members complained, and heavy-handed disciplinary committees were brought into play; every incident was grist for the media mill.

One of the harbingers of this new era was Jim Laker, who in 1956 at Old Trafford had taken nineteen Australian wickets, the most astonishing feat in all Test match history. In 1959 he retired, after thirteen years with Surrey, at the fairly early age of thirty-seven, and the following year wrote a book that got him banned from the pavilions of both the Oval and Lord's. Laker's chief offence was in criticising Peter May, his captain both for Surrey and England. May was a glorious batsman, to whom responsibility had come early, but he was also highly sensitive and introverted and, before he was thirty, hagridden by stomach ulcers. Laker was tempted into indiscretion by the lure of the sensationalist trend – and by the hypocrisy that still festooned the game.

On the previous winter's tour of Australia he had been considerably irked by the high-handed manner of F. R. Brown, the manager. Brown, colourful but anachronistic, had sought to restore something of feudal discipline, for example by his insistence that the professionals should not refer to his assistant , E. D. R. Eagar as 'Desmond' but as 'Mr. Eagar', and had aroused indignation by laying down paternalistic drinking rules. But Laker was mostly upset by the anomalies of the amateur distinction. The professionals wryly accepted that the amateurs should now get not only expenses but compensation for loss of earnings. They had been startled on the voyage out, however, by the rumour that this compensation was to be tax-free, like their expenses. Laker commented that he had seriously thought of turning amateur, adding sardonically, 'I might have been better off.' As for Peter May, in the same week that he won £500 from an Australian newspaper for scoring a century between lunch and tea, it was announced that he had turned himself into a limited company.

So far from ending these anomalies, MCC had since 1956, under the presidency of Sir Walter Monckton, better known as the confidant of Edward VIII, bent their energies towards trying to keep amateurs in the game. Diana Rait-Kerr's official history afterwards explained that

> this was not, as popularly stated, for the sake of the 'old school tie', but with a
> sincere desire to regain and preserve the unfettered spirit of high adventure,
> which, since the Golden Age, had been the amateur's priceless contribution to
> cricket.

The difference was lost on most people at the time and has become no clearer since. Public school and Oxford or Cambridge was still the royal road to cricketing success. Leisure, coaching, good wickets, good fixture lists and easy access to the magic circle were crucial elements in the making of a Test-match player: it is no accident that May, Sheppard, Cowdrey, E. R. Dexter and M. J. K. Smith were among the best batsmen of the time.

The best way of keeping amateurs in cricket would have been to reorganise the first-class game so that it took place mainly at weekends, public holidays and in August. As it was, apart from shamateurs most gentlemen cricketers – out-of-practice schoolmasters during holidays, for example – did nothing to raise the standard. Yet the Monckton committee recommended no change, and the buck was passed to the incoming president, the Duke of Norfolk no less, the Earl Marshal of England. The duke was not one of your modern Harvard Business School aristocrats, nor even Oxford, for he failed the entrance examination. But his admirers spoke of his bluff common-sense and he was nothing if not independent-minded.

The committee he led, however, were all amateurs and shamateurs and inevitably interested parties. A conference of county clubs found only two in favour of change: even the professionals did not come out publicly in favour. The buck, as Norfolk complained, 'had been firmly passed back to the special committee'. And in 1959 they concluded that the distinctive status of the amateur was not obsolete, was of great value to the game and should be preserved.

In order to achieve this they adopted a definition of an amateur so loose as to be worthless: employment as secretaries and so forth, writing, broadcasting and even advertising were no bar to amateur status, nor was 'broken-time' payment on overseas tours. Only overt payment for actually playing and broken-time for home matches were forbidden. They expressed a pious hope that the counties would adopt a standard policy over expenses, and set up a standing committee to watch points.

By February 1962 they were reconsidering their position and anxiously debating the alternatives of allowing 'broken-time payment', as the Northern Rugby Union had done in 1893, or ending the distinction altogether; a majority came down in favour of abolition. The duke was ready to throw in the towel, reporting to the Advisory County Cricket Committee: 'Try as we may to retain it, amateur status as we have known it is at an end.' The counties, startled by this blunt appraisal, stalled for time and asked for a memorandum. The duke's committee, when they came to spell out their proposal, took fright and changed their minds, recommending the status quo by a single vote.

But that November the Advisory Committee put an end to the shilly-shallying, and from the following season there were no gentlemen and players, only cricketers. There were obviously still many opponents of the change, notably the editor of *Wisden*, who thought cricket 'in danger of losing the spirit of freedom and gaiety which the best amateur players brought to the game'. (Chaps like Johnny Douglas and Douglas Jardine, perhaps. Or even Trevor Bailey.) But in *The Times*, John Woodcock pointed out that E. R. Dexter, England's dashing young amateur captain, had recently admitted that he made a good deal more from cricket than he did from business. As Michael Melford of the decidedly unrevolutionary *Daily Telegraph* put it, what was being abolished was merely 'a form of legalised deceit'.

CHAPTER NINETEEN

A Different Game

NINETEEN SIXTY-THREE was a bad year for traditionalists. The Beatles had become 'top of the pops' – whatever that meant. Then the Profumo scandal rocked the government, and amazed the populace by glimpses of the sexual antics enjoyed in London society. Cricket's establishment suffered extra pangs. Not only did they lose their amateur purity, but the county clubs were tempted into playing a truncated, mutilated version of the game. Back in 1956 the Altham Committee had floated the idea of a single-innings knock-out competition, but could see no way round the problem of how to finish matches in a day. The press had been nagging away at the idea ever since, but it was only dire necessity that eventually drove the Advisory County Cricket Committee to take it up. Attendances at county matches had dropped from nearly 2 million in 1950 to just over 700,000.

Yet another committee of enquiry was set up, producing even gloomier statistics. They revealed, for instance, that between 1955 and 1960 the counties' expenditure had exceeded 'normal cricket income' by an average of £120,000 a year. Their recommendations – faster, truer pitches, brighter cricket, more determination to entertain – were less compelling. So, reluctantly and with much trepidation, the knock-out cup idea was resurrected. There were two main kinds of objection to it: first, the kind of cricket it would produce, second, the source of the money to stage it. Both can be seen as the kind of élitist smoke-screen that had prevented cricket from responding to social change over the years. Equally, however, they reflect a more fastidious age, both culturally and morally, now only dimly remembered – when splitting infinitives was a serious crime, 'gay' meant light-hearted and 'ecstasy' meant joy, actors kept their clothes on, four-letter words were gutter language and the new premium bonds were thought a 'squalid raffle'.

The worry about limited-over cricket was that it would denature the game by removing the necessity of bowling the other team out: this would further encourage negative bowling and discourage spin. Spectators showed from the outset that these were risks they were prepared to run to see a match finish in a day, often in great excitement, and in fact as experience bred greater sophistication the fears, for the most part, proved groundless. On the positive side furthermore, the contest between bat and ball was sharpened by the time constraint and by the vast improvement in fielding.

The second concern was part of the wider anxiety that county clubs were selling their souls by resorting to all manner of dubious ways of augmenting their incomes. The real shellbacks amongst the membership, of course, still thought gate-money a vulgar and deplorable necessity. Now the small lotteries and 'pools', long practised even before they became legal in 1960, became a staple: when Yorkshire in 1964 agreed to accept a contribution from its supporters' club, every county was being subsidised in this way. Apart from the moral scruples of a despairing minority there was a worry that the money was being raised from non-cricket activities, including football, and was in the gift of people outside the committees.

Industrial sponsorship was then a rarity in British sport, but the prospect of television coverage awoke interest. It began in 1957 when Col. Whitbread brewer and former National Hunt rider, rather than buying air-time established a Gold Cup, to help the sport as much as profit from this new form of publicity. The Hennessy brandy family were also keen on steeplechasing, and soon sponsoring races became an accepted and popular form of advertising. Placards and hoardings could be displayed to advantage during the races bringing extra revenue. Cricket grounds were also well suited to this, which curiously enough was permitted on BBC as well as Independent Television. Hence by 1963 the cricket authorities, already wedded to BBC television sought a sponsor for the offspring they had sheepishly produced and promised a final to be held at Lord's at the season's end as the climax.

The reason for seeking outside funding, with all its dangers of 'cheapening the game', was the counties' fear that the expenses of putting on the new competition might be doubled or trebled if the weather intervened, and yet would bring in only one day's gate. The first sponsors, Gillette, the razor-blade people, were asked to underwrite these possible losses to the tune of £6,500. It was an immediate success. The final was greeted with astonished enthusiasm by the press. The *Daily Mirror*'s Peter Wilson, the leading sports writer of the day, marvelled that 'Lord's, the temple of tradition', could be transformed, on a cold damp September Saturday, into 'a reasonable replica of Wembley', 'a sell-out with rosettes, singing, cheers, jeers and counter-cheers. This triumphant sporting experiment ... may not have been cricket to the purists, but by golly it was just the stuff the doctor ordered.'

II

Cricket's financial prospects had been further improved by the Test series against the West Indies, who were establishing themselves as at least the equal of the Australians, and a tremendous attraction to crowds boosted by thousands of the 'black Englishmen' who were coming to live and work in an otherwise cheerless promised land. The matches were blood-and-thunder affairs but by then the tit-for-tat stridencies of the fast bowling conflict had become an accepted part of international cricket. There was also a postcolonial edge as country after emerging country put English batsmen on their mettle, and the virility cult was allowed full play: helmets were still thought namby-pamby.

South Africa was a special case. Always the apple of MCC's eye, her tightening racialist policies evoked little hostility in the world of cricket. Jim Laker's sharp comments about police discrimination in *Over to Me* were thought part of the bloody-mindedness that earned him the establishment's displeasure. Chauvinists had taken more notice of his blood-chilling description of the Afrikaner Peter Heine, exasperated in the 1956–7 series by Trevor Bailey's obduracy:

> Halfway between a sneer and a growl Heine said, 'I want to hit you, Bailey ... I want to hit you over the heart.' He meant every word of it.

By 1960 South Africa had become a Republic and was soon to leave the Commonwealth, and from the moment the touring team arrived there were demonstrations against them. But most cricketers were more concerned about the young fast bowler Geoff Griffin, selected for the tour in spite of having been no-balled for throwing in South Africa.

The sequel showed the reality behind the fiction that umpires were the sole judges of fair play within the laws. A year earlier the umpires had been assured of the support of MCC and the counties in rooting out certain bowlers with suspect actions. This had resulted in Harold Rhodes of Derbyshire being no-balled by Paul Gibb, the former Yorkshire amateur,[1] and Griffin being called in some matches but not in others – including the first Test. In the second, at Lord's, Griffin got a hat-trick. However, although the South African captain kept him away from Sid Buller, the best-known and most outspoken English umpire, Frank Lee, at the other end, called him eleven times. England won by an innings, and the match ended early in some disorder. Then Buller no-balled Griffin in the exhibition match that followed.

The throwing saga was complicated by a simultaneous experiment to try to stop fast bowlers 'dragging' across the line.[2] It was now time to clear the decks for the visit of Australia in 1961. Peter May and his team had been troubled the previous winter by the fast but erratic Ian Meckiff, whose action was suspect. MCC had agreed a new definition of throwing with the Australians, but for some impenetrable reason agreed not to implement it on the forth-coming tour until 7 June. Instead, umpires who thought any Australian erred were asked to send confidential reports (on the appropriate form) to MCC. This furtive procedure proved unnecessary, as Meckiff, having lost form, was not picked. England, for their part, had chosen Tony Lock, said to be a reformed character, or at least to have reformed his action. But to be on the safe side, MCC asked 'Gubby' Allen, chairman of the selectors and of the cricket committee, to give a stern warning to Lock. He did this so effectively that poor Lock took 3 for 250 in the three matches he played. The Australians didn't seem to care whether his action was fair or not.

In one sense the upsurge in throwing was part of the challenge-and-response that had characterised the development of cricket from the beginning – a calculated attempt to prevent the batsman anticipating the direction and trajectory of deliveries. But it was also a new twist (as it were) in the quest for speed, reflecting a growing taste for violence that was afflicting society as a whole. (There was particular concern for the effect of films and television on the young – young people that were better fed than ever before, and so more energetic; better off and so more able to indulge their fantasies.) The West Indies were now discovering a seam of fast-bowling talent that was to set the standard for the rest of the century. Some of its early products lacked a certain refinement: one, Roy Gilchrist, was sent home from India for bowling beamers, and in 1962 a new discovery, Charlie Griffith, had cracked the skull of the Indian captain Nari Contractor, who ducked, but not low enough. And the word was that, every so often, when he wanted extra speed, Griffith threw.

The Lord's Test of 1963 is remembered not for calypsos or the wiles of Ram and Val, but for the naked hostility of Hall and Griffith. Wesley Hall had a classic bowling action, but his sheer speed was alarming: it was he who broke Cowdrey's wrist in the first innings. He contributed his share, too, to the bruises that covered Brian Close's torso as he bravely counter-attacked. Yet it was Griffith, with his mixture of yorkers and 'throat' balls rising from a length, and his disregard of the convention that tail-enders shouldn't receive bouncers, who caused most consternation. Behind the stories of English gallantry that were added to the corpus there was a less creditable backstairs story.

125,000 spectators, paying £56,000 at the gates, had watched that Test match, enthralled to the last ball, though it had ended in a draw. Millions had listened to the radio or watched the television coverage. The whole series had been highly lucrative, despite England's 3–1 defeat. The team were heroes, battered and bruised in defeat, and the crowd loved the sheer excitement, the pity and terror of it, though the drama of cricket had degenerated, as Greek tragedy had degenerated into Roman excess. This drawing power clearly affected MCC's moral judgement, and, just as they had shut their eyes to the problem of the bouncer that was soon to engulf cricket, they also decided to forget for a while their purge of throwers. The party had been spoiled by the umpires' interference over Griffin in 1960. So Charlie Griffith mysteriously acquired immunity in 1963. No umpire, not even the bold Buller, called him that season. And the players (including Dexter, who began by treating Griffith with disdain) complained only privately.

The plot thickened in 1964 when the West Indies played in three exhibition games in England. One umpire sent a confidential report to MCC saying that he would have no-balled Griffith had they not been exhibition matches. MCC, in the person of Donald Carr, assistant secretary, replied commending his discretion and saying MCC would consider the matter in due course. If they did so they neglected to pass on the information to the West Indies or Australia, who were about to engage in a highly controversial series.[3] Dexter, meanwhile, condemned Griffith's action in his newspaper column; so did Richie Benaud, the former Australian captain, now a journalist; and afterwards the leading Australian players said publicly that they would never play against Griffith again

MCC next did the thing they were really good at: they belatedly set up a sub-committee to consider the problem. The sub-committee spawned an adjudication committee, ready to pronounce on any action referred to them. Their only noteworthy achievement was to consider the case of Harold Rhodes with the aid of moving cameras and X-ray photography. Rhodes, under a cloud of suspicion since 1960, was finally cleared in 1969. They also produced a new definition of throwing, a somewhat otiose activity since imprecise definition had never been the problem. However, the end of the throwing phase was hastened by the use of slow-motion cameras, an increasingly potent force in cricket. The bigger problem of the bouncer, of course, remained, for faster pitches did not merely mean brighter cricket.

III

The appointment of twenty-five-year-old E. R. Dexter as England captain in 1961 was yet another attempt of the despairing elders to brighten up cricket following the somewhat tense regime of Peter May and their occasional experiments with Cowdrey, who was too assiduously diplomatic for command. Young Dexter had no such problem. One of nature's charismatic leaders, a C. B. Fry in all but intellect, he had already led Radley, Cambridge and Sussex as to the manner born and did not share the general surprise when the England job came to him. Nor did the abolition of amateur status cramp his style: he had been well paid from the start, and he continued to be known, with a mixture of admiration and scorn, as 'Lord Ted' throughout his career.

His was no dedicated vocation:

> I got into it by finding I could do it successfully at a certain level and wanting to
> know whether I could do it at the highest level. Once I discovered I could,
> cricket became a great turn-on. Then I began to wonder what I was doing in
> this business.

Now this, of course, is quite a healthy psychological state for an intelligent
man to be in. Even Fred Titmus, the committed professional, could write,

> Just because you love playing cricket doesn't mean you don't get bored with it
> sometimes ... Cricket is my job. I am as prone to be bored with it on occasions
> as someone who goes to work in a shop, an office or a factory every day.

But Dexter, the emblem of the longed-for new golden age, was inclined to
show his boredom.

J. M. Brearley, a more conscientious England captain of the next decade,
reckoned this was his main weakness:

> In all three matches I played under him in South Africa in 1964–5 there were
> periods when he had lost interest and was more concerned with getting his golf-
> swing right at square leg than with who should be bowling what or with what
> field.

Equally it might be said that all is not well with a game and its organisation
when it has that effect on its leading practitioner.

Dexter certainly did his best to cheer the game up when his mind was not
otherwise engaged. He soon startled the tunnel-visioned, however, by accepting an invitation to stand for Parliament at the 1964 election. They need not
have worried, for the task he had undertaken was to wrest Cardiff South-East
from James Callaghan, a Labour heavyweight. Failing, he abandoned politics,
and returned to more congenial outside interests such as golf, his weekly
column in the *Observer*, flying, the turf and roaring round the countryside in
fast cars.

In 1965 this last saved Dexter from the tedium of doing the international
cricket circuit a second time. He broke his leg and reviewed his future:

> At the time there was no real money to be earned [from cricket]. I thought it
> was about time I got a real job and started making a reasonable living to support
> my family.

Three years later he was back:

> My business wasn't terribly enjoyable and I wasn't that good at it. Why do it

when I could be running about on the international cricket field enjoying myself
and doing a much better job?

This phase did not last long either, and though he retained an involvement
with cricket after retirement his off-the-field contributions (as chairman of
selectors and prospective discoverer of fast-bowling talent) tended to be
merely eccentric. Yet as an attacking batsman unequalled in his time, and as
an influence for good in a world grown grim with the modern version of
'more than a game', he was a breath of fresh air.

IV

Not the least of Dexter's contributions was to help popularise one-day cricket
and to take Sussex, who won the first two Gillette Cups, from the ranks of the
also-rans for the first time since William Lillywhite had transformed bowling.
Despite the Cup's success no one in the game saw it as anything other than a
means of helping out the counties financially. After the first competition
several outsiders applied to join in – not only the Minor Counties and the
Universities (which still meant Oxbridge). All were briskly told to find their
own honeypot.[4] Yorkshire, who had continued winning championships under
the aggressive Brian Close, felt relaxed enough to win a couple of Gillette
Cups (in spite of scepticism about limited-over as distinct from time-limit
cricket) and thus gave it a certain credibility amongst the agnostics.

Yorkshire's grip on the Holy Grail loosened slightly in 1961 when they
narrowly lost the title to the unconsidered Hampshire – sustained, Yorkshire
patriots reckoned, by the bowling of Derek Shackleton, who came from
Todmorden, and the batting of Roy Marshall, a Barbadian. Hampshire's
captain, Etonian Colin Ingleby-Mackenzie, who startled earnest cricket
followers by telling a BBC interviewer that the basis of Hampshire's training
was 'wine, women and song', was determined to enjoy the game, win or lose.
His sporting outlook in the matter of declarations made him highly popular
with opponents and led to reciprocal gestures, of the kind not accorded to the
'give 'em nowt' men of Yorkshire, and this greatly helped in the championship race.

Hampshire's victory delighted neutrals and brighter cricket enthusiasts,
and there was naturally much talk of the Hambledon spirit. Swanton
reminded *Daily Telegraph* readers

> that Broadhalfpenny Down is the very cradle of cricket. We can imagine
> William Beldham chanting a Te Deum somewhere aloft, John Small striking
> triumphant chords on his violin.

Yorkshire quickly restored normality and won the championship five times in the next seven years. But these were the last years of glory for Yorkshire, and arguably for the championship itself.

By the mid-1960s attendance of customers paying at the gate for county matches had dropped to a little over half a million, and even membership numbers were beginning to fall. Partly this was a sign of the times. Fred Titmus admitted frankly, 'if I were not a player ... I wouldn't find time very often to spend a whole day at a county game.' Even Saturday football gates had fallen off because of the various counter-attractions. And most people had to work during the week. In Yorkshire, though, they believed that something else was going wrong, fundamentally wrong. County cricket, they argued, should be rooted in the soil of the county: otherwise it would become like soccer, a soulless urban affair. Counties with less soil and a smaller membership weren't so sure.

Worcestershire's two championship wins in 1964 and 1965, though inspiring purple passages about the Lyttletons and the Fosters, had given notice of what was to come. Only a couple of locally born players supported the array of imports, led by Tom Graveney from Gloucestershire and including two from overseas. Most counties were now fast losing their regional distinctiveness, and, just like soccer teams, were looking beyond their own coaching schemes and nursery clubs to ready-made imports. And they eagerly approved the recommendation from the Clark Committee[5] in January 1967 of a shorter qualification period for one of the two overseas players allowed to each county.

But that was as much innovation as they could take. The editor of *Wisden* sympathised:

> For the past twenty years, we have had one change after another *including the abolition of the distinction between amateur and professional* [my italics] ... Small wonder that the ordinary follower of the game has become utterly confused ...

He thought most of cricket's troubles stemmed from the alteration of the lbw law in 1935, and wrote wistfully of repeal. The Clark Committee had steered clear of such profundities and, amazingly, professed 'optimism for the future, in view of the unimpaired interest in County cricket'. Nevertheless, they made a few proposals alongside the pious hopes for positive attitudes and improved wickets.

The main one – reducing three-day matches to allow for more one-day competition, including a separate one-day championship – was overwhelmingly rejected. 'It's a lot of tommy rot,' judiciously opined Wilf Wooller, the Glamorgan secretary. Glamorgan's gate receipts in 1966 had dropped to £5,344, the lowest since the war. Hampshire, with chronically creaking finances, were so fed up with experiments that they wanted no changes for three years. Sussex wanted more three-day games, not fewer. Derbyshire and

Northamptonshire feared that dropping midweek matches would mean losing members.

Yet something had to be done to increase revenue. So it came about that, although the Clark Committee referred specifically to 'the continuous grind of six days per week cricket', the chosen solution was to play seven days. Opinion polls had shown that the public were in favour of Sunday cricket: so also were the members. The government had started consultations with sporting bodies on relaxation of the Sunday observance laws in 1961, and games could now be started at 2 p.m. But only charity and benefit games took up the option until, in 1966, Rothman's, the tobacco people, launched the International Cavaliers, playing forty-overs televised matches against a different county side each Sunday, usually for a cricketer's benefit.

Now, in the deadlock following the rejection of the Clark plan, a solution of brilliant simplicity was devised – simply elbow out Rothman's and have a county league. Playing on a Sunday meant that the county championship could remain untouched – apart, that is, from the trifling inconvenience of having to break off a three-day match that had started on the Saturday and play a forty-overs game, often against the same opponents, on the Sunday.

Sponsors were found easily enough, in a rival tobacco firm, and the John Player Sunday League began in 1969. In its first year attendances came to 280,000, almost as many as the six-day aggregate for the county championship, which had dropped to 327,000 paying at the gates. The players did not relish giving up their rest day, but they were glad of the extra money it brought. They had got far behind the soccer players, whose star was in the ascendancy following the recent victory in the World Cup. Surrey, for example, one of the richer counties, paid capped players a retainer of £624, rising to £678 after ten years, plus match fees of £7 and a £3 winning bonus; good players could expect to earn between £800 and £1,000. Yorkshire's senior players, still the élite, might get £1,000 to £1,200, but this depended heavily on results.

Test cricket, which kept the counties afloat, was also the magnet for players, who got £100 a match. A winter tour, paying up to £1,000, was another great attraction. The very best players probably made £2,000–£2,500 a year, but the average for those below Test level was nearer £850–£900. A new factor was the influx of overseas players, the first wave of whom included Keith Boyce (Essex), Mike Proctor (Gloucestershire), John Shepherd, Asif Iqbal (Kent), Farokh Engineer, Clive Lloyd (Lancashire) Garfield Sobers (Notts), Rohan Kanhai, Lance Gibbs (Warwickshire), Barry Richards, Gordon Greenidge (Sussex) and Majid Khan (Glamorgan). What they were paid was more difficult to pin down, but (with the exception of the highly exceptional Sobers) probably ranged from £1,500 to £2,500 a year. This was a gamble for the counties and made their finances even more precarious – half of them were in the red and Somerset were on the verge of bankruptcy – so, not for the first time, cricket was at the crossroads.

V

So, indeed, was the country. The Labour Government, vainly trying to control prices and incomes, were proving an easy target for the rampant trade unions. The cost of living, not profitability, became the criterion in wage-bargaining as not only the white-hot technological revolution but a projected 'national plan' was jettisoned. The strongest unions did best and no one gave much thought to the lowest-paid – women and ethnic minorities. The average (male) weekly wage in 1964 was £20 and by 1970 this had become £28; prices were increasing at only half this rate. As motor cars and other former luxuries became necessities for the new Britain, so government expenditure rose to meet the expanding health and social services, including redundancy payments, social security, rent rebates and benefits for the disabled. The education service also needed money, as the school-leaving age was raised to sixteen and pressure grew for comprehensive schools. (The public schools remained untouched, and higher education developed on comparably class-based lines, from Oxbridge through lesser universities to 'public sector' polytechnics.) Yet the discovery of North Sea oil and gas made it difficult to interest the unions in wage restraint, and proposed legislation to curb their power had to be hastily withdrawn.

Things were somewhat different in the dream-world of cricket, but a glimpse of future reality came with the brief appearance on the industrial relations scene of Fred Rumsey, a Somerset quick bowler, who made the first moves towards a Cricketers' Association in 1967. Only forty of the 300-odd players came to the first meeting, in some cases specifically to argue against forming a trade union. There had always been a curious Jeeves-like snobbery in cricket dressing-rooms, and there was little enthusiasm for following the path discovered by Jimmy Hill, founder of the Professional Footballers' Association. Most county secretaries and chairmen did not look kindly on the new development, either. But the pioneers won some influential friends, and were specially lucky that John Arlott, one of the more liberal cricket writers, agreed to become their honorary president. Even so, recruitment was slow, and it needed a donation from the John Player Organisation before a paid secretary could be appointed – Jack Bannister, of Warwickshire.

More favourable winds were beginning to blow, however. The Labour Government had slowly got round to doing something about setting up a Sports Council, as recommended in a report commissioned by the voluntary organisations. The amateur side of sport now looked forward to more support from public funds. Cricket's institutions, heavily dominated by MCC, a wealthy private club, were quite unsuited to acting as a spokesman for the amateur interests. So in a prudential display of democracy and concern for the whole of cricket, MCC (even more slowly than the Government) regrouped. They set up a Test and County Cricket Board as a new ruling body for the professional game, assembled a National Cricket Association to supervise all the rest, and left MCC in place as the law-makers and administrators of Lord's. These three were put under a supreme body called the Cricket Council. In practice, however, MCC, who provided the secretariat of all three sub-units and whose president and treasurer became the chairman and vice-chairman of the council, still called the shots.

An incidental benefit for the Players' Association was the man chosen as chairman of the TCCB, Cecil Paris. As John Arlott wrote in the *Cricketer* twelve years later:

> Probably the most influentially enlightened early attitude ... from the official side was shown by Cecil Paris ... who recognised it and its potential before many players did so.

And as a tangible sign of his enlightenment Paris arranged a grant of £750 a year, which effectively kept the association alive until, with one or two negotiating successes under its belt – at Middlesex and Somerset, for example – membership became the norm.[6]

The new regime was not otherwise, however, noticeably liberal. Indeed, it was stern in pursuit of brighter cricket. In Tests Ken Barrington, an amiable but anxious accumulator of runs, was disciplined in 1965 for making a big score but too slowly, and two years later the young Geoffrey Boycott, already a hard case, was also dropped for a similar offence. Trueman was given a final warning by Yorkshire, after a series of indiscretions, for not submitting newspaper articles for approval. Dexter, who did the same thing twice, was actually suspended for a month. Close, a brave and successful captain of England, was sacked in 1967 after blatant time-wasting in a county match. A headstrong fellow with too much pride for his own good, Close declined to apologise to the assembled establishment coterie for what he saw as none of their business.

The Government were not directly blamed for this outbreak of insubordination but they were held responsible for creating an atmosphere of moral decay. Not only were they thought deplorably lax on law and order – failing to control violence, drug-taking, 'pop festivals', peace rallies, racially inspired disorder, student unrest, the Rolling Stones, mini-skirts and hot pants – but in 1967 they legalised homosexuality and abortion and put 'family planning' advice on the health service, and the following year made divorce by consent possible after two years. Wilson's bungling, Walter Mittyish foreign policy brought tears of rage to imperialist eyes – trying to forsake the Empire for the European Common Market but being outflanked by de Gaulle, bamboozled by Ian Smith, run out of Aden, and, getting into a fearful mess in Northern Ireland, sending in the British army. And all the time the flow of immigrants, mostly from ethnic minorities, raised the temperature of debate.

The Cricket Council, for all its reach-me-down show of political correctness, had got off to a bad start with the Labour Government – and anyone with remotely liberal values – over South Africa. Close had been replaced by the circumspect, Warnerish M. C. Cowdrey, a weaker captain, but one out of the right stable, a former gentleman. He believed strongly in 'building bridges' with South Africa's racist regime and, having found himself on the wrong end of a West Indian crowd disturbance in 1967–8, looked forward to the next stage of shuttle diplomacy on the projected tour of South Africa the following winter. There was, however, a largish fly in the ointment – a 'Cape Coloured' cricketer called Basil D'Oliveira. 'Dolly' had come to Britain in 1960, and, helped by John Arlott, joined Middleton in the Central Lancashire League. He went on to qualify for Worcestershire and to play for England and looked a likely prospect for the South African tour.

To save possible embarrassment, the ex-Prime Minister Sir Alec Douglas-Home, recently president of MCC, had called on Dr Vorster, the South African premier, early in 1968. On return he gave MCC (privately, of course) the not very surprising intelligence that D'Oliveira would not be an acceptable visitor. His advice, however, was not to deal with a problem that might not arise, but to see whether Dolly was in fact selected. Cowdrey was much impressed by this example of Sir Alec's 'wisdom and integrity', and tells in his autobiography how he and his fellow-selectors thereafter fearlessly based their decisions entirely on cricket criteria. It did not look that way, and there were many occasions during the convoluted affair when Cowdrey records that 'people leaped to the wrong conclusion' and 'those who suspected collusion were convinced the politicians had won.'

One such was John Arlott, when, within days of making a huge score in the final test against Australia, D'Oliveira was left out of the touring party: 'There is no case for leaving out D'Oliveira on cricketing grounds,' he wrote in the *Guardian*, adding prophetically: 'This may prove, perhaps to the surprise of MCC, far more than a sporting matter.' Another critic was the Revd David Sheppard, by then Bishop of Woolwich, who advocated suspension of sporting links with South Africa at a specially convened meeting of MCC. He was supported by Mike Brearley, but not many other leading cricketers. When the Cricketers' Association held a referendum in 1970, in the middle of the strife-torn Springbok rugby tour, about the TCCB's proposal to invite the South African cricketers the following summer, only about half the members bothered to vote, and they were overwhelmingly in favour.

With an election pending the government were not anxious to appear heavy-handed, though they made no secret of their displeasure. The Sports Council, chaired by the Minister for Sport, urged reconsideration. So did the

Archbishop of Canterbury, the Chief Rabbi and the chairman of the Race
Relations Board. South Africa had been expelled from the Davis Cup and the
Olympic Games and thirteen countries threatened to withdraw from the
forthcoming Commonwealth Games in Edinburgh. Nevertheless, the Cricket
Council decided 'by a substantial majority' to go ahead. And an appeal from
Jim Callaghan, the Home Secretary, got nowhere. The election was now only
two weeks away, and there was real danger of disruption. Callaghan, avuncu-
lar patience exhausted, called in the chairman and secretary and formally
requested them to cancel the tour 'on grounds of broad public policy'. And
only then – 'with deep regret' and 'considering they had no alternative' – did
the Cricket Council climb down from the high moral ground of 'freedom
under the law' they felt they occupied.

VI

The dispute over South Africa was a further cause of dissension in county
dressing-rooms. As the vast majority were strongly opposed to the cancellation, either from conviction or from pragmatism, it was not a major cause, but
one amongst many. Few English cricketers, whether ex-gentlemen or ex-
players, seemed to enjoy their cricket, and their faces grew even grimmer as
the overseas players increasingly became the decisive factor in domestic
competition.

The misery was not confined to the traditionally weaker counties. Surrey,
surprisingly inept at the one-day competitions, had behind-the-scenes problems, financial in origin, that lost them players like Bob Willis and Roger
Knight by special registration, unwillingly conceded. After a rare championship win in 1971 they dwindled into mediocrity. Middlesex, whose
committee's high-handed attitude to pay had led to the formation of one of
the earliest branches of the Players' Association, oscillated between the dismal
and the undistinguished. Nottinghamshire were an embarrassment to their
supporters: even the great Sobers could not wholly conceal their plight. On
the other hand Kent, who had broken with tradition by appointing Leslie
Ames as team manager, a new and daring concept, also trampled on Lord
Harris's grave by opening their doors wide to overseas players and other
shrewd imports. But, led by the ultra-dedicated Cowdrey, they used this
strong base to bring on young local players like Underwood and Knott and
successfully made the transition from 'Big Six' to 'modern giants'.
Lancashire, too, drawing on the cosmopolitan traditions and brisk methods of
their senior leagues, did well: the experienced Jack Bond shrewdly built a new
young side round Clive Lloyd and Engineer, which dominated first the new
Sunday League and then the Gillette, brought the crowds back to Old
Trafford and caused envy across the Pennines by their championship results.

The 1960s were to be Yorkshire's last years of glory in any kind of cricket.

The decline had as much to do with the clash of personalities and sheer bloody-mindedness, in both players and administration, as with cricketing ability. Their employment policies were Dickensian. When Ray Illingworth, after twenty-seven years with the club, asked for a three-year contract for 1969 he was told by Brian Sellers, chairman of Yorkshire's cricket committee, to 'bugger off'. He signed for Leicestershire as captain and over the next nine years not only took them to unprecedented heights in the championship but also captained England with distinction. Meanwhile Yorkshire's own captain, Brian Close, left amid clouds of smoke to join Somerset and, at the age of forty, to transform their fortunes. Ironically, though he was supposed to dislike the one-day game and to share Yorkshire's traditional xenophobia, he laid the foundations of a successful multi-national one-day side.

Though stemming from high principle, Yorkshire's recruitment policies were hopelessly anachronistic, not only disastrous in playing terms but laying them open to accusations of racism. In 1969 seventy-six MPs signed a Commons motion asking that the Race Relations Act be amended to allow Yorkshire to continue on their chosen path. This turned out to be unnecessary. (As the Race Relations Board explained, somewhat to the county's surprise perhaps, Yorkshire birth does not in itself confer colour, race or ethnicity.) But the publicity was unwelcome at a time when Enoch Powell's calls for repatriation of immigrants were getting him dropped from the Tory leader, Edward Heath's, shadow cabinet. And it led to more serious questioning of Yorkshire's recruitment practices. As there were so many Pakistani families in and around the Bradford area, people asked, how was it none of their youngsters, born in the county, seemed to come into the reckoning.

Yorkshire not only lost players to other counties and steadfastly refused to import outsiders, but their native source of supply was dwindling. League cricket had been caught up in the vogue for over-limit games. A few leagues held back – notably the Lancashire, Birmingham and North Staffordshire – but most of them enthusiastically embraced the opportunity to eliminate draws, including the Bradford, Huddersfield, North Yorkshire, Sheffield, and Yorkshire Leagues and the Yorkshire Council. Over-limit cricket got young players into bad habits early on and further restricted their chances of learning how to play long innings. The compensating advantage that the greater emphasis on fielding hastened the retirement of older players took rather longer to permeate the system.

Throughout the North the leagues were caught up in social change as never before. The idyllic picture painted by Fred Root of tightly knit local communities sharing in support of their local Lancashire League teams gave way to modern methods of fund-raising through the bars and one-armed bandits of social clubs, and too often depended heavily on the dedication of a few for their administration. There were still plenty of star overseas players, as the Test-match circuit widened and air travel made life simpler, but they tended not to command quite such high fees, nor to attract such great crowds. Edwin Kay, secretary of the Central Lancashire League, referring to the enormous hand-outs ambitious clubs needed from other than cricket sources, said in 1980, 'Cricket clubs with a good social side will probably survive, but social clubs with a cricket side will find it very difficult.'

The most significant social change, however, was the conversion of the South to the vulgar competitive practices of the North. MCC had not been alone in finding themselves, as a private club, cut off from the prospect of government aid through the Sports Council. So were the Club Cricket Conference, the staunch upholders of southern purity. They soon faced anther difficulty. A Trojan horse was discovered in their midst when Raman Subba Row, late of Cambridge University and England, and now of Old Whitgiftians, led a movement for the formation of a Surrey League. The CCC old guard resisted strongly but found themselves outflanked, and the new league began its life in 1968. Hertfordshire, Essex, Kent, Sussex, Middlesex soon followed, and by 1973 there were twenty-three leagues in and around London, and rumours that fastnesses like Devon would not hold out much longer. By 1975 inter-league competitions – sponsored by a brewery – were in full swing, and ten years later the Club Cricket Conference had fifty leagues: friendly games, often held on Sunday, were distinctly unfashionable.

Subba Row and his henchmen, it later emerged, had hoped to set up an organised, pyramidal structure with promotion and relegation. This ambition failed because the senior leagues saw no reason to expose themselves to indignities of the kind familiar to soccer clubs. They could not, however, prevent ambitious players from changing clubs, or ambitious clubs from seeking to induce them to do so, and the reformers did not entirely give up hope that logic would one day prevail.[7] Meanwhile they had achieved the quite remarkable feat, assisted by the great leveller, the television sitcom, of narrowing the North–South divide.

Televising over-limit games at first-class level was a remarkable stimulus to local competitive cricket. Apart from leagues there was a great upsurge in national knock-out competitions of various kinds, with the *Cricketer* magazine to the fore in organising them, inspired by their proprietor and managing director, B. G. Brocklehurst, a former captain of Somerset. First came an élite tournament for select old-boy teams; then in 1969 the National Club Knock-out, for some 250 clubs in membership of the NCA; and in 1972 the National Village Championship. This concept, delighting both romantics and moderns, was an outstanding success, offering the prospect of a final at Lord's to village teams all over Britain.

One thing all these competitions had in common was a need for sponsorship, the most exotic being Moët et Chandon's for the public-school types. The competitions found sponsors readily enough at first, but mounting costs and varying industrial and economic circumstances have since led to bewilderingly frequent changes of name for the competitions, and a mounting feeling amongst the more sensitive that the whole modern game was part of some board-room battle rather than a dynamic institution with a soul and a will of its own. The feeling was increased, furthermore, by the suspicion that, for all these somewhat self-conscious attempts to revive Merrie England, the country where it all started was now but a part of a multi-national enterprise. International one-day matches against the Australian tourists began in 1972 as the Prudential Trophy, were an instant success and have proliferated under various banners ever since. Even more ominous, the Prudential Cup, a smaller-scale copy of soccer's World Cup, began in 1975 and Lord's, rather like Wimbledon, became a stage on which overseas actors were the stars.

VII

In those early days, however, there was still no serious challenge to the supremacy of the Test matches, and it was there that discontent with the new post-amateur ethos showed up most strongly. The England dressing-room was, admittedly, not the most cheerful of places under the new dispensation. The appointment of Alec Bedser as chairman of selectors was highly signifi-cant, not merely because he was a former professional but because he was a bowler, and so not inclined to optimism. (When he was knighted some years later it confounded one of his own gloomy observations: 'The last bowler to be knighted,' he used to say, 'was Sir Francis Drake.') He was also in awe of 'Gubby' Allen (a more natural candidate for the tap) and a great believer that young people had been ruined by soft living, school buses and so forth. His lack of social graces was remarked upon, *de haut en bas*, by E. W. Swanton, the acknowledged expert on such matters.[8]

For Swanton, Cowdrey was the obvious and natural captain for England, not merely for his Kent origins but for his good breeding (another way of saying the same thing), and when necessity propelled the plebeian Raymond Illingworth into the limelight the Swanton features must almost have displayed emotion. There is much elevating material on the subject of 'man-management' in the chapter 'Cricket in Distress' in Swanton's book *Sort of a Cricket Person*, to which serious students of the English caste system should refer. The highlight is Swanton's encounter with a disgruntled member of the England touring party in Australia, who was upset by the last-minute arrangement of an extra Test match, and who made the mistake of saying 'that the sooner these things were arranged by professionals the better'. In a classic Swantonism, E.W. commented:

> It was a cricket-writer, I fancy, who remarked that to listen to a few of these fellows talking was, he imagined, rather like a meeting of shop stewards.

Cowdrey, who had been asked to be Illingworth's vice-captain on this Australian trip, took a long time deciding, but eventually bit the bullet. As he wrote in his autobiography: 'To me only one thing mattered. Would cricket – the whole game – be richer for our visit?' He meant spiritually richer, of course. And he found himself the odd man out in this modern-style touring party. Illingworth's style of captaincy was combative. When the truculent fast bowler John Snow – a vicar's son who wrote verse – was warned for intimidatory bowling, he remonstrated with the umpires in full view of the television cameras. And later, when the crowd threw beer cans at Snow, Illingworth led the team off the field in protest, instead of enduring in dignified silence.

Swanton's view that 'the Ashes [had] been re-taken at a heavy and wholly unnecessary cost in terms of sportsmanship' was not shared by the popular press, and Illingworth was warmly praised for the team spirit he had built up in the face of adversity. Snow was an illustration of the way change was coming into cricket, no matter what the guardians thought. This was the age of the anti-hero, moody and violent, and Snow provided what the public wanted. He may have struck a responsive chord, too, in the bosoms of some upholders of the virility cult amongst the cricket establishment. But this was mayhem on a scale far beyond that of the body-line tour – and the targets could be tail-enders as well as recognised batsmen: one was hit in the face and another laid flat by a blow on the back of the head.

But we were into another cycle of tit-for-tat as the Australians produced first Lillee and then Thomson, both of whom outdid Snow for speed and ferocity, and the ghost-writers competed for the savagery of their revelations. 'I try to hit a batsman in the rib-cage ... and I want it to hurt so much that the batsman doesn't want to face me any more,' wrote Lilley's. Thomson's was more forthright: 'I thought stuff that stiff-upper-lip crap. Let's see how stiff it is when it's split.' It was not, according to orthodox canons, quite cricket. Yet, writing in the 1973 *Wisden*, the former Australian captain Richie Benaud reckoned the controversies of recent times had been good for cricket:

> I doubt if cricket has ever had such beneficial publicity through all avenues of the media, and rarely has the financial return been better for the game's administrators.

CHAPTER TWENTY

Mammon's Turn

MONEY, IF NOT YET quite the all-consuming topic it later became, was more talked about in the Britain of the 1970s and 1980s than it had ever been. The raging inflation that swept the country – an average of 14 per cent a year from 1970 to 1980; 6.5 per cent from 1980 to 1990 – and the monetarist measures deployed in the hope of containing it set everyone in a helter-skelter scramble for survival. These were also years in which leisure became an important industry – the amount of money spent on sport in 1980 was nearly £600 million, and some 110,000 earned their living from it, a growth of 42 per cent on 1970 and 76 per cent on 1960. Sport was also an important political issue, and successive governments found it expedient to minister to the nation's addictions. The chosen method was to assist in its grass-roots development. The problem was that in most sport by that time it took only a couple of small steps up the ladder before the novice was engulfed in professionalism. There was no choice, as there once had been, between amateur and professional routes to excellence. 'Amateur' in cricket, as in everything else, was becoming a term of abuse, connoting second-best.

The guardians, sitting on committees of MCC's Cricket Council, went their various ways about getting a slice of the cake for their sport. The independent Sports Council set up by the incoming Heath government was given £5 million annually to disburse, and the sum (if not the value) was doubled before they left office. Only the National Cricket Association, which had taken over the work of the MCC Youth Cricket Association, was eligible for a share of this largesse. The Test and County Cricket Board, which controlled the professional side of the sport, and MCC itself, which was a wealthy private club, were left to their own devices. The choice, as for many other cherished archaisms – people as well as institutions – seemed to be between starving to death in genteel poverty or joining in the rat-race. In the end the TCCB did neither with any great conviction. But they tiptoed a little further along the primrose path of commercial sponsorship, hoping the end would justify the means.

They made a clumsy enough start, since their first step was to take 'tobacco money'. In 1972, just as government health warnings began to appear on cigarette packets, the TCCB launched a new competition, the Benson and Hedges Cup. Moral issues apart, this added another burden and another complication to the overcrowded county programme, dissipating the interest as throughout the season players and supporters had to keep switching their attention from one competition to another. Some attempt was made to give the new venture a distinctive image – the important new in-word – by starting it out with zonal leagues before proceeding to the knock-out stages, but the Benson and Hedges in all its twenty-six years of life never quite overcame the sense of being one competition too many. In retrospect it may indeed illustrate the dangers of too hastily and too greedily rushing into every sponsorship deal without a carefully thought-out overall plan.

The league stage of the Benson and Hedges aroused little spectator interest and was often handicapped by early-season weather. On the positive side, the sponsorship was generous, the later stages pulled in the crowds and some hitherto unfashionable counties came to the fore, including Illingworth's Leicestershire and Close's Somerset. (Somerset, indeed, adorned by two celebrated West Indians, Vivian Richards and Joel Garner, as well as the young English all-rounder, Ian Botham, were the team to beat in one-day cricket in the late 1970s and early 1980s.) The enlargement of the circle of successful clubs did not revive interest in the county structure: there was no reality any longer in what had been a natural division in Victorian times. Urban encroachment as the cities became the centres of economic and political power had torn the heart out of the counties: one, Middlesex, in fact existed solely as a cricket team, and its supporters were sophisticated urbanites who united in resistance to the opposition – upstart invaders – rather than in warm feelings of county allegiance. Only in Yorkshire, where they were still debating whether to retain the old restrictions on players born outside the county, was the intrinsic belief in county identity still strong, and Yorkshire were generally thought to be flogging a dead horse. The county-cricket programme itself did little to revive flagging passions as the teams played in an array of competitions in higgledy-piggledy fashion throughout the season. The players made no secret of their preference for the three-day game, which, however, fewer and fewer spectators turned up to see and which had little appeal for the television companies. This paradox was heightened by the fact that most establishment critics from the outset wrote off one-day cricket as an inferior version of the real thing. Thus in *Wisden* 1974 Gordon Ross compared one-day cricket to 'pop' music and the standard game to Mozart. 'Pop', he argued, might bring in the crowds but aesthetically there was no comparison. This, though silly snobbery, was harmless enough. But, more dangerously, Ross went on to claim that one-day spectators were not true cricket supporters. The Gillette Cup Final crowds who came to support 'our county', he reckoned, 'might have come just the same if it had been any one of half a dozen sports'. His point was obscure, but his intention was plain enough. As always, the real thrust of these vague, airy comparisons was directed at soccer, which had shown the way along the slippery slope to money-making and to all manner of nameless concomitant vulgarities that cricket thought it could rise above, whilst still taking the money, of course. MCC/TCCB thus introduced one-day cricket for quite the wrong reasons, believing it to be an inferior product, a cheap and cheerful sideline that would swell the coffers with the minimum of disruption to the existing programmes. So they simply tacked it on as an extra chore for the players and a tit-bit for the members. The paying customers saw things rather differently, but their views carried no more weight than they had ever done.

Before long it began to be noticed that one-day cricket-goers often not only dressed like football fans but also behaved like them, especially when primed with drink – cheering, booing, and singing disreputable songs. Lancashire, who had one of the best of the early one-day teams, soon had a particularly noisy and triumphalist following, home and away, and this was reckoned – in southern and trans-Pennine circles at least – somehow to stem from the osmotic influence of Old Trafford's neighbouring soccer ground, part of an urban malaise. It was not so easy to explain how it was that Somerset's travelling supporters had a similar reputation. And by 1977, Michael Melford, resident sage at the *Daily Telegraph*, sickened by Gloucestershire supporters, was ruminating on the difficulty of stopping pitch invasions:

> The trouble is that the only known way, apart from the erection of high fences, is an appeal for good sense and good behaviour, qualities not nowadays pre-eminent in an out-of-season football crowd that has been sozzling all day.

Unfortunately for these pillars of conventional wisdom, the authorised version, with or without proletarian followers, was not always quite as Mozartian as *Wisden* made out. 1974 was a cold, wet summer which put a dampish blanket on the championship, which was already handicapped by operating under yet another innovation designed to enliven proceedings, i.e., limiting the first innings to a hundred overs with a single new ball. Worcestershire, the champions, fined for slow over-rates, were unrepentant: 'It is the price we have to pay for success,' said their captain, Norman Gifford, as their prize money was reduced from £3,500 to £500. Nor were the Test matches any more inspiring. India performed poorly and Pakistan manifestly did not enjoy their visit, for on their return home their President, A. H. Kardar, an old Oxford man at that, called for neutral umpires on future tours of England. And by modern, materialist standards it was a disaster: the counties' share of the profits dropped by £160,000 to £460,000.

Several counties were in serious trouble – Gloucestershire lost £30,000 –

and even the previously secure Middlesex and Yorkshire lost heavily. The lifeline was the injection of sponsorship funding, and the appeal of the one-day competitions. The Cricketers' Association, shedding some of their earlier scruples, behaved as trade unions in all walks of life were doing: in 1973, for example, they threatened disruption of matches in order to secure a share of the TCCB's income from television, then some £150,000. For the most part, however, increases in players' earnings came at the cost of a heavier work-load and conditional upon results: for instance the John Player League's £12,850 prize money included £2,000 for the winners, pools for those who hit most sixes and took most wickets and a prize of £250 for the fastest televised 50. The sponsorships increased to keep pace with inflation: in 1975 Gillette doubled their original £15,000 and newcomers Benson and Hedges rounded theirs up to £100,000. But however big the prizes, they had to be won. County players had no guaranteed minimum wage, and the gap between the glittering prizes of the successful Test players and the rewards of rank-and-file county men grew wider.

These ambiguities led to a further deterioration in the concept of cricket as a game superior to the others, with distinctive character-building qualities – a noble game, as it used to be called. Now the personality cult – another feature of the publicity-conscious age – interacting with the intense partisanship of modern supporters, began to erode team spirit. The most obvious instance was that of Yorkshire, where after Close's departure the captaincy was given not to anyone with leadership qualities, but to Boycott, a by-word for self-centred dedication to the cause of trying to make himself into the world's greatest batsman. As a former team-mate, Richard Hutton, wrote in the *Cricketer*: 'As long as he scores runs, in whatever fashion is irrelevant, even if detrimental to the team effort, nothing else seems to matter.' Things were so bad that after his first disastrous season (1971) the committee called the team together to 'clear the air', but the critics fell back in the face of Boycott's forceful defence of his position, and he remained in post for six more seasons of almost unrelieved gloom for the faithful. Yet he retained a strong personal cult following, almost in inverse proportion to the team's poor performance.

Boycott had built up a strong national following for his resolute batting in the crises that frequently beset the England team. But ironically, part of the reason for his retaining the Yorkshire captaincy was his curious decision to step out of the Test arena for a while to escape the 'pressures and tensions' of international cricket. The editor of *Wisden* clearly thought this was a euphemism for escaping the bouncers of Lillee and Thomson, who scythed through England in the winter of 1974–5. *Wisden* was scathing, too, about 'the huge benefit of £20,639 which Boycott reaped during 1974', commenting:

Boycott, at 34, is not a young man with the years on his side in which to adjust.

England's needs are immediate. It is high time the Yorkshire captain came to terms with himself.

But there was still a long time to wait before the dismal situation resolved itself. Boycott was too old to adjust, even if adjustment had been in his nature. To Boycott cricket was neither a mere game, nor a way of life, but rather an instrument for the cultivation of batting perfection, Boycott-style. Thus in 1977 he was recalled to the Test team at Headingley and before thousands of idolatrous fans duly compiled his hundredth century and put England on course for an innings victory and a 3–0 series win against Australia. The following season he was dismissed from the Yorkshire captaincy despite having made over 2,000 runs – far more then anyone else. By this time Yorkshire had engaged Raymond Illingworth, first as manager and captain, a further rebuff to Boycott, and later as manager alone, with the young, enthusiastic but temperamental wicket-keeper, David Bairstow, as captain. It was a recipe for disaster on and off the field. A Yorkshire reform group that had broken off from the main committee now dedicated themselves to Boycott's reinstatement. Others, notably Brian Close, now chairman of the cricket committee, were equally convinced that Boycott was the main cause of all the county's ills.

Boycott was largely a local phenomenon. The continuing bouncer war was a more widespread menace. England's Peter Lever, entering into the hostile spirit of things, came nearest to causing an actual fatality in 1974–5 when a deflected bouncer laid out the New Zealand tail-ender, Ewan Chatfield, as England proceeded to an innings victory. Poor Chatfield's heart stopped and he had to be given mouth-to-mouth resuscitation. The West Indians' latest crop of fast bowlers – Roberts, Holding, Daniel – who had laid England low in 1976, moved E. W. Swanton to write a letter describing their tactics as 'about as disgraceful as was that of the Australians at times on the last MCC tour'. He deplored the umpires' failure to apply the full rigour of the law.

In fact the game was in the grip of forces more powerful than the umpires or even of MCC, the law-makers. That summer a Mr D. E. Fair wrote to *The Times* arguing that it was wrong that 'an umpire should have to persuade an aggressive and skilful bowler to observe artificial self-restraint'. The problem was, he reckoned, that people had grown too big for the traditional cricket pitch. When the traditional 22-yard length had originally been adopted the average man was 5 feet $4^3/4$ inches tall, compared with 5 feet 9 inches in 1976: in compensation therefore the pitch length should be increased to $23^3/4$ yards and a further 0.17 inches should be added every subsequent decade. But logic did not come into cricket – except that of the turnstiles, newly discovered, but now beginning to exert an hypnotic influence on the authorities. The public loved the vicarious thrill of fast bowling whirling round a batsman's ears, and took an even more sadistic pleasure out of seeing opposing batsmen flattened.

On the other hand the despised one-day cricket needed no such extraneous thrills, and millions throughout the world were developing a taste for it.

II

By 1975 England had ceased to be the unquestioned leaders in world cricket. It was no longer politically correct to talk about the British Commonwealth and by the same token the International Cricket Conference was somewhat less Anglocentric than of yore. But tradition and prestige still counted for a good deal. MCC might by then be more shadow than substance, but the club still owned what was probably the finest cricket ground in the world. Lord's was still the place for the great international occasion. It was the obvious place for the Prudential Cup, the first international limited-over tournament, later known as the World Cup. The takings, despite England's mediocre showing, came to £200,000 and the final between West Indies and Australia was watched by 26,000 people and took a record £66,000.

Australia stayed on after the Cup for the resumption of the bouncer war. Obliged to discard the shell-shocked batsmen of the previous winter, England had to look for coarser-grained but tougher customers. They discovered the kind of hero so beloved of tradition as to be part of the national self-image – the quiet, unassuming chap who stands up to the bully. This was David Steele, a thirty-four year old from unfashionable Northamptonshire whose grey hair made him look even more venerable, and who wore glasses. Having long given up hope of being picked for England he found himself having to go in to stop the rot against Lillee and Thomson.

Steele recalled the scene as he walked out at Lord's:

> People were looking at me. I could hear them muttering, 'Who's this grey old bugger?' as I walked past. Tommo stood with his hands on his hips. I said, 'Good morning, Tommo.' He said, ' Bloody hell, who've we got here, Groucho Marx?'

Scorning thigh pads and chest-protectors – just a towel or two stuffed in his clothes – Steele made 50 and went on to have a splendid series. That England staved off total disaster that summer also owed much to the courage of John Edrich and the wicket-keeper Alan Knott, and, not least, to the aggressive approach of Tony Greig, who replaced the nice-mannered but ineffectual Scot, Mike Denness, after the first Test.

Denness himself was an emollient successor to Illingworth, whereas Greig, born in South Africa of expatriate parents, represented the return swing of the pendulum. Greig's appointment aroused dismay amongst English nationalists. This was not generally for his specifically South African connections, which only troubled a handful of liberals. The TCCB's deep regret at having to cancel the planned 1976–7 tour of South Africa, on account of the Commonwealth leaders' Gleneagles agreement which excluded South Africa from sporting contests, was probably shared by most cricketers.

The purists' concern was that Greig, though captain of Sussex, was a carpet-bagger, not normally resident in England. That winter, *Wisden* noted, he had played cricket for Waverley, a Sydney club, for a fee of some £12,000. And when Greig subsequently fell from grace, accused of disloyalty, John Woodcock, the eminent cricket correspondent of *The Times*, explained to his readers:

> What has to be remembered, of course, is that he is an Englishman, not by birth or upbringing, but only by adoption. It is not the same thing as being English through and through.

Greig's other disadvantages as an England captain – his gamesmanship, his mastery of the art of needling opponents, his violent mood swings, impetuosity and so forth – were presumably also attributable to his insufficient Englishness. Pycroft had explained it all long before. However, some, in the summer of 1976, were convinced that his declared intention to make the touring West Indians 'grovel' was attributable specifically to his South African background. Certainly the remark enraged the touring captain, Clive Lloyd, and gave added spice to the bowling, as forty-five-year-old Brian Close and thirty-nine-year-old John Edrich joined Steele in the firing line, and Greig confessed himself frightened for the first time in his life. But it was all astonishingly good for business and the TCCB found themselves with a total of £950,000 to share out at the season's end from their various enterprises. This was an increase even in real terms, a qualification that everyone had to get used to making in those ultra-inflationary times.

Greig, meanwhile, who so far had not won a match as captain, found welcome relief on the tour of India with its slow bowling traditions. *Wisden* cooed with satisfaction over England's victory and Greig's inspired and inspiring leadership. It was also pleased that the Cricket Council had dealt so promptly and conclusively with the accusation that England's bowlers, Willis and Lever, had been guilty of ball-tampering. They had adopted the unusual practice of sticking gauze strips to their foreheads with vaseline, purportedly to keep the sweat from running into their eyes, but the Indian captain, Bishen Bedi, had complained that they were in fact using the sticky substance to keep the shine on the ball. The Cricket Council, after telephoning the England captain and manager, utterly refuted the foul allegation.

III

That winter's tour was, however, to be remembered chiefly for the Centenary Test match, commemorating the anniversary of the first match played on level terms between English and Australian players (see Chapter Nine). More precisely it was remembered for the subsequent discovery that Greig, the England captain, had used the intervals of play to recruit members of his team to the service of Kerry Packer, son of an Australian media tycoon. Packer had tried to negotiate with the Australian Board of Control for the right to televise matches exclusively on his commercial Channel 9, and when they peremptorily refused had decided to run his own international contests, hiring all the teams.

Greig's sorties on Packer's behalf were conducted in great secrecy, and no one at Lord's had any inkling of what was in store. All the talk was of the great news that a sponsor had been found for the county championship: Schweppes were offering £360,000 for three years, a generous sum considering the limited amount of television coverage that could be expected. Even when in April rumours began to circulate that a number of South Africans had signed to play for Packer in an eight-week series in various parts of the world, no one thought much about it. The Australian tourists arrived on schedule, armed with contracts newly negotiated with the ABC (£12,000 a man and a pension scheme, the word was), and old-stagers shook their heads at what things were coming to. Then Packer announced that he had signed thirty-five Test players, including thirteen Australian tourists and four current English players, Greig, Knott, Snow and Underwood.

The TCCB's response was to relieve Greig of the captaincy, because of the breach of trust, and to call a meeting of the International Cricket Conference (formerly the Imperial Cricket Conference, adapted to accommodate loose cannons like South Africa and Pakistan), where it was agreed that no action be taken for the immediate series, but that afterwards five conditions be imposed on players who contracted to play for Packer.[1] These conditions were not wildly unreasonable, but were paternalistic in the best MCC traditions. However, this soon became academic, for when the ICC met Packer he insisted on his original demand of exclusive television rights, the ABC saw this as blackmail and refused, the ICC stood by them and the trial of strength resumed.

Packer signed another dozen or more players, including two current English Test men, Dennis Amiss and Bob Woolmer, to play what he called 'Super-cricket' and what the establishment referred to as a 'circus'. This was a conscious attempt to relate the Packer scheme to Old Clarke and the All-England XI, which was a horror story told in the best circles about a dastardly plot to wrest the game from MCC's lawful grasp. In 1866 the happy ending had come when MCC had laid down the conditions on which they would engage the rebels for future matches. In 1977, when the TCCB and ICC tried to do the same, they found themselves in court answering an application for an injunction and damages from the Packer organisation and three of their contracted players, headed by the infamous Greig. Furthermore, they lost the case with costs, some quarter of a million pounds.[2] As a *Guardian* leader put it, 'Mr Kerry Packer may be a bounder and a cad. But he is a legal bounder and a High-Court-sanctified cad.'

To rub salt in establishment wounds, Richie Benaud, who emerged as the brains behind Packer's scheme, announced that it would not be played under MCC laws, which he had the temerity to call mere 'rules', and preparations gleefully began for World Series Cricket (WSC). Furthermore, it was evident that some counties were more concerned to retain the crowd-pulling power of their overseas players than to uphold TCCB dignity. Sussex expressed relief that they were not to be deprived of the services of Greig, Snow and Imran Khan, the Pakistani star. Gloucestershire's treasurer likewise declared himself 'ticked pink' that Mike Procter and Zaheer Abbas would be staying. The Hampshire captain, R. C. M. Gilliatt, of Charterhouse and Oxford University, said it was 'good news for Hampshire cricket'. There was, of course, much huffing and puffing from choleric upholders of tradition, but as the TCCB made no move to appeal against the judgment there was little they could do but seethe.

Loyalist indignation was further aroused when Sussex declined to follow England's lead, and renewed Greig's captaincy for the 1978 season. (Nottinghamshire proposed and Lancashire seconded a motion to expel Sussex from the championship.) Kent followed a more politically correct line when they removed Asif Iqbal as captain, but they were careful not to try to dispense with his services as a player. All but the fiercest accepted that the counties had little choice but to honour existing contracts with the 'rebels' (though it was assumed that it would be a different story a year later: the judgment had said nothing about renewing contracts). Warwickshire took a similar line. Stiff upper lips were *de rigueur* and crossed fingers were hidden under board-room tables.

Two things saved the bacon, if not entirely the face, of officialdom. First, World Series Cricket was not the immediate runaway success Packer had predicted, for although it attracted television audiences of a sort, and floodlit matches were a great novelty, the jazzed-up proceedings did not seem to stir up any great concern for who won or lost. Second, the assault on the citadel had led to some rallying round amongst lovers of the authorised version. The TCCB landed £1 million sponsorship from Cornhill Insurance for the Test matches. Fees went up from £3,000 to £5,000 (plus winning bonuses) for tours and from £200 to £1,000 for each home match. Players were thus given pause before they rushed to sign for Packer, and some English players of a certain age or temperament saw this as an opportunity to thin the ranks of overseas players on the county scene, which they now dominated. Personal ambitions and old feuds came into play.

World Series Cricket put a further twist in the ravelled skein of Geoffrey Boycott's fortunes. Not everyone was as pleased as *Wisden* with the choice of

Mike Brearley, the Middlesex captain, to replace the alien Greig. Sceptics who thought his batting below standard also pointed out that he had not spoken out against the Packer 'circus', and hinted darkly that the only reason he hadn't actually joined them was because he wasn't good enough to be made an offer: Boycott, by contrast, had been amongst the first to be invited but had ostentatiously refused. Instead he had offered his services to England in her hour of need, and had scored his hundredth century on his home ground, as England took advantage of Australia's greater disarray to put it across them in that summer's Tests.

The Cricketers' Association had members on both sides of the argument – which essentially was whether Packer's intervention was likely to benefit all cricketers or would merely further widen the gap between the stars' pay and that of the rest. At the time the basic pay of the 150 or so capped English players averaged about £2,600 a season, rising to perhaps £3,000 with bonuses. Test players averaged nearer £5,000, which was the normal minimum for overseas stars, some of whom commanded £10,000 or more, and the immediate effect of World Series Cricket was to increase the disparities. Boycott further developed his role as champion of the loyalist cause in Pakistan in the winter of 1977–8. When the Pakistan Board of Control lost their nerve and proposed to select three Packer players, Boycott, as acting captain, led a dressing-room revolt.

This, without helping intra-ICC relations, was a setback to the rebels' hopes of breaking up the fragile alliance. Greig vented his spleen in the *Sydney Sun*, claiming that Boycott had had a special reason to fear the return of the Pakistan rebels – the pace of Imran Khan. Greig was suspended by the TCCB for breaking his contract and Sussex dolefully dismissed him as captain and 'allowed him to go' during the year. As ICC's united front began to crumble under pressure from West Indies and Pakistan, neither of whom could afford to adopt high moral principles, discussions began with WSC, who were going to greater and greater lengths to try to drum up interest, notably fast bowling of such ferocity that helmets ceased to be regarded as wimpish. 'Roller-ball cricket', traditionalists called it.

Neither side was yet ready to concede, but cynics were already predicting that money would have the last word. When John Arlott, president of the Cricketers' Association, reported in August that ICC had made a 'considerable advance towards accommodation' with Packer, the writing was already on the wall. Kent announced that they would re-sign their Packer players for 1979 on the grounds that if they didn't other counties would. And when Warwickshire announced shortly afterwards that, in view of a letter from the other players,[3] they did not propose to renew Dennis Amiss's contract, it caused a great furore amongst the members, for Amiss had had his best season ever for the club: 'Why should we suffer when Kent don't intend to?' the dissidents asked. But when they asked for a special meeting, arranged for late

September, Amiss himself asked for it to be called off, advised, apparently, by the Cricketers' Association, who were confident that a settlement would be reached during the winter.

Little more needs to be said about this ignoble episode in the affairs of the noble game as the saga lurched towards the inevitable surrender by the ICC. English disapproval of Packer was alloyed somewhat at the outset by the fact that his impact was greatest in Australia, whose Test teams dwindled into insignificance as a result. Conversely, though the Australian Board made war-like noises, the Australian public made it clear that, while not everyone liked the frenetic WSC approach, they certainly were not going to pay to see their reserves trampled on by the Poms. The English public, meanwhile, became relaxed enough in their unaccustomed supremacy over the old enemy to indulge in a nostalgic North v. South, Gentlemen v. Players debate about the claims of Boycott and Brearley to the captaincy. One side followed the lead of John Woodcock of *The Times*, who backed the Middlesex captain despite an average of under 20 in his previous twelve Test matches – 'because England are at ease under Brearley and play the better for being so'. A diametrically opposed minority view was expressed by Albert Hunt, a Bradford contributor to *New Society*: the north-country 'professional' Boycott, having swallowed his pride and gone out to tour Australia under Brearley, had been unchival-rously denied the opportunity to practise at a crucial stage in the tour by the Cambridge 'amateurs' Brearley and the manager, Doug Insole.

This unique reversal of roles may indeed have affected Boycott's perfor-mances. So also may his dismissal as Yorkshire's captain two days after the death of his beloved mother and a couple of weeks before the tour began. Boycott himself even blamed his personal troubles for his deplorable outburst against one of the umpires, whom he called a cheat when he gave him out. Anyway Boycott was glad to get the tour over and returned home, intent on pressing hard for a ban on Packer players at the Cricketers' Association meeting in April 1979. This was expected to be a stormy affair, but it turned out to be an anti-climax, for the members were advised to take no decisions but to await developments. By the end of the month it was all over: the Australian Board had done a deal, conceding Packer's exclusive television rights, and the wind went out of loyalist sails with a rush.

IV

In the immediate aftermath it became customary to blame World Series Cricket for all the ills that were afflicting the first-class game. A longer perspective suggests that all it did was tear down the moth-eaten curtains of the old regime, letting in the glaring light of the modern world. And while this has undoubtedly led cricket into some crazy antics, bizarre marketing ploys and a decline in standards, both of taste and behaviour, what institution, including the arts, politics and religion, has not gone the same way? If we regard sport as merely an escape from reality, the incursion of modernity may seem an aberration; if we see it as something more significant, then we can perhaps console ourselves that cricket was being kept alive and was not destined to become a museum piece, too refined to survive in the outside world.

And survival could not be taken for granted in any walk of life in Britain in the 1980s and early 1990s. They were turbulent times for the islanders and the tattered remnants of their empire. The British economy hit its worst recession for fifty years, and society had not seemed so deeply and bitterly divided in living memory. Things had gone rapidly downhill since Edward Heath, in 1974, had challenged the miners' union on the issue of who should govern the country – and lost the election. There had followed episodes of mounting violence on strike picket-lines, National Front marches, and inner-city riots with racial undercurrents and a mounting hostility to the police. Not least, there were IRA outrages in the wake of the latest Ulster troubles, now magnified, as all else, by the power of modern technology and the insatiable appetite of the burgeoning mass media. Centrifugal tendencies in Scotland and Wales were only relatively less serious, as the national anthem began to be a painful ordeal. These controversies were intensified by the most divisive issue of all, entry to the Common Market, and by the disputes over North Sea oil and nuclear energy, underlining the limits of British autonomy against the encroachments of international collaboration and multi-national industrial companies.

Parochially, unemployment, fuelled both by wages outstripping production and by the belated, self-defensive rush towards automation, began shooting up towards the 2 million mark and beyond, with wide regional and sectional varia-tions. The 'winter of discontent' of 1978–9, in which the public sector weighed in with a series of strikes, brought to power the 'Iron Lady', Margaret Thatcher, whose bitter medicine everyone had to swallow. Fortified by the unifying effect of victory in the Falklands, she was confirmed in her mission of teaching the unions, the local authorities, the professions, economic 'wets' and backsliders in general a monetarist lesson. Britain became a neo-Darwinist society in which winning was what, in the new idiom, it was 'all about'. And there were plenty of new winners in Thatcher's Britain, which conformed closely to Oscar Wilde's depiction of cynicism – knowing the price of everything and the value of nothing. The street-smart were the admired models for youth and there was plenty of money around for them.

Class allegiance had already begun to disintegrate in the 1960s: as respect for authority declined, the working-class young began to hanker after the fruits of capitalism and their middle-class counterparts to reject convention. The expanding student class expected good jobs and began to behave as if they were key workers rather than a privileged élite. But as, with recession, the gap between qualified and unqualified grew wider and 'degrees in flower-arranging' lost credibility, Sir Keith Joseph, a Conservative intellectual, began to try to steer higher education towards more purposeful goals. At secondary level the Labour notion of comprehensive education was enthusiastically pursued by 'one-nation' Tories, with the effect of helping to preserve and strengthen the independent schools despite their escalating fees. In higher education the distinctions between polytechnics and universities were swept away in the interests of economical expansion.

Money thus was emerging as the main determinant of people's role in society. Work, for most, was no more than a means of making a living. And as leisure became an increasingly important industry, so the best exponents of sport, particularly if they had no other marketable skills, expected to make money from it, like their innumerable dependent sub-species (from writers and broadcasters to equipment makers and suppliers of drink). As with the arts, sport became indistinguishable from show business (at least in those aspects that attracted most public attention and money). In cricket Packer had merely accelerated the process by undermining the traditional sources of authority.

Indeed at the time of the Packer heresy, England was in some trouble, whether cricket was considered as an entertainment or as a healthy outdoor activity. As a spectator sport (excluding that viewed on television) it was second only to football in 1979, but it was a very poor second, and by 1983 it had fallen behind rugby and horse-racing as well. More seriously, people were no longer playing the game as they had done in the immediate post-war years. In 1965, according to the Government Social Survey, cricket had ranked alongside angling as the most popular outdoor sport for adults; by 1980 it was tenth, below golf, tennis and even bowls.[4]

The recession had no doubt contributed to the sharpness of the more recent decline, from 600,000 in 1977 to 500,000 three years later, as recorded in the General Household Survey: cricket was an expensive sport. Consumer spending on cricket gear amounted to some £23 million, the biggest share on bats, of which the best even then could cost well over £50. 140,000 of all sizes and prices[5] were sold at home and abroad in 1977, but the number fell to 100,000 in 1980. Cricketers also needed a level ground and an even more level pitch to play on. Private clubs, many of them set up by industry as an amenity for their workers, provided most of the better pitches, and although many local authorities were active they were rarely able to reach high standards.

As for adults, so for schoolboys. Nine out of ten men surveyed in 1965 had played the game before they were fourteen, two-thirds of them at school. (Like smoking, the addiction tends to set in early or not at all.) But by 1980 there was some decline in state-school participation. Rising costs and the elaborate facilities required were one reason, but the decline also coincided with the widespread introduction of comprehensive schools. On philosophical as well as organisational grounds many of these bigger schools offered a wider range of recreational activities than the space-consuming élitist pursuit to which Lewis Carroll had taken exception in Victorian Oxford. An anti-team-games ethos in some schools caught media attention. Also, state-school teachers, like other public sector workers, were caught up in the trade union struggle to improve pay and conditions, and fewer volunteers were available for unpaid overtime. Comprehensive schools generally played more cricket than the old secondary modern schools, but often less seriously than in the old grammar schools. A 1982 article in the *Times Educational Supplement* complained, for instance, that less than half the 130 secondary schools in Hampshire took more than a casual interest.

In the comprehensive era the pillars of school cricket were still, as ever, the independent schools. Preparatory school headmasters, entertaining old boys' teams during the holidays, could not quite fill the gap left by country-house cricket. There was no modern equivalent of Sir Julien Cahn, house parties were smaller and sported fewer gaudy blazers, but, according to R. L. Arrowsmith in *Barclay's World of Cricket*, 'Lord Porchester at Highclere, the McAlpines at Marchwiel, the Blofelds at Hoveton, the Rothschilds at Hovingham, Robin Leigh-Pemberton at Torry Hill and Captain Hawkins at Everdon' kept the flag flying. So did the wandering clubs from I Zingari, Free Foresters and the county foundations – Band of Brothers, Hampshire Hogs, Somerset Stragglers and the like – to the multiplicity of old boys' clubs, some of whom were distinguishing themselves in the new club competitions and leagues.

But, particularly as Oxford and Cambridge started to lose their dominance and Durham and Loughborough headed a new wave of university cricket, public-school élitism began to lose its focus. In the nineteenth century, cricket had been taken up by the schools that trained the nation's leaders as a moral force in education: their products had taken over the first-class game and shaped it for their pleasure. In the modern era, when cricket had become a branch of the leisure industry, the main body of recruits from the public schools were likely to be those intent on entrepreneurial exploitation of their talents, just like the ground staff apprentices from the working classes.

The characteristic modern instrument of democracy is competition, and the English Schools Cricket Association, straddling both state and private sectors, now provided even more opportunities than it had done in Denis Compton's day for the talented working-class boy. The Somerset branch, for instance, played their part in developing the most celebrated English cricketer of the period, Ian Botham. Botham was a secondary-modern schoolboy, though not the kind who played in the street with a lamp-post for a wicket, but one who used to infiltrate games on the grammar-school playing fields adjoining his home. The network of talent scouts linking the county and the Lord's ground staff did the rest – but Somerset still took on more public-school than secondary-modern schoolboys when they signed Botham.

V

Compton and Botham. The juxtaposition is irresistible, for Botham was to illuminate the world of cricket as Compton had done thirty years before. The association is not, however, one that Compton relished. Botham's off-the field antics – including drug-taking, pub brawls and generally rowdiness – were not to Compton's liking. As the cricket-addict and television presenter Tony Francis put it, 'These rushes of blood persuade Compton that he does not wish to be mentioned in the same breath as Botham.' And as to cricket, Compton was equally scathing: 'Don't associate me with him! He was over-rated. Botham only did well because all the best players had joined Packer.'

But a player can hardly be blamed for the quality of the opposition he faces, and Botham was the biggest single reason why, when faced with the Packer threat, English cricket did not succumb. He emerged just at the right time to keep loyalist spirits up, and, more importantly, after the crisis was over, to supply the glamour and excitement that Packer, Greig and Benaud had recognised the public wanted. Botham was, in terms of his importance to the English game at the time, the equivalent of W. G. Grace, though of course lacking the Old Man's stability of character, shrewdness and long-headedness. Botham also elevated off-the-field horseplay to a fine art, and the more he earned (hundreds upon hundreds of thousands of pounds) from his various commercial ventures, the grosser his manners became.

Every lurid detail of sportsmen's lives, private or public, was by this time being fed to avid readers by an increasingly sensationalist press. Botham himself contributed a highly paid (and ghosted) column to the *Sun*, the most popular paper. Those interested in the interaction of the media men and their temperamental subject-matter should read Don Mosey's acidulous biography of Botham. Here we simply note part of Denis Compton's reply to the *Sun* when, in 1985, he was libelled by Botham after criticising his bowling tactics:

> Botham's not a nice chap ... I suppose this is the new generation. His example to the young is awful.

Yet for both the young and the not-so-young, Botham was the great hero who swung round the Headingley Test of 1981 with a thrilling 149. (His friend Bob Willis, who himself contributed a marvellous bowling performance, afterwards revealed that throughout the match Botham was, in his admiring phrase, 'drunk as a skunk' every night.) He could have burned down the pavilion and been forgiven. By then, he had already been England's captain for a brief, disastrous period. Apart from his technical inadequacies his social skills had not been great, particularly in reaction to criticism. He had a point, perhaps, in taking exception to the crude attack by Henry Blofeld in the *Sunday Express* – 'Botham captains the side like a great big baby' – but an England captain is not supposed to seize his critics by the throat. Even his impressive charity walk to Land's End was studded with allegations of drug-taking and clashes with the police.

The decline in moral standards was not confined to the players. The TCCB, desperately anxious to protect their box-office appeal, merely went through the motions of disciplining Botham on several occasions when he stepped out of line. Their attitude towards his drug-taking was astonishing. When he was convicted of possessing cannabis in 1985 they decided to take no action, though threatening severe measures against future offenders. And when the following season he confessed, in a long newspaper article, to having been a 'pot' smoker, he was suspended for two months. As his biographer, Don Mosey, put it, 'he had been very, very leniently treated indeed'.

It can hardly be argued, as some did at the time, that the Packer affair brought about a deterioration in standards of behaviour in cricket, but there certainly was a fairly sharp deterioration on and off the field. And the English contribution to it was considerable. Perhaps it was a coincidence that they were performing badly, too. The star players in England came from overseas. Far too few native-born players were of the quality to compete for Test places, and those who held them did not seem to regard it as a privilege. By 1986 the veteran political columnist, John Junor of the *Sunday Express*, observing the tattered flag of imperial supremacy being dragged through the mud, wrote of 'the snivelling, long-haired, money-conscious yobboes who now represent England'.

VI

The Packer affair was not the only thing to ruffle official feathers in 1977. That was also the year of the Gleneagles agreement, in which the Commonwealth countries undertook, *inter alia*, 'to discourage contact by their nationals with sporting organisations, teams or sportsmen from South Africa'. The British Government subscribed to this but did not take it to apply to cricketers who spent their winters coaching there, and they drew the line at withholding passports or other means of enforcing it. The Cricket Council's view was plain: an emergency committee in 1978 declared South Africa ready, racially speaking, to return to Test cricket. They failed to persuade other members of the ICC, notably India and Pakistan, however. The United Nations also drew up a blacklist of offenders and many of the Commonwealth countries kept a sharp eye on this.

Guyana, who even before Gleneagles had refused entry to teams led by such 'bridge-builders' as Warwickshire business man Deryck Robins because of his links with South Africa, was one such. Presumably, therefore, the TCCB knew they were asking for trouble when they chose Robin Jackman, the Surrey bowler, for the 1980–1 West Indies tour, for he regularly played and coached in South Africa. Nevertheless, the team, with Jackman, were instructed to present themselves in Guyana, and when he was refused entry they declined to play. The governments of the other islands, though huffing and puffing, put cricket and its touristic potential first and the trouble blew over after a while.

Then in October 1981 the Indian Government refused to accept two players, one of them Boycott, because they were on the blacklist, and it seemed for a time that that winter's tour might be cancelled. Political point made, however, India accepted Boycott's assertion that he disapproved of apartheid, a claim supposedly based on his playing cricket with black children in the West Indies. He stayed with the tourists long enough to break the Test runs aggregate record, then became fatigued during the next match and went off to play golf. He then returned to England, needing time to recuperate from the pressures of batting, his dealings with the Yorkshire committee and life in general. Then it emerged that Boycott had been busy all year, Greig-like, recruiting English players for a South African tour.

Recalling the Packer defections, Christopher Martin-Jenkins, editor of the *Cricketer*, wrote,

> There is less guilt on this occasion, perhaps, [because] there has been a strong feeling within county cricket that something should have been done to reward the South African cricketers for doing all they could to play cricket multi-racially.

And a South African reader wrote:

> Double standards abound. England is South Africa's chief trading partner. There are no barriers there. Our gold and minerals are too valuable for a country which consistently shuts one eye.

The TCCB perhaps saw the force of this, but they had already issued warnings and with Tests against both India and Pakistan scheduled for the summer they had no alternative but to take action, excluding the rebels from Test cricket for three years. The Cricketers' Association agreed with this action and the rebels prudently did not appeal.

Much interest centred on who did and who did not sign up with South African Breweries for the tour. Some, like Amiss, Underwood and Woolmer, were already WSC rebels and presumably brought the same simple financial criteria to bear on this second problem as on the first. Conversely, Botham and the accomplished young David Gower felt able to decline. Gower, described by the *Guardian* as a 'laid-back, charming Goldilocks', probably thought it not worth all the fuss. Botham, originally offered £50,000 and later even more, still turned it down, either out of loyalty to his friend and Somerset team-mate, Viv Richards, or because, as Boycott implied, the money still wasn't enough. As his solicitor said at the time, 'A major point with Ian was that ... it could have ended his Test career, and could well have meant the loss of future contracts in the United Kingdom.' He certainly had no money worries, and when in 1990 he was invited to go on another South African 'rebel' tour under the Middlesex captain Mike Gatting, he reportedly pulled out only when the organisers would not meet his demands of £600,000. Even allowing for inflation (at 6.5 per cent per annum) his price had gone up more than somewhat. The standard fee was probably only a tenth of that but even so exceeded what all but the very best Test players could hope to earn.

The most surprising 'acceptor of the proffered rand' was Graham Gooch, in his prime as a player and widely regarded as England's best prospect as captain: according to the *Cricketer* he was already making £20,000 a year from Test cricket, plus a minimum of £8,000 from Essex and probably another £15,000 from endorsements and other side-shows, and had a benefit in the offing. The English rebels were fortunate in that their county bases for their South African excursions remained solid, for all of them were retained by their clubs. And the heat of adverse public opinion, insofar as it was on them at all, was soon deflected to the rebel West Indians, who made a highly successful tour of South Africa in 1983.

An organisation calling itself Freedom in Sport, with the backing of business interests in Australia and South Africa and ambitious to spread worldwide, campaigned against the blacklist, proclaiming the rights of sportsmen to ply their trade without political interference. This undoubtedly reflected the view of most county professionals. Some few, however, took a different stance. Asif Iqbal, of Kent and Pakistan, in a powerful piece in the *Cricketer* in April 1982, declared it 'the height of hypocrisy to condemn apartheid, but to have no qualms about fraternising with those who perpetrate it'. It was 'a lot of nonsense to pretend that sport and politics can be completely dissociated at international level. What eleven players represent in a Test match is not a cricketing entity, but a political state.'

Freedom in Sport thought they saw a way round that. Was not MCC a private club? Why should they not organise a tour of South Africa? A Conservative MP, John Carlisle, put the proposal to the MCC, but found the committee firm in their support of the TCCB and ICC in seeking to preserve Test cricket and discourage renegade ventures. The truth of Asif's contention was being demonstrated, in fact, for MCC was now an integral part of the state's arrangements for the support of cricket. The MCC tour idea came to nothing in the end. All the same, the great Edrich and Compton were amongst the group of members who donned their old sweaters and marched along the streets to Lord's in the cause of liberty. The sudden, dramatic reversal of fortunes in South Africa saved English cricket from impaling itself fatally on the hook Asif Iqbal had warned of. Black South Africans proved to be a more tolerant and forgiving people, and though the pace of economic and social reform disappointed some, cricket would seem to have made rapid strides towards an integrated 'level playing field' system. South Africa's return to Test cricket, after twenty-two years out in the cold, was highly successful, both in economic and in playing terms.

CHAPTER TWENTY-ONE

Heavy Weather

THOUGH GENERALLY EUPHORIC about the 'boom' that had followed Packer's intervention, Asif Iqbal had some negative things to say about cricket in Britain's painfully emerging multi-cultural society. He was clearly slightly baffled by the lack of logic behind what went on. For example, he was scathing about the peculiar English attitude, bred in the public schools, that regarded protective headgear as somehow effeminate. He could not understand the 'senseless ballyhoo' against wearing helmets that swept the country as batsman after batsman got hit on the head in the bouncer wars: 'I cannot see how it is a sign of anything but the grossest stupidity to guard your shin but not your head.' Nor did he share the contempt of the purists for the coloured uniforms popularised by Packer and now used in English one-day games, noting wryly, 'Surely colours are amoral things.' And he had no sympathy with the blimpish view that the game had been debased by professionalism and the Packer extension of it. He responded with some blimpish views of his own. In Asif's opinion bad cricketing behaviour was a reflection of the general lowering of social standards:

> One has only to walk into any comprehensive school in England to appreciate this, and one need hardly labour the point that comprehensive schools at least have not been 'contaminated' by Channel 9.

He acknowledged, of course, that some of the wilder excesses may have been spurred by the extra money that had come into the system, but it was 'not the only, or even the main factor responsible for such behaviour'. Asif saw clearly that the traditional structures of cricket had not produced true professionalism:

> Professionalism in a lawyer or an engineer is supposed to be an attribute, but when used in a cricketing context the term somehow insinuates indiscipline, boorishness – everything in fact that is traditionally not cricket.

Asif also sternly criticised 'governing bodies that chose quite unashamedly to ignore recent deplorable happenings'. He cited particularly a very bad case involving the England captain, currently Keith Fletcher of Essex.

Fletcher had been appointed after Brearley's brief return to preside over Botham's heroics in 1981. Fletcher was a county captain and a better batsman than Brearley, but in other ways, including social and educational background, was less impressive. The tour of India that followed Fletcher's appointment was an immediate corrective to the press talk of a new golden age. Fletcher had grandly announced before leaving, 'Sport ... can only help bring nations closer together – and even closer ties will be forged this winter.' But quite apart from the political problems over apartheid and the United Nations blacklist, the cricket itself was poor stuff. Mutual suspicion and hostility were the keynotes as India won the first Test and took care not to lose the rest. The sheer boredom of it was punctuated by unseemly incidents, the worst of them involving Fletcher himself, who expressed his annoyance at being given out by knocking the bails off. The tour manager, Raman Subba Row, instead of disciplining Fletcher, defended him, declaring it 'a gesture of disappointment rather than dissent'.

Asif Iqbal, with some justification, regarded this as preposterous: 'I am afraid we will need much more honesty than that.' The dishonesty was not an attempt to deceive the public, but a mixture of misguided loyalty and self-deception, things the British have always been good at. It is an aspect of the xenophobia that appears to afflict island races, like the bar-parlour consensus that whereas every other nation in the European Union cynically subscribes to regulations that they have no intention of observing, British governments alone take them seriously. In sport, where the unconditional loyalty of the supporter is part of the suspension of disbelief that transforms otherwise trivial activities into religious rituals, enthusiasts tend not to want correct decisions from referees or umpires but partiality. But one is entitled to expect a less prejudiced view from the people who run the game.

'Not cricket', like loving your neighbour, was always a doctrine that implied access to some superior external moral force if ordinary mortals were to be able to live up to it. And in the modern materialist world, which has a distinct shortage of spiritual authority, it has failed progressively to attract even lip service. The 'not cricket' side of Fletcher's Indian tour was further imperilled by the BBC radio commentators, who not only fell below traditional standards of objectivity themselves by exuding scepticism about umpiring decisions, but invited streams of players into their commentary box to enliven the proceedings and encouraged them to give vent to their feelings. These included not only righteous indignation but the assumption that only British umpires were any good – because, of course, as everyone hastened to explain, they were drawn from the ranks of retired county cricketers. In the aftermath of the British Raj and with South Africa still a controversial issue, the impression of condescension was unfortunate. Asif Iqbal entitled his survey of the state of the game after the Packer transformation, 'RACIAL SPLIT THREATENS CRICKET'S BOOM'. He saw the dangers of South African apartheid and the hypocritical attitudes it induced: 'Sportsmen felt themselves singled out by the Gleneagles agreement, but it was the height of hypocrisy to condemn apartheid but to have no qualms about fraternising with those who perpetrate it.' And South Africa was not the only source of racial friction. An internal measure that cricket needed to take as a matter of urgency, Asif thought, was the appointment of neutral umpires. Such a step would not, of course, mean that umpiring mistakes would not occur, Asif agreed, but it 'would at least ensure that they are seen for what they really are – a genuine and human error of judgement – and not something else, the mere suggestion of which is at best embarrassing, and at worst possibly degrading'. Events in the next few years involving Asif's native Pakistan were to reinforce his point emphatically.

II

There was, as we have already noted, a long history of acrimony over umpiring between Pakistan and England. A new instalment of the saga began in 1982, when the TCCB agreed to a request from the Indian touring team to replace David Constant by another umpire. The TCCB, of course, denied any lack of faith in Constant, paying his match fee, but it set a dangerous precedent. Then later in the season they refused a similar request from Pakistan, with predictable results. After a controversial decision in the deciding Test, the Pakistan captain, Imran Khan, formally announced that his team had no confidence in Constant.

Five years later, on Pakistan's next tour, they objected to Constant again, and the TCCB refused them again. This greatly inflamed feelings during a season in which there was racial trouble in the crowd at a one-day international in Birmingham. The Pakistan manager lost no opportunity to criticise English umpires, especially Constant, whom he called a 'disgraceful person'. The English team for their part found it hard to avoid showing dissent (as 'not cricket' and the TCCB required them to do). Their patience was greatly strained in the Headingley Test when the Pakistan wicket-keeper twice claimed catches that had in fact bounced ('not cricket', perhaps, but a thing not unknown even amongst English cricketers, arising from the extreme difficulty for a wicket-keeper of telling whether a ball he scooped from near the ground lodged directly in his glove or was taken on the half-volley).

As television slow-motion replays became better and better and human fallibility was increasingly displayed, umpires' judgements were more likely to be criticised than cricketers' discourteous reaction to them. At Headingley in 1982 one aggrieved batsman was Ian Botham, who swore at the Pakistan wicket-keeper and called him a cheat. Umpire Ken Palmer bravely interposed his person between the two. Another, less excusable, dissenter was Chris Broad, afterwards a television commentator, who was to be at the centre of several gruesome episodes in the next few seasons. The first, entirely predictable, repercussions occurred that winter when England were touring Pakistan.

Peter May, chairman of selectors, strongly disapproved of dissent, but conduct on overseas tours depended very much on whoever the TCCB chose as tour manager. Weak or over-trusting ones tended to be brushed aside by strong-minded captains (as, notoriously, Warner by Jardine) or at least to feel the need to show solidarity with them. In the post-Packer era the former amateurs appointed by the TCCB as tour managers bore little resemblance to grandees like Gubby Allen or Freddy Brown. On the 1987–8 tour of Pakistan the TCCB manager was Peter Lush, hitherto a public-relations man. He was in nominal charge of a party that also had a team manager, Micky Stewart, and a captain, Mike Gatting, both battle-hardened professionals.

In the first Test Lush had to deal with Broad, who, when given out by umpire Shakoor Khan, refused to leave the crease until persuaded to go by his partner Graham Gooch. This extraordinary conduct, reminiscent of Leicester v. Coventry two hundred years earlier (Chapter Four), was expected to incur a heavy fine, but Lush merely reprimanded Broad and that evening issued a statement casting doubt on the quality of the umpiring. This encouraged the captain, Gatting, the archetypal plain, blunt man, into an intemperate diatribe on the same subject. England had lost by an innings, and Gatting began by complaining that 'obviously in this match we weren't competing on an even basis'. He went on to sledgehammer his point home:

> When we come to Pakistan the umpiring is always the same. I've never seen it as blatant as this. I warned the younger players beforehand what they could expect, but until you've experienced it you can't comprehend how the game is played out here.

And much more to that effect.

Gatting claimed, furthermore, that nine of England's twenty wickets had fallen to bad decisions, eight of them from umpire Shakoor Rana. This particular official, it must be said, did not enjoy a good reputation with overseas players, Australian and New Zealand as well as English. He was clearly well thought of at home, however, so it was not surprising that Pakistan, grossly insulted by Gatting and Lush, should feel obliged to reappoint him for the second Test. One can only imagine Shakoor Rana's frame of mind when late on the second day he saw Gatting making what he took to be a surreptitious sign to a fielder to move without the batsman's knowledge. He stopped play and volubly rebuked Gatting. Gatting in turn angrily denied the charge and added a few observations on the umpire's ancestry and general character.

The television cameras and the new, intrusive device of a sound-effects microphone installed by the pitch made public the full horror of the exchanges that followed – arm-waving, expostulations, accusations and counter-accusations of cheating – and at close of play Shakoor Rana, declining to stand again until he had an apology, reported Gatting for using 'foul and abusive' language to him. Gatting for his part felt aggrieved rather than contrite. Eventually, after two days of stalemate, he was instructed to apologise and did so minimally and gracelessly.[1] The enormity of what had occurred was obscured in a welter of partisan reaction, encouraged by the sensation-hungry media. For instance, Tom Graveney, one of the many former internationals engaged as television expert summarisers, launched an attack on the 'chronically low' standard of umpiring in Pakistan.

Perhaps the most depressing feature of all this was that Raman Subba Row, chairman of the TCCB, who had flown out to Karachi, ostensibly to smooth things out with the Pakistani authorities, in fact awarded every member of the team a special hardship bonus of £1,000. For all the proliferating layers of management coming into the game, no one seemed able to stop the rash of bad manners that afflicted it. For example, Broad, already twice fortunate to escape serious punishment, again showed dissent at Karachi over a lbw decision. Then in the special bi-centenary Test in Sydney at the end of the Pakistan tour, after making top score, he petulantly knocked a stump out when he was dismissed. This time it was the manager, Micky Stewart's, turn to warn him about his future conduct.

III

Gatting, by any standards, was lucky to survive as England captain. But those who ran the game, which was now not short of money, especially at international level, seemed incapable of rational management, a skill for which neither service at the crease nor service in committees is adequate preparation. And the point was reinforced when, six matches later, Gatting was relieved of the captaincy for bringing the game into disrepute, this time for off-the-field cavorting with a barmaid – an offence not previously thought heinous but something Peter May, chairman of selectors, was not prepared to countenance during a home series. Not long afterwards Gatting's ghosted autobiography was published, suitably spiced up by a chapter on the Pakistan tour, and he was fined £5,000 for a breach of his contractual obligation not to write about a tour within two years.

The TCCB fielded three other captains (Emburey twice, Chris Cowdrey and Gooch) in that summer's series against West Indies, which they lost 4–0. Gooch, a fine batsman, but a somewhat blinkered fitness fanatic, had been chosen to lead that winter's tour to India, but this proved to be an error, not for cricketing reasons, but because the Indian government refused to admit him under the Gleneagles agreement, and the tour was cancelled. It was about this time that the veteran Alec Bedser was reported as saying: 'All I know about Gleneagles is that they have a nice golf course there.'

Bedser had long been retired as chairman of selectors. Peter May had put his own stamp on the post, but was in the same cautious, conservative tradition. When May retired in 1988 there was a general feeling that something slightly more adventurous was now needed. What they got instead was a much-publicised 'new era'. No less a personage than 'Lord Ted' Dexter, having reached yet another crossroads in his career, was persuaded – for a consideration – to take on the chairmanship of selectors, in between his other business enterprises, his golfing and his astrology. The new era proved rather better at attracting publicity – not all of it good – than at achieving anything more solid, and there was much uncertainty – and some wrangling – arising from Dexter's distinctive management style, which might be described as 'hands-off'. The fallen star, Gatting, had hoped to be recalled under the new dispensation, and, indeed, it was rumoured that Dexter tried to get him back for the 1989 Australian visit. Gatting was certainly strongly supported by Stewart, the team manager, but in the end he was declared *persona non grata* by TCCB's cricket committee chairman, 'Ossie' Wheatley, a Cambridge contemporary of Dexter.

The replacement Messiah chosen this time was David Gower, a fine batsman and a charming man but a lily of the field rather than a toiler or spinner, and, as he had already demonstrated in his first spell of captaincy, unable to motivate a losing team either by exhortation or industrious example. Gower led another losing team in 1989. Some of the reasons were nothing to do with him. The extra pressures being put on cricketers to play day in, day out in various competitions was beginning to take its toll, particularly on bowlers; batsmen, for their part, were suffering more injuries than in the past, not least because of the constant emphasis on high-speed intimidatory bowling. Altogether thirty-one players were needed for the series.

Another handicap for the selectors was players' availability for winter tours, which the TCCB decided should be a criterion for selection at home, eventually agreeing to pay retainers to keep them on ice. A current counter-attraction was another South African 'rebel' tour. A troupe of disaffected players, including Gatting, Emburey and Broad, had signed for this, a circumstance apparently known to Dexter and Stewart but not disclosed to Gower, who by this time had lost his Messianic appeal. As Botham put it,

> While Gower was displaying all the politeness and good manners Dexter had wanted him to show, Border [the Australian captain] had got on with the job of stuffing the Poms.

Botham perhaps overstates the case, presenting a crude model of captaincy, but whatever the rights or wrongs of it, the selectors, then and later, went on seeking gentlemanly leaders. (Technically the distinction between Gentlemen and Players had been ended in 1963 but it was still detectable in the committee rooms at Lord's and seemingly deeply enshrined in the unconscious of many cricketers themselves.) The barriers of educational and family background were not easily forgotten, especially by the older generation. Gower himself was a new man. A public-school boy from Kent, he forsook the established Cowdrey-dominated orthodoxies and secured a contract with the more frankly entrepreneurial Leicestershire, adopting a less class-distinctive accent to match, in keeping with the new fashions in voguish society, and with broadcasters and the acting profession, which increasingly dominated British life. Even Botham, a more naturally demotic hero-figure, was acutely aware of the social gap that lay behind Dexter's preferences and the somewhat different, 'lower-deck' outlook of the other selectors. Micky Stewart, in particular, disapproved of Gower's flippancy and was much more comfortable with the ultra-conscientious early-morning jogger, Gooch. Alec Bedser, the delightfully crusty ex-professional who had been unpaid chairman of selectors for seventeen years, was scornful about the entire new system:

> This Dexter-Stewart-Gooch thing is a lot of bullshit. Ted gets £20,000 a year for a job I did without pay. Micky gets £30,000 and a car and there's a whole bunch of players like David Gower who get a Test salary whether they're in the team or not.

The social dynamics of the selection process changed from time to time, but somehow the overall effect was the same. Thus Dexter's departure in 1993 coincided with that of Graham Gooch as captain, which left the way open for Michael Atherton, a young Cambridge graduate of whom much was expected. But Cambridge graduates were not the same as in Dexter's day: whatever his qualities – and he became England's longest-serving captain despite the team's indifferent playing record – they were not those of the old Varsity stereotype. Atherton suggested rather the pre-war Lancashire or Yorkshire professionals, and his chief gift, both as batsman and in his dealings with the selectors and the media, was a dogged determination to survive. A spin-off was a less-than-debonair outlook which communicated itself, through body language and occasional utterances, to his team – sometimes, it was widely believed, affecting their performance adversely. It was this that eventually led to his having to step down at last from the captaincy after a bad series against the West Indies in 1997–8. An incidental casualty was the doctrine of 'not cricket', to which young Atherton clearly did not subscribe.

'Not cricket', though ailing, was still part of the mythology of the game, but Michael Atherton pricked the bubble once and for all in an episode that shocked Ian Botham, the advocate of uncompromising captaincy, who called it 'a dirty business'. This was a punning reference to Atherton's initial departure from the straight and narrow, when, in July 1994, fielding in a Test match against South Africa, he was revealed by the television cameras pulling his hand from his pockets and rubbing the ball in a manner that strongly suggested contravention of Law 42.5 by using an artificial substance to alter the condition of the ball. Indeed, it later came out that he had been carrying dirt in his pockets for that express purpose. Regrettably, however, when called before the match referee, Atherton dissembled and the (Australian) match referee, apparently unable to contemplate the possibility that an England captain might depart from the truth, accepted his explanation. Luckily, too, for Atherton, Raymond Illingworth, Dexter's successor, was an authoritarian type who decided to take matters into his own hands. Confronting Atherton, he quickly ascertained the true facts, then fined him the maximum permitted, £1,000, for having dirt in his pockets and £1,000 for lying about it to the match referee. Illingworth calculated, correctly, that this would pre-empt any more serious action from the referee and ICC.

And so ended one of the sorriest episodes in all the high-minded annals of the noble game. In earlier times Atherton would have been discreetly ditched. Now he recouped his fines by writing a book, *A Test of Cricket*, in which he commented, 'I am not alone in thinking that the laws should be changed to allow certain actions which the players tacitly accept as part and parcel of the game.'

Clearly the finer points of etiquette and sportsmanship now had to give way before the supreme duty of satisfying the British public's burning desire for their national team to win. The public also had a somewhat conflicting desire, stemming from the same intense 'patriotism', for it to be a truly national team. The continuing dominance of overseas players in county cricket had led to a slightly more restrictive approach to registration in 1982, but there were two other trends which, whilst troubling 'Little Englanders', actually greatly strengthened the Test team. One was the entry to county cricket of the children of immigrants from Britain's former Empire. Middlesex's Roland Butcher, in 1980, was the first of these to be selected for England, and he was followed by a notable band, who added to the drama as well as the quality of English cricket at a trying time: Gladstone Small and Devon Malcolm, bowlers who on their day matched the great West Indian fast men of the period; all-rounders Chris Lewis and Philip de Freitas, both oddly enough from the same London comprehensive school. Slightly later came the stylish batsmen Nasser Hussain and Mark Ramprakash, both suburbanites and 'college boys' but blazing a trail for many other talented young British Asian cricketers of less affluent backgrounds looking for a way to make their mark in society. These new Englishmen were not always regarded in the same light as the more traditional sort. Dexter's own view of the situation appears to have been somewhat muddled: Ian Botham in a recent book recalled how the chairman of selectors sounded off in a radio programme: 'What chance do we have of building up a new pace attack when a county like Derbyshire open their bowling with an attack comprising a West Indian, a South African and a Dutchman?'

The Dutchman was in Dexter terms a near-miss, for he was in fact Ole Mortensen, a Dane, but Alan Warner, the 'West Indian', had actually been born in Birmingham and the 'South African' hailed from Maidstone in Kent. 'What chance have I got,' he spluttered, 'if the chairman of selectors thinks I am a Springbok?'

Some Springboks did, of course, make their way into the team. A second liberalising trend in registration began with the improved pay and conditions following the Packer intervention. The basic minimum for county players (fixed at £5,850 in 1982) was not a lot even then, but many earned double that and the rewards for Test players (£1,400 for home matches and £7,850 for tours plus £200 for every previous tour) were much better and increased rapidly over the next decade. The prospects were good enough to attract, especially, players from South Africa while it was still excluded from Test cricket. Two South Africans in particular did England notable service, first Allan Lamb, then Robin Smith, qualifying for English counties and providing much-needed stiffening against the latest crop of West Indian and Australian fast bowling. A third young man, Graeme Hick, a Zimbabwean, had such immense talent and performed so well in county cricket that the English public were on edge waiting for him to satisfy the seemingly endless qualification period for international cricket. Hick did not after all quite live up to expectations – no one could have – and so found out the brittleness of selectorial favour. In 1998, when recalled to the colours for yet another trial, he told a reporter that he was never quite at ease in the England dressing-room, partly because he felt that his place always hung by a thread.

This feeling was also experienced, even more strongly, by West-Indian-born Devon Malcolm: 'They don't pick me all summer and then suddenly it's win us a Test match, Devon,' he told the *Independent on Sunday* in 1995. 'People expect me to do it every time. If I don't I'm dropped. It does seem I'm singled out.' He certainly had experienced a dramatic change of status from the hero who had routed the South Africans on a fiery pitch at the Oval in 1994 – 'You guys are history!' he told them – to the humiliation of having the chairman of selectors and the bowling coach deem his bowling action defective in South Africa the next winter, and seek to remedy it in public by special net practice sessions. His particular grievance was against the combative Raymond Illingworth, but he might well have taken mild exception to his treatment by Illingworth's predecessor, the increasingly eccentric Ted Dexter, who had referred to him as 'Malcolm Devon' at a press conference.

In 1993 one of the most transient of England captains, Chris Cowdrey, son of the bridge-building Colin,[2] had urged that 'Lord's ban non-Englishmen playing for England ... kick out Robin Smith and Graeme Hick, and lock the door forever on Allan Lamb'. The feeling, shared by racially inspired cranks and 'Little England' politicians, was that, when it came to the pinch, men without the pure native blood coursing through their veins could not be relied on to give their all. This doctrine, long since discarded with regard to county cricket, could hardly be sustained on any rational or equitable employment principles. In any case, beggars can't be choosers. The embattled TCCB, desperate to restore some semblance of respectability to England's deteriorating Test record, welcomed all the talent they could persuade the ICC to accept as legitimate. As the supply of South Africans dried up, Andy Caddick from New Zealand and the Hollioake brothers, born in Melbourne, helped make up the deficiencies.

IV

It was not enough. By the summer of 1998 the sports pages were full of the fact that England had not won a major series for a dozen years. They had last won the Ashes in the winter of 1986–7, an age ago, when they had been led by the socially unacceptable Gatting, and helped by significant contributions from the ageing war-horse Ian Botham, the temperamental Chris Broad and the injury-prone Gladstone Small. In the intervening years they had won occasional Test matches, sometimes narrowly avoided defeat and usually doggedly stuck to their task, but they had also suffered a few spectacular defeats and it was these that had been remembered by the press, which gave the impression of a deplorable descent from a previous peak of perfection. This blissful state, for which no documentary evidence was produced, was nevertheless vividly, if patchily, remembered. The impression was that England, until dragged away to win the Second World War, had enjoyed a golden age, with only occasional setbacks against Australia, and none against lesser lights. These recollections were cold comfort in the face of the gloomy evidence of more recent years, during which the cricketing nations' performances had been systematically recorded on the computers of giant accountancy firms and assessed comparatively. According to these 'ratings', England stood only sixth in the pecking order, jostling for position with New Zealand and the newcomers Sri Lanka rather than with the acknowledged champions, Australia and the West Indies. There seemed every chance that South Africa, restored to the fold in 1991, would depress England's ratings further still. It was a mark of Britain's diminishing confidence in the rapidly changing world that the public should be so depressed about this, that it should matter so much. Not that the man in the street would have been quite so gloomy had he not been bombarded with headlines like 'ENGLAND COLLAPSE AGAIN' and elaborating text implying culpable slackness and negligence and suggesting that the natural order of things had been over-

turned. Newspapers, with their limited life-span, tend to have a correspondingly narrow perspective and not to burden their readers with balanced views
arising from cyclical theories of history or anything likely to lessen the drama
of the moment. And these regular mishaps touched upon a sore point.

British pride at introducing so many modern sports to the world was
diminished rather than increased by the rapid advances the newcomers had
made. Indeed, they felt not paternal pride but something more like senescent
resentment at youth's success. Certainly much more was read into defeat on
the cricket field than the mere loss of a game would seem to merit. When
England faced South Africa in the summer of 1998, the view of the gloomier
pundits was that the crunch point had been reached. At the start of the season
The Times headed its review of prospects 'ENGLAND DESPERATE FOR A
TRUE CHAMPION' and described the season stretching ahead as 'like some
Siberian tundra'. It spoke of the feeling, hard to dispel, that 'in the new order
[i.e. the 'cool Britannia' of the new Labour government]' cricket was seen as a
mere hangover from the past. By July, one match down, newspapers were
writing of the forthcoming Old Trafford game as the 'Test they dare not
lose'. They certainly dare not if they wished to escape the lash. The peril of
the situation (we were told) was increased because the first half of the season
was being conducted in the shadow of the soccer World Cup. The encroachment of soccer on the short summer cricket season always provoked some
pardonable irritation and, increasingly, envy, but this time it went far beyond
that. *The Times* went so far as to say that 'cricket was struggling to hold its
place in the nation's sporting psyche'.

It was certainly remarkable how differently cricket and soccer were treated
by the press. The soccer team performed indifferently, to put it kindly, but
were extended every indulgence: the media in their endless coverage and
post-match analyses gave the impression that England had only narrowly
failed to win the whole competition. By contrast, the chief interest in the
cricket seemed to be how badly England might do. The cricketers' every
move was scrutinised for signs of weakness or potential error. Why this
should be so is hard to fathom, but presumably it had something to do with
confusing slick public relations with good performance.

But there was also undeniably something in the air, as the end of the
century drew near, that favoured the soccer style of life. It was a vogue that
touched all classes. The previous Prime Minister, John Major, had been a
keen cricketer and had achieved mild publicity thereby, but when he lost the
election a marked change came upon the land. When Mr Blair's children met
the young royal princes it was reported that they played soccer together; soon
cricket, to the fashion-watchers, began to seem like yesterday's game. At the
same time, in professional soccer a new and even flashier breed of manager
and player caught the headlines and produced the requisite soundbites.
Hence, while Glenn Hoddle and his men were portrayed as gallant losers,

England's cricketers were given short shrift. *The Times*, after England had lost one match, wrote disdainfully of 'the manner of England's surrender at Lord's' and described the next match melodramatically as the 'Test they dare not lose'. In fact England went on to win the series, though not without mishaps along the way. At Old Trafford the ground was but half full and the mood despondent. After a promising start England lost 6 wickets for 11 runs and were booed off the field for the second evening in succession. Next day South Africa made a big score and England seemed to be in for a heavy defeat. A big stand between Atherton and Stewart improbably saved the game, however, and thereafter, as the South African captain put it, the pendulum swung.

One symptom was that umpiring decisions, which before had seemed to the partisans to favour South Africa, now seemed to go the other way. Umpires had long ceased to be appointed by the participating countries, so there was no chance of another Shakoor Rana-like episode. Umpires were now drawn from an international panel selected by the ICC, and well enough paid for this to be a full-time year-round career. There were also now third umpires, armed with television cameras, to adjudicate on close run-out or stumping decisions, but the debates about doubtful lbw and close catch decisions, which were shown from all angles and in slow motion on television, continued as vociferously as ever. When the pendulum swung, one of the indicators was that bad umpiring decisions now seemed to go in England's favour. The South African captain, Cronje, accepted this as one of those things – 'win some, lose some'. His English counterparts had not been so philosophical when they were up against it. Ramprakash was disciplined for dissent at Lord's, and many thought Stewart ought to have been.

With the pendulum, the press now swung to the other extreme and the national drums began to beat, ever more insistently, as England had the better of a hard-fought game at Headingley. They had won a series at last. *The Times* was fulsome in its praise: in a special article their former correspondent (also the former editor of *Wisden*) John Woodcock summed up the situation: 'Experiences such as yesterday of the England side are wonderfully beneficial. If I were to pick out two such from all the Test matches I have seen one would be the Sydney Test of 1954–55 and another would be the Headingley Test of 1981. I left them both feeling quite *transformed* [my italics] and each time England went on to great things.' True, that Australia had then been the opponents, 'but in the present circumstances beating South Africa means no less.'

This debatable point need not be challenged, for within a week *The Times* (this time *sans* Woodcock) had changed tack again, with a headline which read 'ENGLAND SENT SPINNING TO HUMILIATION'. She had in fact lost to Sri Lanka in a one-off Test match. This was admittedly not very good, but it scarcely deserved the sackcloth and ashes treatment. What was considerably underplayed was what a thoroughly enjoyable game this extra match had been. Sri Lanka had been denied a Test series on the grounds that they would not attract the crowds, but this was shown to be nonsense – the Oval was full on all five days. The spectators basked in hazy sunshine and saw a basketful of runs and some very fine spin-bowling. The Sri Lankans endeared themselves to everyone – except, perhaps, the England fielders – by their stylish batting – orthodox but rapid – and then moved around coolly and purposefully in support of their cunning bowlers, plotting England's destruction. In particular they had no tearaway fast men firing missiles at the batsmen, and this completed the picture of a charming rather than a wildly exciting experience, capturing some of the elements of the game that tend to be missing from the typically modern blasting match. In particular the element of display that captivated players and spectators in the past was briefly restored – more of those moments, when, after a cover drive, the spectators, before applauding the power of the stroke and its addition to the score, catch their breath and cry, 'Aa-ah!' This, it may not be too much to claim, is the very essence of cricket. At any rate the game is reduced by its absence, and we should be grateful to the Sri Lankans for showing us what we so often miss in the whizz-bang world we have created. There is an irony in this, for, as noted earlier, Kipling, almost exactly a hundred years ago, had explained the gulf between east and west in terms of English madness and magic:

> How is this reason (which is their reason) to judge a scholar's worth
> By casting a ball at three straight sticks and defending the same with a fourth?

It is not that the English have lost their magic in the meantime – simply that they have taught it to pupils so apt as to put their old masters in the shade. And unfortunately the masters, missing an old educational trick, have learned too little in return. There was a refreshing sense that the Sri Lankans really enjoyed their cricket. And the most gratifying thing was that this communicated itself to the spectators, who loved them for it even when they were putting it across the England bowlers. And it can hardly have been a coincidence that this was the one Test match of the summer that was not marked by poor crowd behaviour, but was governed by factors quite outside the usual decisive one of winning or losing that had been prominent in the earlier games.

V

Misplaced patriotism was not the only reason for poor behaviour, of course. Indeed, some of the reasons were only marginally to do with cricket, which simply provided an audience for attention-seekers. The most curious of these, the solitary streakers, who removed their clothes and ran across the field, seem to have been motivated by sheer exhibitionism, rather than any social or political cause. Lord's was subjected to its first (male) streaker in 1975. This seemed a symbolic act of wanton vandalism, if not sacrilege: several members were treated for shock. It was widely thought that the floodgates were opening and that the worst excesses of Sodom and Gomorrah were nigh. But streaking had grown no worse by 1998, and there were hopes that the fashion had worn itself out, basically through being ignored, particularly by the television cameras, with whose aid these exhibitionists had hoped to expose themselves to the world at large. A more abiding problem was the tendency of young males to band together and lace themselves with drink, which Englishmen of all ages seem to need to help them shed their natural inhibitions in public. And some of them, so far from casting off clothing, adopted various forms of fancy dress: thus troupes of Disney characters, penguins, nuns, 'Mr Blobbies' or assorted fruit and vegetables descended on the stands, infiltrated the crowds and engaged in high-spirited and often boorish behaviour.

In 1998 the Lancashire authorities, convinced that drink was the root of the problem, ordained that for the Old Trafford Test no drink should be brought into the ground (except by county members, who were deemed to be trustworthy). Richard Hutton, editor of the *Cricketer*, had commented on events at the first Test at Edgbaston, where drunks and chanters of foul-mouthed nonsense had done their utmost to spoil the game for the 'silent majority'. Hutton was incensed at the appalling and intrusive behaviour of the crowd in the 'popular' sectors of the ground. He also complained that 'some of the most expensive seating areas are now within earshot of the disgusting language that passes for ordinary conversation'. Yet he also complained about the authorities' attempts to remedy matters:

> The place was swarming with security guards, almost all with hair shaven down to their brains, ostensibly to contain this social evil. It is intolerable that perfectly law-abiding and respectable citizens should be subjected to Gestapo-like searches before they can take their seats.

His 'solution' went totally against the tide of democratic opinion. The authorities, he reckoned, 'should double or even treble the price of tickets in the over-populated areas, to equate with the social costs that their inhabitants impose. In that way the hooligans can be seen to be subsidising those whose days at cricket they are determined to ruin.' This suggests something less like a bunch of irreverent drunks and more like terrorists determined to wage a class war. In fact it is doubtful whether the class element was as pronounced as Hutton implies.

For one thing, the 'popular' side seats were by no means cheap, at £20 or more. In any event 'men behaving badly' was a fashion prevalent in all sectors of society. The alcohol that fuelled their rowdiness was surprisingly often champagne rather than beer. Economic sanctions were thus not likely to single out the trouble-makers. Life was like that in the 1990s. So perhaps the Edgbaston security guards, whatever their haircuts, were a better way of going about it. The searching was presumably for contraband liquor. (God knows what the *Cricketer* would have had to say if the Lancashire members had been subjected to the indignity of searches.) But concern for the liberty of all free-born Englishmen reached the ultimate in absurdity when the Headingley authorities, having decided that obtrusive and outlandish costumes were a disruptive influence, decided to deny entry to those wearing them. The media at once began to treat this as a denial of basic human rights; the BBC put out a radio programme in which a Mr Cheeseman, a lecturer in sociology, argued eloquently for his right to attend cricket matches, peaceably and quietly, dressed as a giant carrot.

Another more serious problem was noted by Richard Hutton: 'It is unhelpful that the England side should give interpretation to the prevailing din as "getting behind the team".' Quite. These rowdy and offensive 'loyalists' were a special case, whose best-known practitioners proudly called themselves the 'Barmy Army'. Matthew Engel, the editor of *Wisden*, laid into these people in a long article in *Wisden Cricket Monthly* in April 1998. What he called their 'mindless chanting ... and endless mantras [could] only detract from everyone else's enjoyment'. They had reached their low point in the third Test in the West Indies in 1998 with an adaptation of a local 'pop' song: 'Who let the dogs out? (Woof, woof, woof, woof, woof).'

The Barmy Army were at their worst on overseas grounds, where (in the West Indies, for instance) English supporters may nowadays far outnumber the home crowds. These types, who are obviously sufficiently well-heeled to be able to afford Caribbean holidays, can be very hard to bear at home, too, especially when the 'patriotism' gets out of hand.

Not so long ago 'Disgusted of Tunbridge Wells' looked askance at the players' coloured clothing that was replacing the traditional pristine white. Now he is in danger of finding himself seated next to a young person with a face painted red, white and blue or the equally vivid colours of the opposition. Perhaps the ground authorities of the future will have to issue their gate-keepers and security guards with paint-stripper, or whatever is the approved humane method of removing the stuff from human skin, and if they do, 'Disgusted' and the more solemn elements of the media can enjoy a great debate about this further invasion of privacy. Alternatively, perhaps we could learn to sit back and enjoy the colours and the various sights and sounds of the modern game.

This, of course, is the sort of question about which MCC or its heirs and assigns traditionally set up committees of enquiry and reach no very clear conclusion. And, conversely, it does not seem to be a question that would trouble the guardians of any other national sport in any other country. The French, for example, seemed positively to relish the carnival atmosphere created by the various gaudily bedecked national groups that came to their soccer World Cup and, almost without exception, winners and losers coexisted happily.

France '98, indeed, most unusually in international sporting events, seemed to add to the gaiety and goodwill of nations. Failing the stiff upper lip, it may be that the answer for English cricket lovers is simply to get off our high horses and enjoy the fun.

CHAPTER TWENTY-TWO

At the Crossroads

THE REVOLUTIONARY NOTION OF 'Middle England' enjoying itself at a cricket match is admittedly an alarming one. Those who feel outraged by the suggestion that cricket is supposed to be entertaining, preferring to regard it rather as something that is good for you, like fasting and prayer, have an easy remedy – avoid Test matches and one-day games and attend only three- or four-day county matches. Here the fastidious may enjoy, in sepulchral calm, the venerable rituals hallowed by time and still held in reverence by traditionalist critics, but actually witnessed by only a tiny handful, mostly members seeking to get their money's worth out of their subscription, and all of them apparently with time hanging heavy on their hands, drop-outs from the helter-skelter existence endured by most people since the Industrial Revolution. That is the stark fact that has to be faced by the marketing men who nowadays control the destinies of first-class cricket. To the untutored mind the task seems formidable – how to interest people, even those who actually like cricket, in spending a day watching a detached fragment of a game? None of the favourite remedies of the past, like 'brighter cricket' or winning matches (which even in their day had had only limited and temporary effect) seem much use. Consider Warwickshire, for example, who were the leading team of the early and middle 1990s – as dominant as Yorkshire had been before the war. Apart from frequently winning the championship, furthermore, they played entertaining cricket, assisted by outstanding overseas players such as Alan Donald, the great South African fast bowler, and Brian Lara, the record-breaking West Indian batsman. They had 7,500 members and lavish new hospitality boxes, but the rest of the vast Edgbaston ground looked pretty desolate during county matches. The committee in desperation at last decided to throw open the grounds to the public free for certain championship matches in order to improve the atmosphere somewhat and give the players a few more supporters to cheer them on – and cheer them up. The experiment was not a great success, and things reached rock bottom one hot Saturday afternoon in August. Very few took advantage of the offer of free seats: the handful who did formed a small oasis in the vast desert of empty seating on the 'popular' side. They did little to improve the atmosphere, evoking protests from the members for their occasional uninformed, usually ribald comments, and finally causing great offence by playing portable radios, not to follow the cricket but to catch the football results.

The cause of county cricket had not been assisted by the introduction of four-day games. The idea was to give young players the chance to develop free from the pressures of the clock. But of course by no means all county players are young, eager strivers after perfection. Parkinson's Law came into operation, and many games drifted along aimlessly. As Boycott put it:

> Extra time actually allows the poorer batsmen to graft out bigger scores, while the fielding side, rarely needing to take wickets in a hurry, sits back and waits for its turn at the crease.

The number of freakish declarations did not diminish. The mixture of three- and four-day games added further to the confusion of followers of the sport – and of those who compiled the fixture lists. As Robin Marlar, erstwhile chairman of Sussex, complained in 1998,

> Four-day games end in three days, there was hardly any cricket on a sunny holiday Saturday, there's no continuity ... The rhythm of our summer game grows faint.

Marlar, who was not only a vigorous county chairman but also one of the best-known cricket writers, was laying about him in the *Sunday Times* in August 1998. His theme was the poor performance of the England and Wales Cricket Board, the latest device to revitalise the game.

From 1 January 1997, the ECB had replaced both the Cricket Council and the Test and County Cricket Board, thus providing a single body responsible for the whole game, recreational and first class. This all-purpose outfit was led by a captain of industry, Lord MacLaurin, formerly the chairman of the Tesco supermarket chain, which he had successfully modernised. As he ruefully admitted, however, his new job was far more complex than anything he had previously attempted. Thus although some counties, notably Lancashire, were enthusiastic about MacLaurin's reforming ideas, not everyone agreed with them. Robin Marlar's piece was amongst the more trenchant criticisms. Stung by MacLaurin's apparent denigration of the counties, Marlar reminded this 'retailer of great distinction' what had happened when Gerald Ratner, the chain-store jeweller, had jocularly referred to his own products as 'crap'. The business had disappeared.

Marlar also questioned the ECB's basic competence, complaining of 'bureaucracy... holding back further development in English cricket.' The ECB had, Marlar grumbled, 'a welter of working parties' and 'a committee in every corner'; as an illustration of its incompetence he cited the muddle over players' contracts. There had been a debate for some years over whether an élite England squad should be contracted to the central authority rather than to the counties, to avoid conflict over how much cricket key internationals should be playing. There were arguments for both sides, and, this apart, it was clearly a complex matter involving the whole long-established and delicate relationship between the counties and the centre: Lord MacLaurin and his board had decided to give it high priority. Then, according to Marlar, the ECB fell foul of its own absurd structures. Two of its committees had embarked separately on the task, neither knowing what the other was up to; and this only came to light, months later, when one of them proposed that players be contracted to the board for the World Cup in 1999. All this, commented Marlar, was symptomatic of a badly run organisation with an absurd structure:

> Tim Lamb is called chief executive, but rightly points out that he is only really head bureaucrat, unable to act without reference to this chairman or that. So cock-ups like this one are inevitable.

Already, Marlar wrote, one key member had been upset by the muddle and had offered his resignation.

Meanwhile, at centre stage Lord MacLaurin had produced, like a magician pulling rabbits from a hat, a set of proposals for reshaping the game from top to bottom. 'Raising the Standard' offered a co-ordinated system putting school and club cricket at the foot of a ladder leading up from divisional competition to the top through a new County Board tournament, modelled on Australian grade cricket, and replacing the Second XI championship by a mixture of first-class counties, Minor Counties and selected 'premier league' clubs playing two-day single-innings matches.

To dwell further on the details of the proposals and the reaction to them would be to stray from the social history of cricket to the minutiae of its current politics and bureaucracy. It seems worth commenting , however, that at long last changes did seem likely to occur. There was, in the country, a general acceptance of the need for change, in order to try to improve the performance of the national team. MacLaurin had sensed this mood and laid plans to match, including financial incentives where appropriate, as for instance in the tricky business of persuading northern league clubs to give up their well-established traditions and compete for a place in the new order. And though not everyone agreed with the notion of introducing a new soft-ball 'development game' in the secondary schools, everyone could see that something needed doing; this was certainly much better than nothing. It was not likely to produce the new Bothams or Comptons the nation dreamed of, but no one imagined that talented youngsters would be content with such limited provision anyway, and the new premier league clubs would be there to offer a path to the top.

Where Lord MacLaurin's blueprint for success seemed less convincing, however, was in its attempts to make the county championship a better preparation for Test cricket. MacLaurin did not pursue the idea of creating some new form of regional tier above the counties. This was fair enough, but it meant that there was little to stretch really talented players at the 'run of the mill' general level of county cricket. There was a fairly widespread view (outside county dressing-rooms) that the 400 or so county players spent a lot of their time in not very challenging pursuits. Harsher critics tied this in with the new levels of pay, pension schemes and so on – county cricket had become too cosy to produce champions, they reckoned. Failing a higher tier, hopes were pinned on making the championship itself internally competitive. There had been clamour for some years for a two-division championship with promotion and relegation: some seemed to think this limited measure would be enough in itself to transform the whole system of cricket. Conversely, some counties saw it as the death knell of all they held dear.

Lord MacLaurin was so nervous of propounding this controversial notion that he offered instead a 'three conference' scheme said to be based on American baseball, which, apart from this grave handicap, was so complicated that it completely baffled everybody, and was laughed out of court. In fact Lord MacLaurin need not have resorted to diversionary tactics. The notion of a two-division championship had caught on with the general public and with much of the press and was not to be obscured by smoke screens. When the 'three-conference' plan was rejected by the First-Class Forum of the ECB in September 1997, it was agreed to continue the discussions. Gradually, support for the two-division championship grew until fifteen months later the forum approved the idea with only Glamorgan dissenting. This, together with the proposed new forty-five-over National League replacing the old Sunday League, and an enhanced knock-out tournament, seemed to offer county cricket a more competitive future, better suited to the public taste.

Not all the public, however. There have always been people who detest change and think one of the advantages of cricket is its adherence to the values of the past. In July 1995, before Lord MacLaurin had begun his work, *Wisden Cricket Monthly* published a long interview with the sub-heading, 'NOVELIST SIMON RAVEN SPEAKS FOR THOSE WHO OPPOSE CHANGES TO THE GAME'. The article began by rehearsing Raven's qualifications to act as spokesman for these reactionaries. It made complimentary remarks about Raven's 'deep knowledge' and his 'dislike of all forms of humbug': he could, we were told, be 'startlingly and joyously politically incorrect'. The main burden of the piece was Raven's implacable hostility to all forms of change in first-class cricket. His pleasures were, of course, 'far removed from the considerations of the "football yobs" at one-day matches'. He liked the 'peace and decency of the longer game': 'It takes up much time, which the modern world would like to turn into money ... I like the fact that it is not modern.' In fact Raven's dislike of the modern game was basically a dislike of its social characteristics. He obviously preferred the neo-feudalism of the days before the abolition of the distinction between Gentlemen and Players. He complained of the 'indifference' of modern cricketers: 'They're doing it for the money. Everyone's got big-headed.' It emerged that his idea of the proper order of things stemmed from memories of his old school, Charterhouse, where the professional, the distinguished international George Geary, was not above whitening someone's pads. Raven also blamed poor leadership for the slack, dour and unsmiling demeanour of the modern players: 'There's too much of the Corporals' Mess in the leadership.' He cited Gooch, Fletcher and the Stewart family.

But however appealing the call of the 'good old days', there is no chance of their returning. For one thing, the Gentleman is gone for ever and amateur, meaning 'unprofessional', is a term of abuse. The Professional Cricketers' Association, indeed, increasingly control the game, with their chairman David Graveney also installed as chairman of selectors. (Those who claim that cricket is incapable of social change should consider the reversal of fortunes of the once-humble players and their erstwhile principal employers, the once-mighty MCC, whose Gentlemen members were the arbiters of taste and fashion and whose honour code was the reality behind the written laws.)

In fact a more compelling argument than Simon Raven's is the conventional received wisdom that the full two-innings game is the one the players prefer, and the old-style championship is 'the one they really want to win'. This may well still be so, but whether the desire extends beyond a preference for being in full-time employment is hard to say. Certainly not many players display outward and visible signs of enjoyment as they go about their daily task. And Lord MacLaurin himself has declared,

> The players are the ones who know how soul-destroying it is to play professional cricket in front of three men and a thermos. Cricket is nothing if no one wants to watch it.

Nevertheless, the players, in the nature of things, have not been in a headlong dash to change the system that sustained them. And according to Ian Botham, many timorous and self-regarding county committees have seen nothing wrong with the game at all. 'For too long,' he bluntly asserts, 'the county clubs have existed on a diet of complacency and romanticism.'

Whatever the cause, the counties certainly showed little sign, before

MacLaurin, of wanting to raise their own standards by any artificial or extraneous devices to induce greater competition. On the contrary, they greeted the 1990s by increasing the number of first-class clubs, welcoming Durham into the magic circle. Durham had given decades of distinguished service to the Minor Counties, and then, uniquely, in the 1970s and 1980s had twice beaten first-class opposition in the new one-day competitions. Sadly, since 1991, they have caused few ripples on the surface of the bigger pond, despite importing a series of veterans from other counties, including Ian Botham and then, more successfully, the Australian David Boon. Lack of playing success has not, however, in the modern world, proved as financially disastrous as it once might have done. This is partly because of the coming of the lottery, which has helped many counties to go in for impressive development schemes without having to save up for them first. It is also partly due to the improved system of raising and distributing profits from the visits of touring teams. And, fundamentally, it is because the balance has swung, in county finances, away from dependence on income from spectators to that from marketing and commercial activity and sponsorship of various kinds. The most powerful influence by far is that of television, which cares little for the county championship. But first the TCCB and lately the ECB have been able to conclude package deals that have not so far interfered with the freedom of the counties to operate in what they see as the best interests of the game. The counties, as a result, though in no danger of becoming immobilised by too much money, are still very much alive, not least as the employers of the 400 or so full-time first-class players, a feature unique to the English system and one that will not be given up lightly.

Certainly, as Warwickshire spectacularly showed, it is possible to make a success of running a county club without attracting cash customers to the four-day game. And this applies, to some extent at least, to the system as a whole. It appears to make surprisingly little difference to the clubs' prosperity, not only how many matches they win, whether four-day or one, but how many spectators they attract.

A study by Richard Hutton (*Cricketer*, June 1998) of the financial performance of the counties in 1997 showed some surprising features. Overall only 3 per cent of their income came from gate-money and only 11 per cent from membership subscriptions. The clubs with the highest levels of overall income, Lancashire, Warwickshire and Surrey, were also the clubs which brought in most commercial and sponsorship income, and most income from members. But the best performance in terms of gate-money came from clubs which attracted less overall income – Kent, Essex, and Somerset – whereas Yorkshire, whilst surprisingly low in overall income, got much the highest relative percentage of it (21 per cent) from members. In sum, the most significant factor in the fortunes of the counties was their ability to attract commercial income, which overall constituted 46 per cent of the counties' total. This does not appear, furthermore, to be necessarily related to championship success.

Glamorgan, the 1997 champions, did well financially, moving into the top five clubs, but Leicestershire, the winners in 1996 and 1998, and also pretty good at the one-day game, languished near the bottom of the list in terms of spectator support, both in gate-money and in membership. There are no very clear or very comforting conclusions for the county championship in its present form. Winning the championship itself may boost gate receipts but this appears to be only a temporary phenomenon. As Richard Hutton put it, 'One good season . . . is usually followed by one of consolidation, at best.' Also there may be non-cricketing factors, such as Glamorgan's growing nationalistic appeal. But either way the direct effect will be small compared with the impact of commercial sponsorship, which seems to depend more on star quality and star individuals than on team success. Hence the continued prosperity of Warwickshire, Lancashire and Surrey. And there was confirmation of what the moneymen are seeking from cricket in October 1998. A television deal concluded by the ECB was for over £100 million, and the contract had gone, not to the BBC, but to Channel Four and Sky Sports, with the specific intention of altering cricket's 'stuffy image'. It is anyone's guess what this may entail, but it seems unlikely to include a lot of four-day county matches.

As we have seen, the cricket authorities over the years have tried to attract the social and economic élite to their games, but the time for this, if there ever was one, has long gone. It is not within the spirit of the age; nor would it make economic sense to try to turn the clock back. In a recent public opinion poll a large proportion of respondents from all income groups said they regarded themselves as working-class. This is not to say that cricket should not be presented as an élite game. As suggested in the introduction, cricket – by contrast with soccer, whose appeal is in its simplicity – is one of the most sophisticated of ball-games, a ritualised conflict in which each side in turn is required to attack and to defend. It requires strategy and tactics. It is a team activity, yet every member has his moment, and leadership is crucial. Not least, its techniques must change: as defence learns to cope with attack, so it offers almost infinite variety. It may well not have mass appeal.

The peculiar economics and structures of first-class cricket, however, have ensured that, so far at least, declining interest in traditional county cricket has not led to any decline in county cricketers' pay. On the contrary: following a deal that brought in satellite as well as terrestrial television in 1995, cricket became richer by £60 million over four seasons – loose change compared with the money pouring into soccer but a dramatic increase even so. By 1998 the average annual pay for county cricketers was over £30,000 a year: one player, Chris Adams, hitherto uncapped by England, had been given a three-year contract worth £200,000 to transfer to Sussex as captain.

In such a climate it is unrealistic to expect the beneficiaries to see the need for radical change, and therefore much will depend on the far-sightedness or otherwise of the leadership of the Professional Cricketers' Association. It is this that will largely determine whether the root-and-branch reforms propounded by the ECB – or whoever next comes up with a blueprint for change – get beyond the committee rooms. It was inevitable, by the same token, that in the reaction to 'Raising the Standard' most attention should be focused on the first-class game.

It is to be hoped, however, that, amid all the excitements of reorganising the first-class game, the ECB do not lose sight of the need to give high priority to attracting youngsters into cricket – whether by launching the new 'development game' or by addressing the long-neglected problems in school and local clubs, providing decent playing surfaces and team equipment, or preferably both. In a country awash with lottery money it should not be too difficult. And, difficult or not, it is absolutely vital to the health of the game. Cricket was originally a schoolboy game, and it is still mainly learned at school, whether as part of the formal curriculum or otherwise. It is not the sort of game that is easily learned in adult life. Nor are adult spectators likely to take to it if they have to learn from scratch a whole set of elaborate rules and conventions, and to appreciate sophisticated batting and bowling techniques.

And finally, it may be worth suggesting that at long last the cricket authorities ought to give due attention to the neglected half of the population. This would not only make commercial sense, but would be a valuable civilising influence, quite apart from questions of social justice – or what is sometimes sneeringly referred to as 'political correctness'. It is not intended, at this last gasp, to launch into a discussion of the women's game (women's cricket has already made a niche for itself as a summer equivalent of women's hockey, whose development it has followed, at a respectful distance, and it is already well chronicled). The time now seems ripe to bring many more women into the men's game. This is not a plea for the recruitment of greater numbers of tea-ladies, or other worthy but patronised female auxiliaries. Nor, at the other extreme, is it a belated part of the campaign to have female members of the MCC – which happily has now been successful. However desirable that may be thought from the point of view of MCC's image, it is of little real significance to the future of the game. Nearer the heart of the matter is the tale of Ms Fiona Foster, aged twenty-four, who has shown what women are capable of. She learned the game at Charterhouse, no less, and played for girls' teams there and at university, and for Surrey Women, before graduating to Blackheath, a men's village team. 'I actually prefer playing for men's sides,' she told *Wisden Cricket Monthly*, 'because I find the men's game more challenging.' She makes light of facing men's bowling. Occasionally a fast bowler will say 'sorry' when he gets her out. She replies: 'It was a great ball.' She hopes to captain the Second XI next year, and says: 'It should be fun.'

This is the spirit that is so often lacking in modern cricket, and if women can help to rekindle it, so much the better, for it represents a distinctive – and healthy – attitude to competition. As the obituary writers affectionately recalled, following his death in 1997, this was Denis Compton's approach. It had all been 'great fun', even facing Lindwall and Miller on a fiery pitch. Compton's abiding memory of all the innings he played in the record-breaking year of 1947 – 'probably the most memorable of all, I think' – 'was for Middlesex against Kent at Lord's, a run-chase, 300-odd at over 100 an hour. We just failed, but it was such glorious fun going for them.' How much better for cricket – and everyone in it – if that could be the spirit in which future England teams approached the game.

EPILOGUE

In Search of Village Cricket

W E SHOULD, IF ONLY FOR COMPLETENESS, take a brief look at the present state of village cricket. For sad but fairly obvious reasons most writing on the subject is fictional. Humorists have made much of the social comedy arising from the juxtaposition of the classes that supposedly occurs: for example, P. G. Wodehouse's young 'man about town', Psmith, declines to play in a village match because on a previous occasion it had been a severe shock to his system 'to be caught at point by a man wearing braces'. This kind of thing works better if it is set in a more class-conscious age: hence 'literary' cricket, and particularly village cricket, is stuck in a time-warp.

Thus assisted by the soothing balm of nostalgia, spiced with humour, the image of village cricket is likely to be a picture-postcard or chocolate-box scene of rural tranquillity with oaks and poplars shading a sun-lit green, thatched cottages and an old church in the background, with perhaps an inn or its sign-board somewhere in the picture, inviting the viewer to travel back in time to a pre-industrial heaven that, if it existed at all, has long since disappeared under the busy roads, semi-detached houses and television aerials of commuter-land, supermarket society. In consequence, as Ronald Mason neatly puts it in his contribution to *Barclay's World of Cricket*,

> Over the origins and context of village cricket the chronicler must hover warily, for its image exists as much in the common imagination as in actuality.

Elsewhere John Arlott gently but firmly complains about the false impression given by the writers on village cricket in the inter-war years, when 'it was thought clever to make jokes about it'. In particular he cites A. G. MacDonnell's acclaimed account in his novel *England Their England*, which most people misremember for its account of 'a comic village cricket match'. In fact, the comedy is provided by a visiting team of literary and arty folk from London – based on an actual team run by J. C. Squire and including such notables as Alec Waugh and the idiosyncratic 'Beachcomber' (J. B. Morton). The older villagers, called gaffers, are respectful onlookers over the tops of their pint pots; those villagers who are playing are thought amusing largely because of their occupations – blacksmith, sexton, rate-collector and so on – which are supposed to determine the kind of cricket expected of them. Drink plays a full part in the frolics, but mainly that of the 'toffs'.

It is no accident that most of the best writing about village cricket comes from earlier times. Perhaps the best is 'The Flower Show Match', a chapter in Siegfried Sassoon's *Memoirs of A Fox-Hunting Man*, which was discussed in Chapter Thirteen. It evokes brilliantly, and with self-directed irony, the time before the First World War, as a designed contrast to the grim reality that followed. Hugh de Selincourt, author of the most renowned example of this genre, *The Cricket Match* (1924), gets away with things like 'quoth Bill' and 'What I needs make that assish scoop for', but succeeds in showing cricket as an integral part of the life of a Sussex village, which we may think deserves to exist, even if it is 'only' fiction. After all, Jane Austen does not reflect the realities of Regency England or the Napoleonic Wars – 'Let other pens dwell on guilt and misery' – but we find other truths – and great delight – in her novels.

We have noted in earlier chapters how the remorseless inroads of urbanisation, and the impact of technology and industrialisation, have transformed the countryside and its villages to the point of near extinction, and how the Arcadian dreams of the new townsfolk, obliged to earn their living there, have replaced the real rurality they left behind with a new sylvan landscape of the imagination – particularly amongst the middle classes, who have benefited most from the industrial and urban revolution. This yearning for imagined days when England was an agricultural community is tied in, too, with new anxieties about the English identity, an age-old concern but intensified by the dissolution of Empire, the advent of the European Union, the latest and worst Irish 'Troubles', and the present government's 'regionalisation' policies – to name but a few.

Two recent studies, *The English Tribe* by Stephen Haseler and *The English* by Jeremy Paxman, have contrasted the serene, secure and superior sense of identity formerly enjoyed by the English with the uncertainties of the more complicated present. 'When, occasionally,' writes Paxman, 'we come across someone whose stiff upper lip, sensible shoes, or tweedy manner identifies them as English, we react in amusement.' Amongst cricket-lovers, he might have added, the amused reaction is more likely to be tinged with affection than amongst non-addicts. At any rate, in both his and Haseler's studies, love of cricket is identified as an important ingredient of Englishness. For Paxman, indeed, it exemplifies the crazy English belief, expressed most lyrically in Newbolt's 'breathtakingly stupid' poem 'Vitaï Lampada', that 'all life's problems could be solved by playing a straight bat'. Stephen Haseler, on

A Social History of English Cricket

the other hand, sees cricket as part of 'theme-park Englishness', which is a product to be marketed as part of the leisure and tourist industry, a valuable export, part of the broader 'heritage industry'. He admits, however, that 'this kind of rhapsodising is not really about the game of cricket.' But cricket is the emblem of that bygone rurality that now exists only in dim old photographs and dusty record books – and in the nostalgia-laden pipe-dreams of the antiquated.

'Village cricket is not what it was,' wrote John Arlott in 1977, 'but nothing is.' He was writing in the *Haig Village Cricket Annual*, itself an indication of profound change, for it was characteristic of our 'Barnum and Bailey world' and its 'paper moon' that village cricket was being tracked down in its remote fastnesses and brought up to the metropolis, indeed to Lord's itself, thanks to the sponsorship of the famous whisky firm. It was the 'dream', so we are told in the august *Barclay's World of Cricket*, of Aidan Crawley, television eminence of the recent past, to see village cricket played at Lord's, an idea taken up as a personal project by Ben Brocklehurst, proprietor of the *Cricketer*, and his wife.

The *Cricketer* undertook the considerable task of administration and communication. They were surprised – agreeably – by the response to their first invitation to compete in 1972. There is some doubt about the numbers involved. The *Barclay's* account puts the number at 'almost 800' and states that it has 'remained at about that level ever since'. On the other hand the *Cricketer* itself, inviting entries for 1999 in the previous July, proudly boasted that 'the competition goes from strength to strength', citing a 'record entry of 657 villages'. Either way it is a remarkable achievement – and the mere numbers are not the whole story, by any means. The competition and its villages cannot be dismissed as figments of cynical admen's imagining, aspects of 'theme-park' Englishness.

The first competition, in 1972, was won by Troon in Cornwall. But Troon is no tourist trap, no part of picture-postcard Cornwall. It is saved by only a thin strip of open ground – but also by a long and important tradition of independence – from being a suburb of Camborne. Camborne, with its twin town, Redruth, was once, long ago, an important mining centre. Around it, in the 1850s, nearly 350 mines employing 50,000 underground workers produced some two-thirds of the world's copper. Most of the mines had closed by early in the twentieth century, when cheaper-to-mine deposits of copper and tin were found overseas. Cornish workers and their families emigrated to America, Australia and South Africa. One such was Jack Angove's father, who went to America. Jack, now seventy-eight, was born in Idaho, USA, but returned to Troon as a child. He first played for the club in 1938 and has served it since then in various capacities, including a long stint as honorary secretary, and has proudly seen his own son follow him as a player in this remarkable club.

Until the 1970s Troon's renown was local. But it was real enough. They played no village-green antics – indeed Troon had no village green – but had been used to the disciplines of league cricket, which had existed in Cornwall since 1905. Its requirements included neutral umpires, one of whose tasks was inspection of pitches. Troon had few problems in this respect, for they had been bequeathed by some benevolent squire, in the distant past, a share in a vast communal playing field, from which they hedged off a splendid cricket ground, which was carefully tended, and eventually, after much legal wrangling, bought by the club. Nevertheless, Troon, as a mere village, was regarded askance by the neighbouring town clubs, who not unnaturally took exception to being beaten, as they quite often were, by this village team. And Troon were a village side – strictly amateur and local. Of the players that won the National Championship, nine were born within a mile and a half of the Troon ground.

I learned, when I visited the club recently, that it had been founded in 1875 through the initiative of the then schoolmaster, and had carried on ever since through communal effort. They had good facilities, but they were not a rich club with wealthy patrons. Nor were they able to attract big money at the gate: quite often indeed they charged no admission, but relied on collections. The club chairman, Gerald Penberthy, said, with a twinkle in his eye, that if they charged admission, all the vice-presidents would get in free, *ex officio*, whereas if there was a collection instead, they would cheerfully dip deep in their pockets. In fact the club's chief source of revenue seems to have been a share in the proceeds of a lottery organised by Plymouth Argyle Football Club. Jack Angove was an agent for this enterprise, controlling a fleet of ticket-sellers – and he gave his commission to the cricket club.

Nineteen-seventy-one was an important milestone. That year they began work on a clubhouse of some splendour, stone-built and spacious, including a comfortable lounge bar and separate snooker and pool rooms, as well as fine committee rooms. A cricket-loving farmer gave them the land. The building cost £7,000 or £8,000. They had saved £3,000, and the local man who built it put up the rest of the money and was paid back – in quick time, it was made clear. By this time Troon were, as the local newspaper, the *West Briton,* made clear, becoming 'a team to be reckoned with'. Each week in the season, the *West Briton* carried at least two substantial reports on matches in the buoyant Senior League, Division 1 West; and early in the 1972 season they reported that 'with a 43-run win over champions Truro, Troon served notice that they will be staking a claim to the title this season'.

Meanwhile at the club there was a low-key debate about whether or not to enter the new National Village Championship. Some felt that it might distract attention from their long-standing objective, winning the league title. Certainly it would put great pressure on the players – and on their wives' and sweethearts' patience – to play two games a weekend. (The Haig competition was to be played on alternate Sundays.) There was also a feeling of diffidence, that they just wouldn't be good enough. Surely the Cup would go to some smart, well-heeled 'village' club from the Home Counties. Amongst the doubters was Jack Angove's father, and though Jack himself had more faith, he could not be sure that going for Cup and League might not prove a mistake. Even if they had a bit of a run in the Cup, they risked falling between two stools. The decision to enter seemed vindicated, however, by the opinion of a local bookmaker, who now played for Camborne, but who had formerly played in Sussex. He believed that Troon had nothing to fear, and reinforced his opinion by backing them to win!

In the event Troon did fail to take the league title, coming second to Truro, but by then they had already won six matches in the preliminary rounds of the National Championship, and the *West Briton* headline read 'TROON PREPARE FOR BUMPER CUP GATE' as they prepared to meet Linton Park of Kent, with extra seating and car parking. And Troon, as it seemed to the *West Briton*, 'won with astonishing ease' against a side that included John Ames, son of Leslie, the legendary wicket-keeper/batsman of pre-war days. Troon lost only one wicket in reaching the target of 168. A record crowd of 2,000 watched the match: there was no admission charge, but a collection brought in £126 and a competition raised a further £118.

This time the cricket was on the front page of the *West Briton*. Its article read, under the headline 'SO LOOK OUT LORD'S': 'Troon are on their way to the sacred centre of cricket. The final is on September 9 ... Troon's opponents are Astwood Bank [Warwickshire]. They have been warned.'

The inside pages carried another story under the headline 'TROON PLAN SPECIAL "UP FOR THE CUP" LONDON TRAIN'. The plan was to hire a train leaving Camborne about 11 p.m. on the Friday night, returning around midnight on the Saturday after the match. The fare would be £3.50. But the train would not run unless at least 500 tickets were sold. As Troon's population was only about 2,500 this seemed a stiff requirement, but in fact 700 tickets were sold. The train-goers were in high spirits as they set off, and seemed to have the best of it, rather than making the long overnight journey by road. But after travelling across Devon the train was unable to proceed beyond Dawlish because of a derailment that blocked the track. The *West Briton* front page report noted that 'all of them behaved nobly, despite their disappointment'. A man who had been on the train said, 'I was very impressed by their patience and tolerance.' He was not making a Cornish point (though he might well have done, for the Cornish are indeed a tolerant people, bearing their disappointments patiently and with good humour). No, he was making a cricket point: he went on,

It showed a sportsmanship so often lacking today ... I wonder what state the train would have been in if it had been carrying football supporters instead.

A train eventually took the passengers back to Camborne, whence the intrepid ones started all over again by car. One man persisted with the railway, however, and eventually found another train. Dick White, the club's general secretary, told me how this fan's enterprise was rewarded by seeing the whole match, and is commemorated by the club, who still have his ticket on display in the clubhouse.

Meanwhile the car-drivers managed to get to Lord's in time to see at least the closing overs. 'It was well worth it,' said one of them. He had been in time to see the Troon captain, Terry Carter, make the winning hit. And quite a hit it was. After a shaky start to the batting, Troon won in style – by seven wickets. 'SKIPPER'S SIX WRITES STORY-BOOK ENDING' was the *West Briton*'s headline. And another article began, 'Home are the champions ... to a village fit for heroes,' and continued, 'It was more like a carnival than a cricket triumph.' The entire centre of Troon was hung with flags and bunting: bed sheets were scrawled with 'welcome' and hung from windows. Scores piled into flag-bedecked cars and drove to the top end of the Redruth bypass to await the red coach bringing the team home.

The 'triumphal route' was chosen by the coach driver and two local constables. A mile-long cavalcade of hundreds of cars escorted the coach. 'This was the day Troon went on the map,' said the senior constable. The crowds never stopped singing: 'Twenty thousand Cornishmen' most of the time, except, appropriately, just outside Camborne, where they sang a ballad commemorating one of Trevithick's early railway experiments – 'Going up Camborne Hill, coming down'. And the *West Briton* printed the score-card under the heading 'THE LORDS OF TROON'.

The following summer the *West Briton* continued the theme as Troon progressed through the early rounds. 'VILLAGE CHAMPS WIN YET AGAIN' signalled their reaching the regional final stage, while at the national semi-final stage it was 'KENT BIG HITTERS FLY IN TO TACKLE TROON CHAMPS'.

The report of the match, headed: 'TROON POWER WAY BACK TO LORD'S', called Troon 'the kings of village cricket and the village of cricket kings' and admiringly recorded their 37-runs victory over Marden: a crowd of 3,000 'virtually exploded with a cacophony of clapping, cheering and the triumphant hooting of car horns'. That year there was no mishap with the special train, and, in the end, no mistake by Troon, though Gowerton (Wales) gave them a hard time in what was labelled by the *West Briton* as the Celt v. Celt match. It was a nail-biting affair – 'a hell of a match', said Terry Carter – but the 1000 Troon supporters saw their heroes win by 12 runs and go home to another tremendous reception. The *West Briton* touched on another aspect of Troon's success:

Troon's great run in the village cricket championship has boosted their hopes of being able to build a new pavilion by 1975, their centenary year.

They had £650 prize money from cup matches plus £500 for winning the final. Otherwise they made £367 from collections and competitions. They duly got their pavilion, but the figures show how near the breadline even the finest village clubs are accustomed to living. It is not only nationally that cricket is the poor relation. It would be foolish to sentimentalise over poverty, which can sometimes breed a corresponding caution that seems like a shrivelling of the soul. But you have only to walk into the Troon clubhouse to feel the warmth of the welcome and, soon, to experience the patience with which they deal with brash and unintelligent questions – the former players who run the club that has meant so much to them all their lives and into which they have put so much selfless service. Undoubtedly, too, they have done a great deal for the village: it is good to see that real community spirit can exist in a village that has seen better days and that lacks all the trappings of 'theme-park England' – if such a place exists outside London admen's offices. Troon has no village green, no maypoles, no touristic party-pieces. What it does have is some dedicated workers for its cricket club, which they will tell you has the best wicket in Cornwall – and the finest clubhouse. And they could, if they would, tell you that they had left the youngsters of today a fine tradition. Of course they are honest enough to admit that they are no longer the 'champs' that the newspapers put on a pedestal.

No one can reign supreme for long in cricket – it's not that kind of a game – and Troon's glory days came to an end, but not before they had again won the championship in 1976, creating a record that has not yet been surpassed. It was in 1983, when they fell at the very last hurdle, losing to Quorndon, to whom all praise, in the final at Lord's, that a certain poignancy entered into the Troon story. The three times they had come back winners thousands had turned out to greet them. In 1983, though, when they lost, it was just a few family and friends – no publicity. 'Not that we wanted it,' a committee member who had been there remarked philosophically, 'that's the way of the world.' And he talked realistically about the present state of the club: 'We don't turn out the cricketers we used to.' Everyone agreed about that and about the reasons. First and foremost there were too many other diversions for today's young people – 'computer games, television and playstations and such like'.

'When we were young ,' said Gerald Penberthy, 'in the evenings we could either play snooker or cricket. And if it was fine we chose cricket – we had a Test match every night out there' – waving his hand to the vast open space of the cricket field. Even through the mists and rain of a January day we could all feel the poignancy of the loss of innocence he was describing, though thank God nobody tried to put it into words.

We went on to discuss more prosaic reasons for the decline. There was no work any longer to keep families with adolescent children there: the young-sters had to go to the towns for work. Partly this was because of the retraction of traditional industries, but social mobility and education also played their part. Today's youngsters were not content with any old job. The best of them looked further afield – and the Troon elders fully accepted this. Indeed they were manifestly proud of the achievements of youngsters who had gone away to 'better themselves', much as their grandparents had done – except that this time there were no promised lands offering industrial jobs – the escape now tended to be into the service industries, the 'white-collar' world as it used to be, now a Technicolor world of opportunity. The Troon clubhouse members were proud of those they had lost through going to college or to find a teach-ing job, just as they were proud of the three Troon boys who had made their way into county cricket, through such devices as distinguishing themselves while on a Butlin's holiday. It was just a pity that as a result of this process Troon CC had lost a little of its erstwhile pre-eminence, but at least they were still able to field three teams and two youth teams.

And, importantly, for all its economic hardships Troon has kept the village flag flying. The village has kept, too, most of its numbers, however different the mix nowadays. And it has kept its Cornishness, unlike many other smaller and more picturesque places in the county. Many of these have lost much more, often through the influx of townsfolk, buying up the best houses, often as second homes or weekend cottages – and forcing the prices up beyond the reach of the locals; this places the Cornish folk who remain, the original villagers, no longer in full control of their own, communal identity. Many are now, indeed, obliged to seek cheaper housing in the towns. And the cricket field, if there is one, may be used only by a town club.

There seem to be no solutions, only palliatives. T. A. L. Huskinson, writing in *Barclay's* in 1983, concludes his contribution: 'Village cricket has changed much over the past twenty years and standards have improved.' He pays due tribute to the National Village Championship, with its prospect of playing at Lord's, but attributes the improvement to the great proliferation of the local leagues. If we cannot have or do not want church spires and village greens, we can at least have leagues. This is the Cornish experience, but it is surely reflected all over the country to a greater or lesser extent. We should not make artificial divisions between town and country, but only between the good and the better, as measured by results – and by the values on which each sets store. It may be very hard to find caperings on village greens these days, but it is easy to find a good local cricket match any weekend, contested for league points and of a high standard. 'Village cricket' in the 'theme-park' sense may have disappeared, but what has not gone is the spirit of clubs like Troon – an amateur ethos without hypocrisy, but full of straightforwardness, decency and generosity – what we might call, if we are not afraid of clichés, the true spirit of English cricket.

Notes

CHAPTER 1

1. Norman French also had a word *wiket* (*wiquet*, *ouiquet?*), meaning a small gate, and a word *beil*, a cross-piece.

2. Though obsolescent as a serious weapon in foreign wars, the longbow (for reasons of economy as well as tradition) was still the standard armament of the local militias. It had a firm emotional hold on Henry VIII himself, and he was responsive to the pleas of the bowyers and fletchers that they were being put out of business by its neglect.

3. It first came to official notice in 1598, in a dispute over 'a parcelle of land' in Guildford, Surrey. A fifty-nine-year-old coroner called John Derrick testified that he and his school-fellows had played 'creckett' there some fifty years earlier.

4. It evidently still had a juvenile image in 1611. Randle Cotgrave's French–English dictionary, published that year, defines 'crosse' as 'the crooked staff wherewith boys play at cricket'.

5. There was by 1601 a Poor Law, designed to spring into action when required, with rate funds not only for poor relief but to pay for materials for them to work on during their enforced idleness. But paupers could not expect to enjoy themselves at the parish's expense.

6. A typical definition put forward by an applicant in 1592 was 'noblemen, gentlemen and merchants, or such as shall be entered in the Book of Subsidies at £10 a year in land or goods'. Subsidies were taxes of 4*s*. in the pound for land and 2*s*. 8*d*. for movable goods.

7. Philip Stubbes, *The Anatomie of Abuses*, 1583.

8. The freedom did not extend to bull- and bear-baiting and interludes, which were banned on Sundays, and bowls, forbidden to 'the meaner sort' at all times.

9. Churchyards, before they became graveyards, had been used over the centuries for games after service, for often they were the obvious and convenient, sometimes the only place to play them; curates and even parish priests were known to join in. But the games, at least those officially allowed by the ecclesiastical authorities, were usually of a simple, juvenile, untroublesome kind: handball, the simplified version of real tennis, had been a particular nuisance, and cricket, however little it had

advanced from 'club-ball', must have been an unwelcome incursion. For the goings-on in Sussex see 'Seventeenth Century Sussex Cricket: East Lavant, 1628' by Timothy J. McCann, *The Journal of The Cricket Society*, vol. 15, no. 2, spring 1991.

10. Apart from Cromwell's 1656 ban in Ireland: as ever, a special case.

CHAPTER 2

1. Gambling debts below this amount could be recovered by civil action, with the defaulter paying a fine of three times the amount, half going to the Crown and half to the plaintiff: debts on bets higher than £100 could not be recovered at law.
2. William Morice was one of the two Secretaries of State who co-ordinated all government business.
3. The guinea, a gold coin from Guinea, West Africa, was introduced in 1606 as currency for the Royal Africa Company equivalent to the silver £1 coins then in circulation. Its value fluctuated, however, and at the time of the match it was worth around 30s. (£1.50). The rate was fixed at £1 1s. (£1.05) in 1717.
4. See note 3 above.
5. Originally 'noumpere' from Old French *non per* – no peer, one set above the rest: a noumpere became an umpire.
6. Translation by Harold Perry for *Etoniana*, December 1922, reprinted in *The Laws of Cricket*, R. S. Rait-Kerr.
7. This stemmed originally from the prudent practice of William the Conqueror, doling out the spoils to his henchmen, deliberately giving them great chunks of land in widely scattered places to reduce the risk of physical empires being founded in his midst.
8. Or, in modern terms, the Rest of England. Teams were usually called after the place they or their leader came from, but metropolitan teams often called themselves, or were called, simply London. No monopoly was implied, however, nor any selection process other than hire by the promoters. When teams called England began to appear, they were simply a miscellany of box-office attractions.
9. Dr Johnson, who was working for the *Gentleman's Magazine* at the time, offended cricket-lovers by defining it in his monumental *Dictionary* (1755) as a game 'in which contenders drive a ball with sticks or bats in opposition to each other!'

CHAPTER 3

1. Comedian was the publisher's description of the author on the second edition of 1771. Love, whose real name was Dance and whose father designed the Mansion House, was an actor and writer of light comedies and pantomimes.
2. First published in the *New Universal Magazine* in 1752 as 'settled by the Cricket Club in 1744'.
3. The previous norm had been only 1 foot high by 2 feet wide. The change in height presumably reflects the trend towards bouncing the ball, with a compensating reduction in width.
4. Charge as in costs.
5. One of the things for which he is remembered is his 1745 note to the Admiralty Board, when first appointed commissioner: 'I'll be at your board when at leisure from cricket.' This was not a derisive gesture, but an explanation.

6. The price was increased to two shillings during the Napoleonic War.

CHAPTER 4

1. Notes on these southern laws were published in Heckmondwike around 1800.
2. 'Blacklegs' were bookmakers, probably so called because they were up to the thighs in mud from hanging round the paddock and starting line at Newmarket.
3. The physical characteristics of the lower orders employed in various categories by the great men were adaptable to sport – tough little grooms became lightweight jockeys, tough big men who started as liveried watermen or bodyguards became exponents of the noble art, and tough, horny-handed men of toil with a certain amount of guile were natural cricketers.
4. Milling was sparring.
5. The old dress was even hazardous for fieldsmen. Beldham says, 'Fancy the old fashion before cricket shoes, when I saw John Wells tear a finger nail off against his shoe buckle in picking up a ball.'
6. From 22 by 6 inches to 24 by 7 inches.
7. Brooks's, formerly Almack's, was the haunt of high-flying Whig gamblers like Charles James Fox, and of the Prince of Wales.
8. Eight years earlier Wellington had been Chief Secretary for Ireland during Richmond's spell as Lord Lieutenant. Now at this crisis, Richmond wanted to show the flag, see the thing through and all that. When his old colleague organised a cricket match at Enghien, Wellington took one of Richmond's daughters to it. The Duchess of Richmond's ball on the eve of Waterloo was the climax of the insouciant approach. No one quite knows how the story of Waterloo being won on the playing fields of Eton got around. Wellington, who denied ever saying it, was indeed at Eton, but he played no games there, only the violin. His only recorded appearance at cricket, furthermore, was in Dublin, when he was ADC to a previous Viceroy. It is not known whether Richmond, an Old Westminster, ever heard the saying.

CHAPTER 5

1. It was a central tenet of the honour code that since gentlemen did not cheat other gentlemen did not accuse them of it. It would have become a duelling matter if allegations had been made. Osbaldeston, who had a very short fuse, fought one against Lord George Bentinck in 1831. Clergymen were obviously more inhibited.
2. After the stoolball era women tended to be cast in the role of admiring spectators. Their first appearance in the canon is in the famous letter sent in 1739 by Mrs Mary Turner of East Hoathly near Lewes to her son: 'last Munday youre father was at Mr Payns and plaid at Cricket and come home please anuff for he struck the best ball in the Game and whishd he had not anything else to do he could play at Cricket all his Life!'

Women may well have gone along to see the fun sometimes, as Trevelyan suggested, but at other times they *were* the fun. Admittedly it was not always cricket: witness the match in 1744 announced in the *Penny Daily Morning Advertiser* between two teams who had 'subscribed for a Holland smock of one guinea value, which will be run for by two jolly wenches, one known by the name of The Little Bit of Blue (the handsome Broom Girl) at the fag end of Kent Street, and the other, Black Bess, of the Mint. They are to run in drawers only, and there is excellent sport expected.'

On the other hand the first time we hear of white as a distinctive emblem of cricket is in the dress of the teams in a women's match on Gosden Common near Guildford in 1745. In this decorous affair, described by the *Reading Mercury* as the 'greatest cricket match that ever was played in the South part of England', eleven maids of Hambledon wearing red ribbons on their heads beat eleven maids of Bramley, wearing blue, before the biggest ever crowd 'of both sexes', and the 'girls bowled, batted, ran and catched as well as most men could do ...'. Two years later, whilst Slindon and Newland were competing with hurling matches for attention, three women's teams from Sussex villages engaged in a series of matches at the Artillery Ground. George Smith evidently thought them worth top money: 'It is to be hoped the paying of sixpence of admission will not be taken amiss, the charges thereof amounting to upwards of four-score pounds.' There were 'several large bets depending' so the excitement may not all have been salacious, but the crowd caused grave disorder and the first match could not be finished.

3. Indeed, most members did not bother about fielding either: as the *Sporting Magazine* put it in 1827, 'it is grievous to know that the majority of gentlemen field badly ... principally [because] in practice their whole attention is devoted to batting, instead of being equally divided between batting and fielding'.

4. Most say it was Harry Bentley, a noted umpire and compiler of the early records of matches at Lord's, but others say Noah Mann, son of the old Hambledon player. Neither would be likely to act on their own initiative in such a matter.

5. Unfortunately Lowth himself had to give up the game through failing eyesight.

6. In 1864 *Baily's Magazine* published an article, by 'MFH', about the preparations at Eton for the MCC match in 1813: 'It was the grand event of the half, conned over for weeks before it came off, and books were made for and against it: bets were hedged according to rule, and the score of the favourites had the scale of odds with the precise regularity of Tattersall's.' The final bet-laying was done in eleven o'clock chapel on whole holidays.

7. There were still only two universities in England: the first college of London University started in 1828 and Durham in 1832. 'Redbrick' began in 1851 with Owens College, Manchester.

8. Scotland had some 2.3 million, and Ireland, ominously, 7.75 million.

CHAPTER 6

1. 145,000 of these were small farmers who hired no labour.

2. For example, in the famous drawing by G. F. Watts, one of a number of lithographs, the pencil sketches for which are in the MCC collection (see p. 5 of the first plate section).

3. The reforms had done little to advance working-class education. In the 1840s roughly a third of adult males and a half of females were illiterate.

4. One of the new gentlemanly fashions. The professionals kept their top hats for some years – it was a status symbol – but the gentlemen affected everything from boaters, as in the public-school matches, to tall caps with shiny peaks.

5. Norfolk subsided after Pilch's departure and went out of existence in 1848: the present club dates from 1877.

6. Osbaldeston (see Chapter 5) was presumably referring to the Old Club when he spoke of the matches he played in Nottingham. Originally they played on the race-course, in the Forest, which was not enclosed, and therefore free.

7. In 1846, F. P. Fenner, a noted bowler for the Town, acquired a piece of land and leased it to the University. The county club, after some very good seasons, dissolved. The present club dates from 1891.

8. W. A. Bettesworth, in *The Walkers of Southgate*, 1900.

9. Friendly societies, in existence from the seventeenth century, were originally poor people's burial and sickness clubs. When embryonic trade unions fell foul of the law in the early nineteenth century, they became one of the few ways in which people in the various trades could get together for mutual benefit. Good employers encouraged, and even contributed to them.

CHAPTER 7

1. 29 August 1863.

2. *A Pattern of Islands*, 1958.

3. Hughes actually wrote 'British', so Lang, a Scot, is aligning himself with the London ascendancy. For a discussion of the wider implications see Derek Birley, *Sport and the Making of Britain*.

4. 'I am desired to express the Committee's unanimous disapproval of any such scheme as may be entertained under the specious name of a Cricket Parliament. The laws that regulate the game of cricket are so excessively simple, the questions that arise are so easily to be met by them and, in fact. they are and have long been acknowledged by the MCC to be quite sufficient authority – that, without dictating to the contrary or desiring anybody, if otherwise inclined, to follow blindly in their steps, the Committee do not see any reason to depart from the course which they have pursued in the spirit of cricket through all difficulties since their first year of existence as a club in 1787.' R. A. FitzGerald to W. M. Kelson, 20 April 1864.

5. The hall was removed from Hyde Park after the Great Exhibition and transferred to Sydenham, where it became a tourist attraction and, over time, the centre of a sports complex, featuring anything from track and field athletics and cycling to soccer, lawn tennis and bowls. W.G. went back there as cricket manager in 1900.

CHAPTER 8

1. John Lillywhite, the umpire in the Willsher no-balling incident, is credited with extending 'not cricket' to include badgering the umpires. *Oxford English Dictionary*, 2nd edn, 1989: '... it is not cricket to keep asking the umpire questions. J. Lillywhite, *Cricketer's Companion*, 1867.' The prerogative was, of course, restricted to the gentlemanly captains by the second Duke of Richmond, who forbade his gamesters to speak.

2. From 1899 the ball became dead when lodged in clothing. Running six runs (at the time equivalent to hitting the ball out of the ground) was fairly common: in 1868 C. A. Absolom, playing for Cambridge University against Surrey, was trying to run a seventh when a throw at the wicket struck his intervening bat: he was given out 'obstructing the field', the first recorded instance.

3. Letter from F. R. Spofforth, who played in the match, with an embargo on publi-

cation before his death. Published in *The Times*, 17 August 1926. Darling's hearsay account is in a book privately printed after his death by his son, *Test Tussles on and off the Field*, D. K. Darling.

4. Alfred Cochrane, *Dictionary of National Biography (1931–1940)*.
5. Spotted or striped shirts, cravats, high-peaked caps, toppers giving way to pill-box hats or hooped, low-peaked caps, large leather belts with snake buckle.
6. The name given to days taken off after a Sunday's roistering.
7. After the famous horse race (founded by Lord Derby and his friends). A derby had come to mean any great contest.
8. George Howitt, a Nottinghamshire man, played a few games for Notts and forty-three times for Middlesex between 1866 and 1876.

CHAPTER 9

1. Son of William Ward, the banker, benefactor of MCC, Ward had stayed on as a curate in Cambridge and became an indefatigable fund-raiser for the University Club, helping them negotiate a thirty-five-year lease of Fenner's and construct a handsome pavilion.
2. A coloured lithograph by 'Spy' (Sir Leslie Ward) issued with *Vanity Fair*, 13 July 1878. Only W.G. (June, 1877) had previously been featured.
3. W. R. Gilbert, a Gloucestershire 'amateur', was a cousin of the Graces. He emigrated to Canada after a scandal over thefts from the dressing-room.
4. Grahame Parker, *The Midwinter File*, Wisden, 1971. See also *Wisden* 1880 and *The Times*, 14 January 1879 and 24 July 1879.
5. Midwinter played for Gloucestershire until 1882, touring Australia with Shaw and Shrewsbury in 1881–2, went back to Australia, touring England in 1884 with Billy Murdoch and then rejoined England in 1886–7 – a remarkable career. The loss of his wife an children drove him insane in 1890 and he committed suicide.
6. The Commonwealth of Australia was not created until 1901: the States were separate colonies.
7. 1879, reprinted in B. Green (ed.), *Wisden Anthology* Vol. 1 (1864–1900), London, 1979. For the Australian perspective see W. F. Mandle, 'Cricket and Australian Nationalism in the Nineteenth Century' in *Sport in Australia*, ed. T. D. Jaques and G. R. Pavia, 1976. Lord Harris's account of the events of 1880 is in *A Few Short Runs*, 1921.
8. Captain Holden did not last long, resigning in exasperation. In 1882 he decided that the touring Australians, as 'amateurs', ought to pay for their own lunches. He also claimed the right to decide such matters as how long the wicket should be rolled between innings. Rude comments about him were chalked on the door of the tourists' hotel, which he, publicly and wrongly, accused the Australian manager of writing.

CHAPTER 10

1. The party was given by Sir William Clarke, a millionaire grazier, the current president of Melbourne Cricket Club, and the ladies of his household were the putative bail- or ball-burners. See R. Willis, *Cricket's Biggest Mystery: the Ashes*, Guildford, 1983. Amongst the subsequent counter-theories the most ghoulish was that the ashes were those of one of the Aboriginal tourists of 1868. See 'New Light

on the Ashes', John Twigg, *International Journal of the History of Sport*, London, September 1987. Bligh subsequently married Miss Florence Rose Murphy, one of the Melbourne ladies who had presented him with the urn. They kept the urn until his death in 1927, after which it was bequeathed to MCC, without further explanation of its contents. On 16 April 1998 it was reported in *The Times* that Rosemary, Dowager Countess of Darnley, had said that the former Miss Murphy, her mother-in-law, told her the ashes were those of a veil she had worn at one of Ivo's matches in 1883.

2. He gravitated to Minor Counties cricket and spent many years running Radnorshire CC. Another meteor was S. E. Butler of Oxford, who in 1871, on a particularly bad Lord's pitch, took all 10 wickets for 38 runs, followed by 5 in the second.

3. Known as 'Round the Corner', Smith, a Cambridge Blue for four years, later went to South Africa, became an actor and, for some reason, was knighted. As Sir Aubrey Smith he became famous in Hollywood epics about the British Raj and celebrated as the founding father, along with Boris Karloff (a Surrey member), of the Hollywood Cricket Club.

4. Shrewsbury did not bother much what code of football it was to be, and the team ended up playing both rugby football and 'Victorian rules' – a transition which proved more difficult than expected, especially as the players enjoyed 'too much whisky and women'.

5 He died from enteric fever fighting in the Boer War.

CHAPTER 11

1. He remained secretary of Surrey CCC until his death in 1907.

2. Hawke dispensed with the services of the gifted England left-arm spinner, Ted Peate, in 1887.

3. In 1896 Hawke dismissed Peate's successor, Bobby Peel, an even better bowler and a good batsman, for getting drunk and urinating on the pitch.

4. *Recollections and Reminiscences*, M. B. Hawke, 1924. This is freely quoted in a light-hearted discussion in *The Willow Wand*, Derek Birley, 1979.

5. Darling says that in the Old Trafford Test match (2nd Test, 1896) Jackson ran Brown out. His memory must have been at fault: it was Jackson who was run out.

6. In MCC collection (see p. 1 of the second plate section).

7. Lohmann held out until after the Test, then apologised and was forgiven. Gunn, of Nottinghamshire, did not apologise, and played only once more for England – at Nottingham in 1899.

8. The Parsees, led by a local doctor, had previously toured England, but Harris was unable to play against them because of parliamentary duties. From 1895, when Harris left Bombay, the Parsees played an annual match against the whites.

9. *Great Batsmen* (1905) and *Great Bowlers and Fieldsmen* (1906).

CHAPTER 12

1. It was, according to C. B. Fry, given an editorial polish by the essayist, publisher and cricket fanatic E. V. Lucas.

2. Mythically, George Hirst said to Wilfred when he came in to bat, 'We'll get 'em in singles,' but this was later questioned by assiduous north-country researchers,

some arguing that the expression 'singles' was not true colloquial Yorkshire – 'wuns' would have been what was said – others convinced that such an injunction would have been quite superfluous, not to say insulting, to a Yorkshireman. In fact they scored thirteen singles and a two. Both participants denied saying anything of the kind, and Wilfred Rhodes went on record as saying that it was 'only a tale'.

3. By Bernard Partridge on 12 May 1904.

4. As a result, a rule was brought in, requiring team-lists to be exchanged before the toss.

CHAPTER 13

1. S. Sassoon, *Memoirs of a Fox-Hunting Man*. The cricket match, from internal evidence, took place in 1902.

2. Wodehouse watched occasional county matches when he was in England, and took the name of his best-known character from Percy Jeeves of Warwickshire, a young Yorkshire-born bowler who was killed in the First World War.

3. C. P. Foley, of Eton, Cambridge and Middlesex, a veteran of the Jameson raid, in *Autumn Foliage*, 1934.

4. Foster wrote a remarkable, mildly idiosyncratic autobiography, (*Cricketing Memories*, 1930) in which he displays a deeply emotional streak. A motor-cycle accident in 1915 ended his cricketing career at twenty-six and his life dwindled sadly away, with the final ignominy in 1950 of a conviction for fraud.

CHAPTER 14

1. John Kipling was killed in action in 1915.

2. After Oscar's death Hornung did his bit, working for the YMCA in France, never losing his faith in playing the game.

3. He died of influenza, the scourge which killed twice as many people as the war, in 1918.

4. Worcestershire did not compete in 1919.

5. A. C. MacLaren, *Cricket Old and New*, 1924. MacLaren, of course, famously chose and captained a team of (non-innovatory) amateurs at the end of the 1921 season and beat the Australians.

CHAPTER 15

1. 'Cradle' cannons and similar techniques, enabling a star like Tom Reece to compile a break of several thousands, had just about killed off the Edwardian vogue for professional billiards by this time. Basket-ball was a recent innovation, imported from America by Madame Bergman-Osterberg's ladies' college. An early version of lawn tennis (1866) had been called pelota; cricketers called it pat-ball.

2. A Lancashire version of the story has the same performance at Old Trafford against someone like Ted Macdonald. The young gentleman this time spars at the first ball but misses, is hit on the pads by the second but given not out, and is clean-bowled by the third. He pays his compliment to the bowling to a group of members as he climbs the pavilion steps, and one of them says, 'Aye, thou wert lucky to get a duck.'

3. Hirst to Eton and Rhodes, somewhat less contentedly in the event, to Harrow.

4. The idea of the senior professional was seen to have value, as a sort of RSM, a link

between commanding officer and troops, and with this in mind two professionals were co-opted to the selection committee: Wilfred Rhodes and Jack Hobbs (one from the North and one from the South!).

5. An honourable exception was Col. Philip Trevor, the veteran *Daily Telegraph* correspondent, who believed Carr had been 'absolutely right' but that Macartney had played the greatest innings he had ever seen.

6. 21 January 1933 (Express Newspapers).

CHAPTER 16

1. *Beyond a Boundary*. C. L. R. James, a West Indian Marxist intellectual, lived in England in the 1930s and wrote for the *Manchester Guardian*, in which his original reports on Constantine in the leagues appeared.

2. In this case the appellant was James Seymour of Kent, whose benefit match seven years earlier had brought him in £930-odd. He had appealed against being charged income tax and eventually won his case. This seems to be a clear case of prejudice, arising from the esteem in which the national game was held in high places, for no similar concession was given to football.

3. Another, Duleepsinjhi, Ranji's nephew, was injured and unable to tour.

4. Allen was not invited to give evidence, nor indeed was Wyatt, who was believed to have misgivings about what had gone on.

5. Larwood wrote afterwards that he did not want to play in the match, that he only bowled half-pace, that it was an easy wicket and that he did not hit anybody.

6. Two cautions, then a further offender to be taken off and not allowed to bowl for the rest of the innings.

7. The ball's circumference was reduced in 1927 from between 9 and 9½ inches to between 8$\frac{13}{16}$ and 9 inches, and in 1931 the wickets were increased from 27 by 8 to 28 by 9 inches.

8. Editor of the *London Mercury*, minor poet and essayist, founder of the literary cricket team, the Invalids, commemorated in the satire *England, Their England*, A. G. McDonnell, 1933.

9. With Allen and Robins trying to save the game for Middlesex on the last evening, Holmes wanted to take the new ball (due in those days after 200 runs) and so bowled an over of 24 boundary-wides and no-balls. See *Wisden*, 1938.

CHAPTER 17

1. The name given to two broadcasters of German propaganda with distinctive, honking 'upper-class' accents: first Norman Baillie-Stewart, a renegade Seaforth Highlander, then the Mosleyite William Joyce.

2. Except in 1940. Eton v. Harrow was not held, and all Lord's public-school matches were called off in 1944 for fear of flying bombs.

3. There were a few near-misses, and a house owned by MCC was destroyed.

4. E. W. Swanton, in *Sort of a Cricket Person*, tells how he and his friend I. A. R. Peebles, then captain of Middlesex, taking advantage of a shipboard conversation, sent a wire to Col. S. W. Harris of the Cavalry Club and extricated themselves from the indignity of serving in the ranks of an unfashionable regiment, getting commissions in the Bedfordshire Yeomanry without further formality.

5. Diana Rait-Kerr, by then the Curator of Lord's treasures, was joint author, with Ian Peebles.

6. After an extraordinary season in which a quite talented but inexperienced amateur, R. H. Maudsley, was asked to share the duty with the deeply experienced Dollery.

7. Counties without recourse to illicit sources relied on donations of members' clothing coupons to buy boots and flannels. Certificates were needed for the purchase of cricket balls.

CHAPTER 18

1 . Walter Hammond, in *Cricket's Secret History*, was scathing about the amateurism of the selectors who had seen fit to drop Hutton after the second Test – apparently because he had drawn away from a few balls from Lindwall. One particular adherent of the virility cult had held this to be culpable and a bad influence on the morale of later batsmen, whereas, Hammond reckoned, Hutton, who had earlier taken a severe blow on the hip-bone, was simply taking prudent care to avoid a recurrence. A less courageous man would have retired hurt, Hammond wrote. Anyway, the selectors chose a wholly inadequate replacement, who was never picked again.

2. As a student he had already played for England and toured Australia with Freddy Brown's team in 1950–1. He led Sussex in 1953, and was thus available for the England job in the Ashes and Coronation year, but thereafter played only in sabbatical spasms. He still managed to captain England when Hutton fell ill in 1954 and was good enough, relatively speaking, to justify a recall in 1956 and to tour Australia in 1962–3.

3. Trueman, famously, liked to go into opposing dressing-rooms and treat them to his views. Bob Berry, the Lancashire left-arm spinner, twelfth man for the day, was reputedly once so exasperated that he cried out, 'Fred, you're just like a canary – all chirp and shit.' Fred, furious, said coldly, 'It's easy to see you're not batting against me today,' and swept out.

4. It was apparently Tom Graveney who, irked by her sweeping criticisms of the team's behaviour and lack of hard information, had suggested that she mind her own business.

5. A select group of retired professionals had been similarly honoured in 1949.

6. MCC had a waiting list that would have taken them thirty years to expunge, and could have increased the subscription substantially and regularly. But to do so would have risked bringing in the 'wrong sort' and would have pained existing members. It was still 8 guineas in 1955.

7. The episode became even more controversial when MCC promptly withdrew an invitation to tour Australia for the same offence. Other counties were ready to employ Wardle, but Yorkshire would not agree to the special registration and he ended up as Nelson's latest spectacular signing in the Lancashire League.

CHAPTER 19

1. Gibb, an amiable eccentric with passion for ice-cream, had turned professional for Essex in 1951 before becoming an umpire.

2. From 1955 MCC had been trying two different methods; one making the position

of the front foot the criterion, the other involving an allowance of 18 inches of drag behind the bowling crease. The former was chosen and adopted by the Imperial Cricket Conference in 1962, but the West Indies did not come into line until 1964. Every fast bowler hated it but it eventually stopped dragging, which had become fashionable through the success of Lindwall, Trueman and Tyson.

3. The matter came to light in 1965 when the correspondence came to the notice of the *Daily Mail*.
4. In the end the top five Minor Counties were allowed in, but only after Gillette had agreed to put in more cash.
5. An MCC committee of enquiry into county cricket, called after its chairman, D. G. Clark, recently retired captain of Kent.
6. It had reached 100 per cent by 1976.
7. They are still (1999) hoping, encouraged by the plans of the English Cricket Board to set up some twenty premier leagues throughout the country, offering inducements of £1000 grants.
8. For example, Swanton rebuted Bedser for alleged insensitive handling of Graveney in 1969. (Roy Peskett, a veteran reporter, told a press box story of John Arlott seeing white smoke coming from a nearby chimney and saying, 'We can relax now, boys, they've elected E. W. Swanton Pope.')

CHAPTER 20

1. Programme and venues to be acceptable to Boards of Control; individual permission to be sought by players; no teams to be represented as national sides; players to make themselves available for Tests if required; existing commitments to sponsors not to be put in jeopardy.
2. The TCCB found some solace in the £150,000 they got from Packer for the television rights of the 1977 England v. Australia series.
3. The letter, quoted in *The Times* on 7 August, asked the committee to take this action: 'We do appreciate the very difficult position in which the Committee finds itself owing to the incredible action of many other counties. We would, however, hope the club committee will not simply bow to parochial pressures.'
4. Participation figures for all sports are, in the nature of things, unreliable, but the Sports Council and various other official agencies have begun to shed a little light in recent years. In 1980 estimated comparative figures were:

Sport	No. of players	% of population	No. of clubs
Cricket	500,000	1.4	14,000*
Soccer	1,100,000	3.0	40,000
Rugby Union	180,000	0.5	1,850

* 4,000 clubs affiliated to National Cricket Association, estimated membership 80,000.

5. Imported willow cost much less and 'budget' English bats could be found for under £30.

CHAPTER 21
1. He scribbled the following on a scrap of paper: 'I apologise for the bad language used on the field at Faisalabad.'
2. Later Sir Colin and, soon after, Lord Cowdrey of Tonbridge.

Bibliography and Further Reading

(a) EARLY CRICKET

Arlott, John (ed.), *From Hambledon to Lord's*, Johnson, London, 1948 (contains Nyren, Mitford, Pycroft).

—— (ed.), *The Middle Ages of Cricket*, Johnson, London, 1949 (includes Denison's *Sketches*, Pycroft's 'Cricket Reminiscences from Oxford Memories').

Buckley, G. D., *Fresh Light on Eighteenth Century Cricket*, Cotterell, Birmingham, 1935.

——, *Fresh Light on Pre-Victorian Cricket*, Cotterell, Birmingham, 1937.

Cuming, E. D., *Squire Osbaldeston: His Autobiography*, Lane, London, 1926.

de Saussure, C., *A Foreign View of England in 1725–29*, Caliban, London, 1994.

Denison, W., *Cricket: Sketches of the Players*, Simpkin, Marshall, London, 1846.

Frewin, Leslie (ed.), *The Poetry of Cricket*, Macdonald, London, 1964.

Haygarth, A., *Cricket Scores and Biographies 1862–1925*, 15 volumes, new edition to be published June 1999 by Southern Books and Publishing Co.

Love, James (James Dance), *Cricket: An Heroic Poem*, ed. F. S. Ashley-Cooper, Richards, Nottingham, 1922.

Martineau, G. D., *Bat, Ball, Wicket and All*, Sportsman's Book Club, London, 1954.

——, *The Field is Full of Shades*, Sportsman's Book Club, London, 1954.

Mitford, John, review of Nyren, *Gentleman's Magazine*, 1833.

Mitford, Mary Russell, *Our Village*, Whittaker, London, 1824–32.

Nyren, J. *The Young Cricketer's Tutor and the Cricketers of my Time*, ed. C. Cowden Clarke, first published 1833; new edition with introduction by John Arlott, Davis-Poynter, London, 1974.

Pycroft, James, *The Cricket Field*, Longman, London, 1851.

Rait-Kerr, R. S., *The Laws of Cricket*, Longman, London, 1950 (includes *In Certamen Pilae*, with translation).

Rhys, E. (ed.), *The Old Country*, Dent, London, 1971 (includes 'A Country Cricket Match' by Mary Russell Mitford).

Thomas, P. F. (H. P.-T.), *Old English Cricket*, Richards, Nottingham, 1923–29.

Trevelyan, G. M., *English Social History*, Longman, London, 1942.

Waghorn, H., *Cricket Scores, Notes, etc.*, Blackwood, London, 1899.

Wheeler, C. A., *Sportscrapiana*, 2nd edition, Caw, Simpkin and Marshall, London, 1868.

(b) MIDDLE PERIOD

Barrie, J. M., *The Greenwood Hat*, P. Davies, London, 1927.

Barty-King, H., *Quilt-Winders and Pod-Shapers*, Macdonald, London, 1979.

Birley, D., *Land of Sport and Glory*, Manchester University Press, Manchester, 1994.

——, *Sport and the Making of Britain*, Manchester University Press, Manchester, 1993.

Box, C., 'The English Game of Cricket', *The Field*, 1877.

Brodribb, G., *The Croucher*, London Magazine Editions, London, 1974.

——, *Felix on the Bat*, Eyre & Spottiswood, London, 1962.

Daft, R., *Kings of Cricket*, introduction by Andrew Lang, Simpkin, Marshall, London, 1893.

Darling, D. K., *Test Tussles On and Off the Field*, self-published, Hobart, 1970.

Darwin, B., *W. G. Grace*, Duckworth, London, 1934.

Duckworth, L., *S. F. Barnes: Master Bowler*, Hutchinson, London, 1967.

Ensor, R., *England*, Oxford University Press, Oxford, 1936.

Frith, D., *The Golden Age of Cricket*, Lutterworth Press, Guildford, 1978.

Fry, C. B., *Life Worth Living*, Eyre & Spottiswood, London, 1939.

Gale, F., *The Life of the Hon. Robert Grimston*, Longman, London, 1885.

Grace, W. G. with Porritt, A., *Cricketing Reminiscences and Personal Recollections*, J. Bowden, London, 1899.

Harris, Lord and Ashley-Cooper, F. S., *Lord's and M.C.C.*, London and Counties Press Association, London, 1914.

Hornung, E., *Raffles, the Amateur Cracksman*, Methuen, London, 1899.

Knight, A. E., *The Complete Cricketer*, Methuen, London, 1906.

Marwick, A., *The Deluge: British Society and the First World War*, Macmillan, London, 1965.

Morrah, P. *Alfred Mynn and the Cricketers of his Time*, Eyre & Spottiswood, London, 1968.

'Old Ebor' (A. W. Pullin), *Talks with Old Yorkshire Cricketers*, Yorkshire Post, Leeds, 1898.

——, *Talks with Old English Cricketers*, Blackwood, London, 1900.

Powell, A. G. and Canynge-Caple, S., *The Graces*, Sportsman's Book Club, London, 1948.

Sassoon, S., *Memoirs of a Fox-Hunting Man*, Faber, London, 1928.

Sissons, R., *The Players*, Pluto Press, Melbourne, 1988.

Standing, P. C., *Cricket of Today and Yesterday*, Caxton, Edinburgh, 1902.

Taylor, A. J. P., *The First World War*, first published 1963; paperback edition Penguin, London, 1966.

Trevor, P. C., *The Problems of Cricket*, Sampson, Low, London, 1907.

Warner, P. F., *Lord's 1787–1945*, Harrap, London, 1947.

Wisden Cricketer's Almanack, Sporting Handbooks, annual since 1864.

Wynne-Thomas, P., *Give Me Arthur* [Arthur Shrewsbury], Arthur Baker, London, 1985.

(c) MODERN PERIOD AND GENERAL

Allen, D. R. (ed.), *Arlott on Cricket*, Collins, London, 1984.

Birley, D., *Playing the Game*, Manchester University Press, Manchester, 1995.

Botham, I., *The Botham Report*, Collins Willow, London, 1997.

Bowen, R., *Cricket: A History of its Growth and Development Throughout the World*, Eyre & Spottiswood, London, 1970.

Boycott, G., *Boycott on Cricket*, Partridge Press, London, 1990.

Calder, A., *The People's War 1939–45*, first published 1969; paperback edition Pimlico, London, 1992.

Cardus, N., *Autobiography*, Collins, London, 1947.

——, *Second Innings*, Collins, London, 1950.

Carr, A. W., *Cricket with the Lid Off*, Hutchinson, London, 1935.

Compton, D. C. S., *End of an Innings*, P. Oldbourne, London, 1958.

——, *Playing for England*, Sampson, Low, London, 1948.

Cowdrey, M. C., *The Incomparable Game*, Hodder & Stoughton, London, 1971.

——, *M.C.C.*, Hodder & Stoughton, London, 1976.

Francis, T., *The Zen of Cricket*, Stanley Paul, London, 1992.

Graves, R. and Hodge, A., *The Long Weekend*, first published 1940; paperback edition Abacus, London, 1995.

Hammond, W. R., *Cricket's Secret History*, Stanley Paul, London, 1952.

Hobbs, J. B., *My Cricket Memories*, Heinemann, London, 1924.

James, C. L. R., *Beyond a Boundary*, Hutchinson, London, 1963.

Jardine, D. R., *In Quest of the Ashes*, Hutchinson, London, 1933.

Larwood, H., *Bodyline?*, E. Mathews & Marrot, London, 1933.

Larwood, H. and Perkins, K., *The Larwood Story*, W. H. Allen, London, 1965.

Marwick, A., *British Society Since 1945*, Allen Lane, London, 1982.

Parkin, C., *Cricket Reminiscences*, Hodder & Stoughton, London, 1923.

Root, F., *A Cricket Pro's Lot*, E. Arnold, London, 1937.

Stevenson, J., *Britain 1914–45*, Penguin, London, 1984.

Swanton, E. W., *As I Said at the Time*, Unwin, London, 1983.

——, *Sort of a Cricket Person*, Collins, London, 1972.

Swanton, E. W., Plumptree, G. and Woodcock, J. (eds.), *Barclay's World of Cricket*, 3rd edition, Guild, London, 1986.

Taylor, A. J. P., *English History 1914–45*, Oxford University Press, Oxford, 1965.

Titmus, F., *Talk of the Double*, Stanley Paul, London, 1964.

Warner, P. F., *Cricket Between Two Wars*, Chatto & Windus, London, 1942.

Wiener, M., *English Culture and the Decline of the Industrial Spirit 1850–1980*, Penguin, London, 1992.

Index

388 *Index*

Walker, Tom 50, 51, 54, 64
'walking' 273
wandering clubs 100, 323
Ward, William 55, 61, 63, 65, 76, 83, 109
Warner, P. F. ('Plum') 157, 168–9, 173, 178, 187, 189, 195, 199, 203, 207, 209, 210, 214, 215–16, 217, 219, 220, 229, 230, 231, 234–5, 236, 247, 248, 249, 251, 253, 258, 263, 266
wartime cricket 206–7, 208, 209–11, 263–9
Warwickshire 144, 145, 153, 188, 201, 211, 271, 318, 319, 345–6, 350, 351
Washbrook, Cyril 279, 280
Wass, Tom 179–80, 209
Wellington, Duke of 56, 57–8, 69
Wenman, Edward 78, 80, 99
West Indies 168, 195, 231, 247, 261, 272, 275, 281, 286, 287, 295, 296, 297, 314, 315, 316, 319, 325, 327, 333, 335, 343
White Conduit club 47, 48
White Conduit Fields 17, 43
wicket
  size 64, 65
  state of the 93, 114
wicket-keepers 78
wide balls 57
Willes, John 64–5
Willis, Bob 305, 316, 324
Willsher, Edgar 97, 98, 100, 101, 116
Wilson, Rockley 217–18, 234

Winchilsea, George Finch, Earl of 43–4, 47, 48, 49, 51
'winter of discontent' (1978–9) 321
winter tours 301, 334
Wisden, John 85, 90, 93, 96–7, 102
Wisden's Cricketer's Almanack 103–4
Wodehouse, P. G. 196, 354
women's cricket 352
Woodfull, W. M. 236, 238, 250
Woods, Sammy 165, 202
Wooller, Wilf 276, 286, 300
Woolley, Frank 180, 209, 231, 244, 253, 256, 263
Woolmer, Bob 317, 326
Worcestershire 151, 177, 202, 203–4, 211, 243, 254, 265, 300, 312
workplace legislation 87, 150
World Series Cricket 318, 319, 320

xenophobia 33, 72, 306, 330

Yardley, Norman 266, 276, 283, 284
Yardley, William 114, 116, 139
York 117
Yorkshire 72, 73, 101, 115, 116–17, 134–5, 140, 156–7, 178, 200–1, 202, 206, 207, 211, 213, 224, 225, 226, 243, 244–5, 264, 265, 280, 288, 289–90, 294, 299–300, 301, 305–6, 311, 313, 350
Youth Cricket Association 278, 310